Everyman, I will go with thee, and be thy guide,
In thy most need to go by thy side.

This is No. 345 of Everyman's Library. A
list of authors and their works in this series
will be found at the end of this volume. The
publishers will be pleased to send freely to all
applicants a separate, annotated list of the
Library.

J. M. DENT & SONS LIMITED
10–13 BEDFORD STREET LONDON W.C.2

E. P. DUTTON & CO. INC.
286–302 FOURTH AVENUE
NEW YORK

EVERYMAN'S LIBRARY
EDITED BY ERNEST RHYS

CLASSICAL

OFFICES: ESSAYS ON FRIENDSHIP
AND OLD AGE & SELECT LETTERS
BY CICERO · INTRODUCTION BY
THOMAS DE QUINCEY

CICERO, born in 106 B.C. at Arpinum, the son of a Roman knight. Went to Rhodes to study law. In 75 B.C. made quaestor, and later praetor and consul. Exiled in 58 B.C. Governor of Cilicia, 52 B.C. In 43 B.C. was proscribed and slain.

OFFICES, ESSAYS, AND LETTERS

CICERO

LONDON: J. M. DENT & SONS LTD.
NEW YORK: E. P. DUTTON & CO. INC.

Q16/3m

INTRODUCTION

NOTES ON CICERO'S CHARACTER

By Thomas De Quincey

NOMINALLY it is not easy to assign a period more eventful, a revolution more important, or a personal career more dramatic, than that period—that revolution—that career which, with almost equal right, we may describe as all essentially *Ciceronian*, by the quality of the interest which they excite. For the age, it was fruitful in great men; but, amongst them all, if we except the sublime Julian leader, none as regards splendour of endowments stood upon the same level as Cicero. For the revolution, it was that unique event which brought ancient civilisation into contact and commerce with modern; since, if we figure the two worlds of Paganism and Christianity under the idea of two great continents, it is through the isthmus of Rome imperialised that the one was able virtually to communicate with the other. Civil law and Christianity, the two central forces of modern civilisation, were upon that isthmus of time ripened into potent establishments. And through those two establishments, combined with the antique literature, as through so many organs of metempsychosis, did the pagan world send onwards whatever portion of its own life was fitted for surviving its own peculiar forms. Yet, in a revolution thus unexampled for grandeur of results, the only great actor who stood upon the authority of his character was Cicero. All others, from Pompey, Curio, Domitius, Cato, down to the final partisans at Actium, moved by the authority of arms: "*tantum auctoritate valebant, quantum milite;*" and they could have moved by no other. Lastly, as regards the personal biography, although the same series of trials, perils, and calamities would have been in any case interesting for themselves, yet undeniably they derive a separate power of affecting the mind from the peculiar merits of the

individual concerned.   Cicero is one of the very few pagan
statesmen who can be described as a thoughtfully conscientious man.

¶ Readers of sensibility acknowledge the effect from any
large influence of deep halcyon repose, when relieving the
agitations of history; as, for example, that which arises in
our domestic annals from interposing between two bloody
reigns, like those of Henry VIII. and his daughter Mary,
the serene morning of a child-like king, destined to an early
grave, yet in the meantime occupied with benign counsels
for propagating religion, for teaching the young, or for
protecting the poor.   Such a repose, the same luxury of
rest for the mind, is felt by all who traverse the great
circumstantial records of those tumultuous Roman times
in the Ciceronian epistolary correspondence.   In this we
come suddenly into deep lulls of angry passions; here,
upon some scheme for the extension of literature by a
domestic history, or by a comparison of Greek with Roman
jurisprudence; there, again, upon some ancient problem
from the quiet fields of philosophy.   And all men are
already prejudiced in favour of one who, in the midst of
belligerent partisans, was the patron of a deep *pacific*
interest.   But amongst Christian nations this unfair
personal bias struck deeper: Cicero was not merely a
philosopher; he was one who cultivated ethics; he was
himself the author of an ethical system, composed with
the pious purpose of training to what he thought just
moral views his only son.   This system survives, is studied
to this day, is honoured perhaps extravagantly, and has
repeatedly been pronounced the best practical theory to
which Pagan principles were equal.   Were it only upon
this impulse, it was natural that men should receive a
clinamen, or silent bias, towards Cicero, as a *moral* authority
amongst disputants whose arguments were legions.   The
author of a moral code cannot be supposed indifferent to
the moral relations of his own party views.   If he erred, it
could not be through want of meditation upon the ground
of judgment, or want of interest in the results.   So far
Cicero has an advantage.   But he has more lively advantage in the comparison by which he benefits, at *every*
stage of his life, with antagonists whom the reader is
taught to believe dissolute, incendiary, almost desperate

citizens. Verres in the youth of Cicero, Catiline and Clodius in his middle age, Mark Antony in Cicero's old age, have all been left to operate on the modern reader's feelings precisely through that masquerade of misrepresentation which invariably accompanied the political eloquence of Rome.

¶ I do not make it a reproach to Cicero that his reputation with posterity has been affected by these or similar arts of falsification. Eventually this had been his misfortune. Adhering to the truth, his indiscreet eulogists would have presented to the world a much more interesting picture; not so much the representation of "*vir bonus cum malâ fortunâ compositus*," which is, after all, an ordinary spectacle for so much of the conflict as can ever be made public; but that of a man generally upright, matched as in single duel with a standing temptation to error growing out of his public position; often seduced into false principles by the necessities of ambition, or by the coercion of self-consistency; and often, as he himself admits, biassed fatally in a public question by the partialities of friendship.[1]

Of the translations that follow, the "Offices" is by Thomas Cockman (first published, 1699); the essays on "Friendship" and "Old Age" (1773, 1777) and the appended selection of Familiar Letters (1753) are by W. Melmoth. It is proposed to add the Orations and the Letters to Atticus in a select later volume.

The following is a list of the English translations of the foregoing works of Cicero:—

Offices: Robert Whittington, 1534 (Wynkyn de Worde); N. Grimalde, 1556, several later editions; J. Brinsley, 1616; R. L'Estrange, 1680, and later editions, ed. by W. H. D. Rouse (Temple Classics), 1900; T. C. Cockman, 1699, several later editions (in Lubbock's Hundred Books, No. 76); G. B. Gardiner, 1899.

Laelius; J. Tiptoft, Earl of Worcester, 1530 (?); J. Harrington, 1550, ed. E. D. Ross, 1904; Anon., 1700; Robert Hicks, 1713; W. Melmoth (with Cato), 1773 (in Lubbock's Hundred Books, No. 76); Benjamin E. Smith, 1897.

Cato; Robert Whittington, 1535 (?); T. Newton, The Worthye Booke of Old Age, etc., 1569; W. Austen, 1671; J. Logan, with

---

[1] From Thomas De Quincey's *Miscellaneous Essays*, "Richard Bentley, and Other Writings " (1857).

preface by Benjamin Franklin, 1744, 1751 (Philadelphia), 1788 (London); with memoir, 1750; W. Massey, 1753; W. Melmoth, 1773.

Letters: Complete translation, E. S. Shuckburgh, 1899-1900 (Bohn); Selections by T. W. (Latin and English), 1575; G. E. Jeans, 1880; 2nd ed. 1887; 3rd ed. 1901; S. H. Jeyes, 1883; R. Y. Tyrrell, 1891; A. Watson, 4th ed. 1891 (Clarendon Press); Anon. (letters as included in Tyrrell's Selection), 1903.

Letters; Ad Familiares: J. Webbe, 1620 (?); W. Melmoth, 1753, 1772, 1778.

Two or more works including the Offices, or Cato, and Laelius: 1481 (Caxton) with Tiptoft's Laelius; T. Newton, 1577; S. Parker, 1704; J. D. 1744; W. Guthrie, 1755; C. R. Edmonds, 1850 (Bohn); Dr. McKay, 2nd ed., 1855; E. S. Shuckburgh, 1900; Cassell's National Library, 1905; King's Classics, 1906.

CONTENTS

	PAGE
THE OFFICES	1
LAELIUS; OR, AN ESSAY ON FRIENDSHIP . . .	167
CATO; OR, AN ESSAY ON OLD AGE	217
SELECT LETTERS TO SEVERAL FRIENDS . . .	263

THE OFFICES

BOOK I

I.—Cicero exhorts his son, a young student at Athens, not to forget his Latin, though he was in a Greek university ; but to mix the studies of both those languages, and also learn to write both as a philosopher and an orator.

DEAR SON MARCUS,—Though after a year's study under Cratippus,[1] and that at such a place as Athens, you ought to have abundantly furnished yourself with knowledge in the doctrines and rules of philosophy ; having had the advantage of so eminent a master to supply you with learning, and a city that affords you such excellent examples ; yet I should think it convenient for you (which is a method I took for my own improvement) always to mingle some Latin with your Greek in the studies of eloquence, as well as philosophy, that you may be equally perfect in both those ways of writing, and make yourself master of either language : for the further-ance of which, I am apt to imagine, I have done no incon-siderable service to our countrymen ; so that not only those who do not understand Greek, but even the learned them-selves will confess, that by reading my works, they have mended their styles, and somewhat improved their reason and judgements.—Wherefore I am willing that you should learn indeed of Cratippus, the greatest philosopher of the present age, and learn of him too as long as you desire it ; and so long I think it is your duty to desire it, as you find yourself sufficiently benefited by it : but withal, I would have you to read my writings, which very little differ from those of the Peripatetics ; for both we and they profess our-selves followers, not of Socrates only, but of Plato likewise. As for the matters contained in them, use your own judge-

[1] The most noted Peripatetic philosopher of that age, and a familiar acquaintance of Cicero.

ment with freedom and impartiality, for I lay no manner of restraint on you: your improvement in the Latin is what I chiefly desire, which I am confident must follow from a careful perusal of them. Nor let any one think that I am vain and pretending when I speak thus: for, allowing to some others the precedence in philosophy, should I assume to myself what is the part of an orator, viz. to speak suitably, methodically, and handsomely on any subject, seeing I have spent my whole life in that study, I think it is no more than what I might reasonably and fairly lay claim to. I cannot but very earnestly desire you, therefore, my dear Cicero, to read my books with care and diligence; not my orations only, but these pieces also that concern philosophy, which are now of a bulk almost equal to them; for though in the former there is more of the force and power of eloquence, yet is the smooth and even style of the latter by no means to be neglected: and of all the Grecians, I find not one that has employed his pen in both these kinds, and been at once successful in the language of the bar, and this other more gentle and easy style of philosophical discourses; unless Demetrius Phalereus may be reckoned for one, who is subtle enough in his disputes of philosophy, but, methinks, in his oratory, wants that spirit and vehemence that is requisite: however, has so much of sweetness in him, that one might know he had been Theophrastus' scholar. Whether I have had any better success in both these ways, must be left to the judgement of others to determine: I can only say that I have attempted them both. And it is my opinion, that if ever Plato had undertaken to plead, he would have been a most copious and powerful orator; and if Demosthenes had studied and discoursed of those things, which he learned of Plato, he would have done it with a great deal of ornament and majesty. The same I think true of Isocrates and Aristotle; each of whom, pleased with his own way of writing, neglected to cultivate and improve the other.

II.—*The reasons why he writes on this subject—The general use and importance of it—What sects of philosophers have a right to lay down any rules or precepts concerning it.*

But having resolved to write something at present, and a great many others hereafter to you, I thought I could begin on no better argument than that which is fittest for your age, and most becoming my authority as a father; for, of all those useful and important subjects, which philosophers have handled so largely and accurately, the precepts they have delivered about Offices or Duties seem of the largest extent and comprehension; for they take in every part of our lives, so that whatever we go about, whether of public or private affairs, whether at home or abroad, whether considered barely by ourselves, or as we stand in relation to other people, we lie constantly under an obligation to some duties: and as all the virtue and credit of our lives proceed from the due discharge of this, so all the baseness and turpitude of them result from the non-observance of the same. Now, though this be a subject which all philosophers have employed themselves about (for, who ever dared to assume that name without laying down some instructions about duty?), yet have some sects of them given such accounts of man's happiness and misery, as destroy the very being of virtue and honesty: for he that makes any thing his chiefest good, wherein justice or virtue does not bear a part, and sets up profit, not honesty, for the measure of his happiness; as long as he acts in conformity with his own principles, and is not overruled by the mere dictates of reason and humanity, can never do the offices of friendship, justice, or liberality: nor can he ever be a man of courage, who thinks that pain is the greatest evil; or he of temperance, who imagines pleasure to be the sovereign good. Which things are all so obvious and plain, that one would think they could never stand in need of a dispute: however, I have largely discoursed on them in another work.[1] These sects, therefore, unless they are resolved to be inconsistent with themselves, ought wholly to abstain from speaking anything about duties; nor indeed can any constant, unalterable, rational rules of them at all be given, unless it be by those who go on this principle—that it is virtue alone, or at least that chiefly, which ought to be desired for its own sake. So that only the Stoics, Academics, and Peripatetics, have a right to lay down any rules on this subject; for as to the opinion of Aristo, Pyrrho, and Herillus, that has been exploded a good while ago; who might have claimed a privilege to treat about duties, as well as the former three, had they but left

---

[1] In his treatise On the End of Good and Evil.

the possibility of choosing, and allowed at least so much difference between things, as to put us into a capacity of finding out our duty, and distinguishing it from that which is not so. I shall follow therefore at this time, and on this subject more especially, the Stoics; not as a bare translator of them, but, according to my usual custom, shall take out of their stores so much, and after such a manner, as in my own judgement I shall think most convenient. Seeing then the whole of our following discourse is designed to be about Offices or Duties, I think it will be necessary for me, in the first place, to determine and fix the signification of the word "Office," which I cannot but wonder to find omitted by Panaetius: for every clear and rational discourse on any subject ought first to begin with an explication of that subject, so that we may have a distinct conception of what we are afterwards to discourse about.

III.—*The whole subject consists of two parts, ordinary and perfect duties; and what they are—The general method he designs to take in the whole work.*

The whole subject of duties then, in its greatest latitude, comprehends under it these two parts: the first is taken up in explaining what is good, and what our greatest good; the second in certain directions and precepts, according to which on all occasions it is our duty to govern our lives and actions. To the first part belong such questions as these, whether all duties are perfect or not? and, whether one can be greater or less than another? with several others to the same purpose. Not but that the duties of this second part, the rules and precepts of which are laid down, have some tendency and relation to our chiefest good; but only it does not so plainly appear, because they seem to concern more immediately the government of our lives and regulation of our manners; and these are they which I design to explain in the following treatise. There is also another distribution of duties, some of them being called middle or ordinary, and others perfect or complete. To the latter, I think, we may give the name of right or straight. By that which we have called right or straight, is meant a virtue that is wholly complete in all its parts, without any manner of flaw or imperfection; and by that which we have called ordinary, such a one as a fair and reasonable account may be given for the doing of it. Now these fair and reasonable accounts are all to be drawn from several heads, which are by Panaetius reduced to three, and may be called general heads of deliberating or doubting concerning any action, whether it should or should not be done. The first is, when it is consulted or doubted, whether the action that is under consideration be honest or dishonest; in which inquiry men are often divided between several opinions. The second is when it is inquired and consulted, whether the action that is under deliberation will supply us with the pleasures and conveniences of life, furnish us with plenty of outward things, such as riches, honours, power, etc., which may put us into a capacity of doing good to ourselves, and to all those for whom we are more nearly concerned; all which inquiry comes under the general head of profit. The third ground or reason of doubting is, when that thing which seems to be profitable for us comes into competition with that which is honest; for then our interest drawing us one way, and honesty pulling us back another, the wavering mind is, as it were, torn in sunder between the two, and is racked with doubting and anxious thoughts. There is no greater fault in any division, than not to take in all the several parts of the matter to be divided; and yet two are omitted in the now-mentioned one of Panaetius: for men not only consult and deliberate whether such an action be honest or dishonest; but also of two honests that are both proposed to them, which is the most so; and in like manner of two profitables, which is the most profitable. From whence it appears, that what he thought was contained in three, ought rather to be divided into five heads. We must then, in the first place, discourse about honesty, and this we shall do under these two inquiries: whether the thing proposed be honest or dishonest? and, of two that are honest, which is the most so? which will make up the subject of our first book. We shall treat in our second of profit or interest under the same heads. And lastly, in our third we shall endeavour to show, when a seeming advantage and honesty come into competition, how a good man should determine his judgement.

IV.—*The excellence of the nature of man—How the several virtues are agreeable to its dictates, and result from them—Wherein honesty in general consists.*

The first thing to be taken notice of is this, that every creature doth by nature endeavour to preserve its own self, its life and body; and to shun and avoid those things which appear prejudicial and hurtful to it; but to seek and procure whatever is necessary for the support of its being, and advancement of its happiness, such as food, shelter, and the like. There is likewise common to all sorts of animals a desire for the continuance and propagation of their several species; together with a love and concern for their young ones. Now there is this special difference between men and brutes; that the latter are governed by nothing but their senses, never look any farther than just to what strikes and affects them at present, and have a very little, or hardly any concern, for what is past or to come: but the former are creatures endowed with reason, which gives them a power to carry their thoughts to the consequences of things, to discover causes before they have yet produced their effects; to see the whole progress, and even the first seeds, as it were, and appearances of them; to compare like occurrences with like, and by joining what is past and what is to come together, to make a just estimate of the one from the other; whereby they are able at once to take a view of their whole lives, and accordingly to make provision for the necessities of them. And the same force of reason makes all men by nature to love one another, and desire an intercourse of words and actions. It begets in them, likewise, a somewhat extraordinary love and affection for their own children; and strongly inclines them to frequent public meetings, and keep up societies one amongst another. For the same reason also they are very industrious to provide for the necessaries and conveniences of life; and that not only for themselves in particular, but for their wives, their children, and others whom they have a kindness for, and are obliged to take care of; which concern is very proper to rouse up the spirits, and make them more vigorous and active in business. But of all the properties and inclinations of men, there is none more natural and peculiar to them than an earnest desire and search after truth. Hence it is that our minds are no sooner free from the thoughts and engagements of necessary business, but we presently long to be either seeing, or hearing, or learning of something; and esteem the knowledge of things secret and wonderful as a necessary ingredient of a happy life. Whence it appears that nothing is more agreeable and suited to the nature and minds of men than undisguised openness, truth, and sincerity. Next to this love and affection for truth, there follows in the soul an impatient desire and inclination to pre-eminence; so that whoever has the genuine nature of a man in him, will never endure to be subject to another, unless he be one that instructs or advises, or is invested with a just and lawful authority for the benefit of the public: whence there arises a greatness of soul, which sets it above all the petty concerns and trifling enjoyments of this present world. It is another, and that too no mean prerogative of our reasonable nature, that man alone can discern all the beauties of order and decency, and knows how to govern his words and actions in conformity to them. It is he alone that, of all the creatures, observes and is pleased with the beauty, gracefulness, and symmetry of parts in the objects of sense; which nature and reason observing in them, from thence take occasion to apply the same also to those of the mind; and to conclude that beauty, consistency, and regularity, should be much more kept up in our words and actions; and therefore command us, that nothing be done that is effeminate or unbecoming; and that so strict a guard be kept over every thought and action, as that no indecency be either conceived or practised by us. From these inclinations and instincts of nature arises and results that honesty we are seeking for; which, however little valued and esteemed it may be, is nevertheless virtuous and amiable in itself; and which we may justly say, though it were commended by no one, is yet in its own nature truly commendable.

V.—*The admirable beauty of honesty—Four general heads from which all the several duties arise.*

Thus, son Marcus, have I given you a rough draught, and just the outlines, as it were, of honesty; which, could she be seen in her full beauty with mortal eye, would make the whole world (as Plato has said) be in love with wisdom.

Now whatever is contained under the notion of honesty arises
from one of these four heads; first, a sagacious inquiry and
observation for the finding out of truth, which may be called
by the general name of prudence: secondly, a care to maintain that society and mutual intercourse which is between
them; to render to every man what is his due; and to stand
to one's words in all promises and bargains; which we call
justice: thirdly, the greatness and unshaken resolution of a
truly brave and invincible mind, which goes by the name
of magnanimity or fortitude: and lastly, a keeping of our
words and actions within the due limits of order and decency;
under which are comprehended temperance and moderation.
Now every one of these several heads, though they all have
a mutual connection and dependence on one another, has
yet its peculiar class, as it were, and respective set of duties
arising from it.   From that, for example, which is mentioned
first, and under which prudence and wisdom are contained,
arises the duty of seeking, contemplating, and finding out of
truth, which is the proper and peculiar business of those
virtues: for it is then, and then alone, that we justly esteem
a man prudent and wise, when we find that he is able to see
and discover the truth of things; and of an active, vigorous,
and piercing mind, to give an account of the reasons of them;
so that it is truth that is the proper object of both these
virtues, and that about which they are only concerned.
The other three heads more peculiarly belong to the active
life, and their business lies in procuring and keeping what is
useful and necessary for the preservation of it; as in holding
up mutual love and correspondence among mankind; in an
elevated greatness and strength of mind; which appears, as
in getting things profitable and pleasant for ourselves and
dependents, so more especially in despising and being above
them.   Then, as for the last, viz. order, uniformity, moderation, and the like, it is plain they belong not only to contemplation, but have also a respect to our outward actions;
since from keeping of these within the bounds and limits
of order and moderation, we are said to observe what is
virtuous and becoming

VI.—*Prudence or contemplation of truth, the first of the general virtues, is the nearest allied to the nature of man—Two cautions concerning it.*

Having thus explained how the whole nature and power of honesty is deduced from some one of these four parts, we are now to discourse of them each in particular. And, first, of Prudence, which is wholly taken up in the knowledge of truth, and has the nearest affinity of any with the reasonable nature of man. For how are we all of us drawn and enticed with the desire of wisdom! how noble and glorious a thing do we imagine it to excel in knowledge! and how mean and reproachful do we count it, on the other hand, to slip, to be in error, to be ignorant, or to be imposed on? In gratifying this so natural and virtuous inclination in the mind of man, there are two grand faults to be carefully avoided: the first is an over-great hastiness and rashness in giving up our assent, presuming that we know things before we really do so. Whoever desires (as I am sure all ought) to avoid this error, must in all his inquiries allow himself time, and diligently consider the matter with himself, before he proceeds to pass his judgement on it. The second fault is, that a great many men bestow abundance of study, and a world of pains, on very difficult and obscure subjects; and such as, perhaps, when they are found out, are of but very little, or no concernment. Would men but be careful to shun these two mistakes, whatever study or pains they might spend on virtuous, worthy, or profitable subjects, it would not without reason be highly commended. Thus Caius Sulpicius [1] was heretofore praised for his skill in astronomy: Sext. Pompeius,[2] since my memory, for his in geometry: many have been famous in the study of logic, and more in that of the civil laws: the more peculiar business of all which parts of learning is the finding out of truth. No man, however, should be so taken up in the search of truth, as thereby to neglect the more necessary duties of active life: for, after all is done, it is action only that gives a true value and commendation to virtue. Not that we are able to be always employed without intermission, but often retire from business to study; beside that the mind, which is in perpetual motion and agitations, of itself will supply us with study and thinking, whether we set ourselves to it

---

[1] C. Sulpicius Gallus.   [2] Uncle to Pompey the Great.

or not. In a word, the general aim and design of our thought, and application of mind, is either the attainment of such things as are honest, and tend to a virtuous and happy way of life, or else the improvement of our reason and understanding in wisdom and knowledge. And this may suffice for the first of our general heads of duty.

VII.—*The second general virtue, which consists in the maintenance of human society—Two parts of it, justice and liberality.*

Of the other remaining three, that which consists in upholding society, and keeping up mutual love and good nature amongst mankind, seems of the largest and most diffusive extent. It comprehends under it these two parts: first, justice, which is much the most glorious and splendid of all virtues, and alone entitles us to the name and appellation of good men; and, secondly, beneficence, which may also be called either bounty or liberality. Now the first thing that justice requires of us is this; that no one should do any hurt to another, unless by way of reasonable and just retribution for some injury received from him: and whatever belongs either to all in common, or particular persons as their own property, should not be altered, but made use of accordingly. Now no man can say that he has anything his own by a right of nature; but either by an ancient immemorial seizure, as those who first planted uninhabited countries; or, secondly, by conquest, as those who have got things by the right of the sword; or else by some law compact, agreement, or lot. It is by some of these means that the people inhabiting Arpinum and Tusculum came to have those lands, which are now called theirs; and the same may be said as to private men's estates. However, since at present, by some of these ways, each particular man has his personal possessions, out of that which by nature was common to all, it is but just that each should hold what is now his own; which, if any one endeavour to take away from him, he directly breaks in on common justice, and violates the rights of human society. "But seeing (as is excellently said by Plato) we are not born for ourselves alone; but that our native country, our friends and relations, have a just claim and title to some part of us;" and seeing whatsoever is created on earth was merely designed (as the

Stoics will have it) for the service of men; and men themselves for the service, good, and assistance of one another; we certainly in this should be followers of Nature, and second her intentions; and by producing all that lies within the reach of our power for the general interest, by mutually giving and receiving good turns, by our knowledge, industry, riches, or other means, should endeavour to keep up that love and society, that should be amongst men. Now the great foundation of justice is faithfulness, which consists in being constantly firm to your word, and a conscientious performance of all compacts and bargains. The vice that is opposite to justice is injustice, of which there are two sorts: the first consists in the actual doing an injury to another; the second, in tamely looking on while he is injured, and not helping and defending him though we are able: for he that injuriously falls on another, whether prompted by rage or other violent passion, does as it were leap at the throat of his companion; and he that refuses to help him when injured, and to ward off the wrong if it lies in his power, is as plainly guilty of baseness and injustice as though he had deserted his father, his friends, or his native country. Now that former injustice, which consists in the wilful and actual wronging another, has oftentimes no other cause but fear; when he, who designedly does a man an injury, is afraid lest himself should be forced to undergo one, if he does not secure himself by doing it beforehand. But, generally speaking, the great source and fountain of all such injustice is the satisfying some irregular and exorbitant appetite; and in a more especial manner, the desire of riches; of which we shall therefore say something in particular.

VIII.—*The desire of riches and honours a cause of injustice.*

Riches then are most commonly desired, either to supply us with the necessaries of life, or furnish us with the pleasures and conveniences of it; or else, as it often is observed to happen in persons of great and aspiring minds, as a means of obtaining an interest in the public, and a power of obliging and gratifying one's friends; to which purpose was that saying of the late Marcus Crassus, that whoever designed to be a leading man in the common-wealth, ought never to think he had estate enough, till he could maintain an army with its yearly revenue. Others take pleasure in splendour and magnificence, in a handsome, noble, and plentiful way of living: all which things have begot an insatiable greediness after money, without which they can never be supported and maintained. Not but that a moderate desire of riches, and bettering a man's estate, so long as it abstains from oppressing of others, is allowable enough; but a very great care ought always to be taken that we be not drawn to any injustice by it. There is another desire that makes men as apt to be forgetful of justice, as that after riches; the thirst, I mean, of empire, glory, honours, etc. For that saying of Ennius, "There is no inviolable faith or friendship in the matter of a king-dom;" though applied by him to that one case only, is yet fully as true in a great many others; for wherever the subject of contention is such, as that only one party can meet with success, and the rest must fall short of what they desire; things are usually carried to so great a height, as that it is very difficult not to break in on faith and friendship. This hath appeared but too manifestly of late, in that rash and most impudent attempt of Caesar's; who has broken through all those ties and obligations, that either by gods or men could be laid on him, for the compassing and getting of that dominion to himself, which he had vainly proposed in his depraved imagination. But in this case, it is one very great unhappiness, that the thirst after honour, empire, power, etc., falls most on men of the greatest souls and most exalted natures; wherefore the greater care ought to be taken that nothing of offence be committed in this kind. Now it makes a great difference in all acts of justice, whether they proceed from some violent passion, which is for the most part of short continuance, or are done with design and previous deliberation: for those that are the effects of a sudden gust of passion ought not to be esteemed of so heinous a nature, as those that proceed from premeditated malice. And this may suffice for the first sort of injustice, which consists in the actual doing of wrong, and the causes of it.

IX.—*Injustice of omission, and the causes of it.*

As for the second, which only consists in seeing another injured, and being wanting to our duty, by not defending him; the causes of that are wont to be several: for some are afraid of offending others, or of bringing a trouble and charge on themselves: others are negligent, idle, or mean-spirited: and a third sort there is, who are so taken up with their own concerns, that they have no time left to regard the oppressed, whom yet it is their duty to save and protect. I am therefore of opinion, that Plato's consequence will hardly hold good where, speaking about the philosophers, he says, " They are wholly taken up in the seeking out of truth, and perfectly neglect and make light of those things which the rest of the world are so eager after, and so contend about; and that therefore they are just." This, I say, I am afraid is a bad consequence; for though, it is true, they keep the first sort of justice, inasmuch as they actually do no wrong; yet they run perfectly counter to the other; for being engaged in their learning and studies, they abandon their friends to be injured by others, whom in justice they ought to have protected and defended. So that it is believed they hardly ever trouble themselves so far, as at all to inter-meddle with the business of the public, if it was not alto-gether, as it were, forced on them. But it were a great deal better would they do it voluntarily; for an action, though honest, is not therefore truly virtuous, unless it be done out of choice, and with a good will. There are others yet, who out of a desire of improving their own estates, or else a morose and unsociable sort of temper, cry, they meddle with nobody's business but their own, that so they may seem to be men of strict honesty, and to injure nobody; and they do indeed avoid the one sort of injustice, but directly run themselves into the other; for they desert the common good and society of mankind, while they bestow neither study, pains, nor money toward the preservation of it. Thus have I laid down the two sorts of injustice, and pointed out to you the causes of each; and have also endeavoured to explain the true nature and extent of justice; from all which ac-count it will be easy to judge, unless we are extremely fond of our own ease, what those several duties are, which at several times are required of us. I say, unless we are fond of our own ease; for the truth of it is, it is a troublesome thing to be concerned in the business of other people: however, old Chremes in Terence thinks "That he ought to be concerned for the good of all men." But be that as it will, forasmuch as the success of our own affairs, whether good or ill, more nearly concerns us, and makes us more sensible than that of another, which appears to us small, as a thing at a great distance; therefore we pass a quite different judgement on the one and the other. And, on this account, it is a very good rule that is given by some men, "that we should never venture on any action, of which we doubt whether it is honest or dishonest:" for honesty quickly would show itself by its own native brightness; and the doubting about it is a plain intimation that at least we suspected some injustice when we did it.

X.—*Justice is altered by an alteration of circumstances—In what cases promises are not binding, and a rigid adherence to the words of a law or bargain is an act of injustice.*

But here it is observable, that the limits of justice are not so fixed, but that they may be altered by an alteration of circumstances; so that what at one time appears to be the duty of an honest and good man, at another is altered and becomes the quite contrary; to deliver up a trust, for example, or perform a promise, and other things relating to truth and faithfulness, are duties which justice itself will allow as, in several cases, to neglect or omit: for respect must be had to those general rules we before laid down, as the ground and foundation of all justice—first, that no injury be done to another; and, secondly, that we make it our earnest endeavour to promote the good and interest of all mankind: so that our duty is not always the same, but various, according to a variety of circumstances. There may be a contract or promise, for instance, the performance of which would bring very great damage, either to the person himself that made it, or the other party to whom it was made. Thus, had Neptune not granted what he promised to Theseus, Theseus had not suffered the loss of his son Hippolytus: for, as the story goes, Neptune having granted him any three wishes, for the third he once in a very great passion desired the death of his own son; by obtaining of which he was afterwards brought into the greatest afflictions. Such promises therefore are not to be kept, as will but bring a mischief on him they were made to; no more are those which tend to the damage of the promiser himself, more than to the profit of him they were promised to.— Again, even justice itself requires us to perform a greater before a lesser duty: you promise, for example, a friend of yours, to assist him in a cause that he has depending, but your son grows dangerously sick in the meantime: here it would be no breach of duty in you, if you should not make good what you promised to your friend; and he himself rather would be much to blame, should he complain of being disappointed by you. Farther, it is plain to any one's sense, that such sort of promises can never be binding as are made by people overawed by fear, or overreached by deceit; most of which are void by the pretor's edicts, and some of them even by the laws themselves. But another great spring from which injuries arise, is some quirk or cavil, and an oversubtle and malicious interpretation of the laws; from whence that saying, " The height of justice is the height of roguery," is now become a daily and common proverb among us. There are frequent examples of this to be met with in our public transactions; as that of him, for example, who, concluding a truce with the enemy for thirty days, made continual incursions into their territory by night; because, forsooth, the truce was not made for so many nights, but only so many days. Just such a crafty and pitiful trick, if the story be true, was that notable cunning of Quintus Fabius Labeo, or whoever the man was, for I have it only by hearsay, who being by the senate appointed arbitrator in a difference between those of Nola and Naples about their bounds; when he came to the place that was appointed for the treaty, took aside the commissioners of either party, and exhorted them privately not to be too eager and greedy in their demands, but rather to take up and content themselves with less, than pretend to any more than what was honestly their due. Both parties did so according to his desire, so that a good quantity of ground was left between them; this he even goes and adjudges to the Romans, leaving that to each party which they themselves had demanded. And is not this now to deceive and cheat, rather than to judge? In all cases therefore such subtle kind of tricks should be diligently avoided.

XI.—*Justice to be kept towards all men—Bounds to be observed in punishing those that have injured us—Laws of war to be strictly observed.*

There are certain duties also to be strictly observed, even towards those that have injured us; for we ought not to go beyond certain bounds, in exacting revenge and punishment of another: in which particular it may, perhaps, be enough to make him that has wronged us repent of the wrong done; so that both he himself may abstain from the like, and others may be discouraged from injuring us for the future. There are certain peculiar laws of war also, which are of all things most strictly to be observed in the commonwealth; for there being two sorts of disputing in the world, the one by reason, and the other by open force; and the former of these being that which is agreeable to the nature of man, and the latter to that of brutes; when we cannot obtain what is our right by the one, we must of necessity have recourse to the other. It is allowable therefore to undertake wars, but it must always be with design of obtaining a secure peace: and when we have got the better of our enemies, we should rest content with the victory alone, and show ourselves merciful and kind to them afterwards, unless they are such as have been very cruel, and committed inhuman barbarities in the war. Thus our forefathers took into their city the Aequians, Volscians, Sabines, and others whom they had subdued; whereas Carthage and Numantia they entirely destroyed. I could wish I might not add Corinth too; but I believe they had something in their eye when they did it, and more especially the situation of the place; which, being so very convenient as it was, they were afraid lest it might be at one time or other an encouragement to revolt. In my opinion it is always our duty to do what we can for a fair and safe peace; in which thing, if people would have hearkened unto me, we might at this time have seen the republic, though, it is true, I cannot say in a flourishing condition, yet certainly not as at present we perceive it, entirely subverted and fallen into ruins. As we are bound to be merciful to those whom we have actually conquered; so should those also be received into favour, who have laid down their arms, and thrown themselves wholly on the general's mercy; and that even though the breach be made in their city walls. Our good forefathers were most strictly just as to this particular; the custom of those times making him the patron of a conquered city or people, who first received them into the faith and allegiance of the people of Rome. In short, the whole right and all the duties of war are most rigorously set down in the fecial laws;[1] out of which it is manifest, that never any war can be justly undertaken, unless satisfaction have been first demanded, and proclamation of it made publicly beforehand. Popillius was commander in one of the provinces, and Cato's son a young soldier under him; and Popillius thinking fit to disband one of his legions, it happened to be the same in which the young man was, who therefore was dismissed among the rest of the soldiers: but having a mind to see more of the war, he notwithstanding this continued still in the army. Shortly after old Cato writes a letter to Popillius, and therein desires him, " that if he suffered his son to remain in the army, he would give him his military oath again;[2] forasmuch as the former being void by his disbanding, he could not any longer fight lawfully with an enemy; " so religiously careful they were in those days of doing nothing that is contrary to the laws of war. There is extant still an epistle of Cato the father to his son, in which he tells him, " that he had heard of his being disbanded by the consul, when he was a soldier in Macedonia, in the war with Perseus; and therefore he advises him not by any means to intermeddle in a battle; because, he says, it is unlawful for one that is no longer a soldier to engage with the enemy."

XII.—*The civility of the old Romans towards their enemies—Some wars are only for empire, others for safety; difference of conduct to be observed in each.*

And here I cannot but observe moreover, that he who is properly called a stubborn enemy, had by our ancestors a name given him, the gentleness of which somewhat lessened the foulness and odium of the thing: for an enemy, among them, signified the same thing that a stranger does now amongst us; as appears from the laws of the Twelve Tables.

[1] The feciales were a sort of priests or heralds among the Romans, established by Numa, whose business it was to determine all cases about the lawfulness of war, leagues, ambassadors, etc.

[2] An oath that was given to the soldiers when they went out to war.

What greater courtesy could be shown than this, to call even an enemy by only the softest and most obliging names? Though the word is now altered, I confess, from that mild to a harsher sense; custom having changed it from what it first properly signified, a stranger, to denote such a one as bears arms against us. We have told you already what previous causes and conditions there should be, before any war can be lawful and just; the same are required even in those wars also, which are undertaken merely for glory and empire; but then all contests of this latter sort should be carried on with less heat and animosities; for as in the differences that happen among citizens, we make a distinction between a violent enemy and a generous rival, in one case nothing but a title of honour, in the other our lives and reputations being concerned; so did our ancestors do in their wars. That which they waged with the Cimbers and Celtibers, was managed as with hateful and implacable enemies; the question then being, not whether of the two should remain a conqueror, but whether should remain a people at all; whereas those with the Latins, Carthaginians, Pyrrhus, etc., were only quarrels about honour and dominion. The Carthaginians were perfidious and treacherous; Hannibal, their great commander, cruel; but all the rest more faithful and merciful. That speech of Pyrrhus is indeed very extraordinary on restoring the captives, when he says,

> I neither gold of you nor price demand:
> Nor will I chaffer, but fight out the war:
> Let steel, not gold, to each their fate decide.
> Whether to you, or me dame Fortune will
> The victory grant; or what the chance of war,
> Shall courage try. And this I add withal,
> That freely I their liberties restore
> To these brave men, whose lives the war has spared,
> Freely I give: do you as freely take,
> In the name of the mighty gods.

A truly royal and princely saying, and worthy of the glorious family of the Aeacidae!

XIII.—*Particular persons bound in justice to keep promises made to an enemy—Justice to be observed towards the meanis slaves—Two ways whereby injuries are inflicted, fraud and force.*

It is also the duty of particular persons, if at any time forced by the necessity of their circumstances, they have made any promise or oath to an enemy, afterwards to see that they perform it faithfully. Thus Regulus was taken in the first Punic war by the Carthaginians, and sent by them to Rome about an exchange of prisoners, on solemn oath given that he would return to them again: first, then, as soon as he was come to Rome, he advised the senate against making such an exchange, and when he had done so, though begged on to stay by his friends and relations, rather returned to a certain punishment than his oath should be broken, though made to an enemy. But Hannibal, in the second Carthaginian war, after our fatal defeat at Cannae, sent ten to Rome under the same obligation of returning again, unless by their interest they could prevail with the senate to redeem their prisoners; who were all by the censors deprived of their privileges as freemen, and tied to pay such and such duties to the public as long as they lived, for not being true to their oaths and obligations. There was one of them thought by a trick to have eluded the force of his oath, but was nevertheless punished for all that: his shift was this. Hannibal had let them depart his camp on the condition afore-mentioned; when therefore they had got a little way out of it, what does he do, but come back to it again, under colour of having forgot to take something, I know not what, with him; and then away he goes out again, discharged, as he thought, from his obligation of returning. And so it is very true he was in word, but not in reality; for in all such oaths we are not to attend to the mere form of words, but the true design and intention of them. But the greatest example of justice to an enemy was shown by our ancestors towards king Pyrrhus. There came a deserter out of Pyrrhus' camp, and offered the senate to despatch him with poison; which they and Fabricius were so far from accepting of, that they gave him up again as a traitor to his master. Thus we may see, that they would not allow any unjust way of dealing, though for the death of a powerful and invading adversary: and so much for the duties required in war. There is one part of justice remaining behind, and which ought by no means to be forgotten by us; I mean that towards the lowest and meanest sort of people: and these are more especially those we call our slaves; in relation to whom, it is a very good rule that is given by some men, that we should use them no otherwise than we do our

day-labourers, make them first do their work, and then pay
them honestly what they have earned. In fine, to close up
this discourse of justice, there are two ways or methods
whereby one man may injure or oppress another; the one
is fraud and subtlety, the other open force and violence;
the former of which is esteemed the part of a fox, and the
latter of a lion; both of them certainly very unworthy of a
reasonable creature, though fraud, I think, is the more
odious of the two. But of all injustice, theirs is certainly
of the deepest die, who make it their business to appear
honest men, even whilst they are practising the greatest of
villanies.

XIV.—*Of liberality, the second part of general justice—Three cautions to
be observed concerning it.*

We have now gone through with the subject of justice;
it remains, in the next place, to go on according to our
method proposed, that we say something likewise of bounty
and liberality, than which there is nothing more nearly
allied to the nature of man. But then we must observe
these following cautions—first, that we take care in all acts
of bounty, that they be not prejudicial to those we would
oblige by them, nor to any other body; secondly, that we
do not in our bounty and liberality go beyond our estates;
and, thirdly, that we duly proportion our kindness, according to every man's merit and deserts. And first of the
former, which is grounded on the great and fundamental
principle of all justice, to which this duty in all its particular
instances should be referred—for he who, pretending to do
one a kindness, does that which is really a prejudice to him,
is indeed so far from being kind and obliging, as that he
ought to be counted a most pernicious flatterer; and to do
any manner of injury to one, that you may show your
generosity and bounty to another, is just one and the same
sort of roguery and injustice, as to enrich yourself by the
spoils of your neighbour. Yet this is the fault of a great
many people, and especially those who are desirous of
glory, to take away from some that which justly belongs
to them, that so they may have to bestow on others; and
they are apt to think themselves extremely bountiful if they
enrich their adherents by any manner of means. But this

is so far from being a duty of liberality, that nothing in the world can be more contrary to it. It ought to be therefore our first care in giving, that what we bestow be a real advantage and kindness to our friend, and no ways an injury to any third person. That action therefore of Caesar and Sylla's, in taking away estates from the rightful proprietors, and giving them to others, who had no right to them, ought by no means to be accounted liberal; for nothing can ever be truly such that is not at the same time just and honest. A second caution to be observed was this: that our bounty be not suffered to exceed our abilities; for they who give more than their estates will allow of, are, in the first place, injurious to their own relations, by spending that wealth on other people which should rather have been given or left to them. Beside that this over-great bounty in giving is usually accompanied with an answerable desire and greediness of getting; which often proceeds even to downright oppression, that so men may have wherewithal to supply this extravagant humour. One may also observe in a great many people, that they take a sort of pride in being counted magnificent, and give very plentifully, not from any generous principle in their natures, but only to appear great in the eye of the world; so that all their bounty is resolved into nothing but mere outside and pretence, and is nearer of kin to vanity and folly, than it is to either liberality or honesty. The third caution was, that our bounty should be proportioned to the merits of the receiver; in judging of which, we are first to consider the man's honesty or manners; secondly, the good-will he bears towards us; thirdly, the nearness of relation, or society that is between us; and, lastly, the benefits we have formerly received from him. It is desirable that all these inducements might concur in the same person; but when they do not, we should bestow our kindness more especially on him, in whom we find the most and weightiest of them.

XV.—*Honesty the first sort of merit—Modesty, temperance, etc., more especially to be regarded—Gratitude a most necessary duty—How to judge of the value of any kindness.*

Now seeing we do not live amongst such as are perfectly and fully wise, but such as are thought to have done very

well, if they are but, as it were, the rough draughts of virtue;
we ought to consider, I think, in the first place, that no one
should wholly be neglected in this case, in whom there
appears any shadow or resemblance of real honesty; but
that those men ought to be principally regarded, who excel
in the quiet and more peaceable virtues of modesty, temperance, and especially this justice, of which I have now been
discoursing a great while: for most times greatness of spirit
and courage, unless it be in those who are perfectly wise
and virtuous, is something too hot, and apt to boil over; the
others are the virtues, which seem more peculiarly to constitute a good man. And so much for the first sort of merit
to be considered, viz. the manners or honesty of the person
we would be kind to. The second was, the good-will which
he bears towards us; as to which it should always be our
principal care to do most for him by whom we are most
beloved. Now in judging of the good-will that any one
bears us, we are not to consider, like boys and children, any
sudden flashes and heats of passion, but rather a constant
and well-settled affection. But if a man, in the next place,
has done us any real service, so that our part is to make a
requital, and not first to lay an obligation on him, it is then
our duty to take some greater care; for of all the virtues,
there is none we are more necessarily obliged to, than gratitude. If then, according to Hesiod's rule, even that which
was no more than barely lent us, is, if possible, to be returned
back with interest again; what abundant returns should we
make to those by whom we have been freely and generously
obliged? What less can we do than be like fruitful fields,
which produce beyond comparison more than was thrown
into them? And if we do services even to those men, from
whom we hope afterwards to receive any favours, ought we
not much more to do the same to those, from whose forward
kindness we have already received them? For the virtue
of liberality containing under it these two parts; in the first
place, the doing a kindness to any one; and, secondly, the
requiting it when done to us; whether we will perform the
former or not, is altogether left to our own choice; but every
good man is obliged to the latter, whenever he can do it
without injustice. But then we are to make a distinction
between benefits, and are there bound to make the most
ample returns, where the obligations we have received are

the greatest: and to judge of the merits of any kindness, we are chiefly to consider in what manner it was done; as whether freely, considerately, and from a principle of good nature: for several people do many things rashly, and with a blind sort of impulse; throwing away their favours on all without distinction; being hurried about, as it were with a tempest, by every mad and frolicsome humour, and every sudden or impetuous passion. A benefit, therefore, when received from such a one, is not to be esteemed of an equal value with those that proceed from a settled judgement and due consideration. But our principal duty, both in doing of kindnesses and making requitals, is to do most for those that stand in greatest need of it, supposing all circumstances else to be equal; the contrary to which appears plainly in the practice and actions of the most part of men; for people choose to bestow their favours on those from whom they expect to receive the most benefits, though the persons perhaps do not at all stand in need of them.

XVI.—*The first sort of alliance is that between all men in general, to all of whom we are bound to render assistance; but with this caution, that we do not thereby make ourselves unable to assist those who are more nearly allied to us.*

The fourth inducement remaining to be spoken to is, the nearness of relation, or society that is amongst men; for the maintenance of which, we cannot do better than to give most to those that stand nearest related to us. But that we may consider, with greater distinctness, the natural principles of human society, we shall here trace it down from the fountain head. The first thing then to be taken notice of is this: that there is such a thing as a fellowship or society between all men in general: the bond or cement that holds this together is reason and discourse, which, by teaching, learning, communicating one with another, etc., easily make men agree together, and unite them all in one natural sort of conjunction and community: nor does anything set us at a greater distance from the nature of beasts; for we oftentimes talk of the courage of them, such as lions and horses; but never a word of their equity, justice, or goodness: and why is this, but because they are destitute of reason and discourse? This is then the largest and most comprehensive of all societies, being made up of men considered barely as such, and so taking in even the whole race and kind of them one with another; the duties of which are, to let every one have a share in those things which by nature were produced for the common advantage and benefit of all; to let what is already determined by laws and civil constitutions remain as it is, without breaking in on any man's right; as to which things, however, we should remember a rule, which is now among the Greeks become a usual proverb, "All things in common amongst friends." But perhaps you may ask what kind of things we suppose them to be which ought to be common to all mankind: Ennius has given us one instance of them, which may easily be applied to a great many others—

> He that directs the wandering traveller,
> Doth, as it were, light another's torch by his own;
> Which gives him ne'er the less of light, for that
> It gave another.

By this one case he sufficiently teaches us, that whatever kindness can be done for another, without any damage or loss to ourselves, it is our duty to do it, though to a stranger. From hence have arisen those general maxims and principles of humanity, not to deny one a little running water; or, the lighting his fire by ours, if he has occasion; to give the best counsel we are able to one who is in doubt or distress: which are things that do good to the person that receives them, and are no loss or trouble to him that confers them. Such things, therefore, being by nature common, should accordingly be kept open for the free use of all men; and of those which are our own we should always be giving something that may contribute to the benefit and welfare of the whole. But because the revenues of particulars are small, and there are infinite numbers of those that want, therefore is this universal bounty to be kept within the limits prescribed by Ennius, " it gives him never the less of light "; that so we may have it still within our power to be liberal to those who are more nearly allied to us.

XVII.—*Several other degrees of relation, with their appropriate rank and duties, here enumerated.*

But there are several degrees of society and fellowship amongst mankind; for to take now our leave of that general and universal one already mentioned, there is a nearer among those who are all of the same country, nation, or language, than which nothing more knits and unites men to one another. There is a closer yet among those who are all of the same city; for a great many things are in common to fellow-citizens, such as markets, temples, walks, ways, laws, privileges, courts of justice, freedom of votes, besides common meetings and familiarities, and abundance of business and intercourse with one another. But there is a stricter bond of alliance still between those who belong to the same family, as taking into it but a very small part of that vast and immense one of all mankind. The closest and nearest of all societies is between man and wife; then follows that between them and their children, and afterwards that of the whole family, who inhabit together and have all things in common; which is, as it were, the first beginning of a city, and ground or seed-plot of a whole commonwealth. Next to this comes the bond of relation between brothers, as also between first and second cousins; who, growing too numerous to live in the same house, are sent out to others, as it were into new colonies. Next after this follow marriages and alliances, and so a new stock of relations that way; from whence comes a new propagation and offspring, which serves to give rise, as was said, to commonwealths. Now that nearness of blood, and the natural love which arises from it, cannot but endear men to one another, is past all doubt; it is a very great matter to have the same relics and monuments of our ancestors, to make use of the same religious ceremonies, and be laid, after death, in the same place of burial. But of all the societies and unions amongst men, there is none more excellent, or more closely knit, than when such as are men of real virtue and honesty, from a certain agreement and likeness of their manners, contract a familiarity and friendship one with another: for virtue and goodness (as we often observe) of necessity moves us wherever we see it, and makes us all have a love and respect for that person in whom we discover it; and as every virtue thus wins on our hearts, and even forces us to love those we believe to possess it, so more especially do justice and beneficence. But when several persons are all like one another in honesty and good manners, then no society can ever be more loving, or more closely united: for

where there are many of the same humour and same inclinations, every one sees, in some measure, his own self, and is
accordingly delighted in the person of another; and that is
brought about, which Pythagoras thought the perfection
of all friendship, that a great many severals are made into
one.   There is another remarkable fellowship or community,
arising from an intercourse of doing and receiving benefits;
which, while it is kept up by a mutual gratitude and kindness of all the parties, cannot but occasion a firm and very
lasting agreement between them.   But when we have gone
over all the relations that are in the world, and thoroughly
considered the nature of each, we shall find that there is no
one of greater obligation, no one that is dearer and nearer
to us, than that which we all of us bear to the public.   We
have a tender concern and regard for our parents, for our
children, our kindred, and acquaintance, but the love which
we have for our native country swallows up all other loves
whatsoever; for which there is no honest man but would
die, if by his death he could do it any necessary service.
How detestable, then, must the wickedness and barbarity
of those people be, who have mangled and rent this their
native country by all manner of villanies, and have made it
their business (nay, and still do so) to bring it to ruin and
utter desolation.[1]   Now if there should happen any contest
or competition between these relations, which of them
should have the greatest share of our duty, we should pay
the first regard to our country and parents, from whom we
have received the most endearing obligations; the next to
our children and family, who all have their eyes on us alone,
and have nobody else on whom they can depend; next in
order to these come our kindred and relations, whose fortune
is generally the same with our own.   To each of these,
therefore, whom I have just now mentioned, we most of all
owe what is necessary for their subsistence: but then, as
for living and eating together, for mutual advising, discourse, exhortation, comforting, and sometimes (if occasion
serves) rebuking, friendship is the properest soil for them;
and of all kinds of friendship, there is none so pleasant as
that which is cemented by a likeness of manners.

[1] In allusion to Julius Caesar, Marc Antony, etc.

XVIII.—*In liberality the necessity of the person is especially to be considered—Greatness of soul, the third general virtue, most glorious and splendid of all.*

But in all these duties of beneficence and liberality, one principal thing to be taken notice of is, what necessity the person we would be kind to lies under, and what he is able or not able to do without our assistance; so that, in some cases, the present posture and circumstances of a man's condition ought more to prevail with us than the degrees of relation. Again, there are certain particular offices, which are more peculiarly owing to some one sort of relatives than they are to another: in the business, for example, of getting in his corn, it is our duty rather to assist a next neighbour than either a brother or familiar friend; but if the business be a case at law, then a kinsman or friend must rather be defended than a next neighbour. These things, therefore, and such like circumstances, should be well considered, in the practice and exercise of every virtue; and our minds should be brought to a kind of acquaintance and familiarity with them, that so we may be quick at the accounts of our duty, and able, by casting up all things together, to see at last what the remainder is, and know what we owe to the several sorts and conditions of men: for as a general, orator, or physician, however well skilled in the rules of his art, can never be perfect without the assistance of practice and experience; just so it is in the case now before us: many have laid down the rules and precepts of virtue and good living, as I myself am doing at this very time; but there is moreover required, to a due degree of height and perfection in it, that one accustom himself to the exercise of them. And thus have I shown how virtue and honesty, from which all our duty does immediately flow, are deduced from those things which concern the society and good of mankind; which was the second general head I proposed to discourse of.

It is to be observed, that whereas there were laid down four general heads, from which all virtue and honesty is derived, whatever proceeds from a brave and exalted mind, that is raised above fortune and all the little chances and accidents of the world, is usually made most account of amongst men. Hence, in reproaches, we find there is nothing more common than such things as these—

> For shame! Young men, and yet have women's hearts!
> While this brave woman plays the man—

Or something like this—

> Dear Salmacis,[1] give spoils that cost no sweat or blood!

Whereas, on the contrary, in praises or panegyrics, those things that are done with a bravery of mind, and have something of extraordinary courage in them (I know not how), we commend in a nobler and loftier strain than we do anything else. Hence Marathon, Salamis, Plataea, etc., are so common a field for all the rhetoricians: hence our Cocles; hence the Decii, the Scipios, Marcellus, and a great many others; and especially the people of Rome itself, are particularly famous for greatness of courage. But the value that is set on military glory appears, from this, that almost all statues are done in the habit and garb of a soldier.

XIX.—*Courage is not truly a virtue, unless it be accompanied with justice, truth, etc.—Men of great souls are apt to be ungovernable and ambitious ; which prompts them to injustice—A man of a truly noble spirit never injures another, but protects from injuries, and scorns the applause of an ignorant multitude.*

But that sort of courage which is seen in the dangers and fatigues of war, unless a man be governed by the rules of justice, and fight for the safety and good of the public, and not for particular ends of his own, is altogether blamable; and so far from being a part of true virtue, as that it is indeed a piece of the most barbarous inhumanity. Fortitude is therefore very well defined by the Stoic philosophers, when they call it "a virtue contending for justice and honesty." No man, therefore, by baseness and treachery, has ever got the name and reputation of true courage; for nothing can ever be virtuous or creditable that is not just. To which purpose that of Plato was admirably well said: "As that sort of knowledge, which is not directed by the rules of justice, ought rather to have the name of design and subtlety, than wisdom and prudence; just so that bold and

[1] Salmacis was the name of a nymph presiding over a stream, which was said to soften and effeminate those that washed in it.

adventurous mind, which is hurried by the stream of its own passions, and not for the good and advantage of the public, should rather have the name of foolhardy and daring, than valiant and courageous." The first thing therefore I would have in a truly courageous man is, that he be a follower of goodness and fair dealing, of truth and sincerity; which are the principal and constituent parts of justice. But here it is one very unhappy thing, that, most times, these great and exalted minds are naturally ungovernable and desirous of rule: so that what Plato observed of the Spartans, that all their customs had no other aim but to get the superiority, may fitly enough be applied to these persons: for the more any man has of this greatness of soul, the more eager he is of being a sharer in the government, or rather of obtaining it wholly to himself: and it is no easy matter to be fair and equitable in all one's actions, which is the proper and peculiar office of justice, while one is endeavouring to make himself uppermost. Hence it comes to pass, that they never will be conquered in any debates, nor overruled by the laws and constitutions of the public; but make it their business, by factions and bribery, to get a strong party and interest in the republic; and rather choose to be uppermost by force and injustice, than equal to others by fair and upright dealing. But the difficulty of it can only serve to make it more honourable, but never its contrary more excusable: for no sort of case or circumstance whatever can excuse any man for being guilty of injustice. Those are therefore your truly brave and courageous men, not who rob, plunder, and injure others, but those who secure and protect them from injuries. But that greatness of mind which is truly such, and, under the direction of wisdom and prudence, makes that honour and credit, which we naturally desire, not consist in the outward imaginary applause, but in the real intrinsic goodness of its actions; and is not so eager of appearing to be greater and better than others, as of really being so: for he that is so mean as to depend on the giddy and ignorant multitude, ought never to be accounted of a truly great and exalted spirit; besides that, there is nothing so easily draws men to acts of injustice as a loftiness of mind, when joined with this foolish desire of applause. This is indeed a very dangerous place, and requires our greatest concern and watchfulness; because you shall hardly find any man, who, when he has gone through labours and difficulties, does not expect this honour and applause, as a kind of reward for his courage and achievements.

XX.—*Wherein true greatness of soul consists—It is an enemy to covet-ousness, to the desire of applause and of power—Produces a calm and unpassionate mind.*

Now all true courage and greatness of mind is more especially seen in these two things: the first is a generous contempt or disregard of all outward goods, proceeding from an opinion, that it is unworthy of a man to admire, or wish for, or endeavour after anything, unless it be that which is honest and becoming; to make himself subject to any one's will; to be a slave to his own irregular passions, or any ways depend on the caprices of fortune. When he has got such a temper of mind as I have now been describing, then the second thing is, that he perform such actions as are glorious and profitable, but withal very full both of labour and difficulty; and extremely dangerous to his life itself, as well as to those things that are requisite for its preservation. Now all the lustre and dignity of these two parts, nay, and I add all their usefulness too, is lodged only in the latter; but the groundwork, as it were, and foundation of all true greatness, is laid in the former: for in that are contained those generous principles, which exalt men's minds, and raise them to a contempt of all worldly things. But that former itself is made up of two parts: the first is an opinion that nothing is truly and really good, but only what is honest; the second, a freedom from all sort of passion or disturbance of mind: for what can more discover a man of a brave and heroic spirit, than to make no account in the world of those things which seem so glorious and dazzling to the generality of mankind; but wholly to despise them, not from any vain and fantastic humour, but from solid and firm principles of reason and judgement? Or what can more show a robust mind and unshaken constancy, than to bear those heavy and numerous calamities, which are incident to mankind in this life, with such a firm temper and fixedness of soul, as never to offend against nature and right reason, or do anything that is unworthy the dignity and character of a wise man? Now it would not at all be consistent or agreeable, that he who bore up so courageously against fear, should be afterwards unable to resist desire; or that he who could never be conquered by pain, should suffer himself to be captivated by pleasure. These things therefore should well be considered, and of all desires, that of money should be avoided; for nothing is a greater sign of a narrow, mean, and sordid spirit, than to dote on riches; nor is anything, on the contrary, more creditable and magnificent than to contemn wealth, if you have it not; and if you have it, to lay it out freely in acts of bounty and liberality. The desire of glory, as I before observed, ought also to be avoided; for it robs a man wholly of his freedom and liberty, which generous spirits ought of all things in the world to maintain and contend for. Neither ought places of power to be sought after; but at some times rather to be refused when offered, at others to be laid down if they can conveniently. We should free ourselves, in short, from all vehement passions and disorders of mind, not only those of desire and fear, but also of sorrow, of joy, and anger; that so the state of the mind may be calm and undisturbed; which will make the whole life become graceful and uniform. Now there both are and have been many, who, to gain this repose of which I am speaking, have betaken themselves to a life of retirement, and wholly withdrawn from all business of the public. Among these the noblest and most eminent of the philosophers; and some men of rigid and severe lives, who disliked the manners of the people or their governors; others have withdrawn themselves into the country, being pleased with the management of their own private fortunes. These men proposed the same end to themselves that kings and princes do, viz. the living so as to want for nothing; to be under the power and control of none, but to enjoy a full and perfect freedom; which consists in living so as one's self best pleases.

XXI.—*Those who live a public and private life compared—Those ought to serve the state who are qualified for the service—Two or three rules to be observed before a man enters on business.*

This then being the common design and end of them both, those who are ambitious of power and authority, think to obtain it by enlarging their fortunes and interests in the world; but these whom I have mentioned as men of retirement, by contenting themselves with their own condition, though but humble and mean. In which they are neither of them wholly in the wrong; but the life of the latter, I mean the retired, is both easier and safer, and begets less of trouble and disturbance to others, whereas that of the former, who give themselves up to affairs of state, and the management of great and important concerns, is more adapted to the benefit and good of mankind, and the getting of credit and reputation in the world. Those people therefore are perhaps excusable, who, being of parts and capacities for learning, give themselves wholly to the study of it, and never at all meddle with public business; and so are those also, who, being disabled by sickness and infirmities, or on any other good and allowable account, have separated themselves from the administration of affairs, leaving the power and reputation of it in the hands of others: but as for those people who have none of these reasons, and pretend to despise those commands and honours, which most men admire; I am so far from thinking it a virtue in them, that I rather esteem it a very great fault. Thus far, it is true, one can hardly condemn them, in that they despise, and make little account of glory and applause; but their true reason seems to be rather this, that they do not care to suffer the labour and fatigue of them, and are afraid of encountering with rubs and repulses, as things that are attended with some shame and dishonour: for you shall often find there are a great many men, who are very inconsistent with themselves in things of a contrary nature: as for pleasure, they despise it with all the severity of a Stoic; but yet are so effeminate, as not to be able to bear the least trouble; are mighty contemners of fame and applause; but extremely concerned at anything of disgrace: which are things that do not very well agree together. Those people then, whom Nature has endowed with abilities for that purpose, should forthwith endeavour to procure themselves places, and manage the business of the commonwealth; otherwise how should the city be well governed, or the greatness of their endowments be made known to the world? But that greatness of soul, and contempt of all human things, which we have often mentioned, together with that calmness and serenity of mind, is requisite in those of a public station, as much, if not more than it is in philosophers, if ever they hope to be free from anxieties, and arrive at any steadiness or uniformity in their lives. Now these things are easier to philosophers than to them; forasmuch as their lives being led in private, require for their support a less number of things, and have fewer within the power and reach of fortune: and if any ill accident should befall them, it is impossible their sufferings can be very considerable. Those men, therefore, that are in public stations, having things of more weight and importance to be taken care of, must in reason be supposed to lie much more open to the assaults of the passions than those who spend their days in privacy and retirement. On which account they should take the more care to fortify themselves with this greatness of spirit, and to free their minds from the grievous torments and disturbances of them. But he who takes on him a public trust, should not only look that the business be honest, but that he himself be qualified for the management of it; in considering which there is a double extreme to be carefully avoided, that he neither despair through a mean timidity, nor yet be over-confident through eagerness of desire: and, lastly, in whatever he sets about, let all things be diligently and carefully put in order, before he goes on to the execution of it.

XXII.—*It is no less great and commendable to manage affairs of peace than of war—Several examples to prove this.*

But seeing most people are apt to imagine that it is greater and more glorious to manage affairs of war than peace, I shall endeavour to lessen this general opinion: for the greatness of that glory, which is given to warriors, has made many people, for no other reason, desirous of quarrels, especially men of the greatest parts and most aspiring minds; particularly if they are qualified for a soldier's life, and their disposition carry them to the profession of arms: but if we would make a just estimate of the case, we should find both greater and more glorious actions done by wisdom at home than by arms abroad. For what though Themistocles be deservedly commended, and his name more illustrious than that of Solon; and though Salamis be brought for the proof of a victory which is commonly preferred to the wisdom of Solon, in constituting and settling the senate of Areopagus; yet, in truth, ought this to be judged no less great and extraordinary than that; for Themistocles' victory was only a service to the commonwealth once; but Solon's counsel will be so for ever, seeing it is by this that the laws of the Athenians, and constitutions of their ancestors, are kept up and maintained. Besides, Themistocles can name nothing in the world wherein he assisted the Areopagus; but Solon on his part may truly say, that he, by his wisdom, was assisting to Themistocles; for the war was carried on by the directions of that senate, which he by his prudence at first appointed. The same may be said of Pausanias and Lysander; for though by their valour they are thought to have enlarged the dominion of the Spartans, yet it is by no means at all to be compared with the laws and discipline of the wise Lycurgus: besides, that it was solely to these laws and this discipline they owed all the courage and obedience of their armies. I, for my own part, was always of opinion that Marcus Scaurus, when I was a boy, was by no means inferior to Caius Marius; nor Quintus Catulus, since I meddled with the republic, to Cneius Pompeius; for armies can signify but little abroad, unless there be counsel and wise management at home; neither was the rasing and destroying of Numantia, by that incomparable person and brave commander, the second Africanus, a greater and more signal piece of service to the republic, than the killing of Tiberius Gracchus by Nasica, though a mere private citizen at the same time. It is true, this action had something of the soldier in it, as being done by force and downright violence, and so does not wholly come under the notion of civil concerns: however, I have brought it as an instance of these, because it was effected by this civil sort of prudence, and without the assistance of a military power. I cannot but therefore still extremely approve of that saying of mine, which I am told some malicious and envious fellows most mightily carp at—

> Let warlike arms give place to the peaceful gown,
> And to the statesman's praise the victor yield his crown.

For, not to say anything of other people, when I sat at the helm of the government, did not arms then give place to the gown? Never was the state in more imminent danger, and yet never were things better and more happily quieted.

Thus by my prudence and careful management, the most impudent and audacious of all the citizens let, as it were, their arms fall out of their hands. What action then was there ever performed in war like this? Or where is the triumph that can be compared to it? For I think I may venture a little to boast before you, son Marcus, whose happiness it is to succeed in the glory, and whose duty to imitate the excellence of my actions: this I am sure of, even Pompey himself, a man the most famous for martial achievements, did me that justice, in the hearing of several, to say,—that his returning home with his third triumph had been to little or no purpose, unless my endeavours and services to the republic had preserved the city for him to truimph in. I conclude, therefore, from what has been observed, that that sort of courage which is seen in the management of civil affairs, is no less deserving than that which consists in the business of fighting; and the former requires more pains and application to be perfect in it than the latter doth.

XXIII.—*The body ought to be so far taken care of, as that it may be able to bear fatigues ; but it is the mind that truly makes great men.*

On the whole, that virtue which consists in greatness and elevation of soul, and makes up the subject of our present inquiry, is obtained by the strength of the mind, not the body: however, the body ought not to be neglected, but by exercise brought to such a frame and condition, as that it may be able to obey the prescriptions of the mind, in performing that business, and bearing those fatigues which are required of it. But still the nature of the virtue we are seeking for, consists in due care and application of mind; in which particular, the public receives as much benefit from gownmen, who manage and take care of its civil concerns, as it doth from soldiers, who are generals of its armies: for they by their prudence have often either hindered the breaking out of wars, or else have occasioned their speedy conclusion; and sometimes too have been the cause of their being undertaken, as the third with Carthage was entered into on the advice of Cato, whose credit and authority prevailed in that case even after he was dead. Wisdom, therefore, and skill in determining civil affairs, is more to be desired than courage in fighting: but then we must always be careful in this case that our design be not the avoiding of war, but the being more useful and serviceable to the public. And as for war, it should never be undertaken with any other aim, but only that of obtaining an honourable peace. It is the part of a brave and unshaken spirit not to be disturbed under any misfortune, or suffer itself in disorder and tumult to be thrown off the saddle, as we usually speak, but always to keep such a presence of mind, as to be able to consult on every occasion, and be hurried on to nothing but what is agreeable to reason and discretion. And as this is the part of an exalted spirit, so is what follows of an elevated understanding; to discover effects even while they are yet in the wombs of their causes, and consider beforehand whatever may happen on either side, and accordingly what is to be done when it does happen; that so he may never be taken unawares, and brought to that lamentable shift of crying out, " I never once thought of it." These are the duties, as of a truly courageous and lofty, so of a wise and judicious mind; but rashly to run and lay about one in battle, and come to wounds and downright blows with an enemy, is but a savage and brutish kind of business: however, necessity so requiring, a man should fight, and choose rather to part with his life than his liberty, or be guilty of any base or dishonourable action.

XXIV.—*Cool and deliberate counsels to be preferred before heat and boldness—It is a duty rather to expose oneself, than the public affairs—They are to blame, who rather venture the loss of their armies, than their own reputation.*

In the business of rasing and plundering cities, there ought to be taken a very special care that nothing of rashness or cruelty be shown; and all true greatness of spirit obliges us, having first considered things calmly and maturely, to pardon the multitude, and punish those only that were principally faulty; and in every state and condition of fortune, to observe the just medium of virtue and honesty: for, as we have already observed of some, that they count it more noble to manage affairs of war than of peace; so you shall find there are a great many others, who imagine that hot and adventurous undertakings have something that is greater and more glorious in them, than cool and deliberate counsels. Now as no man ought, by too warily avoiding of dangers and labours, to get himself the name of a coward; so, on the other hand, care should be taken that we thrust not ourselves into hazards and difficulties, where there is no manner of occasion for it; than which there is no greater folly on earth. It is a duty, therefore, in attempts of any danger, to imitate the practice of skilful physicians, who always to light and inconsiderable diseases apply none but easy and gentle remedies, but in desperate cases are forced to have recourse to desperate cures. It is a madness, therefore, while all things are calm and in a peaceful state, to desire a storm; but to keep off the mischiefs of it when it does happen, is the part of a wise and a prudent man; and so much the more, if the good to be obtained, by getting well rid of it, outbalance the evils you may be brought into by the attempt. The danger of some actions only relates to the person that undertakes them, but that of others to the whole republic; and again, a man's life is endangered in some, in others his reputation, and the good-will of his citizens. It is our duty then, in the former case, more willingly to expose and endanger ourselves than the whole state; and in the latter, to fight for our glory and reputation more readily than any other conveniences whatever. Yet the contrary to this appears plainly in the practice of a great many men, who are willing to spend their estates and lives for the good of their country, but will not bear the least diminution of their honour, though the present occasions of the republic require it. Thus Callicratidas, admiral of Sparta, in the Peloponnesian war, after he had done many signal services, at last was the occasion of ruining all; for when he was advised to retreat with his navy from Arginussa, and not venture giving the Athenians battle, he utterly refused it, and told his advisers, that if this whole navy should chance to be lost, the Lacedaemonians could fit out another; but that he for his part could never fly, without an irreparable loss of his honour. And here the Lacedaemonians had, though a great, yet a tolerable blow; but that other was mortal, and put a full period to the Spartan greatness, when their leader, Cleombrotus, only for fear of being somewhat ill-spoken of, unadvisedly ventured to fight

Epaminondas. How much better did Fabius Maximus do? concerning whom Ennius has these words:

> One man our state has saved by wise delays:
> For he regarded not the foolish prate
> Of idle people; but the city's good;
> Therefore his growing fame now flourishes
> More when his deeds are passed.

The same kind of fault should also be avoided in civil administrations; for a great many men are afraid to speak out what they really think, though perhaps it is for the best, for fear it should give any offence to others.

XXV.—*Rules to be observed in the government of the state and the administration of justice.*

Those who design to be partakers in the government should be sure to remember those two precepts of Plato; first, to make the safety and interest of their citizens the great aim and design of all their thoughts and endeavours, without ever considering their own personal advantage; and, secondly, so to take care of the whole collective body of the republic, as not to serve the interest of any one party, to the prejudice or neglect of all the rest: for the government of a state is much like the office of a guardian or trustee; which should always be managed for the good of the pupil, and not of the persons to whom he is entrusted; and those men who, whilst they take care of one, neglect or disregard another part of the citizens, do but occasion sedition and discord, the most destructive things in the world to a state: whence it comes to pass, that while some take part with the popular faction, and others make their court to every great one, there are but very few left who are concerned for the benefit and good of the whole. From this root have sprung many grievous dissensions amongst the Athenians; and not only tumults, but even destructive civil wars in our own republic; things which a worthy and truly brave citizen, and one who deserves to hold the reins cf the government, will shun and detest; and will give himself so to the service of the public, as to aim at no riches or power for himself; and will so take care of the whole community, as not to pass over any one part of it. Such a one will scorn, by the mean arts of calumny and a false accusation, to bring others into hatred

and disrepute with the people, but will always adhere to
what is just and honest, and never be drawn from it, whatever offence may be taken by others; nay, will rather part
with his life itself, than do anything that is contrary to the
virtues I have mentioned. Eager ambition, and contending
for honour, is of all things most ruinous and destructive to
a state; concerning which Plato had said admirably well,—
"that for men to contend and fall out with one another,
about which should be chief in the management of the state,
is just as if the ship's crew should go together by the ears
about who should be master or pilot of the vessel." And
the same philosopher has given us this for a rule—"that
only those men should be reckoned enemies who have taken
up arms in opposition to the republic; not those who would
govern it after their own schemes." Such was the dissension between P. Africanus and Q. Metellus, without any
great bitterness or animosities between them. Some people
think it the part of a brave and heroic spirit to show heat of
anger and passion against an adversary; but what they say
is by no means to be regarded; for it is certain, on the other
hand, that nothing is more laudable, nothing more worthy
of a great and brave person, than clemency, meekness, and
gentleness of spirit. In cities that are free, and where all
men in common enjoy the same privileges, courtesy, and
affability, and a calm and undisturbed temper of mind are
peculiarly requisite; for to fret on every unseasonable visit,
or at every impertinent and troublesome petitioner, makes
a man sour and morose in his humour; which, as it brings
no manner of good to himself, so it gets him the hatred and
ill-will of others. But though meekness and clemency be
laudable virtues, yet no farther than as they leave room for
a just severity, whenever the occasions of the public require
it; without which a city can never be well governed. Now
every reproof and chastisement in the first place, should be
always free from contumelious language, and not inflicted
for the sake of the person chastising or reproving another,
but for the good and advantage of the whole republic.
Diligent care should be taken, in the next place, that the
penalty be proportioned to the nature of the crime; and that
some do not pass without ever being questioned, while
others are punished for the same misdemeanours. But of
all things, anger should be excluded in punishing; for who-

ever comes to this work in a passion, will never observe that
due mediocrity, which equally abstains from too much and
too little, so strictly required by the Peripatetic schools;
and they have very good reason indeed to require it; but
then I cannot but wonder they should commend anger, and
say, Nature has given it us to good ends and purposes: for
that in truth ought in no case to be allowed of; and it were
heartily to be wished that the governors of a state would, in
this particular, be like the laws themselves, which punish
offenders according to justice, without being anyways
guided by passion.

XXVI.—*Greatness of soul requires an even temper, free from haughtiness
in prosperity, and dejection in adversity—In prosperity we should
especially consult our friends, and have a care of flatterers—How
an estate should be got, improved, and used.*

Another great duty of fortitude is, not to be haughty,
disdainful, and arrogant when Fortune favours us, and all
things go forward according to our wishes: for it shows as
much meanness and poorness of spirit to be transported
with good, as it does with ill fortune; whereas, on the other
hand, nothing is more brave than an evenness of temper in
every condition, and (as is reported of Socrates and Laelius)
a constant retaining the same air in one's countenance, without ever seeming puffed up or dejected. I find that Philip,
the king of Macedonia, was inferior to his son in the outward
glory and splendour of his achievements, but very far above
him in good nature and condescension: therefore the father
kept always the character of a great person, whereas the son
often was guilty of base and dishonourable actions. It is
a good rule therefore, I think, which is given by some men,
that the higher our station in the world is, the more care
we should take of our lives and actions, that they be kept
within the compass of lowliness and humility. Panaetius
tells us it was a usual saying with his scholar and familiar
friend Africanus,—" that men who give the reins to their
vicious appetites, and are high and presuming on the greatness of their fortunes, should be dealt with like horses, when
grown fierce and unruly by frequent engagements; for as
these are delivered to breakers to tame, and to be made fit
for riding; so those should be brought within the barriers

and limits of reason and philosophy, to teach them the uncertainty of all human things, and the great volubility and changeableness of fortune." We should also in prosperity more especially make use of the counsel of our friends, and pay more respect and deference to their advices than we were wont to do: at the same time also we should take great care that we do not give overmuch ear to flatterers, nor suffer ourselves to be wheedled and imposed on by their deceitful words: for there is nothing wherein we are more apt to be mistaken, than in this particular; every one having such a fond conceit and opinion of himself, as to think he deserves those applauses which they give him. Hence spring innumerable errors in our lives; whilst men, puffed up with a vain imagination and mistaken notions of their own great merit, are exposed to the raillery of all the world besides, and are cheated into great and dangerous mistakes. And so much may suffice on this head. From what has been said we may easily gather that those who are over affairs of the public do the greatest actions, and such as express the most bravery of mind; their business affording them more opportunities, and there being more men who are concerned in this, than in any other method of living whatever. But after all, we cannot but acknowledge there are, and have been, a great many noble spirits, even in a life of retirement and privacy, who, being sequestered from the business of the world, have given up themselves to inquiries after truth, and the great concernment of the practice of virtue; or else leading a life in the middle, as it were, between the statesman and philosopher, have been delighted with the management of their own private fortunes: not scraping up money by all manner of ways, or hoarding it so as to make nobody the better for it; but parting with it freely for the sake of their friends, or to serve the republic, when occasion required it. Now this private estate I would have, in the first place, to be honestly come by, not by any base, scandalous, or invidious way of gaining: then let it be distributed to the uses and necessities of as many as is possible, provided they are worthy and deserving people; and let it be increased by such ordinary methods of saving and good husbandry as are agreeable to the dictates of reason and prudence; and, lastly, let none of it be spent in debauchery and luxurious living, but in acts of munificence and liberality towards others. Whoever observes these measures laid down, let his way of life be either public or private, may perform all the duties of magnanimity, constancy, and greatness of soul, as well as of sincerity, fidelity, and doing good to mankind.

XXVII.—*The virtues contained under the fourth head of honesty—Whatever is honest is becoming ; honesty and decency being really the same thing—Two sorts of decorum, and the nature of each defined.*

We are now in the next place to speak of the fourth, and only remaining part of virtue or honesty, under which are comprehended bashfulness, temperance, modesty, government of the passions, and the observing a just order as to time and place in our words and actions; from all which arises a certain engaging kind of beauty and gracefulness, which serves to set off and adorn our lives. Under this head is contained that becomingness, which is in its nature so closely united and riveted to honesty, that there is no way left of pulling them asunder; for whatever is becoming is likewise honest, and whatever is honest is likewise becoming. The difference between them is so very small, that we may better conceive what it is, than explain it; for whatever becomingness there is in any action, it immediately arises from the honesty of it. From hence it appears that becomingness does not peculiarly belong to this one part of honesty, whereof we are now undertaking to discourse, but shows itself also in each of the three former. To reason, for instance, and discourse according to the rules of prudence; to go about nothing but after due consideration, and on every occasion to be quick at espying and defending the truth, are things that are becoming; whereas to be deceived, to be in an error or mistake, and to be imposed on, are very unbecoming, as well as to be mad or beside oneself. So again, all actions of justice are becoming; but those of injustice are both scandalous and unbecoming. The same may be said as to the actions of fortitude: whatever is done with a manly courage and bravery of mind, as it is worthy of, so it becomes a man; but whatever, on the other hand, shows any cowardice or meanness of spirit, is as contrary to becomingness as it is to true virtue. I conclude therefore that the decency whereof I am now discoursing appertaineth

to each of the four parts of honesty; and so appertaineth,
as not to stand in need of any mighty reach of understanding to perceive it, but is easily discoverable at the first view;
for there is something of becoming contained in the very
notion and idea of all virtue, from which it is distinguished
by the mind alone, and not by the nature of the thing itself.
Just as the beauty and good colour of the countenance can
never be separate from the health of the body, so this becomingness of which we are speaking, in itself is all one, and, as
it were, incorporate with virtue and honesty, but may be
distinguished from it by thought and imagination. Now
there are two kinds or sorts of it; the one universal, which
belongs to the nature of honesty in general; the other particular, and contained under this, which belongs to the several
parts of it. The former is used to be thus defined; decorum,
or becoming, is that which is congruous or agreeable to that
excellent part of the nature of man, by which he is distinguished from the rest of the creation. As for the latter,
which is contained under this, it is usually described and
defined to be that which is in such manner agreeable to the
nature of man, as withal to show something of temper and
moderation, with a certain sweet air of gentility and good
manners.

XXVIII.—*Poetical decorum defined—Decency relates both to the actions
of the body and mind—The nature or mind of man consists of sense
and reason—The former of these ought to obey the latter.*

That this is so, will more plainly appear, if we consider
that decorum or convenience of manners, which the poets
aim at in all their writings; concerning which, were it any-
wise necessary to my present purpose, I might largely discourse. Suffice it at present for me only to observe that the
poets are then said to keep this decorum, when each of their
persons is brought in saying and doing those things which
are suitable to the character he bears in the world. Should
Aeacus, for example, or Minos say,

> Ev'n let them hate me, whilst they dread me too; [1]

or,

> The child's entombed in its own parent's bowels; [2]—

---

[1] A verse out of Ennius.

[2] A verse which the poet Accius puts into the mouth of Atreus, who
had killed the children of Thyestes, and served them up to him at
a banquet.

it would be an offence against the rules of decency, because they pass in the world for men of justice and honesty; but let the same be said by a cruel Atreus, and the whole theatre shall clap and applaud it, because it is a saying very agreeable to his character. Now the poet can judge what is becoming and convenient for every person, according to the character which he bears in the poem: but Nature has given every one of us a character, by endowing us with that nobleness and excellence of being, whereby we are set above all other creatures. The poets, then, there being so great a variety of characters, can see what is becoming and convenient for all, even the most vicious; but we have got only one character to live up to,—I mean that which is assigned us by Nature herself; a character of temperance and modesty, of constancy and moderation. And the same Nature having also taught us that we ought to be careful of our carriage and demeanour towards the rest of men, hence it appears of how large an extent that becomingness is, which belongs to the nature of honesty in general, and also that other, which is seen in the exercise of the several kinds of it: for as the beauty and comeliness of the body draws the eyes to it by the fit composure of all its members, and pleases us only on this account, because all its parts correspond with a kind of proportion and harmony; so this decorum, which gives a sort of lustre and grace to our lives, engages the approbation and esteem of all we live with, by that just and due order, consistency, and regularity, which it keeps up and maintains in our words and actions. We ought to have, therefore, a certain respect and reverence for all men, and desire to be approved not only by the best, but by all the world; for not to care a farthing what it is people think of one, is a sign not only of pride and conceitedness, but indeed of having perfectly abandoned all modesty. But here we must observe, that there is a great deal of difference between that which justice, and that which this modesty, respect, or reverence demands, in relation to other people. It is the duty of justice, not to injure or wrong any man; of respect, or reverence, not to do anything that may offend or displease him; wherein more especially the nature of that decorum we are speaking of consists. These things then being thus explained, I suppose it may clearly enough appear what that is which we mean by becoming. As for the duties prescribed by it, the first thing to which it conducts us is, to demean ourselves suitably and agreeably to our nature, and do nothing that may anyways stain or deface it; for whilst we take this for our guide and conductress, it is impossible we should ever go out of the way; but by her shall be led through all the paths of wisdom, truth, and understanding; of justice and beneficence towards the society of mankind; and of true magnanimity and greatness of soul. But the nature of decency is more peculiarly seen in the fourth part of honesty, concerning which we are now discoursing; and relates not only to the motions of the body, but more especially to those of the mind also; each of which then are approved and becoming, when they are such as are proper and suitable to nature. Now the whole of the nature or mind of man is made up of only these two parts: the first consists in the sensitive appetite; by the blind and extravagant impulse of which he is hurried and transported from one thing to another: the second is reason, which shows and instructs him in the way of his duty, telling him what he should do, and what not do: whence it follows that it is reason which ought to be the governing faculty, and the appetite to be subject to the commands of it.

XXIX.—*Our actions should neither be rash nor careless, etc.—Watchfulness and consideration necessary for the subduing of the passions—Moderation to be observed in jests and diversions.*

Every action therefore should be free, as from precipitancy and rashness on the one hand, so from all carelessness and negligence on the other; nor should anything be done, for which we cannot give a sufficient reason; which is almost the very definition of duty. In order to this the passions must be brought under the power of reason, so as neither through hastiness to run before its orders, nor through coldness and heaviness to disregard them when given; but all their motions must be so quieted and restrained, as to bring no uneasiness or disturbance to the mind: and from this calm and peaceable state of the soul arises that constancy and moderation we have mentioned; for when once the passions grow unruly and extravagant, and refuse to be guided in their desires and aversions by the rules of prudence, they will run without question beyond all bounds and measure; for they abandon and cast off their allegiance to reason, which they ought to obey by the constitution of nature. By this means are all things turned topsy-turvy; and not the mind only, but even the body also, put very much into disorder and confusion. Do but mark those who are inflamed with a vehement anger or desire; who are transported with fear, or an over-great joy; and you will see an alteration in their countenances, voices, gestures, and all their actions; which sufficiently gives us to understand (that we may return again to the duty now before us) how necessary it is to restrain and give check to the movements of the appetite, and to be always watchful and standing on our guard, that so we may neither be careless and inconsiderate, nor do anything rashly and at all adventures: for mankind were never designed by Nature merely to sport and idle away their time, but to follow after grave and serious studies, and business of greater importance than play is. Not but that jesting and diversion are allowable, provided we use them but as we do sleep, and other such necessary refreshments of nature, viz. after the discharge of our serious and more important duties. And even then we must see that our jesting be neither excessive nor immodest, but such as is handsome and becoming a gentleman; for as boys are allowed not all kinds of sports, but only such as have nothing that is vicious or ill in them; so in this jesting we should allow ourselves nothing but what is agreeable to honesty and good manners. We may therefore observe that jesting or merriment is of two sorts; the one clownish, abusive, scandalous, and obscene; the other handsome, genteel, ingenious, and truly pleasant. Of this kind are several instances to be met with, as in our Plautus, and the old Greek comedians; so in the writings of the Socratic philosophers: to which we may add the ingenious sayings of several men, such as are collected by the senior Cato, and usually go by the name of Apophthegms. There is no great difficulty then to distinguish between a genteel and a clownish jest; the one, if brought in at a seasonable time, and when a man's mind is disengaged from business, is becoming for a gentleman; the other, for no man at all indeed, when base and unhandsome things are dressed up in filthy and obscene expressions. Our plays and recreations must also be kept within their due bounds; and care should be taken that we do not run out into great excesses, and suffer the pleasure which we take in them to carry us into anything that is base or unbecoming. Hunting, and the exercises of the Campus Martius, supply us with examples enough of creditable and manly recreations.

XXX.—The excellence of man's nature necessary to be considered : wherein it consists—The difference of men's particular natures or dispositions shown by a number of examples.

But in all inquiries concerning what becomes us, it is of very great moment to be constantly reflecting how much man's nature excels that of beasts and inferior animals. These have no taste or relish for anything but the pleasures of the body, towards which they are carried with a great deal of eagerness; whereas nothing is more agreeable and nourishing, as it were, to the mind of man, than learning and contemplation. Hence he is always seeking or contriving something that is new, and is greatly delighted with seeing and hearing, for the increase of his knowledge: and if there is any one too much addicted to sensual pleasures, unless he is transformed into a mere brute; (for some such there are, who are men in name, and not in reality) but if, I say, any one is too much addicted, and suffers himself to be conquered by pleasure; yet, for very shame, he will hide and conceal his propensities towards it as much as possible. And what is this now but a plain indication that sensual pleasures are unbecoming the dignity of a reasonable creature, and ought to be despised and rejected by him? and that whoever sets any value on them should be sure to take care that he keep within the limits of reason and moderation? Hence it follows that we should not have any respect to pleasure, but only to the preservation of our health and strength, in our victuals, clothes, and other conveniences belonging to the body. And does not the consideration of the same dignity and excellence of our natures plainly inform us how base and unworthy a thing it is to dissolve in luxury, softness, and effeminacy; and how brave and becoming it is, on the other hand, for a man to lead a life of frugality and temperance, of strictness and sobriety? And here we must observe that Nature has given us, as it were, a double part to be acted in the world: the first is extended to all men in common, forasmuch as we are all of us partakers of reason, and that prerogative of our nature, whereby we are exalted above other animals; it is this that conducts us in the finding out our duty, and from it all honesty and becomingness arises: the second is appropriate to each in particular; for as there is a great deal of difference in bodies, some being nimble and proper for running, others more lusty, and fitter for wrestling; some of a noble and majestic air, others of a sweet and engaging kind of beauty; so there is no less, or rather a far greater variety in humours. Thus Lucius Crassus and Lucius Philippus were men of a great deal of wit and pleasantry: Caius, the son of Lucius Caesar, of more than they, and a great deal more studied: whereas the young Drusus and Scaurus at the same time were men of extraordinary gravity and severity. Laelius had abundance of mirth and gaiety; his familiar, Scipio, much more ambition, and greater austerity and strictness of living. Amongst the Greeks, Socrates is said to have been one that was of a very easy and facetious humour; that always loved to be merry and jesting, and was a mighty artist at hiding his meaning under witty ironies and droll expressions; whereas Pericles and Pythagoras got themselves credit by being of exactly the contrary temper. Hannibal, among the Carthaginian generals, and, amongst our own, Fabius was crafty and subtle; one that knew how to disguise his intentions and keep his counsel; that could make show of one thing whilst he was really designing another; of exquisite skill for contriving of stratagems, and preventing those laid by the enemy against himself. In this kind the Grecians give Jason the Pheraean, and Themistocles, the preference before any others; and there is one thing of Solon's, which shows he had his share of this cunning and subtlety, when he feigned himself distracted to save his own life, and withal to do a good piece of service to the public. There are others to be found of just an opposite humour, who think it unlawful to do anything by stratagem and underhand dealing, but are all for simplicity and plainness in their actions; lovers of open and undisguised truth, but haters of everything that looks like a trick. There are some that will undergo anything in the world, fawn and crouch to any manner of

person, if they can but obtain their own ends and designs by
it; as Marcus Crassus, we know, did to Sylla: of which sort
of crafty and complying kind of people Lysander the Lacedaemonian is said to have been the chief; whereas Callicratidas, who was admiral of the navy next after Lysander,
was quite the contrary. Again, there is as great a variety
in men's ways of discourse, as in their humours and com-
plexions; some who are able to speak very nobly can yet
suit their language to the humours and capacities of the
ignorant vulgar; as I remember Catullus, father and son, as
also Mucius Mancia could do; and I have heard old people
relate the same of Scipio Nasica; but his father, on the contrary, he who, by slaying Tiberius Gracchus, put a full end
to his ruinous attempts, had none of that affable way of
speaking. No more had Xenocrates, the most rigid and
severe of all the philosophers; and for that very reason was
noted eminent. In short, there is almost an infinite number
of these different natures and characters in men, not one of
which is in itself to be condemned.

XXXI.—*Every one should follow his own genius, so far as it is innocent*

The more easily then to arrive at that decorum of which
we are speaking, let every one stick to his own peculiar
character and humour, provided it has nothing that is vicious
in it: I say, provided it has nothing that is vicious in it; for
we should always take particular care to do nothing that
is contrary to that universal character which Nature has
imprinted on every one of us; but, saving the reverence we
owe to that, then to live according to our own particular
one, so as to follow after that kind of study, and apply ourselves to that course of life which is most suitable and agreeable to our own inclinations, though others perhaps may be
more useful and important; for it is in vain to struggle
against the bias of your nature, or to engage in that sort of
business in which you can never arrive at any perfection.
From what has been said it more fully appears what that is
which we call becoming; since nothing can be such that is
done, as we say, in despite of nature, *i.e.* contrary to the
bent and tendency of a man's genius. Now it is certain, if
anything in the world is becoming, it is a constant uniformity

in our whole lives and particular actions; which it is utterly impossible we should ever maintain, so long as we run counter to our own inclinations, and foolishly follow after those of other people: for as we should use our own native language, which all are supposed to understand best, and not lard our talk, as a great many do, with expressions out of Greek, who are therefore deservedly laughed at by others; so we should keep to one constant tenor and regular conduct in our lives and actions, so that nothing may be in them which is not well suited and of a piece with the rest. And this difference in the characters or natures of men is of so great moment, as that in consequence of it one man may be obliged to make away with himself, whilst another, though like him as to all other circumstances, may be obliged to the contrary. Cato, for instance, and those who in Africa surrendered themselves to Caesar, were all of them under the same condition; and yet any of the rest might perhaps have been blamed for it, had they murdered themselves as Cato did, because they were men of less strictness in their lives, and less severity in their manners. But Cato was a person whom Nature had endowed with incredible firmness and strength of soul, which he had augmented by perpetual constancy, and unalterably adhering to his once undertaken designs and resolutions: it became his character therefore to die, rather than to see the face of the tyrant. How many things did Ulysses undergo in his tedious wanderings, when he was forced to be at the pleasure of women (if Circe and Calypso may be called women), and by fawning words, and fair complaisant speeches, wheedle himself into the favour of all he met with! How did he bear the contemptuous usage of his servants and maids, even in his own palace, that at last he might arrive at his wished-for end! Whereas Ajax, according to the character we have of him, would rather have died a thousand deaths than ever have sub-mitted to such mean compliances. These observations should teach us all to look carefully every one into himself, and consider well what is his peculiar genius, and endeavour to make the best use of it that he is able; and not to be foolishly trying experiments, to see how he can succeed in what is another body's talent; for it is certain, that nothing becomes a man so well, as that which is best suited to his own inclinations. Every one therefore should inform himself thoroughly which way his humour and genius lies, and be severe in examining what he is well fitted or not fitted for: otherwise the players may seem to be wiser than we are; for they, when they pitch on what they will act, do not always choose those parts that are best, but those that are best suited to their humours and abilities. They that have the ablest voices, for instance, Epigoni, or Medus; they that have most action, Menalippa or Clytemnestra; Rupilius, whom I remember, had always the part of Antiopa, and Aesop very rarely that of Ajax. And shall actors observe this in choosing their parts, and wise men not do it in choosing their business and way of living in the world? We should therefore apply ourselves especially to that which we find most agreeable to the bent of our natures; but if we should chance to be driven on anything which is not so proper for our parts and talents, we should make it our business, by care and application, if not to go through with it the most perfectly that is possible, yet at least with as few faults as we are able. And let us rather labour to avoid those vices which we are naturally inclined to, than try to arrive at those excellences and perfections which we were never made for.

XXXII.—*Duties arising from men's several stations and professions in the world—What usually determines men in the choice of a way of life.*

But beside those two parts which I have already mentioned, there are still two others remaining behind: the one is allotted us by time and chance; the other we ourselves choose voluntarily to ourselves. To the first appertain one's being a king, a general, or a magistrate; coming of a great family; having riches and power; together with the contraries of all these; which are all of them things that depend on fortune, and alter according to the difference of times. As for the second, it is altogether left to our own choice what sort of calling we have a mind to be of: accordingly some choose to study philosophy, others the civil law, and a third sort eloquence; and of the virtues themselves, some are desirous of being eminent in one kind, and some in another. Now those men whose fathers or ancestors have been eminent in any one kind, for the most part endeavour to excel in the same; as Quintus, the son of Publius Mucius, did in the civil law; Africanus, the son of Paulus, in martial achievements: and some, not content with the glory of their ancestors, have added something else of their own to it; as that Africanus, whom I just now mentioned, who, besides his great fame for military exploits, made himself noted for his learning and eloquence. The same did Timotheus, the son of Conon, who was equal to his father in the glory of war, and obtained that of learning and ingenuity besides. But it happens sometimes, that omitting to tread in the steps of their fathers, some take new methods and designs of their own; which, generally speaking, is the case with those who are born of mean parents, and propose to rise and make their fortunes in the world. Each of these things should be thoroughly considered and revolved in our mind, whenever we deliberate what will become of us. The first thing then to be determined is, what sort of men we design to be, and what course of living to take to in the world, which is a case of all others the most hazardous and difficult: for when people are young, and consequently most foolish, they generally pitch on that way of life which then best pleases their unexperienced fancies: so that they are fixed and engaged in a certain course before they have the judgment to discern what is best. Prodicus, indeed (as I find it in Xenophon) tells us this story concerning Hercules,—" That when he was a youth, which is the proper season allotted by Nature for choosing a way of life, he withdrew himself into a solitary place, and there having found out a couple of ways, the one of pleasure, and the other of virtue, he sat musing, and considered awhile with himself, which of these two he had best to follow." Such a thing as this might happen to Hercules the son of Jupiter; but it is not for us to expect the same, who each of us take whom we please for our patterns, and suffer ourselves to be drawn as they lead us. We have most of us principles instilled by our parents, and follow their customs and manners of living; others are guided by popular opinion, and like that best which takes the most. However, there are some, whether it be out of mere good fortune, or a happy temper and disposition of soul, or lastly, by the care and instructions of their parents, that pursue right methods and ways of living.

XXXIII.—*The principal thing to be regarded in the choice of a profession is one's own genius ; next to that, one's fortune in the world—After a man has determined, he should adhere to his choice, without great reasons to the contrary—Cautions to be observed in the imitation of our ancestors.*

But those of all are the most difficult to be found, who having sufficient natural parts, or sufficient improvements of learning and education, or both these together, have withal had due time to consider with themselves what is the best course of life they can follow in the world. Now in this deliberation, the principal thing which we ought to regard is, each man's peculiar nature and genius: for since the decorum of each particular action, as before was observed, is taken from the disposition of the person that does it; surely that disposition should be carefully consulted before we determine on our whole way of living; it is otherwise impossible we should keep a due tenor and consistency in our lives and not sometimes falter in the performance of our duty. But though Nature in this case has much the greater sway, yet Fortune comes in for a share next after her; both of them therefore should be duly consulted in making choice of a calling, but more especially Nature; for Fortune is inconstant and often changing, but Nature is firm, and will abide by us; so that for the former to oppose this latter, is like a mortal power's contending with an immortal. That man, then, who has chosen a way of living that is suitable to his nature, provided that nature be no ways vicious, should make it his next care never to alter it; for nothing is less becoming than a humour of changing: but if on trial he should find that he was mistaken in the choice of his method, as it is very possible that such a thing may happen, there is no way left but to unravel again what is already done. If the times themselves favour the making such a change, it may be the more easily and conveniently done; but if not, it must be brought about gradually and insensibly, according to that rule which is given by wise men. Whenever you design to break off any friendship or displeasing acquaintance, you should loosen the knot by little and little, and not try to cut it asunder all at once; and when by this means we have changed our course of life, great care should be taken that we may seem to have done it on very good reasons. But having before recommended the imitation of our fathers and ancestors, I must here interpose an exception or two: in the first place, then, we should take great care not to follow them in anything that is vicious or blamable; nor, secondly, should we attempt it when we find our constitution will not carry us through with it. Thus, for instance, the son of the former Africanus, who adopted this latter, being son to Paulus, by reason of the weakness and indisposition of his body, could not so well tread in the steps of his father, as his father had done in those of his grandfather. But then if a man be of such a constitution, as that he is unable either to plead at the bar, or to harangue the people, or conduct an army, he should take the more care that he does those things which are in his power; such are the duties of justice and fidelity, of modesty, temperance, and liberality; the performance of which may serve to make amends for his want of the others. Now the noblest inheritance that can ever be left by a father to his son, and far exceeding that of houses and lands, is the fame of his virtues and glorious actions; and for a son to live so, as is unworthy of the name and reputation of his ancestors, is the basest and most abominable thing in the world.

XXXIV.—*The respective duties belonging to each age—Vice doubly evil in old men—The duties of magistrates, private citizens, and strangers.*

And since each age has its respective duties belonging to it, and the same things become not both young and old, I must add something also on this distinction. It is required then of the younger sort of people, that they pay due reverence to those that are old, and choose out the best and most approved among them, by whose counsel and direction they may steer their lives; for indeed the unskilfulness and inexperience of youth does stand in some need of the prudence of old age to be its guide and director. This age especially should be kept from all loose and effeminate living, and be inured to labour, and enduring hardships both of body and mind; that so they may be able to bear the toils and fatigues of business, whether in peace or war; and if they do at any time slacken their mind, and give themselves up to their pleasures and refreshments, great care should be taken that they exceed not the limits of temperance and modesty. And in order to this, it would be very convenient, if some aged people would keep a constant eye on their sports and recreations. As for old men, it is their duty to lessen the labours of the body, and employ more frequently those of the mind; and make it their business, by prudent and wise counsels, to do what good they can to the younger sort of people, to their friends and dependants, and more especially to the republic: and old men of all things should especially be careful not to languish out their days in unprofitable idleness. Luxury and riot is unbecoming in all, is perfectly scandalous and intolerable in old age; but should lust and wantonness come into the bargain, those who are guilty of it are doubly faulty; for, first, they bring a shame and disgrace on themselves, and withal make the young men more shamelessly wicked. Besides these duties already mentioned, it may not be amiss to say something of those which peculiarly belong either to magistrates, private citizens, or strangers. First, then, a magistrate ought to consider that he does in his person represent the whole city, and accordingly is bound to maintain the credit and dignity of it: that he is to preserve the laws, and see that all people have their due rights; remembering that these things are committed to his trust, which he is bound to render up faithfully and honestly. It is the duty of those in a private capacity to live as the rest of their citizens do, neither debasing themselves below their just height, nor endeavouring to raise themselves up above it; and to follow those things which are honest and peaceable in the commonwealth: these are they whom we usually call and account good citizens. And, lastly, for strangers and sojourners in a place, it is their duty to follow their own business, and not intermeddle with anybody's else; not to take on them what no ways concerns them, or be curious in prying into the secrets of a state with which they have nothing to do. By observing these rules we may, generally speaking, be sure to find our duty, whenever it is inquired what is suitable and becoming for such a person, such a time, or such an age: I shall only add, that in all our designs, and all our undertakings, nothing is more becoming than constancy and regularity.

XXXV.—*Decorum shows itself outwardly in three things : rules of modesty taken from Nature in the frame of our bodies.*

But since this decorum of which we are speaking is seen more especially, and discovers itself in our actions, our words, and our carriage and exterior ornaments of the body, and consists in one of these three things, in a certain kind of natural beauty and comeliness, in pertinence and well-timing our words and actions, and such other kind of ornaments and outward embellishments as are proper for the business one is going about (things which it is no easy matter to express, but I hope I am understood, and that is sufficient), and since that care which we ought to take, of making ourselves agreeable to those we converse with, consists in a due regulation of these, I shall proceed to discourse of them each in particular. In the first place, then, it may be worth our observing, how much care and concern has been shown by Nature, in ordering the frame and composition of our bodies: those parts which were handsome and agreeable to the sight, she has placed in view; but those which could not be so handsomely shown, these she has been careful to conceal and cover. The Cynics therefore are wholly to be rejected, and some of the Stoics little better than Cynics, who laugh at and blame us for calling those things by their proper names which are really dishonest and scandalous in themselves, while we count it a shame to speak plainly of those, in the doing of which there is no manner of dishonesty. —To rob, for example, to cheat, and lead a sensual life, are actions in themselves the most shameful and scandalous, and yet it is not counted immodest to name them; whereas an action that is honest and creditable in itself must not be plainly mentioned, for fear of its giving offence to chaste ears. This, and much more to the same purpose, they commonly urge against bashfulness; but let us follow where Nature has showed us the way, and whatever may offend either the eyes or the ears, that let us shun in our carriage and conversation. In all our postures and gestures of body, such as standing, walking, sitting, and leaning; nay, in our very countenance, in the cast of our eyes, and motions of our hands, we should be careful to keep and observe what is becoming; in which there is a double extreme to be avoided, that of too much niceness and effeminacy on the one hand,

and that of mere clownishness and want of breeding on the other. We should therefore take care to be strict observers of these rules of modesty, especially being such as even Nature herself has directed us to.

XXXVI.—*Two sorts of beauty, one proper for men, the other for women— Rules regarding apparel, walking, and outward ornaments—More care should be taken to keep decency in the motions of the soul—How this may be done.*

But since there are two sorts of beauty in the world, one of which consists in charms and sweetness, the other in gracefulness and majesty, the former of these should be left to the women, and the latter only be thought proper for the men. Hence it follows, that these should avoid all unmanly ornaments and niceness in their habits, and the same in the motions and gestures of their bodies; for all people hate the affected motions and carriage of those who would be taken for masters of a genteel air; and your actors on the stage have a great many foolish impertinent gestures, which are very displeasing and offensive to the spectators: and in each of these kinds, what is simple and unaffected is always best liked and approved by the world. In order to have a true graceful comeliness, you must endeavour to keep a good colour in your face; and the way to do that is to use frequent exercise. Nor do we forbid men the use of all ornaments and graces to recommend them, but only of those that are too exquisite and affected: so far they are allowable, as they are necessary to keep a man from being thought a clown, and from showing a disrespect for the persons he has to do with. And the same rule may serve very well for our clothes; in which to be moderate, as in most other cases, is certainly the best way. We should also avoid an effeminate softness and slowness in our gait, like those that are marching along in procession; and no less an over-great hastiness and speed, which only begets a deep panting and breathing, distorts the face, and perfectly changes the whole air of the countenance, which discovers a lightness and inconstancy of humour. Now if the motions of the body deserve all these pains and concern about them, how much care should we take to keep those of the mind within the limits prescribed them by nature and right reason, which never can be done any other way, than by keeping the soul in such an even temper, as not to be concerned or dejected at anything; and by a constant care and application of thought, so as to mind nothing but what is honest and becoming. Now the motions of the soul are of two sorts, some of them proceeding from the reasonable or thinking, others from the sensitive and passionate part: the former is busied in nothing but searching and finding out of truth; by the latter we are pushed and driven forward to action. It is our duty therefore to employ our thoughts about laudable objects, and so to reduce and overrule the passions, as that they may ebb and flow in obedience to reason.

XXXVII.—*Decorum shows itself in speaking—Rules about the manner, subjects, and measures of public oratory and our common talk.*

Another great instance in which this becomingness shows itself, is our speech and discourse: but whereas of this there are two sorts, the one proper only for argument and contention, the other for common and ordinary talk; we should make use of that when we plead at the bar, or speak in the senate and public assemblies; of this when we meet and discourse with our friends, when we walk in any of the public places, or are sitting at table, and over a glass of wine. There are teachers of rhetoric who give rules about the former; but there are no rules given about the latter; not but that I think there might be some invented; but the business is, there is nobody to be found that would study them if they were; otherwise masters would never be wanting, if there were but learners that would study and employ them. Hence we are almost overrun with rhetoricians, though no small part of the rules which they give, viz. those that concern either the words or the sense, may be very well applied to our ordinary discourse. The voice is that whereby we can talk, and convey our inward thoughts from one to another; in which there are two things chiefly required; first, that it be clear; and, secondly, harmonious. Each of these must be the gift of Nature, and is not attainable any other way; but where they are naturally, practice and exercise will increase the one, and imitation of those who speak sweetly and agreeably, better the other. This was the principal thing in the two Catuli, which made them

be counted men of judgement and learning; though they
had some skill in the matter it is true, and so had some
others as well as they; but this one thing recommended
them so much, that they were esteemed the most perfect
masters of the Roman language. The sound of their voices
was pleasing and harmonious; they neither slurred over
things negligently in their pronunciation, nor yet were too
exact in expressing every letter, the former of which would
have made their speech obscure, and the latter affected.
They never spoke so as to strain their voices, but equally
avoided the double extreme, that of faintness and sickliness,
as it were, on the one hand, and of too much loudness and
elevation on the other. Crassus' discourse was full as witty,
and not near so barren, as that of the Catuli; yet these had
as great a reputation as he on the score of good speaking.
Caesar, who was brother to the elder Catulus, was far more
facetious and witty than any of them; so that in court,
when before the judges, he would do more by his easy
familiar way of talking than others could do by all the
powers of their eloquence. Each of these things should be
diligently taken care of, if we desire to act decently on all
occasions. Our common discourse then I would have to be
such as that wherein the followers of Socrates excel; easy
and good-natured, without any stubbornness or stiffness in
opinion: let it be seasoned with mirth and pleasantness,
and not be too tedious, pert, and assuming, as though it
had a right to the attention of the hearers, and nobody else
had anything to do with it; but think it reasonable, as in
all other cases, so in this of discourse, to let every man
fairly take his own turn. But especially, in the first place,
it ought to be considered, what is the nature of the subject
we are discoursing on; if it be serious, we should handle it
with seriousness; but if it be merry, with gaiety and brisk-
ness. But the most important thing to be taken care of is,
that our talk do not discover any viciousness in our manners;
which is apt to appear by nothing so much as by falling too
foul on those that are absent, either by turning them into
ridicule, or misrepresenting them by malicious reproachful
language. Now the subject of discourse in common conversation is usually one of these three things; either our
own private domestic concerns; those that relate to the
commonwealth in general; or, lastly, some matter of study

and learning: therefore when our talk begins to ramble from these, we should always be careful to fetch it back to them again. But whatever subjects present themselves (for we are not all pleased with the same things, nor with anything equally at all times, but whatever subject, I say, we are on), we should consider how far our discourse may be entertaining; and as we could find a time when to begin, so we should learn when to make an end.

XXXVIII.—*Discourse should be free from passion and heaviness—In quarrels we should avoid passion—To boast of oneself very unbecoming.*

It is a general rule for the conduct of our lives that we make it our business to be free from passion; that is, from all violent motions of the soul, which reject and cast off their allegiance to reason. This should be applied to the matter now before us; and all our discourse should be calm and dispassionate, without any transports of anger or desire; as also, on the other hand, without deadness and heaviness, or any such vice: and in every company we should carefully endeavour to show a sort of kindness and respect for those persons with whom we converse. It sometimes comes to pass that chiding is necessary; in which we may be allowed a little to raise our voices, and to use more sharpness and authority in our expressions: however, we must be careful that we do not discover any passion; but let it rather be seen that we come to such corrections as physicians do to cutting and scarifying wounds, but seldom, and with a great deal of regret and unwillingness: and indeed we should never come to them at all, unless it be necessary, and when no other methods will do any good: and even then, when we are forced to it, we must be sure, as was said, to avoid all anger; for whatsoever is guided by its influence and directions can never be done with any prudence or moderation. Our rebukes should be generally mild and gentle: but nevertheless such, as may carry some weight and authority along with them; observing a mean betwixt too great easiness, and breaking out into angry and contumelious language. And whatsoever sharpness we may express in our reproofs, we should let the person so corrected know that we do it altogether for his good, and not for any by-ends or self designs. In the quarrels we have even with our greatest adversaries, whatever dirty language may be thrown on us, it is the best way to keep our minds calm and sedate, and never let anger break in; for whatever is spoken or done in a passion can neither be consistent with the rules of gravity, nor be approved of by those who are present in the company. Lastly, it is a very unbecoming thing for a man to boast of himself in discourse, and especially when that which he says is false; which is but to imitate Bragga-docio in the comedy, and make himself the laughing-stock and jest of the hearers.

XXXIX.—*What sort of house is fitting for a person of honour—Three rules to be observed for the keeping of decorum in our actions.*

And since we take in, or desire at least to take in, all the several branches of duty, we must not forget to add a word or two about what sort of house is becoming a gentleman or a person of honour. Now the main end of building is lodging, and other necessary uses of a house; and therefore the draught or contrivance of it should be suited accord-ingly: but we should not so much regard bare necessities, as not to have an eye to convenience and magnificence. Cneius Octavius, the first of that family that was ever consul, built himself a noble and magnificent house on the Palatine hill, which is said to have gained him a great deal of reputation; insomuch, that the people coming usually to see it, the very house was supposed to have gone a great way toward advancing its owner, though a kind of upstart, to the dignity of consul. This some time after was pulled down by Scaurus, that so he might make his own somewhat the bigger by it: but whereas Octavius, by building his house, had made himself consul; this man, on the contrary, by enlarging of his, though the son of a great and most eminent citizen, not only caused himself to lose that office, but was moreover brought into shame and dishonour, and at last utterly ruined. It is well if a man can enhance that credit and reputation he has gotten by the splendour of his house; but he must not depend on his house alone for it; for the master ought to bring honour to his fine seat, and not the fine seat bring honour to its master. But, as in all other cases, a man should not have respect to himself alone, but

*c 345

to other people also; so it is in this of a nobleman's house, which ought to be made very large and capacious, because he must keep up the laws of hospitality, and entertain multitudes of all sorts of persons in it: for a fine and large house that gives entertainment to nobody, serves but to reproach and upbraid its owner; and especially if it were used to be frequently visited under its former master; for it is an odious thing to have passengers cry, as they go along,

> Ah! good old house, alas thy present lord
> Is widely different from thy former one!

which may justly be said of but too, too many in our own days.[1] Care should be taken, especially when a man builds himself, that he be not too extravagant in his magnificence and expenses; which is a very ill thing, though it had no other harm in it but only that one of giving a bad example: for most men are apt, more than in anything else, to imitate the great ones as to this particular. Where, for example, shall we find the man that rivals the famous Lucullus in his virtues? Whereas how many have done it in the stateliness and magnificence of his country-houses! But there certainly ought to be some bounds fixed and prescribed to these things, and those to be according to the rules of moderation; but the measure whereby we are to judge of their being moderate, is their subserviency to the ornaments and conveniences of life: and so much may suffice on this head. As for our actions, the way to maintain this decorum in them is constantly to observe these three following prescripts: first, that we keep all our passions and appetites under the government and direction of reason, than which there is nothing of greater efficacy towards the constant preservation of our duty: secondly, that we consider the quality and moment of the thing of which we go about; that so we may proportion our endeavours accordingly, and take neither more nor less pains about it than it really deserves: and, lastly, that in all these exterior circumstances, which are only designed for a genteel show and grace of the action, we should keep within the measures of prudence and moderation. Now the best measure we can observe is this; to keep our eyes fixed on those rules of decorum I have

---

[1] In allusion to some of Caesar's party, and particularly Marc Antony, who inhabited a house which had formerly been the residence of Pompey.

before laid down, and never to transgress them. But of these three rules the first is the most important, that the sensitive part be kept obedient to the reasonable.

XL.—*Order to be observed in our words and actions—Wherein it consists —The duties arising from it.*

It remains in the next place that we should speak of that order which is to be observed in our words and actions, and of the proper seasons and opportunities of them. And here will fall under our consideration, not that which by us is most commonly rendered moderation, and signifies the keeping within due bounds; but that which contains, in the notion of it, the preservation of order. We shall crave leave, however, to call even this latter by the name of moderation, which is thus defined by the Stoic philosophers —" Moderation is the knowledge of putting whatever we say or do in its proper place." Whence it appears, that order and the well-placing of things are but different words to express the same notion: for order is defined by the same sect of men to be the ranging of things in their fitting and proper places. Now the place of an action they tell us is, the season of time for doing it; so that, in short, by moderation here (in the sense of the word which I have just now given), we mean no more than the knowledge of well-timing whatever we do. Prudence may be defined the same way too, about which we have spoken at the entrance of this work: but now we are discoursing of temperance, moderation, and such like virtues. What the duties of prudence are, is sufficiently explained in its proper place; what those of modesty, and such other virtues as serve to recommend us to those we converse with, and make up the subject of our present inquiry, remains now to be considered. In the first place, then, we ought to observe such a due regularity and order in our actions, as that the several parts of our whole lives, like those of a regular and coherent discourse, may agree and be suitable one with another: for what is more unseemly, and contrary to good manners, than when we are engaged about serious business, to bring in some pleasant and merry discourse, that is proper for a feast, or over a glass of wine? If a man had some considerable cause on his hands, or business that required attentive thinking, could any one blame him for being very thoughtful as he walked or rode? But should he show himself so at a feast among company, it would be counted a great piece of rudeness and ill-breeding, and this for not observing the difference of seasons. Now as for those things, which notoriously offend against the rules of good manners, such as for a man to sing openly in the streets, or any other gross and apparent absurdity, these are so easy to be observed by all, that we need give no rules or directions about them: but we ought more especially to employ our care in avoiding those little unheeded indecencies, which are hardly understood by the generality of mankind. And as the least fault or disagreement in the notes is immediately perceived by a skilful musician, so we should take all imaginable care that there be no disagreement in our lives and actions; and that so much the more, as the harmony in our lives is of much greater consequence than that in our music.

XLI.—*Decency to be observed in the most trivial actions—We should observe what is unhandsome in others, and correct it in ourselves; asking the advice of experienced persons—Some particular duties to be observed by all good men.*

As therefore the delicate ear of the artist can quickly discover the least fault in his music, so, would we take as much care in detecting and censuring our vices, we might from the least and most trivial matters make several observations that would be much to our advantage: from the moving of our eyes, for example; from our way of smoothing or wrinkling our brows; from the merry or sorrowful air of our countenances; from our laughter, freedom, or reservedness in discourse; from the raising or falling the tone of our voices, and a great many other such little kind of circumstances, we might easily judge what is handsome and becoming us, and what is repugnant to the rules of our duty, and to that which our nature or character requires. Now in this particular it is a very good way to observe first in others how each of these suits, that so we may avoid and correct in ourselves whatever we see bad and misbecoming in them: for, I know not how, we can sooner spy faults in other people than we can in ourselves; on which account there is no better way to correct any learner, than for the master to mimic his faults before him; that so he, perceiving their deformity in another, may the sooner be brought to amend them in himself. Another good way is, whenever we are in doubt and suspense about a duty, to go to some learned or experienced person, and ask his advice on the matter in question before we resolve and determine with ourselves; because, generally speaking, when left to themselves, men are apt to be guided too much by their own inclinations and natures: and in asking this advice we should diligently observe, not only what every one tells us in words, but what his real inward opinion is, and what reasons and grounds he may have for such opinions: for as your statuaries, painters, and poets, use to set their works out to be publicly viewed, that so they may be able to correct such faults as are generally found by spectators in them; and as they consider with themselves and their friends, what oversights or mistakes they have been guilty of in them; so should we make use of other people's judgements as well as our own, and do or not do, correct or alter a great many things on their advice. As for those things that are settled by custom and civil constitutions, I shall give no directions at all concerning them; for they are sufficient directions of themselves: I shall only observe that it is a great mistake in any one to imagine, because such men as Aristippus and Socrates have ventured to say or do a great many things which are contrary to rule and received custom, that therefore he may be allowed to do the same; for these were persons of extraordinary merits, and almost more than human perfections; and on that account might demand some privileges, which are not to be granted to the rest of the world. But as for the practice and manner of the Cynics, it is wholly to be discarded; for it is a plain offence against the rules of modesty, without which nothing can be virtuous and becoming. It is our duty to pay a respect and deference, as to all those that are virtuous and courageous, who consult the good and advantage of the republic, and serve or have served her in any of her interests; so to those also who bear any office or command in the state. We should pay, in like manner, a peculiar regard and reverence to old age; never resist any public magistrate; make a distinction between citizens and strangers; and of strangers themselves, between those in a private and public capacity. In fine, not to mention any more particulars, we ought in all cases both to keep ourselves, and endeavour to uphold and maintain among others that common correspondence and universal society that is among all mankind.

XLII.—*Of the several sorts of trade, which are creditable and which not —Husbandry particularly commended.*

As for trades and the ways of getting money, which of them are creditable and which otherwise, I have only these few things to observe: first, all those are unworthy ways of gaining which procure one a general hatred and ill-will; as that of the usurers and tax-gatherers, for instance: secondly, those arts are mean and ungenteel, in which a man is paid for his work, not his skill; for the very receiving a reward for one's labour is like taking of earnest to bind himself a slave. Nor are they to be esteemed as better than mean and ordinary people, that buy things up by wholesale of the merchants, to retail them out again by little and little; for what they gain is but a very poor business, unless they are guilty of abominable lying, than which there is nothing in the world more scandalous. Again, all handicraftsmen have but a mean sort of calling; and it is impossible that a work-house should have anything that is genteel in it. Farther yet, all those trades are pitiful and low, that purvey and cater for the satisfying men's pleasures; fishmongers, butchers, cooks, etc., as Terence reckons them up; to which we may add, if you please, perfumers, dancing-masters, and those who supply us with dice or cards. But arts that have something of knowledge and skill in them, or those that are useful and necessary for the public; such as physic, for instance, or architecture, or the instruction and education of youth in good manners;—these are very creditable and commendable in those whose rank and condition is suited for such employments. As for merchandise, it is sordid and mean, when the trade that is driven is little and inconsiderable; but when it takes in a great quantity of business, and, bringing home goods from every country, sells them out again without lying or deceiving, we can hardly say but that it is creditable enough: nay, it is most certainly very commendable, when those who are concerned in it only design (after they are sated, or rather contented with what they have gained), to betake themselves wholly from the haven to the country, as before they had done from the sea to the haven, and there enjoy quietly their private possessions. But among all the methods of enriching oneself, there is no one better, no one more profitable, and pleasant, and agreeable, no one more worthy of a man and a gentleman, than that of manuring and tilling the ground; concerning which I have spoken at large in my Cato Major, whence you may borrow what is necessary to be said on this subject.

XLIII.—*The duties of prudence, or finding out truth, and those of justice, or maintaining human society, compared: the preference given to the latter.*

And thus have I finished what I had to say on the first question; and, I think, sufficiently made it appear how the particular instances of duty are to be drawn from the several heads of honesty. But it often comes to pass that those very things themselves which are honest, rival as it were, and come into competition with one another, so as to make it be another question, of two that are honest, which is the most so; which is a point not mentioned at all by Panaetius: for the whole of virtue receiving its rise from those four fountains;—first, prudence, or the knowledge of truth; secondly, justice, or doing good to the community and society of mankind; thirdly, fortitude, or greatness of soul; and, lastly, temperance, or moderation;—it cannot but happen that several of these must be compared together before we can be able to satisfy ourselves which it is our duty to prefer. First, then, if the duties of justice, or preserving the community, and those of prudence, or the knowledge of truth, should come into competition one with another; the former, I think, should take place of the latter, as being more consonant to the dictates of nature, which may easily be proved by this following argument. Suppose a wise man to be in such a place as afforded him all the conveniences of life, and all the opportunities of leisure in abundance, so that he might study and contemplate everything that was any ways worthy his knowledge or contemplation; yet were he wholly deprived of all company, and had nobody ever come near him to be seen, he would quickly

be tired, and grow weary of his life. Again, the principal
of all the virtues is that sort of wisdom which comprehends
the knowledge of things both divine and human; that is, the
society and relation of men with the gods, and with one
another. If then this, as most certainly it is, be the greatest
virtue, it follows, that duties which flow from society must
as certainly be the greatest; for the deepest knowledge and
contemplation of nature is but a very lame and imperfect
business, unless it proceed and tend forward to action.
Now the occasions wherein it can show itself best consist
in maintaining the interest of men, and of consequence
belong to the society of mankind: whence it follows, that
the maintaining of this should in reason take place before
learning and knowledge. Nor is this any more than what
all good men show they judge to be true by their actions
and practices: for who is there so wholly addicted to contemplation and the study of nature, as that, if his country
should fall into danger, while he was in one of his noblest
researches, he would not immediately throw all aside, and
run to its relief with all possible speed; nay, though he
thought he might number the stars, or take the just dimensions of the whole world? And the same would he do in
the case of any danger to a friend or a parent. From all
which things it undeniably appears that the duties of knowledge and searching after truth are obliged to give way to
the duties of justice, which consist in upholding society
among men; than which there is nothing for which we
should be more concerned.

XLIV.—*Man by nature a social creature—Knowledge of little use, unless
it do good to the world—Necessity not the reason of men's joining in
societies.*

Nay, those very men, who have spent their whole lives
in philosophy and learning, have yet always endeavoured,
as much as they could, to be serviceable to the interest and
good of mankind: for many brave men, and very useful
members of their several states, have in great part been
made such by their institutions. Thus Epaminondas, the
famous Theban, was indebted for his education to Lysis,
the Pythagorean; Dion of Syracuse, for his to Plato; and

the same may be said of a great many others: even I myself, whatsoever service I have done the republic—if, at least, it may be said that I have done it any service, must wholly ascribe it to that learning and those instructions I received from my masters. Neither is their teaching and instructing others determined to the time of their living here; but they continue to do it even after they are dead, by the learned discourses which they leave behind them: for there is no one point they have left unhandled, relating either to the laws, customs, or discipline of the commonwealth; so that they seem to have sacrificed their leisure and opportunities of study to the benefit of those who are engaged in business; and thus we see how those men themselves, whose lives have been spent in the pursuit of wisdom, have nevertheless endeavoured by their learning and prudence to be some way profitable to the community of mankind. And for this one reason, persuasive speaking, if joined with prudence, is a greater accomplishment than the acutest thinking, if destitute of eloquence: for thinking is terminated in itself alone, but speaking reaches out to the benefit of those with whom we are joined in the same society. Now, as bees do not therefore unite themselves together, that so they may the better prepare their combs, but therefore prepare their combs, because they do by nature unite themselves together; so men, and much more, being creatures that naturally love society, in consequence of that, seek how they may find methods of living happily in it. Hence it follows, that the knowledge of things, unless it is accompanied with that sort of virtue which consists in defending and preserving of men, *i.e.* in the maintenance of human soicety, is but a barren and fruitless accomplishment; and even greatness of soul, without a regard to this society and conjunction, is very little better than savageness and barbarity. Thus we may see, that the getting of knowledge is a duty of much less concern and moment than the preserving this society and union amongst men. It is a very false notion that hath been advanced by some people, that necessity alone was the motive to this society, which we have so often mentioned; and that men would never have associated together, but that they were not able, in a solitary life, to furnish themselves with the necessaries of nature; and that every great and exalted genius, would Providence supply him with food and the other conveniences of life, would withdraw from all business and intercourse with mankind, and give himself wholly to study and contemplation. This is not so; for he would avoid solitude, endeavour to find a companion in his studies, and always be desirous of teaching and learning, of hearing and speaking: from all which things it is abundantly evident that the duties belonging to human society should in reason take place before those which relate to inactive knowledge.

XLV.—*The duties of maintaining society not always preferable to those of temperance, modesty, etc.—What duties of justice ought to take place of others.*

It ought perhaps to be inquired here, whether the duties of this society, which is thus agreeable to the principles of nature, ought always to be preferred before the duties of temperance, decency, and moderation. Indeed I think not; for some things are so very highly scandalous and abominably wicked, that a wise man would hardly be guilty of them, supposing he could bring safety to his country by it. Posidonius has heaped up a great many instances of things of this nature. These then must never be done for one's country; nor will one's country ever desire that they should: for the best of it is, it is impossible such a conjuncture should happen, as can make it be the interest of any republic to have wise men be guilty of such abominable actions. We may lay down this then for a certain conclusion, that when several duties come into competition, those should take place before any others which relate to the maintenance of human society: for wise and considerate acting is the end of all knowledge and prudent thinking; and by consequence, the former is more valuable than the latter. And so much may suffice on this subject; for I think I have sufficiently cleared the way, so that hereafter there will be no difficulty to know which duties are to be preferred. Those very duties which relate to society are of different rates and degrees among themselves; but it is no hard matter to see in what order they ought to be performed: as, in the first place, those to the immortal gods; secondly, to our native country; thirdly, to our parents; and so on to all others in their respective places. What has been said in a few words on this last head, I hope is sufficient to make it appear that it is usual for men not only to doubt whether such and such an action be honest or dishonest; but also, of two, that are both of them honest, which is the most so. This is one of those two heads which I at first observed were omitted by Panaetius. Let us now pass on to the remaining part of our proposed division.

BOOK II

I.—*Subject of this second book—He applies himself to the study of philosophy, as his greatest consolation amidst the calamities of his country.*

WHAT those duties are, son Marcus, which honesty and virtue require of us, and how they arise from their several fountains, is, I think, plain enough from the former book. I am now in the next place to speak of those others which wholly regard the convenience of life, and are requisite for the getting and enjoyment of those things which serve for our comfortable subsistence here, such as interest, riches, etc. And here I told you the common heads of deliberation were, what is profitable and what unprofitable? and, of several profitables, which is more, and which most of all such? Concerning which I shall begin to speak, after I have premised but a word or two in vindication of myself and my present undertaking: for though my books have excited several both to the reading, and even writing of philosophy; yet I am now and then apt to be afraid, lest some, who are otherwise very good men, should hate and despise the very name of that study, and wonder at me for bestowing such portions of my time and pains in so very fruitless and insignificant a manner. To whom I answer, that so long as the republic was governed by those, to whose care and management she had intrusted herself, I was ever diligent, and employed all my thoughts for her good and preservation: but when one man [1] had seized her wholly to himself, and there was no place left for my counsel or authority; and when I had lost those extraordinary persons, who had been my companions in labouring for her interest, I resolved not to sink into anguish and despair, which had wholly overwhelmed me if I had not resisted them; nor to follow such pleasures or idle ways of living as were improper, and unbecoming a man of learning. I could heartily wish,

[1] Julius Caesar, who, having conquered Pompey, got the whole power of Rome into his hands.

had it so pleased the gods, that the republic had continued in its ancient condition, and never fallen into the hands of those men who are not so much for changing as overturning everything! I would then, as I did in its flourishing circumstances, spend my time rather in business than writing; and what I did write would not be things of this moral nature, but my public orations, as I have often done. But when the poor state, which had taken up all my care and thoughts, and for which I had laboured with all my power, was utterly ruined and sunk into nothing, there was quickly no room left for such orations, either at the bar or in the senatehouse: and my active mind, which had always been employed in that kind of studies, now not being able to lie wholly idle, I thought I could find out no better way to get rid of those troubles which oppressed my mind, than by returning again to the studies of philosophy. I had spent a good part of my time in these whilst I was young, for the improvement of my reason; but when I came once to be a candidate for places, and devoted myself to the service of the public, I had little time left for philosophical inquiries, only so much as could be spared from the business of my friends and the state; which was wholly taken up in nothing else but reading, without any leisure at all for writing.

II.—*The commendation and definitions of wisdom and philosophy—The opinion of the Academics, and why they dispute against everything.*

However, then, we have this advantage in the midst of all our miseries and calamities, that by them we are brought to the writing of those things which were not sufficiently known amongst us, though nothing in the world more deserves our knowledge: for what is there, O ye gods! more desirable than wisdom? what more excellent and lovely in itself? what more useful and becoming for a man? or what more worthy of his reasonable nature? Now those who are busied in the pursuit of this are called philosophers, and the word philosophy signifies no more, if you would take it literally, than a certain desire and love for wisdom: and wisdom is defined by the old philosophers, the knowledge of things both divine and human, together with the causes on which they depend; the study of which whosoever finds fault with,

I confess I cannot perceive what it is he would commend;
for what study is there that brings so much quiet and satisfaction to the mind, if these are the things which we propose
to ourselves, as theirs, who are always searching out something which may contribute to the welfare and happiness of
their lives? Or if it be virtue and constancy that we desire,
either this is the method of obtaining them, or else there is
not any to be found in the world. To say there is no art in
those weightier concerns, when none of the most trivial
matters is without art, becomes only those who talk without
thinking, and deceive themselves in the most important
business: but if there is an art of attaining virtue, in what
other way do we hope to find it, if this be forsaken of which
I am now speaking? But these things used to be more fully
handled, when we excite and persuade men to cultivate
philosophy; which I have endeavoured to do in another
work.[1] My design at present was only to show why I
particularly chose this study; being thrust from all business
and concern in the government. There are others, and
those men of no small learning, who object against me, and
ask if I am not inconsistent with myself, who affirm, that
nothing at all can be known, and yet have discoursed on
several subjects, and at this very time am laying down rules
and directions about duty? I could wish those persons had
understood our opinions a little more thoroughly; for we
are not of those whose minds are perpetually wandering in
uncertainties, and have nothing whereby to determine their
assents; (for what sort of mind must a man needs have, or
rather what life must he needs lead, when he is utterly
debarred from all liberty of disputing, and observing any
regular conduct in his actions?) nor yet of those others, who
call some things certain and others uncertain: but rejecting
both these, we say some things are probable, and others
improbable. Is there anything then that should hinder me
from approving of that which I think most probable, and
laying aside that which I think the contrary? Or where
is the inconsistency, if, leaving that arrogant pretence of
demonstrating, I am neither too rash nor presumptuous in
my opinions, which of all things in the world is the farthest
from wisdom? Now this is the reason why we Academics
dispute against everything, because what is probable could

---

[1] A book entitled Hortensius, unfortunately lost.

not appear without comparing the arguments on either side of the question. But these things are cleared, I think, accurately enough in my books entitled *Academical Questions*. But you, my son, are already engaged in the study of a most noble and ancient philosophy,[1] and have got Cratippus for your master and instructor, who is hardly inferior to its most glorious founders: however, I would have you acquainted with our doctrines,[2] which are very little different from those of your own sect. But it is high time now to return to our purpose.

III.—*The knowledge of honesty is of greatest moment—Profit and honesty really the same—The division of things profitable and hurtful to men.*

There being then, as was before observed, five general heads of deliberating and consulting for the finding out our duty; two of which relate to what is honest and becoming; two to the use and conveniences of life, such as plenty, power, riches, etc., and the fifth to the teaching us how we ought to choose, if any of the former should seem to contradict and run counter to one another;—we have gone through with that wherein honesty is the question, with which I desire you would be more especially acquainted. The point which now comes under consideration is what usually goes by the name of profitable; concerning which custom is mightily in the wrong, and by little and little has brought it to such a pass, as to make a distinction between profit and honesty; and settle it as a constant and received maxim, that a thing may be honest without being profitable; and again, may be profitable without being honest; the most pernicious error, and most destructive of all goodness, that ever could have crept into the minds of men. The greatest, however, and most eminent philosophers, have been always so strict and severe in their writings, as to make the three natures of justice, profit, and honesty be blended and interwoven together in reality; and distinguishable only by an act of the mind: for whatever is just, say they, the same is also profitable; and whatever is honest, the same is also just; whence it follows, that whatever is honest, the same must be also profitable. Did people but consider this matter as they ought, they would not, as now they commonly do,

---

[1] The Peripatetic.　　　　[2] The Academic.

admire a crafty and subtle sort of fellows, and esteem that wisdom which in truth is roguery. This error therefore should be wholly rooted out of the minds of men, and all should be taught, that if they ever hope to obtain their ends, they should not set about it by the ways of knavery and underhand dealings, but by justice and integrity in their designs and actions. Now all things that tend to the good and preservation of the life of man, are either inanimate, such as gold, silver, the productions of the earth, and such like; or animals, which have natural powers, inclinations, and appetites. Of these some are unreasonable and others reasonable: the unreasonable are horses, oxen, and other sorts of cattle; to which we may add bees, which produce and make something that contributes to the convenience of the life of men; the reasonable are gods and men. The means for procuring the favour of the gods is to live a religious and holy life; next to the gods, there is nothing so capable of contributing to the happiness and welfare of men as men themselves. The same distribution may serve for those things which tend to the hurt and inconvenience of men. But because it is believed that to hurt is incompatible with the divine nature, the gods for that reason are excepted here; so that men are supposed, of all things in nature, to do both the most service and disservice to one another: for, first, those things which are called inanimate are most of them owing to the industry of men; which we neither could get if it were not for their labour and art in procuring them, nor afterwards use without their assistance: for where should we have such a science as physic, as navigation, or agriculture? How should we gather and preserve our corn, and the rest of our fruits, if it were not for men? and then how should those commodities which we want be imported, or those with which we abound be exported, if there were not men to do each of these works? In like manner how could stone be fetched out of the quarries for our necessary uses? How could iron, brass, gold, and silver be dug and drawn out from the bowels of the earth, did not men set their hands to work for these purposes?

IV.—*The advantages arising from men's joining in society.*

So houses, which serve to defend us from the extremities of heat and cold could neither at first have been made by mankind, or afterwards, if by earthquake, tempest, or length of days, they had fallen to decay, have been repaired or rebuilt, had not men joined together in one common society, and learned to borrow help and assistance of one another. To this industry of men we are also indebted for conveyances of water, for making new channels and arms to rivers, and for turning the streams after such a manner, as thereby to water and fatten our grounds; for throwing up banks to defend us from the waves, and making of new harbours in convenient places. From all which instances, and a great many others, that might easily be produced, it is abundantly manifest that the fruits and advantages reaped from those things which are called inanimate, are entirely owing to men's labour and industry: secondly, those we receive from unreasonable animals, how very little and inconsiderable would they be if they were not augmented by the same people's industry? for who was it but men that first discovered the uses to which beasts in their several kinds might be serviceable? and how at this time could we feed or break them? How could we keep them, and get the most profit and advantage by them, without the endeavours and assistance of the same men? It is they that destroy us those creatures which are hurtful, and procure for us those which may be serviceable to us. Why need I mention a multitude of arts, which are absolutely necessary to our wellbeing here? for what help or succour could those that are sick, or what pleasure those that are healthy, find? how could mankind be supplied with victuals, and other conveniences or comforts of life, if it were not for that number of callings in the world, which are wholly designed to provide them of such things; by means of which men have improved their way of living, and are raised to a condition so far above that of unreasonable animals? Again, cities could neither have been built nor frequented without a community and society of men: hence have arisen all laws and customs; the bounds of equity and justice have been settled; and a certain and regular method laid down for the conduct of men's lives. This has brought modesty into request, and filed off the natural roughness of men's tempers; has contributed to the greater security of their lives, and established such a commerce and correspondence among them, as by mutual giving and receiving of benefits, by bartering and changing one commodity for another, one convenience for another, supplies them to the full with whatever they stand in need of.

V.—*Nothing the cause of so much good or evil to men as they themselves are to one another—What is the office of virtue.*

We dwell much longer than we need on this subject: for who does not see, which Panaetius has spent many pages to make out, that neither a general in war, nor a statesman in peace, could ever perform any glorious exploits, or do any notable service to the public, without the concurrence of other men's endeavours? To confirm this assertion, he brings in Themistocles, Pericles, Agesilaus, and Alexander, and tells us that no one of all these, without the assistance of others to support them, could ever have achieved such glorious actions. What he tells us is undoubtedly true, and such a number of witnesses altogether superfluous. And as men thus receive most extraordinary benefits, from agreeing and conspiring to lend mutual assistance; so, we shall find, on changing the scene, that there are no misfortunes or calamities so great as those which they bring on one another. Dicaearchus, a learned and eloquent peripatetic, has written a whole book concerning the destruction of men; where, first having reckoned up all other causes of it, such as inundations, pestilences, and famines, and even sudden incursions of furious wild beasts, by which he assures us some whole nations have been devoured; and then placing on the other side, wars, seditions, and such like misfortunes, which men were the occasion of; he endeavours to show, at the foot of the account, that a great many more have been destroyed by these than by all other accidents or calamities whatsoever. This then being indisputably true, that the goods men enjoy, and the evil they suffer, proceed for the most part from men themselves;—I lay down this as one principal part of virtue, to procure the good-liking and favour of men, and so to engage their endeavours and affections, as to make them still ready to do us any kindness. It is the business therefore of laborious callings to supply us with all the conveniences of life, which may be had from the use of inanimate beings and unreasonable animals; but to gain the affections of men on our side, and beget in them always a readiness and desire to advance our interest is a work that requires the wisdom and virtue of the greatest men: for the whole work and exercise of virtue in general consists in some one of these three things: the first is a knowledge, in all we undertake, of what is agreeable to truth and sincerity; what is becoming and suitable to every one's character; what will be the consequence of such or such actions; what are the materials out of which things are made, and what the causes that first brought them into being: the second, a restraining the violent motions and passions of the soul, and bringing the irregular inclinations of the appetite under the power and government of reason: the third is a skilfulness of address in our carriage, and a winning demeanour toward the rest of men, with whom we are joined in one common society; that so by their help we may be supplied in abundance with all those things which our natures stand in need of; and by the same may be enabled, should any injury be offered us, to keep ourselves secure from the violence of it; and not only so, but to revenge ourselves also on the guilty person, and inflict such punishments as are according to the rules of humanity and justice.

VI.—*How far the power of Fortune reaches—The several reasons why men favour any one, or submit to his authority.*

What means should be used for gaining and securing men firm to our interests, we should mention immediately, but we have one observation to make beforehand: there is no one but knows that the power of Fortune is very great, both as to the good and ill success of our actions: for when she favours us we quickly arrive at our desired haven; but when she turns against us, we as quickly are shipwrecked and run aground. Now of those events which depend on fortune, there are some that do but rarely come to pass; such as storms, tempests, shipwrecks, ruins, fires, etc., which proceed from inanimate beings; and from brutish animals, kicks, bites, pushes, etc., all which, as I said, do but rarely happen; but the overthrows of armies, as of three but a while ago,[1] and a great many others at several times; the

---

[1] That of Pompey at Pharsalia; his eldest son's at Munda in Spain; and Juba and Scipio in Africa.

deaths of commanders, as lately of a great and extraordinary person;[1] the hatred and violence of the enraged multitude, and, as a consequence of that, the banishments, flights, and utter undoings of well-deserving citizens; as also on the other hand prosperous successes, such as honours, commands, victories, etc., though they are all of them fortuitous things, yet they cannot succeed either the one way or the other without the assistance and endeavours of men. This being noted, we are now to discourse of those ways and methods whereby men are drawn and inclined to be for us, and to endeavour all they can for our interest and advantage; on which if we seem to dwell longer than we should do, I desire the usefulness of the subject may be considered, and then we may possibly be thought too short. Whatever then is contributed by men toward any one's advancement in riches, honours, power, etc., is always done on some of these motives; first, that of kindness, benevolence, or goodwill, when for some reasons they love any person; secondly, honour or admiration, when they respect any one for his virtues, and think he deserves to be highly promoted; thirdly, confidence, trust or reliance, when they think they may safely confide in a man, as one that will certainly take care of their affairs; fourthly, fear, when they stand in any awe of his power and authority; fifthly, hope, when they expect to get something from him, as when princes or popular men promise great donations; and, last of all, hire, when they are drawn to it by money or presents; which is much the most pitiful and sordid way, as for those on the one hand that are taken by it, so likewise for those that endeavour to make use of it; for it is never well when people shall attempt to get that by money which ought to be the reward of virtue and merit. However, seeing sometimes one must have recourse to this method as a refuge, I shall give some rules for our direction in the use of it; but first speak of those that are more nearly related to virtue and honesty. In much the same manner, and for several such reasons, men submit to the power and authority of another, either because they have a kindness for him; or have formerly received some obligations from him; or respect him for his worth; or hope they shall get something by it;

[1] Pompey, who, after his defeat at Pharsalia, flying into Egypt, was there treacherously murdered.

or fear they shall be forced to it, if they do not do it voluntarily; or are drawn by fair promises and large donations; or, lastly, as we see it too often practised in our own republic, are downright hired to it.

VII.—A governor should endeavour to make himself loved, and not feared.

Now of all those methods, which tend to the advancement and maintenance of our interest, there is none more proper and convenient than love, and none more improper and inconvenient than fear: for, as it is very well observed by Ennius, whom men fear they also hate; and whom they hate they wish out of the world: but that no force of power or greatness whatever can bear up long against a stream of public hate, if it were not sufficiently known before, was of late made appear by an instance of our own: and not the violent death of that tyrant [1] only, who by force of arms oppressed the city, which now most obeys him when taken out of the world, but the like untimely ends of most other tyrants, who have generally been attended by the same ill fate, is a manifest token that the hatred of the people is able to ruin the most absolute authority; for obedience, proceeding from fear, cannot possibly be lasting; whereas that which is the effect of love will be faithful for ever. It is well enough in those who by open force have reduced any nation, and accordingly rule it with a high hand, if they do sometimes use rigour and severity, like masters towards their slaves when there is no other way of holding them in subjection: but for those who are magistrates in a free city, to endeavour to make themselves feared by the people, is one of the maddest and most desperate attempts on the face of the earth: for though a man should by his power and greatness oppress the laws and overawe liberty by terror and threatenings, yet still they will find time to recover again; first, by the private resentment of the citizens, and afterwards by their choosing, in secret counsels, some worthier person to free them from the oppressor: and Liberty, after she has been chained up awhile, is always more fierce, and sets her teeth in deeper, than she would otherwise have done if she had never been restrained. Let us therefore embrace and adhere to that method which is of

[1] Julius Caesar.

the most universal influence, and serves not only to secure us what we have, but moreover to enlarge our power and authority; that is, in short, let us rather endeavour to be loved than feared, which is certainly the best way to make us successful, as well in our private as our public business: for those who desire to have others to be afraid of them, must needs be afraid of those others in their turns. What, for instance, shall we imagine of the elder Dionysius? With what eternal fears and apprehensions must he needs be racked, when, daring not to venture his throat to any razor, he was forced even to singe off his beard with coals? Or what of Alexander, who was surnamed the Pheraean? In what torment, think we, must he perpetually live, when, as it is usually reported of him, he dared not so much as to rise from table, and go to his own wife Thebe's chamber, whom he loved with an entire affection, without a barbarian, and him, as it is said, too, a branded Thracian, to lead the way with his naked sword; and would always despatch some of his guards before him, to search all the clothes and coffers of the women, for fear lest any weapon might be concealed within them? O miserable and unhappy man, who could think a barbarian, one who carried the marks of his condition in his forehead, would be faithfuller to him than his own wife! Neither, it seems, was he mistaken in it; for he was afterwards murdered by her instigation. Nor indeed can any authority, how absolute soever, subsist very long when it is thus generally feared. Phalaris himself, who is particularly remarkable for his barbarous cruelties, may serve for a witness to this truth; who was not destroyed by domestic treacheries, like that Alexander whom I just now mentioned; nor yet by some few men conspiring his death, like our late tyrant; but by a general insurrection of all the Agrigentines falling on him at once. Again, did not the Macedonians revolt from Demetrius, and all with one consent march over to Pyrrhus? And when the Lacedaemonians grew insolent and tyrannical, did not their allies on a sudden forsake them, and show themselves idle and unconcerned spectators of their ruin at Leuctra, without ever stirring one foot to their assistance?

VIII.—*The just and gentle government of the old Romans contrasted with the fatal consequences resulting from an opposite course.*

I much rather choose, on such a subject, to bring instances from foreign, than our own nation. However, I cannot but observe thus much, that so long as our empire supported itself, not by the methods of injustice and violence, but rather by actions of kindness and gentleness, wars were undertaken to protect its allies, or defend its honour; and accordingly their issues were attended with mercy, or at least no more rigour than was absolutely necessary. The senate then was a kind of port and refuge for princes and nations to have recourse to in their need; and our officers and commanders made it their greatest glory to defend their provinces, and assist their allies, with justice and fidelity. This city, therefore, was not then the empress so properly as the protrectress of all the world. This conduct and method of managing the state began by little and little to wear off before, but utterly vanished immediately after the victory of Sylla; for people began to think nothing could be unjust to their confederates and allies, when once they had seen so great cruelties exercised even on their very fellow-citizens. This man, therefore, was in a just cause, but which was followed by a cruel and most unjust victory; he having had the boldness and impudence to say, when in full market he was selling the goods of some honest and wealthy men, and whom he himself knew to be Roman citizens, that he was going to make sale of his own booty. But there has come one after him,[1] whose cause was impious, and his victory yet more scandalous and inhuman; who did not stop at selling private men's estates, but involved all our countries and provinces together in one common calamity. Hence we have seen, after havoc and devastation made in other countries, as it were by way of prelude to the loss of our own empire, the city Marseilles drawn along in triumph; and that very place, without whose assistance our former generals never brought a triumph from beyond the Alps, has now found one that could have so much impudence as to triumph over its own destruction. I might bring in a great many other examples of most impious treatment that hath been shown towards our allies;

[1] Julius Caesar.

but this single instance is abundantly sufficient, being one of the basest that was ever committed before the face of the sun. The truth of it is, we have deserved these misfortunes; for if others had not escaped without punishment for their wickedness, this man could never have arrived at that insolence; who, though he has left but few heirs to his estate, I am afraid will have a great many wicked ones of his ambition: for as long as some dissolute and profligate fellows remember that former inhuman auction, and are in hopes one day of seeing the same again, they will always be for propagating civil dissensions. Thus Publius Sylla, who was so busy in that mentioned, when his kinsman was dictator, was never contented till he had managed a worse and more inhuman auction six-and-thirty years after; and another, who was scribe in that former dictatorship, in this latter was advanced to be treasurer of the city. By all which it is easy enough to perceive that we are never to expect we shall be free from civil wars so long as people hope to make their fortunes by them. We have therefore only the walls of our city remaining entire, and even they, as it were, expecting to feel the effects of their abominable wickedness; but as for the republic, it is absolutely sunk into ruins and nothing. And all these misfortunes have fallen on us (that I may return to the subject which occasioned this digression) by our choosing to govern rather by fear than love. What then ought particular persons to expect, when tyranny and oppression could bring all these evils on the whole Roman empire? This then being so manifestly plain, that love is a most powerful motive to obedience, but fear a most weak and dangerous one;—it follows, in the next place, that we should discourse of those means, whereby such a love, joined with honour and confidence, may most easily be got. Now this is what all men do not equally stand in need of; but each should consider his own way of living, and accordingly judge what is most convenient for him; whether to be beloved by the generality of men, or only by some few and select persons. This however we may lay down for certain, as a first and most necessary rule in this case, to procure at least some faithful and sincere friends, who may have a true kindness and esteem for us. As far as this reaches, there is very little difference between even the greatest and meanest of people, and all sorts of them are almost equally concerned to endeavour after it. As for honour, glory, and the general good-will of all the citizens; these indeed are things which are not alike useful and necessary for all. However, for those that have been able to get them, they are very good helps, as for most other purposes, so for the obtaining of faithful friends:— but of friendship I have treated in another work, which is entitled *Laelius*.

IX.—*What the ingredients of true glory are—By what means the love and confidence of the people may be obtained.*

Let us now proceed to discourse of glory; though that too is a subject on which I have two books already extant:[1] however, I shall briefly touch on it here, because it is a thing of such weight and moment towards the successful management of the most important affairs. True and perfect glory, then, is always made up of these three ingredients: first, the love and good-will of the multitude; secondly, their trust and reliance on a man; and, lastly, their valuing and admiring him, so as to think him a person that really deserves honour. The means of getting these three from the multitude, to give one short and easy rule, are very much the same as from particular persons. However, there is another peculiar way of approaching the people, and gaining admittance into the hearts and affections of all men in general. Of those three then, which I just now mentioned, let us first see the ways of obtaining love. Now the love of the people is moved by nothing so much as by bounty and doing kindnesses: next they are pleased with a hearty desire and inclination towards it, though a man have not wherewithal to exercise it: thirdly, the very name and reputation of having beneficence and liberality, justice, and fidelity, with the rest of those virtues which give a kind of smoothness and agreeableness to our conversation, is of very great efficacy in getting us the favour and love of the multitude: and the reason of it is, because honesty and decorum delight us of themselves, and by their own native beauties and excellences move and engage the hearts of all men: which seeing they appear with more lustre and virtues, which I just now mentioned, it follows, that by

---

[1] They are both lost.

nature we must love those people in whom we suppose such virtues to reside. And these are the principal causes of men's loving us: there might, I confess, be some others given, but not of equal weight and importance with these. We are to speak in the next place of their trusting or confiding in us; for the compassing of which, it is necessary we should be supposed to have two qualifications, viz. prudence and justice; for we trust those men, whom we believe to understand matters better than we do, to be wise enough to see things before they are arrived, and in the management of them, if any danger should happen, to be ready at finding out ways and expedients to disentangle themselves from the perplexities of it, in which men imagine that all true and profitable wisdom consists. But when a man is found really just and faithful, that is good, we place so much trust and confidence in such a one, as not to entertain the least suspicion of deceit or injury. To such a man therefore we think we may wisely, and with a secure confidence, entrust our safeties, our children, and our fortunes. Justice therefore, of these two virtues, has much the more strong and effectual tendency to procure this credit and confidence from the people; for that, even without wisdom, can go a great way towards the obtaining of this end; whereas wisdom, without that, is unable to do anything: for the more shrewd and cunning any person is, the more he is suspected and hated by the world, if he be not counted honest and upright withal. Justice, therefore, in conjunction with wisdom, can make a man be trusted as far as he pleases: justice without the other can do a great deal; but the other without that is of no force at all.

X.—*What men are usually the objects of admiration—The difference between despising and having an ill opinion of a man.*

Some men perhaps will be ready to wonder, since it is so generally agreed on by philosophers, and has been so often asserted by myself, that whoever has one must have all the virtues; why I should speak of them separately now, as though it were possible for a man to have prudence without having justice at the same time. I answer, that the way of expression is highly different, according to the difference of the subjects we are treating of; whether they are such as require a niceness and subtlety in handling, or to be suited to the capacities of ordinary people. I do but speak here with the vulgar therefore, when I call one man courageous, another just, and a third prudent; for in treating on a subject which concerns the people, we must make use of common and ordinary expressions; which is what has been done by Panaetius himself. But to return to our purpose: of the three ingredients, which we said were required to the making up of glory; the third was this—that men should admire and value us so, as to think we are persons that really deserve honour. Now, generally speaking, they are apt to admire whatever they see great, and beyond their apprehensions; and likewise in particulars, if they discover any excellency which they never expected. They admire, therefore, and extol them even to the skies, in whom, as they think, they have found any rare and extraordinary qualities; but as for those others, who have neither virtue, spirit, nor courage in them, these men they wholly despise and set light by: for they cannot be said to despise all those of whom they entertain but an ill opinion. They are far from thinking well of your roguish, backbiting, cozening sort of fellows, who are never unprepared for the doing man an injury; but by no means despise them for all that; their contempt, as was said, lighting only on those who neither do good to themselves nor others, as we commonly speak; that is, who spend all their lives in mere idleness and sloth, without ever minding or taking care of anything. Those who are esteemed to excel in virtue, more especially draw men to wonder and admiration; who keep themselves free, as from all other things that are base and unbecoming, so more especially from those sorts of vices which the rest of mankind cannot so easily stand against. Pleasures, for instance, are very alluring and charming mistresses, which are apt to ensnare the better part of the soul, and entice it aside from the paths of virtue; and pain, on the contrary, racks and torments us, so that the dread of it carries most men beyond the bounds of reason. Thus again, when life and death, riches and poverty, are the things in question, there are very few men but are wholly transported with desire of the one and abhorrence of the other. When a man therefore has got such a great and exalted soul, as that he can look on all these things with indifference, and closely pursue and adhere to Honesty, in whatever shape she presents herself; then it is that Virtue appears with such a brightness, as that all the world must admire her beauties.

XI.—*Justice, and a contempt of riches, especially causes of men's admiration.*

Such a constitution of soul therefore as can make a man despise all these goods or evils, begets him a mighty esteem and admiration; but especially justice, which single virtue serves to give men the name and denomination of good, seems much the most admirable to the generality of people; and not without reason, it being impossible for any one to be just who is afraid at the approaches of death, of pain, of banishment, or poverty; or prefers those things which are contrary to these before the great duties of justice and honesty. And more particularly yet, men admire those, whom they find unconcerned as to the matter of money; and count them tried, as it were like gold in the fire, who have been able to withstand the temptations of it. Justice therefore of itself is sufficient to procure those three things that are requisite to glory; in the first place, the love and good-will of the people, because its chief aim is the being serviceable to very many; secondly, their confidence; and, thirdly, their admiration; for the same reason, because it neglects and despises those things which the rest of men pursue with such eagerness and passion. Now, in my opinion, not only the being in a public station, but every method of living whatever, requires the help and assistance of men; as for the other ends, so particularly for this, that we may have some familiar friends to converse with; which it is no easy matter for a man to obtain, without at least the show and reputation of honesty. Hence it follows, that it is necessary even for those men themselves, who have withdrawn from the world, and chosen the quiet and retirement of the country, to be reputed at least men of honesty and integrity; and that so much the more, because otherwise they will certainly be counted dishonest; and then, having nothing of guard or defence, they must needs be exposed to perpetual injuries. The same justice also is necessary for those, if ever they hope to succeed in their business, who buy, sell, let, hire, and are concerned in the commerce and affairs of the world: nay, it is a thing of such powerful moment and universal influence, as that those who live only on villanies and wickedness can never subsist without something of justice: for should any thief steal from another that belonged to the same confederacy, he would immediately be expelled, as unfit to be a member even of a society of robbers; and should the leader himself not distribute their booty according to the measures of justice and honesty, he would either be murdered or deserted by his company. Nay, it is said that your robbers have some certain statutes, which they are all of them bound to observe among themselves. Theopompus tells us of a certain rogue, one Bardylis, an Illyrian, that got a great power by the fame of his justice in dividing the prey: and Viriatus, the Lusitanian, got a much greater, to whom even some of our armies and generals were forced to yield, till he was beaten and weakened by that Caius Laelius, who was surnamed the Wise, in the time of his pretorship; who brought down his haughtiness to so low an ebb, as to render the war easy for those that came after him. If justice then be of so great efficacy, as to raise even the power of pirates; of what mighty force must we suppose it to be in the midst of laws, and in a well-constituted republic?

XII.—*What made men at first choose kings and make laws—The justest men usually made kings, and why—Glory must be founded on solid virtue.*

It was for the sake of enjoying the benefits of this justice, the great use of which we have now been discoursing of, that the Medes heretofore, as we are told by Herodotus, and I am apt to imagine our own ancestors too, chose always the honestest persons for their kings: for the poorer sort of people, being oppressed by the richer, had recourse to some one of remarkable virtue, to save and protect them from violence and injuries; who, constituting measures of equity and justice, bound the greatest to observe them as well as the meanest. And that which was the reason for their choosing kings, in like manner put them on enacting laws: for men have always desired to enjoy such a right, as all sorts of them might have an equal share in, for otherwise indeed it would be no right at all; which, when they could get by the justice and honesty of some one person, they were contented with him, and never looked any farther; but when they could not, they were driven to a necessity of inventing laws, which could never be partial, but use the same language to all ranks and conditions. It is very plain, therefore, that those men were usually chosen to be kings who were counted by the people men of honesty and integrity; but if they were held prudent and wise withal, the people thought there was nothing they might not obtain by their conduct and management. By all means therefore let us constantly follow, and stick close to justice; as for its own sake (for otherwise indeed it will not be properly justice), so for the increase of our honour and reputation. Now as it is not sufficient for a man to get riches, unless he has the wisdom to dispose of them, so as thereby to furnish out all his expenses, not only those of his bare necessities, but those of his bounty and liberality too; so neither is it enough for a man to get glory, unless he knows how to make use of it with discretion; though what Socrates says is very excellent to this purpose, that the readiest way, and, as it were, shortest cut, to arrive at glory, is really to be what one desires to be accounted. Those people therefore are highly mistaken, who think of obtaining a solid reputation by vain shows and hypocritical pretences; by composed countenances and studied forms of words: for true glory takes deep root, and grows and flourishes more and more; but that which is only in show and mere outside, quickly decays and withers like flowers; nor can anything be lasting that is only counterfeit. I might bring a great many pregnant examples for the proof of these assertions; but for brevity sake I shall content myself with those of but one single family. Tiberius Gracchus, the son of Publius, will always be praised and had in admiration, as long as there shall any memorials remain of the Roman achievements; but his sons, on the contrary, were not in their lifetimes approved of by good men; and since their decease have been numbered among those who were justly slain.

XIII.—*Courage in war, temperance, and friendship with the wise and good, great recommendations of young men.*

It is the business therefore of those who desire to get true glory strictly to discharge all the duties of justice: what those are, we have shown already in the former book. I shall now proceed to lay down some directions, how a man should appear before the world what he is in himself; though that of Socrates is certainly the wisest that can possibly be given, to make sure in the first place that he really is in himself that which he desires to appear before the world. For when a young gentleman is just come into the public, and is already known and remarkable in it, either by the fame of his father's actions (which, I think, son Marcus, may be your case), or by any other means or accident whatever, the eyes of all are immediately on, and every one is inquiring after what he does, and how he steers his life; and, as though he were set in the public view, so none of his actions, or so much as his words, can be long kept in secret: but those, who at the beginning and entrance of their lives, by reason of their meanness, are unknown to the world, as soon as they arrive at years of discretion, should set before their eyes the most honourable places, and bend all their studies and honest endeavours towards the obtaining them; which they ought to do with so much the more boldness, because men are so far from envying youth, that they rather encourage and forward them in their progress. The first thing then that sets a young man off, and recommends him to the public, is courage and bravery in martial affairs; by which a great many amongst our forefathers, who were scarce ever wholly disengaged from wars, very nobly distinguished and signalised themselves. But you, my son, have had the misfortune to light on the times of a civil war, wherein the one party was wicked and detestable, and the other unfortunate and unsuccessful; in which, however, when Pompey had given you the command of one wing, you got much praise from that great commander and all his army, by your riding, darting, and patiently abiding all the fatigues of war. But as for this piece of your rising glory, that, and the whole constitution of the republic, are both of them fallen to the ground together. But I never designed so to model this discourse, as that it should be proper for none but you; but that it might be applicable to all men in general: I shall go on therefore to the remaining part of it. As then, in all things, the functions of the soul are more noble and excellent than those of the body, so the effects of our reason and understanding are greater and more powerful, as to this particular, than those of mere strength. Now of these there is none that can more recommend and adorn a young man than temperance and sobriety, duty and respect to his natural parents, love and good-nature towards his friends and relations. Another good way for young people to get known, and have a good reputation, is often to attend on some great and wise men, who are thought to study the good of the public: for when they are observed to be frequently with such, the people are presently apt to imagine that they will be like those men whom they choose for their patterns. Thus P. Rutilius, when he was young, had the general vogue of a very honest man, and an able lawyer, because he frequented the house of Mutius. As for Crassus, whilst he was very young, he was not beholden to any one else, but obtained of himself everlasting honour, by undertaking that noble and glorious accusation, when at that term of years, wherein others are commended if they begin but to study and exercise the art (as we have it recorded of the famous Demosthenes); at that age, I say, did Crassus make it appear that he could perform that laudably, in the open courts of justice, which he might, without disparagement, have been studying at home.

XIV.—*Affability very powerful to obtain men's love, but eloquence much more—To defend more laudable than to accuse ; but the latter in some cases honourable enough—Defending the accused especially honourable, when it is against some powerful oppressor.*

But of speaking or discourse there are two sorts; the one proper only for common conversation, the other for pleadings and debates in public. Of these two, the latter, which is what we call eloquence, is apparently more powerful towards the attainment of glory; but yet it is inexpressible of what influence courtesy and affability are, in the business of obtaining men's love and affections. There are extant letters of Philip to Alexander, Antipater to Cassander, and Antigonus to Philip; in which these most wise and prudent princes (for such we are told they really were) advise each his son to speak kindly to the multitude, and try to win the hearts of both them and the soldiers by gentle words and familiar appellations. But that other discourse, which is proper for pleadings and harangues in public, does oftentimes move and transport the whole multitude: for when a man speaks to them fluently and plausibly, they are presently wrapped into a strange admiration, and cannot but conclude, as soon as ever they hear him, that he is wiser and more knowing than the rest of men are. But if there be modesty joined with the power and weight of his eloquence, there is nothing in the world can more raise their admiration; and especially too if he be a young man that speaks. Now the subjects and occasions that stand in need of eloquence are more than one; and several young gentlemen, in our own republic, have made themselves eminent in several of them: some, for example, by speaking in the senate-house, and others by pleading in the courts of justice. Of these ways, the latter is most fruitful of admiration; the duties of which are only two, defending and accusing. It is much more commendable to defend than to accuse: however, this latter has oftentimes brought men to a considerable reputation. We mentioned the example of Crassus but just now; and Marcus Antonius, when he was a young man, did the same; and nothing got Sulpicius so much credit for his eloquence as his brave accusation of Caius Norbanus, a very seditious and troublesome citizen. This, nevertheless, must be done but seldom, or indeed never, unless it be undertaken on the behalf of the republic, as it was by those three whom I just now mentioned; or, secondly, on the account of some injury received, as by the two Luculli; or else for the sake of those under our protection, as was formerly done by myself for the Sicilians; and by Julius for the Sardinians against Marcus Albutius: in like manner Fusius made his industry be taken notice of, by his accusing Aquilius. Once then, or so, it is allowable enough; but by no means often. However, should the commonwealth call a man to it, he might do it often on her account, it being no disgrace to be often employed in taking vengeance on her enemies: yet, even in this case, it is still the best way to be moderate and cautious; for he shows himself a man of very unnatural and merciless temper, or rather indeed not a man at all, but a savage monster, who can endure to make it his very business and employment to bring many people into danger of their lives: besides, that it is dangerous to the person himself too; and not only so, but even scandalous and shameful, to get himself the odious name of an accuser; which of late was

*D 345

the fortune of Marcus Brutus, a person that had sprung of a noble family, and son of that Brutus who was so particularly famed for his skill in the civil laws. It is another rule of duty more especially to be taken notice of, and which cannot be broken without manifest villainy, never to bring an innocent person into danger: for since kind Nature has given us eloquence, to serve for the good and preservation of all men;—what can be more wicked or inhuman, than to turn it to the ruin and destruction of the best of them? It is our duty then never to accuse the innocent; but we need not, on the other hand, make any scruple of speaking sometimes in behalf of the guilty, provided he be not wholly villainous and abominable: for this is no more than what the people desire, than what custom authorises, and the common bowels of humanity incline us to. It is the duty of a judge to endeavour after nothing but the real truth, but an advocate sometimes may speak up for that, which carries no more than an outward appearance of it; which, I think, I should hardly have ventured to say, especially in writing a philosophical discourse, but that I perceive it was the opinion of Panaetius, a person of as great and considerable authority as any among the Stoics. But defending is that which brings the largest returns both of glory and interest; especially if one happen to be assistant to those who seem injured and oppressed by the power of some great one. This was my fortune, as a great many times, so more especially in my younger days, when I stood in defence of Roscius Amerinus against all the greatness and authority of Sylla; and you know the oration, which I then spoke, is at this time extant.

XV.—*Two sorts of liberality—Better to help men by our labour and industry than by our money—The inconveniences of the second sort of liberality—Measures to be observed in it.*

Having given this account of the particular duties which young men must do for the attainment of glory, we are next to discourse of beneficence or liberality. Of this there are two sorts; the one of which consists in obliging those who need it by our labour and industry, the other by our money. The latter of these two is much the more easy, especially for those who have plentiful fortunes; but the former, on the other hand, more glorious and magnificent, and more suitable to the character of a brave and exalted soul: for though there is a good-will and generous readiness to oblige shown in either, yet in the one case we are indebted to the chest, in the other to the virtues and abilities of the person. Besides, those sort of kindnesses, which are done by the assistance of money, or the like, within a short space of time draw their own fountain dry; so that this liberality doth, as it were, eat out its own bowels; and the more you have formerly obliged in this kind, the fewer you will be able to oblige for the future. But now, on the other hand, he whose generosity shows itself in labour, that is, in virtue, and being active for another's good, the more men he hath formerly shown himself kind to, the more he will have ready to assist him ever after; besides, that by the custom of doing good offices, he gets a kind of habit, and grows much more expert in the art of obliging. Philip, the father of Alexander the Great, reproves his son sharply in one of his epistles for endeavouring to purchase the good-will of the Macedonians by giving them donations. " In the name of wonder," says he, " what method of reasoning could lead you into such a thought, as to imagine that those men would ever be faithful to you whom yourself had corrupted with money? What! do you design to be thought, not the king, but only the steward and purse-bearer of the Macedonians? " That steward and purse-bearer is admirably well said, because it is so scandalous a business for a prince; and that calling donations a corrupting the people, is better yet; for those who receive them are perpetually the worse for it, and only made readier to expect the same again. Philip wrote this to his son alone, but it may serve for a direction to all men in general. I think we may take it for granted, therefore, that that sort of bounty, which consists in doing kindnesses by our labour and industry, is more virtuous and creditable, can oblige more people, and has more ways of doing it than that other has. Not but that sometimes a man should give; nor is this sort of bounty to be wholly rejected; nay, one ought oftentimes to distribute some part of one's money to those who are well-deserving persons, and stand in need of such assistance; but still it must be done with great prudence and moderation: for some men have squandered away whole estates by inconsiderately giving, which is certainly the foolishest thing in the world; for so a man disables himself ever after from doing that which he takes most delight in. But the worst thing is this, that profuseness in giving is usually accompanied by unjust ways of getting: for when by this means men have parted with what is their own, they are forced to lay hands on that which is another's: and by this means they miss what is their principal design, viz. the obtaining men's love by their bounty and generosity; for they get more hatred from those whom they injure, than good-will from those whom they hoped to oblige by it. We ought therefore neither so to lock up our riches, as that even liberality itself cannot open them; nor so to keep them open, as if they were common to all men in general: the best way is, always to observe a due medium, and give more or less in proportion to our estates. In fine, we should do well to remember a saying, which is now grown so common as to be a proverb among us, " Bounty has got no bottom: " for how indeed is it possible there should ever be any end of it, when those who are used to it look to receive again; and others, from seeing them, are taught to expect the same?

XVI.—*How liberality and prodigality differ—What the chief advantage of riches—Public shows to the people very foolish.*

Of those who give largely, there are two sorts; the one of which are prodigal, and the other liberal. The prodigal are those who consume vast sums in making public feasts, and distributing portions of meat to the people; or in providing gladiators to fight with one another, or with wild beasts in the theatres; or in making preparation for other such sports, and recreations of the multitude: things that are forgotten in a very short time, if ever at all thought on after once they are over: but the liberal are those who dispose of their money in redeeming poor prisoners, in helping their friends and acquaintance out of debt, in assisting them towards the marrying their daughters; or putting them into some method of making or increasing their fortunes. I wonder therefore what should come into Theophrastus' head, who, in a book of his which he wrote concerning riches, amongst several noble and excellent things, has been guilty of one very grievous absurdity; for he runs out mightily in commendation of magnificence, and giving public shows or donations to the people; and thinks the supplying of such expenses as these the very principal fruit and advantage of riches: but in my opinion, it is both a much greater and more durable advantage to be furnished with money for those acts of bounty, of which I have just now been giving some instances. But Aristotle, with much more reason and judgement, reproves us for not being amazed at those sums, which are daily thrown away to caress the people—" Should any one," says he, " when a city is besieged, and reduced to great straits, give a large sum of money for a little cup of water, people would wonder at it strangely, and hardly be persuaded to believe it at first; but afterwards, possibly, on farther consideration, would be ready to pardon it, because it was a case of mere exigence and necessity: but yet we can see, without any admiration, those vast charges and infinite expenses which men put themselves to for no reason in the world, neither for the relief of any want or necessity, nor yet for the increase of their glory and dignity: and that pleasure of the multitude, which is principally aimed at, is of the shortest continuance; and only tickles and soothes up the meanest of the people, who themselves will forget the satisfaction they received as soon as ever the show and recreation is at an end." He adds, moreover, with a great deal of reason, " that children, indeed, and some trifling women, together with slaves, and the more servile part of those who are free, might perhaps take a pleasure in such foolish kind of pastimes; but that men of true prudence, and those who judge of things by the rules of reason, can by no means either commend or approve of them." I know it is a custom in our republic, and has been from the time of our good forefathers, to expect and demand, even from the soberest citizens, something that is splendid and magnificent in their edileships. Hence Publius Crassus, who was surnamed the Wealthy, and really was such, in his office of edile was very magnificent and noble in his entertainments; and Lucius Crassus, a little while after, was fully as generous, though colleague of Mucius, the most moderate man living. Next after these came Caius Claudius, the son of Appius; and a great many others, viz. the Luculli, Hortensius, and Silanus. But Publius Lentulus, when I was consul, exceeded all others that ever went before him; who was afterwards followed and copied by Scaurus.

But of all these shows that have been given to please and entertain the people, those of my friend Pompey were the greatest and most magnificent, exhibited when he was the second time consul. In all which cases it is easy to see what is my opinion.

XVII.—*Expenses to please the people must be proportioned to one's estate, and confined within moderate limits.*

No man however should be so far moderate as to draw on himself the suspicion of avarice. Mamercus, a person of very great riches, was repulsed from the consulship, for no other reason but because he refused to be edile first: if such things therefore are demanded by the people, and allowed of, though perhaps not desired by good men, they must even be performed; but so as to keep within the compass of your estate, as I myself did: nay, though they should not be demanded by the people, yet they might wisely enough be presented them, on a prospect of gaining some more considerable advantage by it. Thus Orestes, of late, got a great deal of credit by giving the people a dinner in the streets, under the notion of paying his tenths to Hercules.[1] Nor did any one ever find fault with M. Seius for selling out corn at an easy rate, in the time of a very great dearth and scarcity: for he got himself free from a great and inveterate hatred of the people, by a cost which, considering he was at that time edile, was neither dishonest nor yet very great; but of all, my friend Milo got the greatest honour, by purchasing gladiators for the defence of the public, which was wholly included in my single safety, and thereby defeating the mad and pernicious attempts of Clodius. Such charges therefore are not to be shunned, when either they are necessary or very advantageous; but even when they are so, we must still not exceed the due limits of mediocrity. L. Philippus, the son of Quintus, an extraordinary ingenious and eminent man, was wont, I confess, to be making his brags that he got all the honours the republic could give him, without ever spending one

---

[1] It was a custom among the Romans to vow the tenth of their income to some god, to make him prosper them in their most important undertakings. Orestes, under pretence of paying this to Hercules, gave a great deal of victuals to all the people in public, that so he might gain their favour.

farthing that way; Caius Curio used to say the same; and even I myself have some reason to boast on this account: for, considering the greatness of the honours I got, and that too by every one of the votes, and the very first years I was capable of them (which is more than can be said by either of those two whom I just now mentioned), the charge of my edileship was very inconsiderable. But the best way of laying out money in this kind, is to repair the city walls, make docks, havens, aqueducts, and the like; things that may serve to the general use and advantage of the public: for though things which are present, and given down on the nail, are more acceptable for a time, yet the memory of these will be more lasting, and continued even down to posterity. I forbear to speak much against theatres, porticos, new temples, and the like, out of respect to my old friend Pompey; but I find them not approved of by the most famous men; particularly not by Panaetius himself, whom I have very much followed, though not quite translated in this work: neither are they liked by Demetrius Phalereus, who blames Pericles, one of the greatest men amongst all the Grecians, for squandering away such a vast sum of money on that noble structure at the entrance of the Acropolis. But I have spoken sufficiently on all this subject in those books which I have written concerning the republic. To conclude, therefore, all such profusions are, generally speaking, I think, to be blamed; but yet, at some times, and on certain occasions, may be rendered necessary: however, even then they must be proportioned to one's estate, and kept within the limits of reason and moderation.

XVIII.—*Liberality to be varied according to circumstances—Hospitality deservedly commended.*

In that other sort of giving which proceeds from liberality, we should not keep constantly to one certain measure, but vary according to the variety of circumstances in the persons that receive. His case, for instance, who struggles at present under some pressing necessity, is different from his, who is in tolerable circumstances, and only desires to improve his fortune. We should lend our assistance in the first place to those who are under the burden and weight of some misfortune, unless they are such as deserve to be miserable: we should be ready however to forward those likewise, who desire only of us our helping hand, not so much to save them from being unfortunate, as to raise them to some higher degree of fortune. But here we must be careful to acquaint ourselves thoroughly with the fitness of the persons; for that of Ennius is admirably well said:—" I take good actions, when ill applied, to become ill ones." Now that which is given to a truly honest and grateful person is paid us in the acknowledgement he himself makes, and in the good-will that is got by it from the rest of the world: for nothing is more pleasing to all mankind than bounty bestowed without rashness and precipitancy; and the generality of men praise it so much the more, because the liberality of every great man is a common kind of sanctuary for all that are needy. We should endeavour therefore, as far as we are able, to oblige many men by such acts of generosity as may not be forgotten as soon as ever they are over; but be remembered by the children and posterity of the receivers, in such manner as to lay a necessity on them of showing their gratitude: I say, necessity; for all people hate one that takes no care of being grateful to his benefactors, and count him that is such injurious to themselves, because he discourages bounty and liberality, and so is a common enemy to all the poorer sort. Besides, this way of giving, whereby captives are ransomed and the meaner folk enriched, is useful and advantageous to the public itself; and has frequently been practised by those of our order, as appears very fully from the oration of Crassus. That other way therefore of expending money, which consists in making shows for the entertainment of the vulgar, ought, I think, by no means to be compared with this: the one comports well with the character of a great and a prudent person; the other of such as cajole the people, and look out for pleasures to tickle the fancies of the unstable multitude: and as it is a duty to be generous in giving, so is it not to be too rigorous in demanding; but in every transaction of buying, selling, letting, and hiring, to behave ourselves towards our neighbours and chapmen with all the fairness and courtesy imaginable; to let go something of our strict and just rights, on certain occasions; to avoid all suits and contentions at law, as far as can reasonably and fairly be expected; perhaps I might add, and even something farther; for in several cases to deliver up one's right, is not only generous, but advantageous too. However, a man should have a decent regard to his estate and fortune; for it is not over reputable to let that be ruined by his easiness and neglect; and yet on the other hand he should carry himself so as to avoid all suspicion of a sordid, mean, or avaricious temper: for it is then a man uses his money as he ought to do, when he shows himself liberal, without ruining his fortune. Theophrastus commends, and with very good reason, another sort of bounty which we call hospitality; for there is nothing, in my mind, more handsome and becoming, than constantly to have the houses of noblemen open, and ready to entertain all strangers of fashion; and it is no small credit and reputation to the public, that strangers never fail to meet with that sort of bounty and liberality in our city; besides that there is nothing can be more useful for those who design by honest means to get an interest in the world, than to recommend themselves to the esteem and good liking of foreign nations, by the help of those people whom they thus entertain. Theophrastus tells us of Cimon the Athenian, that he showed his hospitality even to all his brethren of the Lacian tribe; and not only made it his own constant custom, but also commanded his bailiffs the same, to keep open house for any one of the Laciadae that should pass that way.

XIX.—*The liberality which consists in doing good offices for others—What sorts of study afford most opportunities of it—We should be careful of not offending some, by obliging others.*

I come now to speak of that sort of bounty, which consists not in giving, but in labouring for another's good; and extends itself, as to the republic in general, so to each member of the city in particular. The civil law principally gives us opportunities of exercising this; for there is nothing more proper to get a man interest and credit in the world, than the managing the law-suits of a great many persons, the assisting them with his advice, and doing for them all that he can by his knowledge and skill in that learning: and therefore I admire the wisdom of our ancestors, as for several reasons, so particularly for this, that the knowledge and interpretation of their excellent civil law was counted a matter of the highest credit and reputation among them. This the greatest men have kept constantly among themselves, till this late sad disorder and confusion of everything: but now the glory of this sort of learning, together with all honours and degrees of dignity, is utterly ruined and fallen to nothing: and to make the matter still so much the worse, all this has happened in the days of one [1] who, as he equalled in dignity all that have gone before him, so he was far above them in the knowledge of the laws. This study then is approved of by most people, and puts it in one's power to assist a great many, and oblige them by kindnesses. There is another sort of knowledge nearly related to this; the art, I mean, of persuasive speaking, which carries more majesty and ornament along with it, and is more pleasing and liked of, by the generality of men: for what is there in the world more extraordinary than eloquence, whether we consider the admiration of its hearers, the reliance of those who stand in need of its assistance, or the good will procured by it from those whom it defends? Our ancestors therefore held this among the chief of their civil professions. Any one then must oblige a great many, and have a large number of clients and dependents, who is able to speak well, and willing to take pains, and (as it was the custom among our good forefathers) is ready to undertake many people's causes, without ever expecting to be rewarded for his trouble. And here I have a fair opportunity offered me to bemoan the great downfall, that I may not say the utter extinction of eloquence; but that I am afraid I shall seem to complain for my own sake only. However, I cannot but with some concern take notice what a great many excellent orators we have lost; how few there are rising, from whom we can expect anything; and how much fewer who are able to perform and do anything; and for all that, how many full of impudence and presumption. Now it is not for all, nor indeed for very many, to be either skilful lawyers or eloquent pleaders: however, there is no one, if he would make it his business, but may do friendly offices to several people; either by begging some kindnesses for them, or by recommending their cases to the judges and officers, or by being industrious in promoting their interests, or, lastly,

---

[1] Ser. Sulpicius, one of the most eminent among the Romans for his skill in the civil law.

by using his endeavours with those who either are able lawyers or eloquent orators; which whoever shall do, will make a great many be beholden to him, and get himself a general interest in the world. There is one thing however of which I would take notice; though I think it is so obvious, that I hardly need to do it; which is, to have a care of offending some whilst he is endeavouring to be serviceable to others: for it often comes to pass, that such do an unkindness, either to those whom they ought to have obliged, or to those who are able to make them suffer for it afterwards; which shows carelessness and negligence if done undesignedly; but if designedly, rashness and imprudence: and if it should happen that we are forced, though unwillingly, to disoblige any person, we must endeavour to excuse it as well as we are able, by showing the necessity we lay under of doing so, and how it was utterly impossible for us to avoid it; and must be careful and industrious to repair the injury, by making some reasonable amends for it afterwards.

XX.—*In conferring favours merit rather than fortune ought to be observed —We should never do an injury to one for the sake of obliging another.*

Now whenever we do a kindness or friendly office to another, we usually regard one of these two things, viz. either the honesty or the greatness of the person. It is easily said, and every one is ready enough to profess, that in placing their favours, they have much more respect to the merits of the person, than to his fortune in the world. This is very fairly and honestly spoken; but yet I would be glad to be shown that man who is more willing to help one that is honest and poor than to get the favour of one that is wealthy and powerful: for who is not readiest to be serviceable to those from whom he expects the most speedy requital? but people would do well to consider more thoroughly the natures of things; for though a poor man, it is true, cannot make a requital; yet, if he is honest, he will acknowledge the obligation: and it was no unhandsome saying, whoever was the author of it, " That in case of a debt, the man who acknowledges it, doth not thereby pay it; and the man who pays it, does no longer acknowledge it; but in case of an obligation, both he who returns it still continues to acknowledge it, and he who acknowledges it thereby sufficiently returns it." But now those, on the contrary, who value themselves on their riches, honours, and flourishing condition, will scorn to acknowledge they are obliged for any kindness; nay, will think they vouchsafe you a signal favour, even whilst you are doing them some considerable service; and will always be jealous and suspicious over you, as though you demanded and expected something from them: but to have it ever said they were defended by you, or to be numbered among your dependents or clients, is as insupportable to them as even death itself; whereas your mean person, when any one does him a friendly office, considers it was done out of respect to himself, and not out of regard to his fortune or condition; and endeavours to show himself sensible of the obligation, not to him only who has done him the kindness, but, as standing in need of some other men's assistance, to those others also, from whom he hopes for the like: and, if he should chance to do another any service, he does not endeavour to cry up and magnify it, but rather to lessen it as much as he is able. Another thing worth the considering is this; that if you defend one that is wealthy and powerful, the obligation reaches only to the person himself, or perhaps just his children; but if you protect one that is needy and forsaken, provided withal he be virtuous and modest, all the lower sort of people immediately, that are not wicked, which is no inconsiderable part of the multitude, will look on you as their safeguard and protection. On all which accounts I am wholly of opinion that a kindness is better bestowed on an honest than it is on a wealthy and fortunate person. We should endeavour, it is true, to the utmost of our power, to be serviceable to all men of whatsoever condition; but if there should happen a competition between them, I am clearly for following Themistocles' advice, who being once asked, how he would marry his daughter, whether to one that was poor but honest, or to one that was rich but of an ill reputation; made answer, " I had rather have a man without an estate, than have an estate without a man." But the mighty respect which is paid to riches has wholly depraved and corrupted our manners; and yet what does it signify to any one of us, that such or such a person has got a plentiful fortune? Perhaps it may be useful to him that has it, though not so neither always; but allowing it to be so; suppose he has got the world more at his command; yet how, I would fain know, is he ever the honester for it? But if a man be honest as well as wealthy, though I would not have him helped for the sake of his riches, yet I would not have him hindered on their account neither; but in every case have it fairly considered, not how wealthy and great, but how good and deserving a person he is. I shall conclude this head with only one rule more; which is, never, for the sake of doing any one a kindness, to venture on that which is unjust in itself, or injurious to a third person: for no credit can be solid and durable unless built on the foundations of justice and honesty; without which nothing can be virtuous or commendable.

XXI.—*The first duty of the governors of a state to secure each individual in the possession of his property : not to burden the people with taxes, a second duty : a third, to furnish the people with necessaries.*

Having thus discoursed of the one sort of kindnesses which are done to particular members of the city; we are now, in the next place, to speak of those others, which are done to them all, and to the commonwealth in general. Now these again are of two sorts, the one more immediately relating to the community; the other reaching down to each member in particular; which latter is more grateful and acceptable. We should show our beneficence, as far as we are able, in both these ways; but especially in this latter, which relates to each one of the particular members: in which, however, one caution must be observed, that nothing be done in behalf of particulars but that which is useful, or at least not prejudicial to the commonwealth in general. C. Gracchus, for instance, made a large distribution of corn to the people; and the effect of it was, that the treasury was exhausted by it: Marcus Octavius was one that was moderate, which was a kindness to the multitude and no ways a burden or grievance to the state; and, accordingly, both the public and all the members of the city received benefit from it. But the principal thing for a governor to take care of is, that each individual be secured in the quiet enjoyment of his own, and that private men be not dispossessed of what they have, under a pretence of serving and taking care of the public: for nothing is more destructive to the peace of any nation than to bring in a new distribution of estates, which was attempted by Philip, in the time of his tribuneship: however, he quickly gave over his design, and did not persist stubbornly in defence of it, as soon as he found it was so vigorously opposed; but in his public speeches and harangues to the people, among a great many things to obtain their favour, he was heard to say one of very dangerous consequence;—That the whole city had not two thousand men in it that were masters of estates: a very pernicious and desperate saying, directly tending to bring all things to a level; which is the greatest misfortune that can befall any people: for to what end were cities and commonwealths established, but only that every one might be safer and securer in the enjoyment of his own? For though men are by nature sociable creatures, yet it was the design of preserving what they had that first put them on building of cities for a refuge. It is a second duty of the governors of a state to see that the people be not forced to pay taxes, as they often were in our forefathers' time, partly because they were always in war, and partly by reason of the lowness of the treasury. This is an inconvenience, which ought, as far as possible, to be provided against beforehand: but if any state should be under such circumstances, as that it must be forced to make use of this expedient;—I say any state, because I am unwilling to suppose so unhappy a thing of our own; besides that I speak here of all of them in general;—but if, I say, any state should be brought to such a pitch, due care must be taken to let the people know that it is absolutely necessary, as affairs now stand; and that otherwise they must needs be inevitably ruined. Again, it is yet farther required of those men who govern and preside in a commonwealth, to see that it be furnished with all the conveniences and necessaries of life. To tell what these are, and how to be provided, would be altogether needless in this place, since it is sufficiently known already; I only thought fit just to touch on it. But in all kinds of business, and managing affairs of a public nature, there is nothing more necessary than always to keep oneself clear and untainted, so as not to lie under the least suspicion of avarice. "I could heartily wish," said Caius Pontius, the Samnite, "that Fortune had reserved me to those times, and that it had been my fate to be then born, whenever the Romans shall begin to take bribes; I should quickly have put an end to their flourishing empire." Truly he must have waited a pretty many ages; for that is a kind of evil which but lately has begun to infest this republic. If Pontius, therefore, were so great a man as he pretended to be, I am very well satisfied with his being born when he was, and not in those times which have lately happened. It is not yet a hundred and ten years ago since Lucius Piso got a law to be enacted against the corruption of magistrates, whereas there had never been any one before: but since that time there have been so many laws, and still every new one more severe than the former; so many persons accused and condemned; such a war stirred up in the bowels of Italy, by those who were afraid of being brought to punishment; such shameful extortion and pillaging our allies, by those who have defied all laws and courts of justice;—that we are rather beholden to the weakness of others, than our own strength or virtues, that we are not utterly ruined.

XXII.—*Examples of contempt of money among the ancient Romans— The honour attached to this virtue—The danger and folly of the project of levelling estates.*

Panaetius highly commends Africanus for his being uncorrupt as to the matter of money. It is a virtue that well deserved his commendation: but I think there were others in that great person, which deserved it much more; to be untainted with money being not properly a virtue of that man as of those times in general. Paulus Aemilius had all the wealth of Macedonia in his power, which amounted to almost an infinite value; so that he brought such a sum into the treasury, as that the single booty of that one general superseded the necessity of all taxes for the future; and yet he brought nothing to his own house but the eternal memory of his name and achievements. Africanus followed the example of his father, and returned nothing richer from the overthrow of Carthage. So Mummius, who was afterwards his partner in the censorship; did he make himself a farthing the wealthier by rasing one of the wealthiest cities in the world?[1] No, he rather chose to make Italy fine with the

---

[1] Corinth, which was rased by Mummius, the same year that Carthage was by Scipio.

spoils of his enemies, than his own house; though in my opinion the ornaments of Italy reflect a bright lustre on his own house too. There is no vice then (that I may return to the subject from which I have digressed) more detestable than avarice; more especially in great men, and such as bear sway in the government of a state; for it is not only mean for a man to make a prey and advantage of the commonwealth, but even impious and abominable. That oracle therefore of the Pythian Apollo, that nothing but avarice should be the ruin of Sparta, doth not seem designed for the Lacedaemonians only, but for every wealthy and flourishing nation. And as avarice is thus very destructive to a state, so to appear upright and regardless of money is the most certain method those in power can make use of for procuring the love and good liking of the people: but those, who, designing to curry their favour, attempt new laws about the levelling estates, so as to force the right owners from their lawful possessions; or propose to make creditors remit all the debts, which in justice are due to them; plainly undermine the two principal pillars and supports of the government: in the first place, concord and unity amongst the citizens, which can never be kept up whilst some are deprived of what is justly their due, and others discharged from the necessity of payment; secondly, justice, which immediately must sink into ruins, if men cannot be secured in the possession of what is their own: for that (as we before remarked) is the chief end and aim of men's gathering into societies, and building of cities, that each one might freely enjoy what is his right, without any danger or fear of being deprived of it. Besides this, the authors of these pernicious designs never get that good-will, which they propose, from their citizens; for, as for those men, who are losers by such a method, it is certain that they will be their enemies for it; and those who are gainers will be sure to pretend that they never desired it, especially in the business of having debts forgiven: there every one dissembles how glad he is of it, for fear it should be thought he was not able to pay them: but those men, to whom such designs are prejudicial, will hardly forget them, but show a perpetual grudge and resentment. And though the number of these, who are thus wickedly befriended, be greater than of those who are injuriously robbed; yet it doth not follow that therefore they are more powerful; for it is not the number, but the quality of the persons that must carry it in this case. Besides, what reason or equity is there when estates have been held for a great many years, or perhaps ages, that the rightful owners should be thrust out from them, and others, that never had any, should come and possess them?

XXIII.—*Evils arising to a state from insecurity of property—The wise conduct of Aratus the Sicyonian.*

For such kind of partial, injurious proceedings, the Spartans once banished Lysander, one of their ephori; and put to death Agis their king, for the same reason; an action unheard of before in that city. This was succeeded by such grievous contentions and discords in the state, as that tyranny and oppression got the upper hand amongst them; the nobles were banished from their native country, and the best constituted republic on the face of the earth was utterly dissolved and brought into confusion. Nor did this mischief end with the Spartans only; but, like a contagion, spreading itself farther, involved all Greece in the same miseries and calamities. Pray, what is it that ruined our own two Gracchi, sons of the famous Tiberius Gracchus, and grandsons of Africanus, but only these controversies about levelling estates? Aratus the Sicyonian is deservedly commended as much on the other hand: he, when his country for fifty years together had been greatly oppressed and overrun by tyrants, went secretly one night from Argos to Sicyon, and made himself master of the city by surprise; and unexpectedly falling on Nicocles, the then tyrant, he put him to flight. This being done, he recalled six hundred of the wealthy citizens, who had all been formerly banished by the tyrant; and by this his arrival, delivered the city from slavery and oppression: but he afterwards found it would be a great deal of trouble to settle the business of their estates and possessions; for he thought on the one hand it was very unreasonable that those men, whom he had restored, should want, whilst others enjoyed what in equity was theirs; and yet it seemed hard on the other side, that men should be thrust out of those possessions, which now they had held for these fifty years: if, more especially it were likewise considered, that it could not but happen in so long a time, that they must have gone, a great part of them, from one to another, either by inheritance, purchase, dowry, or the like, and therefore were possessed by the present incumbents, without having injured the rightful proprietors. On these considerations, he judged it necessary, both to bear with the latter in the enjoyment of what they had, yet to satisfy the former, whom it justly belonged to: and finding a large sum of money was requisite to settle this business as it ought to be, he told them he had occasion to go to Alexandria, and ordered they should not concern themselves about it till his return. He goes accordingly with all possible speed to his old friend Ptolemy, who at that time was reigning in Alexandria, being the second king after the founding of that city. Having told him his design of settling liberty in his country, and the reasons that put him on undertaking that voyage, he quickly prevailed on that wealthy prince to supply him with a quantity of money for his assistance: with this he immediately returns to Sicyon, and choosing out fifteen of the principal citizens to help him with their counsel on this occasion, he heard both the causes of those who possessed what had belonged to others, and of those who had lost what had been formerly their own. At last, he so managed the whole business, as that the estates being set at their true values, some were persuaded to part with what they had, and take an equivalent in money for it; and others to neglect the recovery of their own, and rest themselves content with being paid its full value. By this means the controversy was fairly determined, and all went home satisfied without grudging or complaining. Here was a great and extraordinary man now! Here was one that deserved to have been born in our republic! This is the true way of dealing with citizens; and not (as hath been practised amongst us twice) to make sale of their goods in the public markets, and have them cried by the voice of the common crier. But this famous Grecian, as was the duty of a wise and extraordinary person, thought it became alike to provide for all; and indeed every magistrate, who proceeds on principles of reason and prudence, will always take care not to make any difference between the interests of his people; but will govern them all by the same rule and standard of justice and equity. Here is one man shall dwell in what belongs to another:

what reason is there I beseech you for this; that when I have bought, built, repaired, and laid out a great deal of money, another should come and enjoy all the fruits of it, in spite of my teeth? Is not this plainly to take away from one that which justly belongs to him, and give to another what he has no right to? As to the project of forgiving debts, I can see no reason in the world for it, unless it be reason that another should buy land with my money; and that he should have the land, but I never have my money.

XXIV.—*Faith the cement of public society—The duties of a good magistrate—How one's health and estate are to be taken care of.*

Care ought therefore to be taken beforehand, which it is easy to do by a great many ways, to keep people from running so much into debt, as may bring any damage or inconvenience to the public; and not, when they are in, to oblige the creditors to lose what is their own, and let the debtors gain what in justice is another's; for nothing so cements and holds together in union all the parts of a society, as faith or credit; which can never be kept up, unless men are under some force and necessity of honestly paying what they owe to one another. This design of having debtors excused from payment was never attempted with greater eagerness than whilst I was consul: men of all ranks and degrees in the state took up arms and formed camps for the bringing it about; whose endeavours I resisted with so much vigour, as that the republic was soon delivered from so pernicious an evil. There never were known greater debts in the city, nor ever more easily and faithfully paid; and pray what was the reason of all this? Why, because when their hopes of defrauding were cut off, they found themselves under a necessity of payment. It is true, there is one who has since been a conqueror, though then he was conquered by my vigilance,[1] that has found out means to effect these designs, at a time when they would bring him no manner of advantage; but such an inclination had that man to villainy, that the bare doing of it was a pleasure to him, without any other invitation in the world. The sum

[1] He means Caesar, who being overwhelmed in debt, was suspected in Catiline's time to favour his wicked designs; and so may be said to have been conquered by Cicero, when he ruined Catiline.

then of what has been said is this, that such as desire the good of the republic must be sure to avoid this sort of liberality, which takes away from one what it gives to another; and must consequently make it their principal care to uphold each member in his proper rights, according to the principles of justice and equity; so as neither to suffer the poorer sort of people to be wronged or oppressed by reason of their poverty, nor the richer to be hindered from keeping or demanding what is justly their own, by the envy of the others; and, in fine, must apply their most earnest endeavours, whether in war or peace, to increase the power, and enlarge the bounds and revenues of the republic. These are the duties and exercises of great men; these are the things which were practised by our ancestors; and whoever pursues the same course will not only bring great advantage to the republic, but gain a mighty interest and reputation to himself. In these rules of duty, relating to things profitable, Antipater the Tyrian, a Stoic philosopher, who lately died at Athens, thinks that two things have been omitted by Panaetius; first, the care of getting and preserving one's health; and, secondly, of an estate. I believe that great philosopher might omit them on purpose, because they are so easy and obvious to every one: however, it is certain they are both of them profitable. Now health is preserved by considering the peculiar temper of one's body, and observing what agrees or does not agree with it; by temperance and moderation in meats and drinks, and other things relating to the welfare of the body, by forbearance and abstinence as to the matter of pleasures; and, lastly, by the skill of physicians, and the like. An estate should be got by nothing that is anyways scandalous or dishonest; preserved by diligence and prudent management; and, lastly, by the same means bettered and augmented. But this whole subject is excellently handled by Xenophon the Socratic, in his Book of Oeconomics; which I formerly translated from the Greek into Latin, when much about as old as you are at present.

XXV.—*The comparing of things profitable one with another.*

The fourth chief head we proposed to speak of was the comparing things profitable one with another; which is oftentimes necessary, however neglected or forgotten by Panaetius: for we used to compare either the goods of the body with those of fortune; or these back again with those of the body; or, lastly, those both of the one and the other amongst themselves. First, the goods of the body are compared with those of fortune; as it is more eligible, suppose, to be healthy than rich: secondly, these back again with those of the body; as it is better to be rich than of a robust constitution: thirdly, those of the body with one another; as health is preferable to pleasure, or strength to activity: and, lastly, those of fortune with one another; as if glory should be preferred before riches, or an estate in the city before another in the country. To this latter sort of comparing may be referred that answer of the senior Cato, who being once asked, what he conceived most profitable in the management of an estate? said, "To feed cattle well." And what second? "To feed cattle pretty well." And what the third? "To feed cattle, though but ill." And what the fourth? "To till the ground." And then the inquirer proceeding still to ask, "Pray what do you think of letting money out to usury?"—"Pray what do I think," replies Cato, "of killing a man?" From what has been said, and a great deal more that might easily be added, it is sufficiently manifest that profits are often compared with one another; and that we had reason sufficient on our side, in making this a fourth head for the finding out our duty: but as for the business of getting an estate, and placing out money to the best advantage, and I wish I might add of applying it to the best uses; there are certain honest men [1] who attend at the exchange that can better inform you than any of the philosophers that dispute in the schools. It is worth while, however, to know these things, because they relate to the business of profit, which has made up the subject of all this book. Let us now pass on to what remains behind.

[1] So he calls, by way of derision, the bankers, changers, etc.

BOOK III

I.—*Difference between the retirement of Africanus and Cicero—
Some good to be drawn out of evils.*

CATO, son of Marcus, who was near of the same age with
Publius Scipio, the first that had the surname of Africanus
given him, tells us it was a usual saying of his, that he was
never less idle than when he was idle; nor ever less alone
than when he was alone: a noble and excellent sentence
indeed, and worthy of so great and wise a person: by which
it appears, that in the midst of leisure he could think of
business, and was used when alone to converse with his
own thoughts: so that he never was properly idle, and
needed no company to entertain him in his solitude. The
two things, therefore, which bring a kind of dullness and
heaviness on others, served but to sharpen and invigorate
his mind, viz. solitude and leisure. I wish I could truly
say the same of myself. But though I am not able to
arrive at that inimitable temper of soul, I desire at least to
come as near it as is possible; and being excluded by open
violence and impious arms, from having aught to do with
affairs of the senate or business of the bar, I wholly betake
myself to a life of retirement; and for that very reason
have abandoned the city, and am often alone, only going
from one seat to another in the country. But, alas! my
leisure is not to be compared with that of Africanus, nor
my solitude with his solitude! for he was employed at that
very time in places of the greatest reputation in the public;
and his leisure was only a voluntary retirement, to give
himself respite from business for a season; and his solitude
only a kind of port or haven, into which he withdrew himself from the disturbances of company: whereas my leisure
proceeds not from any desire of respite, but from a want of
business to employ myself about: for what proper work
can I find to do, when there is no more a senate nor any
courts of justice remaining entire, in which I might honour-
ably show myself: therefore, whereas it was my former

custom to appear much in public, and in the eye of my citizens; I now, on the contrary, hide myself from them, to avoid the very sight of such packs of villains as are everywhere abroad; and as much as is possible confine myself to solitude. But since this is given us for a rule by the learned, that when several evils are threatening us at once, we should not only choose to undergo the least, but extract some advantage out of them, if it be possible; I therefor, in the midst of all these present misfortunes, gain the small advantage of quiet and retirement (though not such a quiet as he might have expected, whose wisdom had formerly procured the peace of the public), and endeavour not wholly to languish out that solitude, which not choice, but necessity has laid on me: though Africanus, indeed, I myself must confess, has got much greater glory by his solitude and retirement; for none of his thoughts are committed to writing, nor any monuments remain of what he did in his leisure, and when he was alone; whereby we are given to understand that he never was idle, nor ever properly alone; because he was always employed in meditation, and his mind was busy in searching out those things which, by thinking, he made himself master of: but I, who have not got such a strength of genius as to be content when alone with the company of my bare thoughts, am forced to apply all my studies and endeavours to the drudgery of writing: I have written more therefore within a very short time, since the ruin of the state, than I did for some years while it was in its flourishing condition.

II.—*The subject of duties the most useful part of all philosophy—An exhortation to his son to be diligent in his studies.*

Now, though all philosophy, my dear Cicero, be rich, as it were, and a plentiful soil, which has not any part of it waste and uncultivated; yet there is no part that is more fruitful in it, or from which more advantage accrues to the husbandman, than that which is employed about offices or duties; whence those precepts and directions are drawn, which lead toward a steady and virtuous way of living. Wherefore, though I doubt not but that Cratippus, the greatest philosopher of our age, is daily inculcating these things to you, and you are receiving them with that atten-

tion they deserve; yet I have thought it not wholly unnecessary to remind you myself of so important a matter,
and could wish that your ears might continually ring, as it
were, with such precepts, and not hear, as far as possible,
anything else. And as this is a method which is useful for
all men, who design to lead virtuous and creditable lives;
so for no one living, perhaps, more than yourself. For consider, you are the son of an industrious father, one who has
borne the greatest honours in the republic, and has got
himself some credit and reputation in the world: people
therefore will expect that you should follow my steps, and
it is your part to see that you answer their expectation.
Besides, it is no small thing you have taken on you, by being
at Athens, and under the great Cratippus; whither since
you are gone, as it were, to a staple and mart of good literature, it will be scandalous for you to return again empty,
and bring a reproach both on the place and your master:
wherefore, dear son, be industrious and diligent, and spare
no manner of pains and labour (if I may call it a labour, and
not rather a pleasure, to study and learn) that you may
make a good use of these advantages before you; and when
all things are thus plentifully supplied on my part, let it
never be said that you yourself are wanting to your own
greatest interest. But I shall say no more on this at present,
having heretofore written again and again to you, by way
of exhortation. Let us now proceed to the fifth and last
part of our proposed division. Panaetius, then, who, without all controversy, has written most accurately on the
subject of duties, and whom in this work, with a little alteration, I have hitherto followed, lays down, as was said, three
general heads, which men use in consulting or deliberating
concerning their duty. In the first it is questioned, whether
the action they are going about be honest or dishonest; in
the second, whether it be profitable or unprofitable; in the
third, how a good man ought to determine the case, if that
which seems honest should come into competition with that
which seems profitable. Of the two former heads he has
given us an account in his first three books, and therein has
promised to go on with the third of them; but has failed,
it should seem, of being so good as his word: which I wonder
at the more on this account; because we are told by his
scholar Posidonius that he lived thirty years after those

books were published. And I cannot but be surprised at the same Posidonius, that having an occasion, in some of his writings, to discourse on this argument, he should do no more than briefly touch on it; especially seeing he himself has observed, that in all philosophy there is no one subject more necessary and important. Some indeed think, whom I cannot agree with, that Panaetius did not forget this part, but omitted it on purpose; and that in plain truth it ought to be omitted, since profit can never be really contrary to honesty: whether it ought to be omitted or not, may perhaps be a question; but whether Panaetius first designed it or no, and yet afterwards neglected it, I think can be none: for a writer certainly, that proposes three heads, and goes through with but two of them, must needs design to discourse on the third; nay, he tells us himself in the close of his third book, that he would afterwards proceed to this remaining part. Besides, we have the authority of Posidonius to vouch it, who in one of his letters has given us a saying of Rutilius Rufus, who was scholar to Panaetius as well as himself; that as never any painter had been yet so bold as to venture on finishing that piece of Venus, which Apelles left imperfect at the island Cos (the beauty of the face making all men despair ever to paint a body that should be answerable to it); so the excellency of that which Panaetius had written on this subject made others afraid of attempting to add that which he had omitted.

III.—*The danger of separating profit from honesty—What the Stoics mean by living according to nature—The most perfect virtue, as it is counted by the multitude, is really imperfect.*

That Panaetius, therefore, did think he was obliged to discourse on this part, is beyond all question; but whether he was mistaken in his judgement or not, when he laid down his head, as the third of deliberating for the finding out our duty, may perhaps be disputed: for whether, according to the opinion of the Stoics, we take virtue or honesty to be the only good; or, according to that of the Peripatetics, acknowledge it so to be the chief good, as that all things else are just as nothing against it;—it is certain, on either of these suppositions, that profit cannot be put in balance against honesty. We are therefore told that Socrates used even to curse those people who disjoined these things in thought and conception, which are one and the same in nature and reality: and the Stoics are so far of his opinion, as constantly to maintain, that whatever is honest must be also profitable, and whatever is profitable must be also honest. It is true, had Panaetius been one of those who assert that virtue is therefore only desirable, because it brings something of profit along with it; like some, who think nothing any farther worth seeking for, than as it begets pleasure, or exemption from pain; we could then have allowed him the liberty of saying that profit is some-times repugnant to honesty: but seeing he was one who thought nothing to be good except that which is honest, and avows, that whatever is contrary to honesty, and appears to us under the notion of profit, can neither, if we have it, make life ever the better, nor if we have it not, ever the worse;—he should not, methinks, have brought in such a deliberation, wherein that which seems profitable comes into competition with that which is honest: for that which the Stoics call their sovereign good (to live in conformity with the dictates of nature), means, I suppose, no more than this: that we should always live agreeably to the rules of virtue; and should use other things, which are suited and adapted to our natural inclinations, no farther than virtue permits and allows them. Now this being so, there are several of opinion that this general head, wherein profit and honesty are compared with one another, was improperly brought in, and that there ought not to have been given any rules or directions on this subject. Now your perfect honesty, which is truly and properly called by that name, is only to be found in your perfectly wise men, and can never be possibly separated from virtue; but those men, who have not this perfect wisdom, must by no means pre-tend to such a perfect honesty, though they may have some shadows and resemblances of it; for all those duties, of which we are treating in these books, have the name of middle ones given them by the Stoics, which are common indifferently to all men in general, and are not confined to any particular number of them. But several get them, either by the peculiar happiness of their natures, or by a constant progress in study and learning; whereas those others, which they call right ones, are perfect and consummate, or (as they themselves express it) have all their numbers, which none can attain to but the perfectly wise. It is true that the vulgar, as soon as they see any action of such a nature, as indeed is no more than a middle kind of duty, are immediately thinking it a perfect and complete one; for the common sort of people cannot tell what is perfect, and by consequence do not know how much any virtue or excellence comes short of it: but finding it answer the highest of their conceptions, they imagine it wants nothing of being as perfect as can be: just as it happens in judging of poems or pieces of painting, and such like; those who are not judges are generally pleased with and praise those things which by no means deserve praise or commendation; because, I suppose, there may be something that is good in them, which serves well enough to take with those that are ignorant, and who have not so much skill as to be able to discover their several imperfections; and, therefore, when they are instructed by those who understand it better, they are brought without difficulty to forsake their opinions.

IV.—*The greatest men not perfectly wise—Profit ought not to be compared with the middle, any more than with the perfect honesty.*

Those duties, therefore, which make up the subject of this inquiry, by the Stoics are counted a kind of second-rate honesty, which is not confined to their wise men only, but is common and open to all mankind; and therefore all those who have any kind of sense of inclination for virtue are very sensibly touched and affected with it: for you are not to imagine, when we call the two Decii or Scipios magnanimous, and give Fabricius and Aristides the appellation of Just, that we set them for patterns of such justice and magnanimity, as we suppose to be in those who are perfectly wise: for they were none of them wise in that exalted sense, which we would here be understood to mean by that word. Nay, those who were counted and surnamed the Wise, such as Cato, for instance, and Laelius, and particularly the famous seven, yet in truth and reality were not such; but by frequently practising that middle sort of duties, had got a sort of show and resemblance of true wisdom. As no profit therefore ought ever to be put in opposition to that which is truly and perfectly virtuous and honest; so neither should any interest, or convenience of life, be set up against that which is ordinarily called so, and which is followed by those who desire to be counted men of honesty and integrity: and we should be as careful to live up to that honesty, whereof we are capable, as the perfectly wise are of keeping close to that which is truly such, and may in strictness of speech be called by that name: for whatever attainments we have made in virtue, they will never stand us in any mighty stead, if we be not thus careful of holding constantly to our duty. What has hitherto been said can be applied to those only who make goodness consist in living according to their duty: but those men, who measure the goodness of things by some profit or advantage which they bring along with them, and who let these prevail with them above virtue and honesty, frequently in deliberating use to put that, which they take to be profitable, into the balance against justice and honesty; but good and wise men never offer to do it. I am therefore of opinion, when Panaetius tells us that men use to deliberate, in considering which of these two they should choose, that he meant no more than what his words strictly signify, viz. that they use to do this, and not that really they ought to do it: for it is infinitely scandalous, not only to prefer a pretended advantage before duty and conscience; but so much as to bring them to the contest and competition, and to doubt whether the one of them should be chosen before the other. If this be so, you will be ready to ask me, " How then comes there to be any doubt at all? And what is it that requires consideration on this subject?" I suppose it is this; that it sometimes happens men are not so very certain whether the action deliberated on be honest or not honest; for that which is usually counted a piece of villainy, is frequently changed by the times or circumstances, and is found to be the contrary. To lay down one instance, which may serve to give some light to a great many others; pray, what greater wickedness can there be on earth, if we speak in general, than for any one to murder, not only a man, but a familiar friend? And shall we therefore affirm that he is chargeable with a crime, who has murdered a tyrant, though he were his familiar? The people of Rome, I am sure, will not say so, by whom this is counted amongst the greatest and most glorious actions in the world. You

will say then, does not interest here carry it against honesty?
No, but rather honesty voluntarily follows interest. If therefore we would, on all emergencies, be sure to determine
ourselves aright, when that which we call our advantage or
interest seems to be repugnant to that which is honest, we
must lay down some general rule or measure, which, if we
will make use of in judging about things, we shall never be
mistaken as to points of duty. Now this measure I would
have to be conformable to the doctrines and principles of
the Stoics, which I principally follow throughout this work:
for though I confess that the ancient Academics and your
Peripatetics, which were formerly the same, make honesty
far preferable to that which seems one's interest; yet those
who assert that whatever is honest must be also profitable,
and nothing is profitable but what is honest, talk much more
bravely and heroically on this subject, than those who
allow that there are some things honest which are not profitable, and some things profitable which are not honest: and
we have very great liberty given us by our academy, so as
never to be tied up to certain tenets, but are left free to
defend what we think most probable.

V.—The ill effects of men injuring others for their own advantage.

But to return to our general rule or measure: there is
nothing on earth then so contrary to nature, neither death,
nor poverty, nor pain, nor whatever other evil can befall
a man, either in his body or fortune, as to take away anything wrongfully from another, and do oneself a kindness
by injuring one's neighbour: for, in the first place, it ruins
all manner of society and intercourse amongst men; since
it is plain, that if once men arrive at such a pass as to
plunder and injure the rest of their neighbours, out of hopes
to procure some advantage to themselves, there must follow
of course a dissolution of that society which of all things in
the world is most agreeable to nature. Should we suppose,
for example, that the bodily members had every one of
them got an opinion, that to draw to itself all the vigour of
its neighbours would very much serve to increase its own;
it is certain the whole body must decay and perish: and
just so, should every one amongst us deprive other people
of their profits and advantages, and take away all he could

get from them, with design of applying it only to his own use, the general society and fellowship of mankind must of necessity be broken: for though it is no more than what Nature will allow of, that each man should look after himself in the first place, and furnish himself with the necessaries of life, before he takes care to provide for other people; yet the same Nature will by no means permit that any one should rise by his thrusting down another, and increase his own fortune by the spoils of his neighbours: and not only Nature, that is the universal law or consent of nations, but particular laws, by which several countries and common-wealths are governed, have commanded likewise, that no one be suffered to do an injury to another for the sake of procuring any advantage to himself: for the very design and end of laws is to keep up agreement and union amongst citizens; which whoever destroys, is by them punished, not with the loss of his goods alone, but with prisons, banish-ment, or even death itself. But nature and right reason, as being at once both a human and divine law too, command this duty with much greater authority; and whoever obeys them (as all men must, who propose to live according to the rules of nature), will never be guilty of coveting what is another's, or applying to his own use what had first been injuriously taken from his neighbour: for certainly great-ness and elevation of soul, as also the virtues of courtesy, justice, and liberality, are much more agreeable to nature and right reason, than pleasure, than riches, than even life itself; to despise all which, and regard them as nothing, when they come to be compared with the public interest, is the duty of a brave and exalted spirit: whereas, to rob another for one's own advantage, is (as has been shown) more contrary to nature than death, than pain, or any other evil whatever of that kind. Again, those men live much more according to nature, who suffer perpetual troubles and labours for the good and preservation, were it possible, of all men (like Hercules of old, whom men, as a grateful requital for his benefits, report to be placed among the number of the gods), than those who consume all their lives in retirement, where they are not only free from disturbances and vexa-tions, but are furnished with all the pleasures and conveni-ences of life; and have, moreover, the advantages of strength and comeliness superadded to them: and accordingly we find it to be so in effect, that all the most great and extraordinary geniuses have preferred all the troubles and difficulties of the former before the quiet and ease of this latter way of living. From all which laid together, it unanswerably follows, that whoever lives agreeably to the dictates of nature can never be guilty of injuring another. In fine, he that injures another to do himself a kindness, either thinks he does nothing that is contrary to nature, or that the doing an injury is a less degree of evil than death, or poverty, or pain, or loss of children, friends, or relations. If he thinks that in wronging and abusing others he doth not do anything that is contrary to nature, it is in vain to dispute any longer with such a one, who takes away from man the distinguishing part, and very characteristic, as it were, of his nature: but if he allows that it is indeed an evil; only thinks that some others, such as poverty, pain, or death, may be worse, he is grossly mistaken, in being of opinion that the ills which touch nothing but the body or fortune can be greater than those which affect the soul.

VI.—*The interest of individuals inseparable from that of the whole community—The rule of not wronging another for our own advantage extends to all mankind.*

We should all of us therefore propose the same end, and every one think his own interest, in particular, to be the same with that of the community in general: which, if each one endeavour to draw solely to himself, all union and agreement amongst men will be dissolved. And if Nature enjoin us, that every man should desire and procure the advantage of another, whoever he be, though for no other reason than because he is a man, it necessarily follows that all men are joined by the self-same nature in one common interest; which, if it be true, then all men are subject to, and live equally under, the same law of nature: and if this be true, too, then certainly they are forbid, by that same law of nature, any ways to injure or wrong one another; but the first of these is undoubtedly certain, therefore the last must needs be so likewise: for as to what is usually said by some men, that they would not take anything away from a father or brother for their own advantage, but that there is not the same reason for their ordinary citizens, it is foolish and absurd: for they thrust themselves out from partaking of any privileges, and from joining in common with the rest of their citizens, for the public good; an opinion that strikes at the very root and foundation of all civil societies. Others there are, who are ready to confess that they ought to bear such a regard to fellow-citizens, but by no means allow of it in relation to strangers: now these men destroy that universal society of all mankind, which, if once taken away, kindness, liberality, justice, and humanity must utterly perish; which excellent virtues whoever makes void, is chargeable with impiety towards the immortal gods; for he breaks that society which they have established and settled amongst men; the closest cement or bond of which is the being of opinion, that for men to injure and wrong one another for their private interests, is an evil that nature is much more averse from than all those which happen either to the body or fortune; nay, and I might add to the mind also, provided only they be not contrary to justice, queen of all the rest. But what (perhaps some men will be apt to say)—if a wise man be ready to perish for hunger, must not he take away victuals from another, though a perfectly useless and insignificant fellow? Not at all; for life itself is not so dear to me, as a settled resolution of doing no wrong for my private advantage. But suppose this good man, almost dead with cold, should have it in his power to take Phalaris's clothes away, one of the most savage and inhuman tyrants, would not you have him to do it? There is no great difficulty in determining such cases; for it is certain, if you take away anything from another, though never so useless and insignificant a creature, for no other end but to benefit yourself by it, it is an inhuman action, and plainly contrary to the laws of nature: but if you are one, who by living will do very great service to the republic, or perhaps to the society of mankind in general, and for that only reason take something from another, it is an action that is not to be found much fault with: but in all other cases, every man is bound to bear his own misfortunes rather than to get quit of them by wronging his neighbour. You will say then, is it not more contrary to nature to covet or seize what belongs to another, than to be in sickness, or want, or any such evil? Yes; but withal it is as contrary to nature to abandon all care of the public interest; for it is a piece of injustice:

whence it follows, that an honest, prudent, and valiant person, whose death would bring a great disadvantage to the public, may take from an idle and useless citizen such things as are necessary for the maintenance of life, without any offence against the laws of nature, which aim at the preservation and interest of the public; provided that he do not make the love of himself, and conceit of his own more than ordinary merits, an occasion of injuring and oppressing others: for he will perform but the duties which justice requires of him, by thus taking care to be serviceable to the public, and upholding that (which I am often forced to mention) universal society between all mankind. As for the question proposed about Phalaris, it is easily answered; for tyrants are not members of human society, but rather its greatest and most pestilent enemies; nor is it unnatural, if it lie in one's power to rob that man, whom it is even a virtue and a glory to murder. And it were heartily to be wished, that this whole destructive and impious race were utterly banished and excluded from amongst men. Just as we cut off those members of the body which have got no longer either blood or spirits in them, and serve but to infect and corrupt the rest; so should those monsters, which, under the shape and outside of men, conceal all the savageness and cruelty of beasts, be cut off, as it were, and separated from the body and society of mankind. Of much the same nature are all those questions, in which the knowledge and understanding of our duty depends on the knowledge of times and circumstances.

VII.—*Honesty alone, or at least chiefly, is desirable.*

I believe then Panaetius would have discoursed on such things as these, but that some accident, or perhaps other business, put a stop to his designs. However, there are precepts enough laid down in his former books to resolve all scruples and doubts concerning them; from which we may learn what that is which is wicked, and therefore to be avoided; and what that, which therefore is not to be avoided, because not at such times, and in such cases wicked. But since I am going, as it were, to crown a work, which was left imperfect by the author of it, though wanting but little of being brought to perfection, I shall follow the method of the geometricians: and as they do not use to demonstrate everything, but demand to have some things allowed them beforehand, by the help of which they more easily explain and demonstrate their designs; so I demand of you, son Marcus, if you can, to grant me this following postulatum; that nothing is desirable for itself alone, but that which is honest: or, however, if Cratippus will not permit you to do that, yet at least, I am sure, you must grant me this which follows; that honesty is desirable for its own sake, above all things in the world: either of the two is sufficient for my purpose, and the one is probable as well as the other, and nothing else besides them is so on this subject. And here, in the first place, we must do right to Panaetius, who does not say, as indeed he ought not, that that which is profitable could ever be contrary to that which is honest, but only that which has the appearance of such: and he often avows, that nothing is profitable but that which is honest, and that whatever is honest is at the same time profitable; and declares their opinion, who first made a difference between those two, to be the greatest evil that ever yet spread itself abroad amongst men. Therefore, when he speaks of a contrariety between them, he means an apparent, and not a real one; which he therefore laid down for one of the heads of his discourse: not as though it were lawful for men ever to give profit the preference before honesty; but only that they might be able to determine themselves aright, if these two at any time should seem to interfere and be inconsistent with one another. This part, therefore, which he has omitted, I shall now supply; not with any borrowed assistance from others, but purely (as we say) by my own strength: for I never had anything come to my hands on this subject that I could anyways approve of, since the time of Panaetius.

VIII.—*Whatever is profitable must also be honest, and whatever is honest must also be profitable—The contrary opinion the great source of all wickedness.*

Whenever therefore anything comes in our view, which carries the appearance of profit along with it, we cannot but immediately be somewhat affected with it; but if, on taking a nearer view, we find there is anything base and dishonest, in that which appeared to be profitable at first, it is our duty to reject it; which is not to deprive us of what is really profitable, but only to let us understand that nothing dishonest can possibly be such. Now if nothing be so contrary to nature as baseness, and nothing so agreeable to nature as true profit (which is certainly so; for she always desires what is right and becoming, and consistent with itself, and abhors the contrary), then it necessarily follows, that whatever is profitable can never have any baseness or dishonesty annexed to it. Again, if we were born for virtue or honesty, and this be the only desirable good, as Zeno would have it, or at least so much more so than everything else, as to outweigh all that can be put in the scale against it, which was Aristotle's opinion; it must certainly follow, that honesty is the only, or however the greatest good: now whatever is good must certainly be profitable; whence it follows, that whatever is honest must also certainly be profitable. It is a villainous error of some bad men, therefore, when anything strikes them with an appearance of profit, to seize it immediately and enjoy it as such, without ever considering its relation to honesty: hence come assassinations, poisonings, and making of false wills; hence stealing, embezzling the public moneys, plundering and oppressing both citizens and confederates; hence the insufferable power and insolence which some men exercise, who are grown too great for the rest of their citizens: in fine, hence ambition, and the desire of rule, have produced their most cursed and deplorable effects, even in free commonwealths; than which nothing can be thought of more odious and detestable: for men look on the fancied advantages of things through a false perspective; but as for the punishment appendant to them (I do not mean of the laws which they frequently break through; but of baseness and dishonesty, which is much the more grievous), that, I say, they never so much as think on at all. Such people therefore are impious and abominable, and deserve to be excluded from all society, who deliberate with themselves, and make it a matter of doubt whether they should choose what they see to be honest or wilfully commit what they know to be villainy: for the very making a question of such a thing is criminal, though one should not proceed so far as to execution. Those things therefore ought not to be deliberated at all on, where the very deliberation is scandalous and dishonest: and whenever we do deliberate on any kind of subject, we should never do anything out of hope and expectations that our actions will be concealed; for we ought to take this as a constant maxim, if we pretend to have made any progress in philosophy; that though we could hide from the eyes of all men, and even of the gods themselves, whatever we go about; yet we should be careful to abstain from the vices of covetousness and injustice, of lasciviousness and incontinency.

IX.—*The story of Gyges, from Plato—No good man can be seduced into the commission of an immoral act, though secure from the fear of detection.*

To this purpose Plato brings in that remarkable story of Gyges. A gaping in the earth being made by reason of some violent showers, as the story tells us, Gyges went down into the hollow of it, and found there lying a brazen horse, with a door in his side. This he opened; and looking in, discovered a dead man's body, of an unusual bulk, with a ring of gold on one of his fingers. This he pulls off, and puts on his own finger; and then coming up, goes and joins himself to the rest of the shepherds; for he was shepherd to the king at that time. Here he observed, that on turning the stone towards the palm of his hand, he became invisible to everybody else, though others did not become so to him; and that on turning it to its proper place, he immediately became visible again, as before: making use therefore of this lucky opportunity, he found out a way to seduce the queen, and by her assistance to murder the king, his lord and master, and to make away those who might prove any hindrance or stop to his designs; nor could any one possibly see or discover him in any of these villainies; so that he quickly, by the help of this ring, from a simple shepherd became king of Lydia. Now had a truly wise man had the keeping of this ring, he would not have thought himself ever the more privileged to be guilty of any action that is wicked or detestable; for good men desire to be virtuous and honest, and not to be secret, that so they may sin without danger. And here some philosophers, men of more honesty than acuteness or subtilty, cry out that this story of Plato is a mere fiction; as though he had said either that it really was, or indeed could be done. No; the meaning and design of this example of Gyges and the ring, is this:—Suppose you could do any dishonest action, for the gratifying a lustful, covetous, or ambitious desire, so as that no one living could either know or suspect it, but both gods and men must be kept perfectly in ignorance; whether in such case would you do it or no? Ah, but, say they, this is an impossible case; though it is not so impossible neither: but that which I ask them is, what they would do, supposing that possible which they deny now to be so. The manner of their arguing is somewhat odd and illiterate; for they still deny the possibility of it, and that they will stand to; not, it seems, understanding what the force and true import of this supposition is: for when we put the question to them, whether they would do such an action or not, supposing they could conceal it, we do not ask them, whether they can conceal it or not, but put them, as it were, to the rack or inquisition; that so, if they say they would gratify such desires on assurance of impunity, we may know them to be villains by their own confession; but if they deny it, they may be forced to grant that every base and dishonest action is barely as such to be shunned and detested. But to return to our purpose, from which we have digressed.

X.—*Men may do what is for their own advantage, provided they inflict no injury on another—The obligations of justice should never be sacrificed to the solicitations of a friend.*

There frequently happen a great many cases which disturb men's minds, and put them into suspense, by the show of some profit which they seem to contain in them: not when men deliberate, whether they should leave and abandon their honesty for the sake of any profit, be it never so great; for that is a piece of wickedness, as was before observed: but, whether that action which appears to be profitable, may not safely be done without transgressing against honesty. It might not seem honest in Brutus, for example, to depose Collatinus his brother consul from his office, whose wisdom and conduct he himself had made use of in expelling the kings: but since the chief men in the government had so ordered, that the kindred of Superbus, and very name of the Tarquins, should be banished the city, and no marks or footsteps be suffered to remain of monarchical government; it was not only profitable thus to consult for the safety of his country, but so honest too, as that Collatinus himself ought joyfully to have acquiesced in it. That which was profitable therefore prevailed, because it was honest withal; which, had it not been, it could never have been profitable. I cannot say the same in relation to that king, by whom this city was first founded; for a bare show of profit got the better over him, when he imbrued his hands in the blood of his own brother, because it seemed more profitable to reign by himself than in conjunction with another: he broke all the ties both of brotherly affection and common humanity, for the obtaining of an end which appeared to be profitable, and yet really was not so. He pretended, however, for a show of honesty, that it was done to revenge an affront of his brother, who leaped with contempt over his new-raised wall; a frivolous excuse, and, if true, not sufficient to serve his turn: by his favour, therefore, whether Quirinus or Romulus, I cannot but think he did a very ill action. Not that men are bound to be careless of their own interests, or to part with that to others which themselves stand in need of; but every one may do what he thinks for his own advantage, provided it be no injury or prejudice to another person. Chrysippus, amongst a great many very good sayings, has this one in particular: "He that is running a race ought to strive and endeavour," says he, "as much as he is able, to get before his antagonist; but must not trip his heels up, or thrust him aside with his hands: so in life it is allowable that every one should get what is useful and convenient for his comfortable subsistence, but it is not so to take it away from other people." But it is nowhere more difficult to keep to one's duty, than in the affair of friendship; for as not to do everything that one handsomely can for the sake of a friend, so to do anything that is base or dishonest, are both of them equally contrary to one's duty. But there is one very short and yet easy rule, which may serve to direct us in all cases of this nature; and it is this; never to prefer that which only seems profitable, such as honours, riches, pleasure, and the like, before a kindness to a friend; but never to do anything for the sake of a friend that is an injury to the public, or a breach of one's oath, or other solemn engagement: for whoever does this, it is impossible

he should ever be a good man. Should such a one therefore be judge in his friend's case, he would not by any means
be biassed in his favour, but would wholly lay aside the
person of a friend as soon as he took on him that of a judge.
Perhaps he might do so much for friendship's sake as to
wish that his friend may have the juster cause, and allow
him as long time to speak for himself as the laws will permit
of; but when he is to give in his sentence on oath, he will
then remember that he calls God to witness, that is, I conceive, his own soul and conscience, the divinest thing that
God has granted to man. It is a good custom therefore we
have received from our ancestors, if we did but observe it, of
desiring the judge to be as favourable to us as his oath will
permit him: the meaning of which request is no more than
this; that he would do so much for us, as I just now said
might very honestly be done by a judge for his friend: for
if men were obliged to do everything presently that their
friends should desire of them, such agreements as these
ought to be counted not friendships, but dangerous con-
spiracies. I speak here only of the ordinary sort of friendships; for in those which are found between perfectly wise
men, there can be no danger of any such thing. Damon and
Pythias, two of Pythagoras' followers, were so closely united
to one another in their affections, that when Dionysius, the
Sicilian tyrant, had appointed a time wherein one of them
should die, and the party condemned had begged a few days'
respite, wherein he might provide for his children and
family, and recommend them to somebody who would take
care of them after his death, the other delivered himself up
in his stead, voluntarily to die in the room of his friend, if
he did not accordingly make his appearance. The prisoner
came back at the day appointed, in order to his execution;
which the tyrant perceiving, was so greatly amazed at their
extraordinary faithfulness, as to desire he might be admitted
a third man in their friendship. In friendship therefore,
when that which seems profitable comes into competition
with that which is honest, the latter should always be
preferred before the former; but faith and religion should
be preferred before friendship, whenever it demands anything that is not reconcilable with virtue and honesty:
which one rule, if but carefully attended to, is sufficient for
the purpose we are now discussing; which is to discover on

every occasion what are those duties which friendship requires of us.

XI.—*In the management of public affairs the appearance of profit makes men relinquish honesty—Examples of the contrary recommended.*

The appearance of profit is also an occasion in public affairs of making false steps, and doing several things that are contrary to duty: thus our fathers, for instance, did ill in destroying and rasing of Corinth; the Athenians yet worse in making an order, that the people of Aegina should all have their thumbs cut off, because they were powerful at sea. This, no question, was thought a profitable decree; for Aegina seemed to threaten their port Piraeum, by reason of its nearness: but nothing can be truly profitable that is cruel; for the nature of man, which we ought to follow as the guide of our actions, of all things in the world is most opposite to cruelty. Those do ill likewise, who banish all strangers, and forbid them the city; as Pennus did in the preceding age, and Papius but lately: for though it is but fair, that he who is no citizen should not have the privileges of those who are (which was made into a law by two very wise consuls, viz. Crassus and Scaevola), yet wholly to exclude them from having anything to do there, is plainly against the dictates and laws of humanity: and as these things are bad in the government of a state, so nothing is more splendid and glorious, on the other hand, than for that, which appears to be the interest of the public, to be rejected in comparison with justice and honesty. Our own commonwealth can abundantly supply us with examples of this nature, as on other occasions, so more especially in the second Punic war; when, after the loss of that fatal day at Cannae, it showed more courage and bravery of resolution, than ever it had done after the greatest successes. There was not any sign of faint-heartedness seen, nor ever any mention of peace once heard of: so great is the glory and brightness of honesty, as that it utterly overwhelms the appearance of interest. The Athenians, knowing they should never be able to resist the Persians, resolved by consent to abandon their city, and carrying their wives and their children to Troezene, to defend by sea the liberties of Greece; and when one Cyrsilus tried to persuade them not

to leave their city, but receive Xerxes into it, they took him
and stoned him; not but that the man would have drawn
them to a thing which was seemingly profitable, but that
seeming profit was really none at all, being contrary to
honesty. Themistocles, after that notable victory in the
Persian war, told all the people in a general assembly, that
he had thought on a thing which might prove of great use
and advantage to the public, but which it was not convenient that everybody should know of: he therefore
desired they would appoint him some person to whom he
might safely communicate it in secret: Aristides was immediately appointed accordingly. Themistocles told him
it would be no hard matter to fire in private the Spartan
fleet, which was laid up at Gytheum, whereby the whole
power of that republic must necessarily be ruined. Aristides, as soon as he knew the business, went back into the
assembly, which was big with expectation of what he had
to say, and let them all know, that Themistocles' counsel
indeed was advantageous, but by no means honest or creditable for the city: the Athenians, therefore, thinking what
was dishonest not to be truly profitable, rejected immediately
the whole proposal, without having heard so much as what
it was, on nothing else but this report of Aristides. How
much better and more honestly did they do than we, who
can suffer even pirates to live free from molestation, and yet
demand tribute of our confederates and allies!

XII.—*A case put, whether that which seems to be profitable be honest or no*
—The arguments on either side of two philosophers differing in
opinion.

Let us lay down this therefore as a standing maxim, that
whatever is dishonest can never be profitable; no, not
though we should arrive at the full possession of all those
advantages which we proposed to obtain by it. Nay, this
very persuasion, that a thing may be profitable, though it
is base and dishonest, is one of the greatest misfortunes
and calamities that could ever have happened to the life of
man. But there often fall out, as was before observed,
some peculiar cases, wherein that which is honest has a
seeming repugnance with that which is profitable; so that
it requires some farther consideration to know whether this

repugnance be certain and real, or whether they may not be brought to a fair agreement. To this head belong such examples as these: suppose we, for instance, an honest merchant, when corn was scarce and extremely dear at Rhodes, to bring a large quantity thither from Alexandria; and withal to know, that a great many ships, well laden with corn, were on their way thither from the same city; should he tell this now to the people of Rhodes, or say nothing of it, but sell his own corn at the best rate he could? We suppose him a virtuous and honest man, and do not here discourse of the deliberation of one, that would hold his peace if he thought it were dishonest; but of one that doubts whether it be dishonest or not. In such sort of cases Diogenes the Babylonian, a man of great credit and note among the Stoics, is of one opinion; and Antipater his scholar, an extraordinary smart and ingenious man, of just the contrary. Antipater would have everything be plainly told, that so the buyer might be ignorant of nothing in what he buys, that the seller himself knows of: Diogenes thinks it enough in the seller to tell the faults of his goods as far as the laws require it; and as for the rest, though, to use no cozening, yet since he is come with design to sell them, to get as much money for them as he can. "Here," may the merchant say, "I have brought my corn; I have exposed it to sale; and sell it no dearer than other people do (nay, perhaps he will say cheaper, there being now a greater quantity than there was before), and, pray, where is now the wrong I have done to anybody?" Antipater argues on a different principle: "What say you?" quoth he: "are not you obliged to do good to mankind, and be serviceable to the society of all men in general? Were not you born under such an obligation? And had not you such principles ingrafted into you by Nature, which it is always your duty to follow and obey, that your single interest should be the same with that of all men; and again, that of all men should be the same with yours? And will you, notwithstanding this, conceal from the people what plenty there is coming, the knowledge of which might be of so great use and advantage to them?" Diogenes perhaps will reply to him thus: "It is one thing to conceal, and another not to tell; nor can I be said to conceal from you now, though I do not tell you, what the nature and essence of the gods is, and what the happiness or chief good of men; things which it would do one much more kindness to know, that that corn will be cheaper, because great quantities are like to be here shortly. But if anything be profitable for you to hear, it is none of my duty to come and tell it you immediately."—" Nay, but you will find that it is your duty," may the other reply, " if you will please but to remember that there is such a kind of thing as a mutual relation and society amongst all men."—" Well, I do remember it," may the other reply again; " but, I pray you, is that society of such a nature, as that no man who lives in it must have anything that is his own? If this be so, then there is no more selling, but we must even give everything away that we have."

XIII.—*Another case put, whether he that sells a bad house be obliged to tell the purchaser it is so—The opinion of Cicero on these questions.*

You plainly perceive, that it is never once said in all this dispute, though such a thing is not honest, yet I will do it because it is profitable, but the one side defends the expediency of it no farther than it is honest, and the other denies that it ought to be done because it is not honest. Again, suppose an honest man were to sell a house because of some defects which he himself knows, though others do not: suppose it to be unhealthful, for example, but esteemed quite the contrary; serpents to annoy all the chambers of it, but nobody to know this; made of bad materials, and ready to fall, but no one to discern this, except the owner only: I demand, if he sells this for more than he expected, and do not tell the buyer of these several faults, whether he do not act like a knave and a villain. " Yes, undoubtedly," answers Antipater; " for what is this better, than not to set a man right when he is out of his way (which at Athens was punished with public execrations), thus to suffer the buyer, as it were, to fall headlong, and run, through a mistake, into very great mischiefs? Nay, it is something worse yet, than not to show a man his way; for it is wilfully and designedly to draw him into mischief." Diogenes, on the contrary, vindicates the seller: " Pray did he force you," says he, " to buy his house, when he did not so much as advise you to it? He set a thing to sale which he did not like, and here you have bought a thing which you did like: for if those men who make it be

published to the world, here is a very good house, and very
well built, to be sold, are not counted deceivers, though the
house be not good, nor at all well built; how much less should
those be counted so, who do not commend their house at all!
for wherever the buyer has the free use of his judgement,
what fraud can there be on the seller's part?   And if a man
is not bound to make good all he said, would you have him
make good what he did not say?   Besides, what, I beseech
you, could be more odd and foolish than for the seller to tell
the faults of his own wares; or what more ridiculous than for
the crier to proclaim, by the proprietor's order, an infectious
and pestilential house to be sold?"   And thus you see there
are some doubtful cases, in which on the one hand men argue
for honesty, and on the other are advocates for profit, so far
as to show that it is not only honest to do that which is profitable, but even dishonest to neglect and omit it; and this is
that seeming opposition we spoke of, which often falls out
between profit and honesty.   But let us now proceed to
determine these cases; for we did not propose them for mere
question's sake, but that we might give them a fair decision.
I am then of opinion, that the corn-merchant ought not to
have concealed from the Rhodians, nor this seller of his house
from the purchasers of it, the several things that are mentioned in their cases.   It is true, not to tell a thing, is not
properly to conceal it; but not to tell that which people are
concerned to know, merely for the sake of some advantage
to yourself, I think is: and there is nobody but knows what
kind of concealing this is, and who they are that make a
custom of it; I am sure not your plain, sincere, ingenuous,
honest, and good sort of people; but rather your shifting, sly,
cunning, deceitful, roguish, crafty, foxish, juggling kind of
fellows.   And must it not necessarily be unprofitable for any
man to lie under this, and a much longer catalogue of such
black and most odious names of vices?

XIV.—*Moral turpitude of those, who are so far from telling the faults of
their wares, that they invent lies to make them appear better.*

And if those men are thus blamable who keep the faults
of their wares secret, what shall we think of those who add
downright lying to it?   C. Canius, a Roman knight, one that
loved to be pleasant, and a pretty good scholar, removing to

Syracuse for the sake of retirement, and not of employment, as he was used to say, gave out he had a great mind to buy some gardens, whither he might invite his friends and acquaintance, and enjoy their conversation without being interrupted. This being reported, there was one Pythius, a goldsmith or banker at Syracuse, who told him, indeed he had no gardens to sell, but such as he had were at Canius' service, if he pleased to make use of them, as much as though they were his own; and, withal, he desired him to come the next day, and take a dinner with him there. When Canius had promised him to come accordingly, what does he do but send immediately for some fishermen (having interest enough, by reason of his calling, with all sorts of people), and desires them the next day to fish before his gardens; giving them their instructions about what he would have them do. Canius came at the time appointed, and Pythius had provided a very splendid entertainment for him. Just before the garden, where he could not but take notice of it, was a company of fishing-boats; and every one of the men in particular brought the fish he had caught, and laid them down before Pythius. "How now, Pythius!" said Canius to him; "what! all these fish here?—all these boats?" "O lack, sir," said the other, "that is no great wonder; all the fish that supply the city must be taken here: this is their common water; none of these people could ever live if it were not for my house." Canius immediately was all on fire, and begged of Pythius that he would sell him the place: he pretended abundance of unwillingness at first; but at length, to make short of it, was brought to a compliance. Canius bought it, together with all that belonged to it; and being very rich, and desirous of the purchase, gave as much for it as Pythius demanded. Security was given and taken for the money, and the whole bargain finally brought to a conclusion. The next day Canius invited some acquaintance thither, and he came himself somewhat earlier than ordinary; but seeing not one of the fishermen's boats there, he now inquired of one of the next neighbours, whether or no that were any holiday with the fishermen; because he saw none of them thereabouts. "Not that I know of," replied the other; "but they none of them ever use to fish here, and therefore I wondered what the matter was yesterday." This put Canius into a lamentable fret: but how could he help himself? for

Aquilius, my colleague and familiar friend, had not then published his court-forms about knavery: on which, when he was asked what he meant by the word knavery, he answered, the making show of one thing, while one is doing another: a very perspicuous and plain definition, as indeed he was a man very happy at defining. Pythius, then, and all others whatever, that make show of one thing and yet do the contrary, are perfidious, wicked, and knavish rascals: it is impossible therefore that any of their actions should ever be profitable, when they are under the scandal of such a number of filthy and detestable vices.

XV.—*All hypocrisy and dissimulation should be discarded—A truly good man is not content with being as just as the laws require.*

If, then, this definition of Aquilius be good, all hypocrisy and dissimulation must be banished from amongst men; so that no honest man will be guilty of either of them, for the sake of buying or selling to his greater advantage. Nay, this knavery or cozenage has always been punished by the laws of the city: witness the twelve tables about the case of guardianship; and Laetorius' law about the overreaching of minors. Nay, where there was nothing of a law against it, it was nevertheless punishable in those judgements of equity; the form of which was, " that all things be done faithfully and honestly: " and the same sort of words are in all other judgements; as when a wife, for example, enters an action for her dowry, on a divorce from her husband, " that things be settled better and more equitably; " when anything had been mortgaged and pawned to another, " that amongst honest men there be nothing done but that which is honest." And could there possibly be any knavery allowed of in that, where the very court-form was, " for the better and more equitable settling of things? " or anything done through deceit and roguery, where these words are publicly read in court, " that among honest men there may be nothing done except that which is honest? " Now there is something of this knavery, as Aquilius says, in all false shows and hypocritical pretences: lying therefore should wholly be banished from all sorts of business and commerce in the world; nor should sellers bring people to bid high for their goods, and enhance their prices; nor purchasers others to bid under value, and so beat them down lower: but each of them, if they come to speak about a bargain, should say at a word what he will give and take. Quintus Scaevola, the son of Publius, going to buy an estate, desired the owner to tell him at one word what it was he must have for it: the seller did so, and Scaevola told him he thought it was worth more than what he had demanded for it, and accordingly gave him a thousand crowns over. Now there is no one but will grant this was done like an honest, but they will not allow it was like a prudent man; any more than if he had sold a thing for less than he might have had for it. Here, now, you may see, is that pernicious opinion, thus to make a distinction between prudence and honesty. Ennius has a saying to this purpose, that he would not give a farthing for a prudent man that could not be prudent for his own advantage; to which I am ready to set my hand, if he and I can agree on one and the same meaning of the word advantage. I find that Hecaton, a Rhodian philosopher, and scholar of Panaetius, in his book about Offices, which he wrote to Q. Tubero, hath laid this down as a wise man's duty, first to conform to the laws, and customs, and practices of his country; and when he hath done that, to make the best improvement he can of his estate; since we ought to seek riches not only for ourselves, but our children, friends, relations, and especially the commonwealth, whose public riches must principally consist in the wealth and stock of its particular members. This man can by no means approve of that action which I just now mentioned of Quintus Scaevola; and there is nothing, he tells us, that he would scruple to do for his own advantage, if it be but permitted and allowed of by the law; for which I think he does not much deserve to be thanked or commended. If, then, to make pretence of that which never was, and cunningly to dissemble the real truth, be pieces of knavery, there are but very few actions that are altogether free from it; and if he alone be an honest man, who does all the good he can, and does no injury to anybody, it will be no easy matter to find one in the world. The result of what has been said is this; to be knavish and wicked can never be profitable, because it is attended with baseness and dishonour; and it always must be profitable to be virtuous and good, because it always is honest and creditable.

XVI.—*The care taken by the Romans to make the seller tell the faults of the thing to be sold.*

In the matter of buying and selling estates, it is provided amongst us by the civil constitutions, that he who is the seller should tell all the faults that he knows of to the purchaser: for the twelve tables ordering no more than this, that the seller should be bound to make good those faults which were expressly mentioned by word of mouth in the bargain, and which whoever denied was to pay double damages, the lawyers have appointed a punishment for those who themselves do not discover the defects of what they sell: for they have so decreed, that if the seller of an estate, when he made the bargain, did not tell all the faults in particular that he knew of it, he should afterwards be bound to make them good to the purchaser. Titus Claudius Centumalus, to give an example, had a house that stood on the Coelian hill, and hindered the augurs as they made their observations from the Capitoline mount; who therefore gave him orders to pull that down which was such a hindrance to their business. Instead of this, Claudius put a bill over the door, that the house was to be sold; and quickly put it off, P. Calpurnius Lanarius being the man that bought it. The augurs in a short time sent him the same orders, and he accordingly took care to perform them: but afterwards, coming to understand that Claudius had not set the house to sale till after he had been ordered by the augurs to demolish it, he brought in against him an action at law, to receive such satisfaction as in conscience and equity he was bound to make him. Marcus Cato, the father of him that is lately dead (for as others are distinguished by the names of their fathers, so he that begot this incomparable person should be named from his son), sat as judge in the case, and gave this sentence on the whole matter; that since Claudius knew this inconvenience beforehand, and did not discover it when he sold the estate, he was obliged in equity to make it good to the purchaser: he judged it therefore to be a part of honesty that the seller should fairly declare to the buyer all the faults which he knows in the thing to be sold. If, then, this judgement were just and equitable, neither the merchant that brought the corn, nor the supposed seller of the infectious house, did well in concealing what either of them knew:

but all the particular sorts of concealing could never be taken notice of by the laws of the city: however, such as could were very carefully provided against. M. Marius Gratidianus, a kinsman of mine, had sold a house to Sergius Orata, which he had bought of the same person not many years before. The house, it seems, paid a duty to Sergius, which Marius never once mentioned in the bargain. The business came at last to a suit in law, wherein Lucius Crassus was counsel for Orata, and Antony for Gratidianus. Crassus insisted very much on the law, which says, that the seller shall make good those faults which he himself knew of, and yet concealed from the buyer: Antony, on the other side, argued for equity; that Sergius could not but know that incumbrance, who had sold the house himself but a little while before; and, therefore, what need was there of telling him of it: that he could not complain of being any ways imposed on, since he knew very well the condition of what he bought. I have brought you these instances, only to let you see that these cunning sort of men were never approved of by our ancestors.

XVII.—*The different methods used by law and philosophy, for the rooting out of knavery—Knavish cunning very different from true prudence.*

But the laws take one way to root out these frauds, and philosophers another; the former meddling no farther with them, than as they break out into open acts, and may, as it were, be laid hold on by the hands of justice; but the latter endeavouring to hinder their breaking out, and to prevent them by precepts of wisdom and reason. Reason therefore requires of us that we do nothing treacherously, nothing deceitfully, nothing merely by outward shows and false pretences. Now is it not treachery to set up a trap, though one does not frighten and pursue the beasts into it? for the simple creatures of themselves will run into it, without being driven. Just so you offer a house to be sold, because of some faults which you know to be in it; and put up your bill, as it were, like a trap, in which some unwary sort of body will be taken. I know that, at present, the depravation of manners and prevalence of evil custom have made this to be counted neither base nor dishonourable, and that it is tolerated by the laws and constitutions of the public;

but I am sure it is not tolerated by the laws of nature: for it is to be considered (I must repeat it again, though I have already mentioned it a great many times), that there is such a thing as natural society, which comprehends all men, and ties and unites them to one another; there is a nearer between those of the same nation, and a nearer yet between those of the same city: therefore our forefathers made a distinction between that law which is common to nations, and that which belongs to each city in particular. Whatever we are bound, by the civil constitutions, to do to our citizens, we are not obliged, by the law of nations, to do the same to strangers; but whatever we are bound by this latter to do to others, the same we ought to do to our citizens also: but the law, which at present we use amongst us, is far from being an original piece, immediately taken from genuine right and true perfect justice; it is only a copy and faint representation of it. However, I could wish we lived up even to this; for it is copied at least from some of the best originals, which were drawn from the truth and nature of the thing. For how excellent is that form in judicial proceedings, "that I may not be defrauded or brought to an inconvenience, by trusting to you and your honesty." And how incomparable that other, "that honest men do nothing but that which is honest and without design." But the great question is, who they are that are honest men, and what it is to do nothing but that which is honest. Q. Scaevola, I remember, the high priest, had used to say, that all those judgements which had "faithfully and honestly" put into their forms, were of marvellous force; and that faithfully and honestly were of very large extent, and belonged not only to wardships, societies, trusts, and commissions, but to buyings, sellings, lettings, and hirings, which relate to the society and intercourse of mankind; and that it was the part of an extraordinary judge to determine exactly in all these cases, what one man ought to make good to another, on only the bare principles of conscience and honesty; especially seeing men differ in their judgements about the greatest part of them. All craft therefore should utterly be banished, and that knavish sort of cunning, which would fain indeed be counted, but is the farthest from prudence of anything in the world; for prudence consists in the making a right distinction between good and evil; but this kind of cunning gives the preference to evil; if, at least it be true (as most certainly it is), that everything is evil which is contrary to honesty. Neither is it only in farms and houses that the laws of the city, which are copied from nature, take care to have cheating and knavery punished; but in slaves they exclude all fraud in the seller: for he that is presumed to know what the slave was, if he does not declare whether he be healthy, a renegade, or apt to steal, is answerable to the buyer, by an order of the ediles: but this does not hold in the case of an heir. From what has been said, it apparently follows, since nature is the fountain whence law in derived, that it is agreeable to the dictates and rules of nature, that no one should endeavour to make his own advantage from the ignorance of another: and indeed there is no greater mischief in the world than this wisdom, falsely so named, joined with baseness and knavery. From this have arisen innumerable cases wherein profit is set up in opposition to honesty: for where almost is there a man to be found, that would scruple to injure and wrong any other, if he could do it with secresy, and without fear of being punished?

XVIII.—It is a wickedness to be a receiver of ill-gotten goods, though you have not assisted in the fraud.

Let us try, if you please, by some examples of that nature, wherein the common sort of people, perhaps, think there is no crime; for we do not speak here of such as cut throats, poison, make false wills, rob, or embezzle the public treasures, who are not to be repressed with words and philosophical discourses, but must be vexed and wearied out with chains and imprisonment; but let us consider here what is done by those who pass in the world for men of honesty and integrity. A will that was forged of one Minutius Basilus, a wealthy person, was brought by some people out of Greece into Italy; who, to make it the more easily pass for good, made Marcus Crassus and Lucius Hortensius, two of the greatest men at that time in the city, joint heirs with themselves, who, though they suspected the whole to be a forgery, yet having no hand in it themselves, made very little scruple of getting an advantage by other people's villany. Truly I am fully persuaded not; though I always loved one of them [1] while

[1] Hortensius.

he was alive, and do not hate the other [1] since he is dead and gone. But when Basilus had desired Marcus Satrius, his sister's son, should bear his name, and had appointed him his heir; ("I nominate him," says he, "lord of my Sabine and Picenian manors") was it any ways a just and reasonable thing, and not rather an eternal blot on those times, that some principal citizens should have a man's estate, and Satrius the heir be put off barely with his name? For if he be unjust, that does not keep off injuries from any of his neighbours, and defend and protect them as far as he is able (as I have shown already in the first book), what sort of man shall we take him to be, who not only does not keep off an injury, but rather, on the contrary, helps to promote it? Nay, I, for my part, am wholly of opinion that estates which are left men by true wills, if got by knavish and servile flatteries, not by a real, but pretended friendship, are scandalous and dishonest. But in such kind of cases it often comes to pass, that one thing seems profitable, and another honest, undoubtedly by a mistake; for the same thing is the measure both of the one and the other, which, whoever perceives not, will easily be led into all sorts of roguery; for he that begins thus to argue with himself, " that indeed is honest, but this is advantageous;" impudently divides, by this gross mistake, those things which by nature are coupled and united; which is the deadly root from which all frauds, wickedness and villainies spring.

XIX.—*The carriage of a truly honest man, when it is in his power to be secretly dishonest—The true notion of a good man.*

If a good man therefore should have such a power, as that by snapping of his fingers he could slip his name cunningly into rich people's wills, he would never make use of it; no, not although he were fully assured, that no one living could either know or suspect it; but give such a power to Marcus Crassus, that by doing the same thing he should make himself heir, where he really was not so, and he would dance, I dare warrant you, publicly in the market-place. But he that is honest, and answers to our notion of a good man, will never take anything away from another for the enriching himself, and filling his own coffers; which whoever admires, let him even confess at the same time that he does not under-

[1] Crassus.

stand what a good man is: for if any one will thoroughly examine his own thoughts, and clear up a little his obscure conceptions, he will quickly be able to tell himself, that a good man is one who does all the good that he can to others, but never any harm, unless by way of reasonable and just retribution for some injury received. I desire to know then; is not that man guilty of harming another, that ejects the rightful heirs, as it were, by a spell, and procures himself to be put in their stead? " How then? " will some men say; "what! would not you have people consult their own interest?" Yes, but withal I would have them understand that nothing can be so that is base or dishonest; which is a necessary maxim for all those to learn, whoever design to be good men. I remember I heard my own father tell, as long ago as when I was a boy, that Fimbria, one who had formerly been consul, was judge in a case of Lutatius Pinthia, a Roman knight, and a very honest man, who, on pain of losing a certain sum of money, was to prove himself to be a good man. Hereon Fimbria plainly told him, that he would never pass judgement on such a matter; lest either by giving the cause against him, he should spoil the credit of a well-approved citizen; or else should be forced, by giving it for him, to pronounce that any one was a good man; which he could not do, considering the infinite virtues and duties that are requisite to the completing any person of that character. This good man then, of whom Fimbria had a notion, as well as Socrates, will never judge anything profitable that is dishonest: whence it follows, that such a one will always be so far from doing, as that he will never so much as think of anything, which he is afraid should be laid open to the rest of the world. And is it not a shame that philosophers should doubt of this, when there is not a peasant in the country but assents to it? for from them we have gotten that common saying, which is now by long usage become a proverb among us, which they bring in to signify the faithful dealing and honesty of a man: " he is one," say they, " that you may venture to play with at even and odd in the dark." The meaning of which, what can it be but this?—that nothing can be profitable but that which is honest and becoming, though a man could be certain of being never found out in it? You see then, according to this proverb, that neither that Gyges, whom we mentioned above, nor that other, whom we just now supposed to have a power by the snapping of his fingers to become all people's heir, can by any means be excused: for as that which is scandalous and dishonest in itself, however it may be hid from the eye of the world, can never be brought to be honest and creditable; so also that which is not honest and creditable can never be brought to be profitable and advantageous, the very nature of things resisting and opposing it.

XX.—*A man loses more by doing an unjust action, than ever he can gain by it, be the reward what it will.*

But when people expect great advantages from their roguery, it is a mighty temptation for them to be guilty of it. Thus, for instance, when Marius was far from any hopes of obtaining the consulship, and had remained in obscurity seven years from the time of his being pretor, so that no one suspected his standing for that honour, being despatched to Rome by Q. Metellus, whose lieutenant he was, an extraordinary man, and a brave member of the republic,—he accused his general to the people of Rome of protracting the war; and told them, that if they would but choose him consul, they should soon have Jugurtha, either dead or alive, delivered into their power. It is true, by this artifice he got to be chosen consul, but he paid for it the price of his honesty and fidelity; who could thus bring a useful and excellent citizen, whose lieutenant he was, and by whom he was sent, into hatred and ill-will by false accusations. Nor did my kinsman Gratidianus act the part of an honest and fair-dealing man, in the time of his pretorship: the tribunes of the people held a common consultation with the company of pretors, about settling the value and rate of money, which at those times was grown to be so very inconstant, that nobody could be certain how much he was worth. They made an edict by common consent, allowing an action against those who transgressed it, and appointing a penalty for those who were convicted. This being ordered, they agreed to meet again in the assembly after noon, and all of them together tell the people what they had done. The meeting broke up, and the rest all departed, some one way, and some another: Marius only, directly from the court went down to the assembly, and by himself alone declared that to the people which all of them had agreed on by general consent.

If you ask now what was the event of this; nothing in the world could have got him greater honour: statues erected for him about the streets, frankincense and tapers burnt at every one of them; and, in short, never was any man more adored by the multitude. These are the things which do sometimes mislead men in deliberating about their duty; when the offence against honesty seems very trivial, but the advantage that is gained by it very considerable. Thus Marius thought it but a little piece of knavery to steal the people's love from the tribunes and his colleagues, but a mighty advantage to be made consul by it, which was what he at that time proposed to himself. But in all these cases there is only one rule, which I desire you would constantly take along with you: be sure, in the first place, that what you count profitable be no way dishonest; and if it be dishonest, then assure yourself that it is not truly profitable. And can we then esteem either the one or the other of these Mariuses good men? Consider a little, and examine your own thoughts, that you may see what idea, what notion or conception, you have of a good man. Is it reconcilable then with the character of such a one, to lie for the sake of his own advantage; to deceive; to raise false reports and misrepresentations of others; to seize that beforehand which others have a right to as well as himself? Certainly, nothing less. And is there anything then of such excellent worth, any profit or interest so very desirable, for the gaining of which one would forfeit the glory and reputation of a good man? Can that which we call by the name of profitable bring us anything so good as what it takes away from us, if it spoil our being counted men of honesty and integrity; if it occasion the loss of our justice and faithfulness? that is, in plain truth, if it change us into brutes? For where is the great difference between altering our shapes and becoming real beasts, and carrying the nature and fierceness of beasts, though under the outsides and figures of men?

XXI.—*To do anything dishonest for the sake of power and authority, not profitable.*

Again, those who neglect all justice and honesty for the sake of power, do not they take just the same method that a certain person did, when he chose to be son-in-law to none but one, by whose daring boldness he might increase his own authority?[1] He thought it a very great advantage, no question, to enlarge his own greatness, by drawing hatred on another; but he never considered how great a disservice he did to his country, and how much scandal and discredit he brought on himself. As for the father-in-law, he had always a couple of Greek verses in his mouth, taken out of Euripides' tragedy of Phoenissae, which I will endeavour to translate as well as I am able; perhaps it may be awkwardly; but, however, so as to make their sense appear—

> If ever we break the ties of right,
> 'Tis when a kingdom is the glorious prize:
> In other things be strictly just.

It was a villainous thing in Eteocles, or rather in Euripides indeed, to exempt that one breach of right from being criminal, which is certainly of all others the most wicked and detestable. Why do we insist then on examples of lesser rogueries, such as making one's cunning and spells, cheats about buying, selling, etc.? Here is a man for you,[2] that has made no scruple of desiring to make himself king of the Roman people, and lord and governor of the whole earth; nay, which is worse, hath accomplished his desire. If any man call this an honest ambition, he must be out of his wits; for he justifies the subversion of our laws and liberties, and esteems the most base and detestable oppression of them a virtuous, laudable, and glorious action: but if any man, confessing that it is not honest to get the dominion in that republic, which has been and ought to be always free, will yet say, it is profitable for him that can do it;— what reproofs shall I use, or what reproaches rather, to recall such a one from so dangerous an error? Good gods! Can it ever be supposed then to be any man's interest, by the most heinous and most unnatural wickedness on earth, to ruin and destroy his own native country; though, perhaps, the man who is guilty of it may afterwards be styled, by his poor oppressed citizens, the father of it?[3] Interest therefore should always be measured by justice and honesty; so that these two words, though of different sounds, should yet be understood to mean one and the same thing. I know

---

[1] Pompey the Great, who chose to be Caesar's son-in-law, marrying his daughter Julia.

[2] Julius Caesar.

[3] Caesar was called so, notwithstanding his oppressions.

the common people are apt to imagine that nothing in the world can be better than to govern; but when I consider the real truth and reason of the thing itself, I find, on the contrary, that nothing can be worse when people arrive at it by unlawful means. Can it possibly be profitable for any man, then, to live in perpetual cares and anxieties? to be day and night racked and tormented with fears, in a life full of nothing but treacheries and dangers? "Many are treacherous and unfaithful to kings," says Accius; "and but few are faithful." But of what sort of kings did he speak this? Was it not of those who, by lawful succession, had received the royal sceptre from Tantalus and Pelops? How many more then must we suppose to be unfaithful to that king, who, with an army of Romans, had oppressed and enslaved the Roman people itself; and had forced that city, which was not only free, but even empress of the whole world, to submit her neck to his tyrannical yoke? What uneasiness of mind must such a one, think you, be continually under! What wounds and twitches of conscience must he needs feel! How, in short, can that life be an advantage to any man, which has this inconvenience inseparably annexed to it— that whoever is so happy as to take it away, will obtain the greatest glory and good-will from all the world? And if these things, which seem most of all to be profitable, yet are found to be the contrary when unworthy and dishonest, this certainly ought to convince us all, that nothing can be profitable which is not honest.

XXII.—*Glory and riches unprofitable if accompanied with injustice, exemplified in several eminent Romans.*

But this has been determined, as at many other times by our wise forefathers, so particularly by Fabricius, then a second time consul, and the whole Roman senate, in the war with Pyrrhus: for when Pyrrhus had voluntarily made war on the Romans, and the contention was held about empire and mastery with a no less powerful than generous adversary, a deserter came secretly into Fabricius' camp, and offered, on condition he might be well rewarded, to return back again with the same secrecy that he came, and to poison Pyrrhus: but instead of encouragement, Fabricius ordered him to be sent back to Pyrrhus, and was afterwards commended by the senate for so doing. If we look no farther now than the outward appearance of what seems to be profitable, here is a dangerous war, and a powerful adversary of the growing empire might soon have been removed by the single assistance of this one deserter: but then it would have been an eternal scandal, not to mention the villainy and wickedness of it in an honourable war, which was waged with a fair and generous enemy, not to get the victory by virtue and courage, but only by base and treacherous practices. Whether was more profitable then for Fabricius, who was such in this city as Aristides was at Athens; or for the Roman senate, which never thought anything dishonourable their interest—to contend with an enemy by valour or by poison? If empire be desirable for the sake of glory, why is not wickedness altogether banished, in which it is impossible there should ever be any glory? But if we are for power at any rate, we should do well to consider that it can never be profitable when accompanied with infamy. That counsel, therefore, of Lucius Philippus, the son of Quintus, was far from being profitable, that those very cities which Sylla had freed for a set sum of money from paying any customs, by the senate's orders, should again be brought under their former contributions; and yet not the money, which they had paid, be returned them. This advice of his was followed by the senate, to the great disparagement and shame of the empire; for even pirates at this rate will sooner be trusted than the Roman senate. "Well, but the public revenues were increased by it, and therefore it was profitable." Heavens! how long will men dare to call anything profitable which is not honest? Can hatred then and infamy be profitable to a state, which ought to be supported by glory and credit, and the love of its confederates? In this particular I often disagreed from my old friend Cato, whom I always thought to be somewhat too headstrong in standing up for the interest of the public treasury, and exacting the tributes with so much rigour, as not to make any allowances to the farmers, and very seldom or never grant anything to the confederates; whereas we ought always to be kind to the latter, and to deal with the former as we would do with our own bailiffs; and that so much the more, because all the safety and welfare of the republic depends on the agreement of the several orders in it. Nor less ill than Philip's was the counsel of Curio, who, in the case of the people inhabiting beyond the Po, though he confessed their demands were but just and reasonable, yet always added, " Everything must give way to the interest of the public." He should rather have said that they were not just, because not comporting with the public interest, than thus have declared they did not comport with it, and at the same time confess them to be just and reasonable.

XXIII.—*Several doubtful cases put by Hecaton the Rhodian.*

Hecaton proposes, in his sixth book of Offices, several questions, such as these which follow. Whether a good man, in time of great scarcity, may refuse to give victuals to the servants of his own family? He discourses indeed on either side of the question; but at last concludes, that he should rather be guided by his interest than humanity. He demands again, if a merchant in a storm be forced to throw his goods overboard, whether of the two he should choose to cast away; a very valuable horse, or a servant that is good for nothing? Here interest and the saving of his goods draw one way, and compassion of human nature another. Should a fool in a shipwreck have gotten a plank, may a wise man take it away from him if he can? He answers, no; because it would be plainly a piece of injustice. But what if the owner of the ship should come, may not he take it away, when it properly belongs to him? No, not at all; no more than he may throw a man out of the ship, under the pretence that the ship belongs to him; for till they have arrived whither the ship was hired for, it does not more properly belong to the owner than it does to the passengers by whom it was hired. Suppose two men that are equally wise, should both of them in a shipwreck lay hold of the same plank; may either of them seize on it forcibly to himself, or should one of them voluntarily yield it to the other? Let one yield to the other, provided that other will be more serviceable to the public, or there is more depending on his life and preservation. But what if these are equal in either of them? Why then there is no more to be said about it, but it must even be left for chance to determine, as though they should cast lots, or play at even and odd for it. What if a father should rifle temples, and dig passages under ground into the treasury; should the son discover him to the public magistrate? No; that were a horrid, unnatural impiety; he should rather, on the contrary, defend his father, if any one else should pretend to accuse him. But what? ought not the interest of my country to be consulted before that of any one else whatever? Yes, undeniably; but then it is very much the interest of your country to have citizens that are dutiful and obedient to their parents. But if a father should attempt to make himself king, or any ways endeavour to betray his country, should a son in such a case hold his tongue, and conceal it? In the first place, let him beg of his father to desist: if that does no good, let him proceed to rebuke, and even to threaten him about it: but if at last he perceive that it directly tends to the ruin of his country, he should prefer its safety before that of his father. Another of the questions he proposes is this:—Suppose a good man to receive, by an oversight, bad money for good, and afterwards come to understand that it is bad; may he pay it for good, if he owes another anything? Diogenes thinks he may, but Antipater not; whom I rather assent to. Suppose a man be selling a vessel of wine, which he knows will not keep; is he bound to tell of this? Diogenes thinks he is under no such obligation; Antipater will have it to be every honest man's duty. These are the things which, whether they are right, and one's duty, or not, are often controverted among the Stoics. In selling a slave, is one bound to declare what his faults are, or not? I do not mean those, which, unless they are told, the law itself commands he shall be returned on our hands; but his being a liar, a filcher, a player at dice, or a drunkard. One is of opinion we ought to declare them, and the other not. Should an ignorant body sell a quantity of gold, and suppose it to be copper; is a good man obliged to tell him that it is gold, or may he buy for a penny what is worth a thousand pence? It is plain enough by this time what my thoughts are, and wherein consists the controversy between the fore-mentioned philosophers.

XXIV.—*Whether a man is obliged to perform all his promises, though at the expense of his life or reputation.*

Are we bound to perform all those promises and bargains, which, in the pretor's language, have neither force nor fraud in them? Here is a man, for example that has got the dropsy, and another prescribes him an infallible cure for it, on condition that he will never make use of it again. The man recovers by its help at present, but falls again some time after into the same distemper. Suppose now that he, to whom he made such promise, will by no means allow him to use the cure again; what would be his duty in such a case? Why, since he, who denies him the request, is inhuman, and it is a thing that will do him no manner of prejudice, it is the best way to take care of his life and safety. A good and wise man is desired by one, who appoints him his heir, and leaves him by will a considerable estate, that before he enters on the possession of it, he should dance at noonday in the open streets; and this he accordingly promises to do, because otherwise the testator would not make him his heir: would you have him perform what he promised, or not? I could wish that he never had promised it at all, which I think would much better have suited with his character; but since he has done it, if he think it dishonourable to dance so in public, the best way will be not to perform such a promise, provided he takes none of the money that was left him; unless the money may be turned to some very great benefit and advantage of the public; so that it would be no disgrace for a man even to dance, when it brings so much good to his country along with it.

XXV.—*Several cases, wherein a man is not obliged to perform his promises and vows, nor to give up a trust.*

Neither is one bound to perform those promises which are hurtful and prejudicial to the persons they were made to. Thus Phoebus, that we may return to our fables, promised to grant Phaeton whatever he should desire; and the mad young fellow desired to get up into his father's chariot: it was accordingly granted him; but before he could get to be well settled in it, he was struck down with lightning. How abundantly better had it been, in such a case, if the father had refused to perform such a promise! The same may be said of another, which Theseus solicited from Neptune. This god had promised to grant whatever he should request; and he, on a false suspicion, desired the death of his own son Hippolytus. He obtained what he asked, which occasioned him great sorrow and affliction. Again, Agamemnon had vowed, for a sacrifice to Diana, the most beautiful thing that was born that year in his whole dominions: to be as good as his word, he was forced to offer his daughter Iphigenia, than whom nothing that year had been born more beautiful. Had it not been better to have broken his promise, than have done such a horrid and unnatural action? In some cases then a man is not obliged to perform his promises; no more is he to restore what was given him in trust. Suppose, for instance, a man in his wits had entrusted you with his sword, and should demand it of you again when he is beside himself; your duty would be not to give it him again; and if you did, you would be guilty of a very great error. Again, should a man put a large sum of money in your hands, and afterwards raise a rebellion against his country, would you deliver up your trust, if demanded by him? Certainly not; for this would be to act against the public interest; which ought to be preferred before everything else. Thus a great many things, which are honest of themselves, we may see cease to be so when the circumstances alter: to perform a promise, for instance, to stand to an agreement, or deliver up a trust, ought not to be done when they become unprofitable. This may suffice to have been said of those things, which a pretended wisdom would fain count profitable, though contrary to justice: but having laid down, in the first book, four general heads, from which all offices or duties are derived, I shall discourse on each of the same in this; and make out, that what is contrary to any of those virtues, is only in show, and not really profitable. Of prudence, then, which a knavish sort of cunning endeavours to imitate; as also of justice, which is never but profitable, we have discoursed already. It remains that we speak of the other two general heads of duty; the one of which consists in the greatness and excellence of a courageous soul; and the other in such a regularity of our actions, as is conformable to the precepts of temperance and moderation.

XXVI.—*That nothing can be profitable which is dishonourable, shown from the examples of Ulysses and Regulus.*

Ulysses thought it would be profitable for him, if what the tragedians tell us be true (for Homer, a writer of the greatest

authority, never once insinuates any such thing); but the
writers of tragedy accuse Ulysses for feigning himself mad,
that he might avoid the war; a design that was by no means
honest and creditable. "Well, but it was profitable," will
some one say, "to stay and govern at his own home, and
enjoy himself quietly in his island Ithaca, together with his
parents, his wife, and son. Is there any such credit in the
daily dangers and fatigues of war, that you can ever think
comparable with living such a life of tranquillity and
security?" Yes, I wholly despise and contemn your
security, being fully persuaded that it can never be profitable so long as it is dishonest. Pray, what would they have
said, do you think, of Ulysses, suppose he had continued in
his pretended madness; when, after his glorious achievements in the war, he had yet these reproaches thrown on
him by Ajax?—

> Though, you all know, he first proposed this oath,
> Yet he's the only man that would have broke it.
> He first endeavour'd not to join in the war,
> Faint-hearted coward! feigning to be mad:
> And had not prudent Palamede found out,
> By cunning, this his impudent deceit,
> The villain, notwithstanding all the ties
> Of sacred oaths, had certainly gone off.

It was much better for him to bear all the hazards, not of
the war only, but of the sea too (as at last he did), than not
to make one among the rest of the Grecians, then resolving,
by consent, on a war with the barbarians. But to remove
the scene from foreign countries, and fabulous relations, that
we may come nearer home, and to a thing that really
happened; M. Atilius Regulus, then a second time consul,
was surprised in Africa by Xanthippus, the Lacedaemonian,
and made a prisoner (Amilcar, father of Hannibal, being the
general of the Carthaginians), and was sent by the Carthaginians to the Roman senate on solemn oath given, that,
unless some remarkable prisoners were restored them, he
should himself return back again to Carthage. Now, as
soon as this man arrived at Rome, he could not but perceive
what appeared to be his interest; but withal was persuaded,
as the event declared, that it only appeared so. The cause
was thus: here he might have stayed in his native country,
and have lived at home quietly with his wife and children;
might have judged his misfortune, received in the war, no

more than what all men in that state are liable to; and might still have continued in his old degree of honour among those of consular dignity. " And who can deny now," will any one say, " that all these things are expedient and profitable? " Who do you think? Why, greatness of soul and true courage deny it. Can you desire any greater and more illustrious authorities?

XXVII.—*Continuation of the story of Regulus.*

These are the virtues by which we are taught to be afraid of nothing, to despise all the outward concerns of life, and count nothing intolerable that can possibly befall a man. Well, but pray what did this Regulus do then? He came into the senate, and told them what it was he was sent about, and refused to give his own vote in the case, forasmuch as he was not to be counted a senator, as being by oath under the enemy's power: and in his speech, which he spoke to the senate on that subject (" fool that he was," some will be ready to say, "and an enemy to his own interest!"), he told them, it was best not to give up their prisoners; that they were young men, and might make able leaders; but that he, for his part, was grown almost useless, and worn away with old age. The senate were so persuaded by his speech, that they resolved the prisoners should be detained in custody; and he himself returned back again to Carthage; not all the love which he had for his country, his friends and relations, being able to detain him: and though he knew well enough what a barbarous enemy and what exquisite torments he was going to return to, yet he thought it his duty, whatever came of it, not to violate his oath. I think he was in a better condition therefore, even whilst he was murdered by being kept from sleeping, than ever he could have been had he stayed at home, and lived under the scandal of being an old captive and a perjured nobleman. " But was not it very great folly and madness, if he would not persuade the releasing of the prisoners, yet to go and dissuade it as much as he could? " Pray, how folly and madness? What! though it were conducive to the good of the republic? Or can anything be profitable to a private citizen, which brings a disadvantage to the commonwealth in general?

Those men who separate profit from honesty wholly pervert the first principles of nature; for we all of us naturally desire our interest, toward which we are carried with so strong a bias, as that it is not in our power to turn the other way: for who is averse from, or rather, who does not most eagerly follow his own advantage? But since we can find out no real advantage, except in what is honest, becoming, and commendable, therefore we count these the principal things; and take the word profit to signify something which only relates to our outward necessities, and the supplying of them, without all that glorious and shining excellence which appears in the actions of virtue and honesty. " But after all is done," perhaps some men will say, " pray, what is there in an oath, that he should be afraid thus to break it? What! was it Jupiter's anger that he dreaded? " But this is agreed on by all philosophers; not only those who maintain that the gods lead an idle life, neither busying themselves, nor disturbing others; but those who affirm they are always busy, and always doing something that relates to the world; —in this thing, I say, they are all agreed, that the Deity neither hurts nor is angry with any one. But supposing the worst, pray what hurt could Jupiter's vengeance have done Regulus, greater than what Regulus did to himself? It could not be anything of religion therefore that hindered him from following what appeared to be his interest. Again, was he afraid of the baseness and dishonesty of the action? As to that, in the first place, always of two evils choose the least; and where was any evil in the baseness of the thing so great as was that of the torments which he endured? Besides, pray, remember that sentence of Accius, which, however, it might be said by an impious king, is yet generally acknowledged to be very well said; who, when one told him, " You have broken your oaths to me," answered, " I neither am, nor have been tied by oath to any treacherous deceiver." Again, they tell us, that as we affirm some things seem profitable which are not so; so they affirm some things seem honest which are not so: as this, for example, of returning to be tormented, rather than break one's oath; which is not honest, though it may seem to be so; because no man is obliged to perform that oath, which was extorted from him by the force of his enemies. And, lastly, they argue, that whatever makes very much for one's profit and advantage, thereby becomes honest, though before it did not seem to be so. This is what is generally brought against Regulus; but let us see and examine all the parts of it in order.

XXIX.—*The first part of the arguments brought against Regulus answered —The sacredness of an oath—Faith to be kept even with those who are treacherous—Laws of war to be preserved inviolable.*

First, then, they say, he could fear no harm from the anger of Jupiter, who neither can be angry nor do harm to anybody. This proves as strongly against all oaths in general, as it does in particular against this of Regulus. But the thing to be considered in people's taking of oaths, is not what danger they are in, should they break them; but what a sacred and powerful obligation is laid on them: for every oath is a religious affirmation; and whatever is promised after such a manner, as it were calling God for a witness to your words, ought certainly to be performed: for now faith and justice require it of us, and not any fear of that anger of the gods, which is not incident to their divine natures;—the faith I mean, of which Ennius has got these incomparable words:—

> O Faith, all-glorious and divine,
> In lofty temples fit to shine!
> Ev'n Jove himself by thee doth swear.

Whoever therefore doth not perform his oath affronts the deity of that divine faith, which was (as Cato in his speech informs us) set up by our fathers in the Capitol itself, even next to the statue of the great god Jupiter. But, secondly, they tell us, supposing Jupiter had been angry with Regulus, he could not have brought any evil on him greater than what Regulus brought on himself. This, I confess, would be very true, if there were no other evil but pain: but that is so far from being the greatest evil, as that it is not so much as any evil at all, if we may credit some of the chief philosophers; among whom, I pray you, let Regulus be counted of no small authority, if I may not rather say of the greatest and most weighty: for what greater testimony can any one desire, than that of a principal man among the Romans, who, rather than be wanting in any point of his duty, chose to undergo the most exquisite torment? " But of two evils," say they, " always choose the least; " that is, in plain words, rather be a rogue than undergo any calamity. Can any calamity, then, be greater than that of baseness and injustice? For if even the filth and deformity of the body be loathsome and offensive; how much more so must that of the mind needs be, when it is covered and polluted with shame and dishonesty? Those philosphers, therefore, who discourse of these things with most closeness and severity, venture boldly to affirm that nothing is evil but what is dishonest; and even those who do it more loosely, yet always acknowledge that it is the greatest of all evils. That saying of the poet indeed is good, " I neither am nor have been tied by oath to a treacherous deceiver; " but it is therefore so, because when Atreus was brought on the stage, he was to make him speak that which was suitable to his character: but if once they begin to lay down this for a maxim; that faith, when given to those who are treacherous, is not to be kept;—they had best have a care that this be not made a refuge and cover for perjury. As for his oaths being made to an enemy; even war itself has laws that belong to it; and faith, except in some very few cases, is always to be kept, even with our greatest adversaries: for whatever you swear, for example, in such a manner, as that your conscience tells you it ought to be done, you are bound most inviolably to perform it; but where it is otherwise, you do not lie under any such obligation; and are not perjured, though you should not perform it. Suppose, for instance, you had sworn to a pirate that you would pay him such a sum if he would spare your life; it would not be perjury, though you should not pay it him: for a pirate is by no means a lawful adversary, but rather a common pest and enemy of mankind; so that no one is obliged to keep his faith or oath with him: for to swear to a thing, and yet not perform it, is not immediately to forswear oneself; but then a man is properly said to be perjured, when he swears, on his conscience (as our form runs), to do such and such things, and yet does not do them: for that of Euripides may be said in some cases to be very good,—" My tongue indeed swore, but my conscience did not assent." But had Regulus, in his case, done anything contrary to the laws and conditions that are kept between enemies, it had been downright perjury: for the Carthaginians, with whom he had then to do, were a lawful adversary, between whom and us there is all the fecial, and several other laws that are common to nations: for had it been otherwise, it is certain the senate would never have delivered up some eminent persons in chains to their enemies.

XXX.—*Examples of several eminent Romans given up to the enemy— Answer to the rest of the arguments brought against Regulus.*

Lucius Veturius and Sp. Postumius in their second consulships were delivered to their enemies, the Samnites; because, being beaten at the passage of Caudium, and the legions being disarmed and sent away with disgrace, they had concluded a peace without any orders from the senate or people: T. Numicius and Q. Maelius, who were tribunes of the people at the same time, because by their authority the peace was concluded, were likewise delivered, that so we might be freed from any obligation of keeping it: and all this was done on the proposal and advice of Postumius himself, who was the person delivered. The case of Mancinus, a great many years after, was exactly the same, who having, without any orders from the senate, made an alliance with Numantia, was the first man that spoke for that bill in the senate-house, which by L. Furius and Sext. Atilius was carried to the people; and which they agreeing to, he was delivered to the enemy. He did more honestly than Sext. Pompeius, who being concerned in the same sort of crime, made interest to be excused from undergoing the same punishment, and by that means escaped it. This man now let the appearance of profit prevail over honesty; but in all the others mentioned, the authority of honesty easily carried it from the pretended profit. But to go on with Regulus: another thing urged by his adversaries is this; that he should not have performed what was forcibly put on him. As though a man of courage could be wrought on by force! "But why," say they, "did he go at all to the senate, being resolved to dissuade the delivery of the captives?" This is to blame him for that, which particularly deserves commendation. He would not depend on his own judgement; but pleading for that which he thought most expedient, left it to be determined by the judgement of the senate: and had it not been for his counsel in the case, the prisoners had surely been sent again to Carthage, and he remained safe in his native country: but this he concluded would be prejudicial to the public, and therefore esteemed it to be no more than his duty to speak what he thought, and endure what might come of it. Lastly, they add, that whatever makes highly for one's profit and advantage thereby becomes honest. I answer, that it may indeed antecedently be such, but can never thereby become such: for nothing is profitable but what is honest; and things do not become honest by their first being profitable, but become profitable by their first being honest. I conclude, therefore, that of all those great and wonderful examples, which might easily be brought on this subject, it will be hard to find any more illustrious and commendable than this of Regulus.

XXXI.—*The sacredness of an oath, among the ancient Romans, illustrated by the examples of Pomponius and Manlius.*

But the only thing that deserves our admiration in all this glorious conduct of Regulus, is his persuading the senate not to restore the captives: as for his returning again to Carthage, it is true we admire it in our days, but at those times he could not have possibly avoided it. The age, I think, therefore should rather be commended for that, than the man: for there is nothing of which our ancestors took greater care, than that the obligation of an oath should be always held as most sacred and inviolable. This appears plainly from the Twelve Tables; it appears from those laws which are called Sacred; it appears from the strict observation of leagues, by which we are obliged to keep faith even with enemies; and, lastly, it appears from the punishments and penalties which have been inflicted by the censors; who in no one thing have been more severe, than in punishing those who have transgressed their oaths. M. Pomponius, a tribune of the people, once entered an action against L. Manlius, the son of Aulus, who had been dictator, for holding that office somewhat longer than he should have done; and amongst other things, brought in this too against him, that he kept his son Titus, who was afterwards Torquatus, from conversation with the world, and had strictly charged him to live solitary in the country. As soon as the son heard his father was in trouble about this business, he is reported immediately to have set out for Rome, and come early in the morning to Pomponius' house. Pomponius was no sooner told of his coming, but he got up immediately, and thinking the youth, out of anger, had brought some complaint against his father, commanded all others to depart the room, and him alone to be brought in to him. As soon as the young man had got into the room, he drew his sword, and swore he would immediately kill Pomponius, unless he would promise him on oath to meddle with his father no farther. Pomponius, out of sudden apprehension of the danger, did swear to him accordingly, and discharged his father from any more trouble; having first reported the matter to the people, and told them why he was forced to let fall his action. Thus strict and conscientious were people, at those times, in observing their oaths. And this Titus Manlius is that very person, who being afterwards challenged by a mighty Gaul, killed him in a duel by the river Anien, and was surnamed Torquatus, from wearing a chain, which he took from his neck. The same man again, in his third consulship, put to flight and defeated the Latins near Veseris. He was indeed a very great and extraordinary person; who, as he showed his love in this case to his father, so he was unnaturally cruel to his son.

XXXII.—*The severity of the Romans against breakers of oaths—Fraud not sufficient to excuse a perjury—The conclusion of this head.*

But as Regulus did well in performing his oath, so those ten who, after the battle of Canae, were by Hannibal sent to the Roman senate, on oath of returning to the Carthaginian camp if they could not obtain an exchange of prisoners, did ill if they did not return accordingly: concerning whom writers have differed in their relations. Polybius, an author of very good credit, informs us, ten persons of considerable quality were sent to the senate; and that nine of them did honestly return to the camp, not having been able to obtain what they went about; but the tenth stayed behind, and remained at Rome. This man, as soon as he was out of the camp, pretending he had forgot to take something along with him, went back thither again; as thinking his returning under such a colour was a very sufficient performance of his oath:

but certainly he was mistaken; for cunning is so far from excusing a perjury, that it aggravates it rather, and makes it the more criminal. This therefore was no more than a foolish piece of craftiness, impudently pretending to pass for prudence: wherefore the senate took care to order that my crafty gentleman should be sent back in fetters again to Hannibal. But the most glorious action of the senate was this: Hannibal had eight thousand of our soldiers his prisoners; not such as had either been taken in battle, or had fled from any imminent danger of their lives, but were left in the camp by Paulus and Varro, the two consuls. The senate decreed that these should not be ransomed, though it might have been done with a small sum of money; for no other end but to let our soldiers see, that either they must resolve to conquer or die: on the news of which, as the same author tells us, Hannibal presently began to be disheartened, when he saw that the senate and people of Rome had so great resolution even in the midst of their misfortunes. Thus, we see, honesty gets the better in the comparison against that which has only the appearance of profit. But Acilius, who has written a history in Greek, says, more of them returned under this pretence to the camp, hoping by such a trick to get quit of their oaths; and that they were all of them branded with shame and dishonour by the censors for so doing. But let us now put an end to this third head; since, from what has been said, it is apparently manifest, that whatever is contrary to the virtue of fortitude, that is to say, whatever is done with a timorous, mean, disheartened, abject spirit, can never be really and truly profitable, because it is wicked, disgraceful, and odious: and such would this action of Regulus have been, had he either, in delivering his sense about the captives, spoken what was for his own, not the public security, or afterwards chosen to remain at home, instead of returning to fulfil his oath.

XXXIII.—*Nothing contrary to temperance can be truly profitable—Pleasure opposite to honesty—The absurdity of those who would have happiness to consist in both—A short recapitulation of this last book—Conclusion, by way of exhortation to his son.*

We have now finished our third head: the fourth and last remains only, which contains in it decency, modesty,

moderation, continence, and temperance. And can anything
be profitable that is opposite to a train of such excellent
virtues? There hath been however a sect of philosophers,
scholars of Aristippus, who were called Cyrenaics; and
others, who had the name of Annicerians given them, that
affirm all good to consist in pleasure, and count virtue itself
therefore only desirable, because of some pleasure which it
brings along with it. But these being now almost worn out
of date, Epicurus is mightily come into vogue, the great
supporter, and, as it were, second founder of the same
opinions. With these we must fight, as they say, with might
and main, if ever we think of supporting the cause, and
maintaining the interest of virtue and honesty: for if what
Metrodorus has written pass for truth, that whatever can
truly be called our profit, nay, all the welfare and happiness
of life, consists in a firm constitution of body, and a well-
grounded hope of its lasting continuance; it is certain, this
profit, nay, this sovereign profit (for such they account it),
must sometimes be set in opposition to honesty. For what,
in the first place, will be the office of prudence? only to
cater and look about for pleasure? How miserable a case is
that virtue in, which is thus made a servant and pander to
pleasure! But what shall be her business in this office? to
taste and distinguish ingeniously betwixt pleasures? Supposing this to be a pleasant business, it is certainly the most
scandalous that could ever have been thought on. Again,
can he that makes pain be the greatest evil have ever such a
virtue as fortitude in him, the very nature of which consists
wholly in despising of pains and difficulties? I know Epicurus on several occasions, and this in particular, speaks
very courageously as to the matter of pain; but we must
not consider so much what is said, as what ought to be said
by a man of his principles, who makes pleasure and pain to
be the ultimate bounds of man's happiness and misery. So
again, if you would hear him about continence and temperance, he tells you abundance of extraordinary things in a
great many places; but he is gravelled (as we speak), and
can never be able to acquit himself handsomely: for with
what face of reason can he commend temperance, who places
his happiness in the enjoyment of pleasures; when the
sensual appetite follows after pleasures, and it is the business
of temperance to correct that appetite? But still they

endeavour, in each of these virtues, to bring themselves off by one little shift or other: thus prudence is admitted, and defined to be the skill of supplying us with pleasures, and defending us from pains: and they make out fortitude as well as they can, by saying it consists in despising death and enduring torments: they do bring in a sort of temperance too, though not without a great deal of straining and difficulty; but, however, they make a shift, after some fashion, by saying, they count it the greatest pleasure, if they can but be exempt from pain and uneasiness. Thus these three virtues stand up pretty well; but Justice, the fourth, totters mightily with them, or rather indeed is quite fallen to the ground, with all those duties which relate to the maintenance of human society: for what kindness, liberality, affability, or friendship, can there be amongst those, who desire these virtues not purely for themselves, but only in relation to their pleasure or advantage? To make short, then, I shall only say, that as I have shown before, that nothing can be profitable which is contrary to honesty, so now I do affirm, that pleasure in general is contrary to honesty: I the more blame therefore Dinomachus and Callipho, who thought this dispute might be brought to an issue, if they joined both pleasure and virtue together, like a man and a beast, as it were, in the same yoke: for virtue can never admit of this conjunction, but abhors and disdains it; nor can ever the sovereign good and evil, which must be one single and simple thing, be made up and compounded of such different principles. But of this, which is a thing of the greatest moment, I have written at large in another work:[1] let us now return to our present subject. What has been said in this last book, I hope, is enough to let any one see how it is his duty to determine his choice, if that which seems useful and expedient for him should come into competition with that which is honest: but if it should be said, that even pleasure carries with it the appearance of profit, let it also be considered, that it never can be brought to an agreement with honesty: for the most that can possibly be said for pleasure (that we may not seem wholly to exclude it), is, that it serves by way of sauce to give a relish to things, but has no true profit or advantage in itself.

This is the present, dear son Marcus, that your father sends

[1] In his treatise " On the End of Good and Evil."

you, and in my opinion it is a very good one; but that will depend on the use you shall make of it: however, entertain, among Cratippus' lectures, these three books, and show them at least the civility due to strangers. Had it been my fortune to have come to Athens (which had surely been done, if I had not been recalled by the cries of my country), you might then perhaps sometimes have heard my lectures: however, since now, in perusing these sheets, you will have my voice, as it were, by proxy, pray, bestow on them as much time as you can, and I am sure you can as much as you please. When I hear you take a pleasure in this sort of studies, it will delight me to talk to you (which I hope may be speedily) face to face; or, however, to write to you, though at never so great a distance. In the meantime, adieu, my dear Cicero; and assure yourself, that though no one in the world is more dear to me than you are, yet you will hereafter be much more so, if I find you take delight in such writings and instructions.

LAELIUS
OR, AN ESSAY ON FRIENDSHIP

To TITUS POMPONIUS ATTICUS.

QUINTUS MUCIUS, the Augur, used to relate, in a very agreeable manner, a variety of particulars which he remembered concerning his father-in-law, the sage Laelius, as he constantly styled him. My father introduced me to Mucius as soon as I was invested with the manly robe, and he so strongly recommended him to my observance that I never neglected any opportunity in my power of attending him. In consequence of this privilege I had the advantage to hear him occasionally discuss several important topics, and throw out many judicious maxims, which I carefully treasured up in my mind, endeavouring to improve myself in wisdom and knowledge by the benefit of his enlightening observations. After his death I attached myself in the same manner, and with the same views, to his relation, Mucius Scaevola, the chief pontiff; and I will venture to say that, in regard both to the powers of his mind and the integrity of his heart, Rome never produced a greater nor more respectable character. But I shall take some other occasion to do justice to the merit of this excellent man; my present business is solely with the Augur.

As I was one day sitting with him and two or three of his intimate acquaintance in his semi-circular apartment where he usually received company, among several other points he fell into discourse upon an event which had lately happened, and was, as you well know, the general subject of conversation; for you cannot but remember (as you were much connected with one of the parties) that when Publius Sulpicius was Tribune, and Quintus Pompeius Consul, the implacable animosity that broke out between them, after having lived together in the most affectionate union, was universally mentioned with concern and surprise. Mucius having casually touched upon this unexpected rupture, took occasion to relate to us the substance of a conference which Laelius formerly held with him and his other son-in-law, Caius Fannius, a few days after the death of Scipio Africanus, upon the subject of Friendship. As I perfectly well recollect the general purport of the relation he gave us, I have wrought it up, after my own manner, in the following essay. But that I might not encumber the dialogue with perpetually interposing "said I" and "said he," I have introduced the speakers themselves to the reader, by which means he may consider himself as a sort of party in the conference.

It turns on a subject upon which you have frequently pressed me to write my thoughts, and, indeed, besides being peculiarly suitable to that intimacy which has so long subsisted between us, it is well worthy of being universally considered and understood. I have the more willingly, therefore, entered into the discussion you recommended, as it affords me an opportunity of rendering a general service at the same time that I am complying with your particular request.

In the treatise I lately inscribed to you on Old Age, I represented the elder Cato as the principal speaker, being persuaded that no person could, with more weight and propriety, be introduced as delivering his ideas in relation to that advanced state than one who had so long flourished in it with unequalled spirit and vigour. In pursuance of the same principle, the memorable amity which, we are told, subsisted between Laelius and Scipio rendered the former, I thought, a very suitable character to support a conversation on the subject of Friendship, and the reasoning I have ascribed to him is agreeable to those sentiments which Mucius informed us he expressed.

This kind of dialogue, where the question is agitated by illustrious personages of former ages, is apt, I know not how, to make a stronger impression on the mind of the reader than any other species of composition. This effect, at least, I have experienced in my own writings of that kind, as I have sometimes imagined, when I was revising the essay I lately inscribed to you, that Cato himself, and not your friend in his name, was the real speaker. As in that performance it was one veteran addressing another on the article of Old Age, so in the present it is a friend explaining to a friend his notions concerning Friendship. In the former conference, Cato, who was distinguished among his contemporaries by his great age and superior wisdom, stands forth as the principal speaker; in this which I now present to you, Laelius, who was no less respected in the times in which he flourished for his eminent virtues and faithful attachment to his friend, takes the lead in the discourse. I must request you, therefore, to turn your thoughts a while from the writer and suppose yourself conversing with Laelius.

For this purpose you are to imagine Fannius and Mucius making a visit to their father-in-law soon after the death of Scipio Africanus, and from that circumstance giving occasion to Laelius to enter upon the subject in question. I will only add that in contemplating the portrait of a true Friend, as delineated in the following pages, you cannot be at a loss to discover your own.

FANNIUS.—I agree with you entirely, Laelius, no man ever possessed more amiable or more illustrious virtues than Scipio Africanus. Nevertheless, let me entreat you to remember that the public eye is particularly turned towards you upon the present occasion, and extremely attentive to observe how Laelius, the sage Laelius (as, by a very singular distinction you are universally both called and acknowledged) behaves under the great loss he has sustained. When I say " by a very singular distinction," I am not ignorant that the late Marcus Cato, in our own times, and Lucius Attilius, in the days of our forefathers, were generally mentioned with the same honourable addition; but I know, too, that it was for attainments somewhat different from those which have so justly occasioned it to be conferred on you. To the latter it was given in allusion to his eminent skill in the laws of his country, as it was to the former on account of the wonderful compass and variety of his knowledge, together with his great experience in the affairs of the world. Indeed, the many signal proofs that Cato gave, both in the forum and the senate, of his judgement, his spirit, and his penetration, produced such frequent occasions to speak of his wisdom with admiration, that the epithet seems, by continually recurring, to have been considered in his latter days as his original and proper name. But the same appellation (and I cannot forbear repeating it again) has been conferred on you for qualifications not altogether of the same nature; not merely in respect to the superior excellency of your political accomplishments and those intellectual endowments which adorn your mind, but principally in consequence of the singular advancement you have made in the study and practice of moral wisdom. In short, if Laelius is never named without the designation I am speaking of, it is not so much in the popular as in the philosophical sense of the term that this characteristic is applied to him, and in that sense I will venture to say there is not a single instance throughout all the states of Greece of its ever having been thus attributed to any man by the unanimous consent of a whole people. For as to those famous sages who are commonly known by the general denomination of " the seven wise men of Greece," it is asserted by the most accurate inquirers into their history that they cannot properly be ranked in the class of moral philosophers. One celebrated Grecian, however, there was, a native of Athens, whom the oracle of Apollo declared to be the wisest of the sons of men, and believe me, Laelius, it is the same species of wisdom which this excellent moralist displayed that all the world is agreed in ascribing to you; that wisdom, I mean, by which you hold virtue to be capable of fortifying the soul against all the various assaults of human calamities, and are taught to consider happiness as depending upon yourself alone.

In consequence of this general opinion I have been frequently asked (and the same question, I believe, has no less often, Scaevola, been proposed to you) in what manner Laelius supports the loss he has lately sustained. And this inquiry was the rather made, as it was remarked that you absented yourself from our last monthly meeting in the gardens of Brutus, the Augur, where you had always before very regularly assisted.

SCAEVOLA.—I acknowledge, Laelius, that the question which Fannius mentions has repeatedly been put to me by many of my acquaintance, and I have always assured them that, as far as I could observe, you received the wound that has been inflicted upon you by the death of your affectionate and illustrious friend with great composure and equanimity. Nevertheless, that it was not possible, nor indeed consistent with the general humane disposition of your nature, not to be affected by it in a very sensible manner; however, that it was by no means grief, but merely indisposition, which prevented you from being present at the last meeting of our assembly.

LAELIUS.—Your answer, Scaevola, was perfectly agreeable to the fact. Ill, certainly, would it become me, on account of any private affliction, to decline a conference which I have never failed to attend when my health permitted. And, indeed, I am persuaded that no man who possesses a proper firmness of mind will suffer his misfortunes, how heavily soever they may press upon his heart, to interrupt his duties of any kind. For the rest, I consider the high opinion, Fannius, which you suppose the world entertains of my character, as an obliging proof of your friendship; but it is an opinion which, as I am not conscious of deserving, I have no disposition to claim. As little am I inclined to subscribe to your judgement concerning Cato; for if consummate wisdom, in the moral and philosophic idea of that expression, was ever to be found in the character of any human being (which, I will confess, however, I very much doubt), it certainly appeared throughout the whole conduct of that excellent person. Not to mention other proofs, with what unexampled fortitude, let me ask, did he support the death of his incomparable son? I was no stranger to the behaviour of Paulus, and was an eye-witness to that of Gallus, labouring under an affliction of the same kind; but the sons whom they were respectively bereaved of died when they were mere boys. Whereas Cato's was snatched from him when he had arrived at the prime of manhood and was flourishing in the general esteem of his country. Let me caution you, then, from suffering any man to rival Cato in your good opinion, not excepting even him whom the oracle of Apollo, you say, declared to be the wisest of the human race. The truth is, the memory of Socrates is held in honour for the admirable doctrine he delivered, but Cato's for the glorious deeds he performed.

Thus far in particular reply to Fannius. I now address myself to both; and if I were to deny that I regret the death of Scipio, how far such a disposition of mind would be right, I leave philosophers to determine. But far, I confess, it is from the sentiments of my heart. I am sensibly, indeed, affected by the loss of a friend whose equal no man, I will venture to say, ever possessed before, and none, I am persuaded, will ever meet with again. Nevertheless, I stand in want of no external assistance to heal the wound I have received. My own reflections supply me with sufficient consolation. And I find it principally from not having given in to that false opinion which adds poignancy to the grief of so many others under a loss of the same kind. For I am convinced there is no circumstance in the death of Scipio that can justly be lamented with respect to himself. Whatever there is of private misfortune in that event consists entirely in the loss which I have sustained. Under the full influence of such a persuasion, to indulge unrestrained sorrow would be a proof not of a generous affection to one's friend, but of too interested a concern for one's self. It is evident, indeed, that the colour of Scipio's days has, in every view of it, proved truly bright and glorious. For tell me, my friends, is there a felicity (unless he wished never to die—a wish, I am confident, he was too wise to entertain), is there a single article of human happiness that can reasonably be desired which he did not live to attain? The high expectations the world had conceived of him in his earliest youth were more than confirmed in his riper years, as his virtues shone forth with a lustre superior even to the most sanguine hopes of his country. He was twice, without the least solicitation on his own part, elected consul; the first time before he was legally qualified by his age to be admitted into that office, and the next, although not prematurely with respect to himself, yet it had well-nigh proved too late for his country. In both instances, however, success attended his arms, and having levelled with the ground the capitals of two states the most inveterately hostile to the Roman name, he not only happily terminated the respective wars, but secured us from all apprehension of future danger from the same powers. I forbear to enlarge upon the affability of his manners, the affection he showed to his mother, the generosity he exercised towards his sisters, the kindness with which he behaved to the rest of his family, and the unblemished integrity that influenced every part of his conduct. They were qualities in his exemplary and amiable character with which you are perfectly well acquainted. It is equally unnecessary to add how sincerely he was beloved by his country; the general concern that appeared at his funeral renders it sufficiently evident. What increase, then, could the addition of a few

more years have made to the glory and happiness of his life?
For admitting that old age does not necessarily bring on a
state of imbecility (as Cato, I remember, maintained in a
conversation with Scipio and myself about a year before his
death), it certainly impairs, at least, that vigour and vivacity
which Scipio still possessed at the time of his decease.

Such, then, was the course of his happy and honourable
days, that neither his felicity nor his fame could have received
any farther increase. And as to his death, it was much too
sudden to have been attended with any sensible degree of
pain. By what cause that unexpected event was occasioned
is by no means indeed clear; the general suspicions concerning it you well know. One circumstance, at least, is unquestionable: that of all the many brilliant days he had enjoyed,
the last of his life was the most completely illustrious. For
it was on the very evening which preceded his death that
he received the singular honour, at the breaking up of the
senate, of being conducted to his house by all the members
of that august assembly, attended by the several ambassadors
both from Latium and the allies of the Roman Commonwealth. So that he cannot, it should seem, so properly be
said to have descended into the regions of the infernal deities
as to have passed at once from the supreme height of human
glory to the mansions of the celestial gods. For I am by no
means a convert to the new doctrine which certain philosophers have lately endeavoured to propagate; who maintain
that death extinguishes the whole man, and his soul perishes
with the dissolution of his body. Indeed, the practice of our
ancestors alone, abstracted from the opinion of the ancient
sages, weighs more with me than all the arguments of these
pretended reasoners. For certainly our forefathers would
not so religiously have observed those sacred rites which
have been instituted in honour of the dead if they had supposed that the deceased were in no respect concerned in the
performance of them. But the conviction arising from this
consideration is much strengthened when I add to it the
authority of those great masters of reason, who enlightened
our country by the schools they established in Great Greece,
during the flourishing ages of that now deserted part of Italy.
And what has a still farther influence in determining my
persuasion is the opinion of that respectable moralist who, in
the judgement of Apollo himself, was declared to be the

wisest of mankind. This incomparable philosopher, without once varying to the opposite side of the question (as his custom was upon many other controverted subjects), steadily and firmly asserted that the human soul is a divine and immortal substance, that death opens a way for its return to the celestial mansions, and that the spirits of those just men who have made the greatest progress in the paths of virtue find the easiest and most expeditious admittance. This also was the opinion of my departed friend: an opinion which you may remember, Scaevola, he particularly enlarged upon in that conversation which, a very short time before his death, he held with you and me, in conjunction with Philus, Manilius, and a large company of his other friends, on the subject of government. For in the close of that conference, which continued, you know, during three successive days, he related to us (as if he had been led into the topic by a kind of presentiment of his approaching fate) a discourse which Africanus delivered to him in a vision during his sleep concerning the soul's immortality.

If it be true, then, that the souls of good men, when enlarged from this corporeal prison, wing their flight into the heavenly mansions with more or less ease in proportion to their moral attainments, what human spirit can we suppose to have made its immediate way to the gods with greater facility than that of Scipio? To bewail, therefore, an event attended with such advantageous consequences to himself would, I fear, have more the appearance of envy than of friendship. But should the contrary opinion prove to be the fact, should the soul and body really perish together, and no sense remain after our dissolution, yet death, although it cannot indeed, upon this supposition, be deemed a happiness to my illustrious friend, can by no means however be considered as an evil. For if all perception be totally extinguished in him, he is, with respect to everything that concerns himself, in the same state as if he had never been born. I say "with respect to himself," for it is far otherwise with regard to his friends and to his country, as both will have reason to rejoice in his having lived so long as their own existence shall endure.

In every view, therefore, of this event, considering it merely as it relates to my departed friend, it appears, as I observed before, to be a happy consummation. But it is much otherwise with regard to myself, who, as I entered earlier into the world, ought, according to the common course of nature, to have sooner departed out of it. Nevertheless, I derive so much satisfaction from reflecting on the friendship which subsisted between us, that I cannot but think I have reason to congratulate myself on the felicity of my life, since I have had the happiness to pass the greatest part of it in the society of Scipio. We lived under the same roof, passed together through the same military employments, and were actuated in all our pursuits, whether of a public or private nature, by the same common principles and views. In short, and to express at once the whole spirit and essence of friendship, our inclinations, our sentiments, and our studies were in perfect accord. For these reasons my ambition is less gratified by that high opinion (especially as it is unmerited) which Fannius assures me the world entertains of my wisdom, than by the strong expectations I have conceived that the memory of our friendship will prove immortal. I indulge this hope with the greater confidence as there do not occur in all the annals of past ages above three or four instances of a similar amity. And future times, I trust, will add the names of Scipio and Laelius to that select and celebrated number.

FANNIUS.—Your expectations, Laelius, cannot fail of being realised. And now, as you have mentioned Friendship, and we are entirely disengaged, it would be extremely acceptable to me (and I am persuaded it would likewise be so to Scaevola) if, agreeably to your usual readiness upon other occasions of just inquiry, you would give us your opinion concerning the true nature of this connection, the extent of its obligations, and the maxims by which it ought to be conducted.

SCAEVOLA.—Fannius has prevented me in the request I was intending to make; your compliance, therefore, will equally confer an obligation upon both of us.

LAELIUS.—I should very willingly gratify your desires if I thought myself equal to the task, for the subject is interesting, and we are at present, as Fannius observed, entirely at leisure; but I am too sensible of my own insufficiency to venture thus unprepared upon the disquisition of a topic which requires much consideration to be treated as it deserves. Unpremeditated dissertations of this kind can only be expected from those Grecian geniuses, who are accustomed to speak on the sudden upon any given question; and to those learned disputants I must refer you, if you wish to hear the subject properly discussed. As for myself, I can only exhort you to look on Friendship as the most valuable of all human possessions, no other being equally suited to the moral nature of man, or so applicable to every state and circumstance, whether of prosperity or adversity, in which he can possibly be placed. But at the same time I lay it down as a fundamental axiom that " true Friendship can only subsist between those who are animated by the strictest principles of honour and virtue." When I say this, I would not be thought to adopt the sentiments of those speculative moralists who pretend that no man can justly be deemed virtuous who is not arrived at that state of absolute perfection which constitutes, according to their ideas, the character of genuine wisdom. This opinion may appear true, perhaps, in theory, but is altogether inapplicable to any useful purpose of society, as it supposes a degree of virtue to which no mortal was ever capable of rising. It is not, therefore, that notional species of merit which imagination may possibly conceive, or our wishes perhaps form, that we have reason to expect and require in a friend; it is those moral attainments alone which we see actually realised among mankind. And, indeed, I can never be persuaded to think that either Fabricius, or Coruncanius, or Curius, whom our forefathers justly revered for the superior rectitude of their conduct, were sages according to that sublime criterion which these visionary philosophers have endeavoured to establish. I should be contented, however, to leave them in the undisturbed possession of their arrogant and unintelligible notions of virtue, provided they would allow that the great persons I have named merited at least the character of good men; but even this, it seems, they are not willing to grant, still contending, with their usual obstinacy, that goodness is an attribute which can only be ascribed to their perfect sage. I shall venture, nevertheless, to adjust my own measure of that quality by the humbler standard of plain common sense. In my opinion, therefore, whoever (like those distinguished models I just now mentioned) restrains his passions within the bounds of reason, and uniformly acts, in all the various relations of life, upon one steady, consistent principle of approved honour, justice, and beneficence, that man is in reality, as well as in common estimation, strictly and truly good; inasmuch as he regulates his conduct (so far, I mean, as is compatible with human frailty) by a constant obedience to those best and surest guides of moral rectitude, the sacred laws of Nature.

In tracing these laws it seems evident, I think, that man, by the frame of his moral constitution, is disposed to consider himself as standing in some degree of social relation to the whole species in general; and that this principle acts with more or less vigour, according to the distance at which he is placed with respect to any particular community or individual of his kind. Thus it may be observed to operate with greater force between fellow-citizens of the same commonwealth than in regard to foreigners, and between the several members of the same family than towards those among whom there is no common tie of consanguinity. In the case of relations, indeed, this principle somewhat rises in its strength, and produces a sort of instinctive amity; but an amity, however, of no great firmness or solidity. The inferiority of this species of natural connection, when compared with that which is the consequence of voluntary choice, appears from this single consideration: that the former has not the least dependence upon the sentiments of the heart, but continues the same it was in its origin, notwithstanding every degree of cordiality between the parties should be utterly extinguished; whereas the kind affections enter so essentially into the latter, that where love does not exist friendship can have no being. But what still farther evinces the strength and efficacy of friendship above all the numberless other social tendencies of the human heart is that, instead of wasting its force upon a multiplicity of divided objects, its whole energy is exerted for the benefit of only two or three persons at the utmost.

Friendship may be shortly defined, " a perfect conformity of opinions upon all religious and civil subjects, united with the highest degree of mutual esteem and affection; " and yet from these simple circumstances results the most desirable blessing (virtue alone excepted) that the gods have bestowed on mankind. I am sensible that in this opinion I shall not be universally supported—health and riches, honours and power, have each of them their distinct admirers, and are respectively pursued as the supreme felicity of human life; whilst some there are (and the number is by no means inconsiderable) who contend that it is to be found only in the sensual gratifications. But the latter place their principal happiness on the same low enjoyments which constitute the chief good of brutes, and the former on those very precarious possessions that depend much less on our own merit than on the caprice of fortune. They, indeed, who maintain that the ultimate good of man consists in the knowledge and practice of virtue, fix it, undoubtedly, upon its truest and most glorious foundation; but let it be remembered, at the same time, that virtue is at once both the parent and the support of friendship.

I have already declared that by virtue I do not mean, with the philosophers before alluded to, that ideal strain of perfection which is nowhere to be found but in the pompous language of enthusiastic declamation; I mean only that attainable degree of moral merit which is understood by the term in common discourse, and may be exemplified in actual practice. Without entering, therefore, into a particular inquiry concerning those imaginary beings which never have been realised in human nature, I think myself warranted in considering those persons as truly good men who have always been so deemed in the general opinion of mankind—the Pauli, for instance, and the Catos, the Galli, the Scipios, and the Phili; for with such characters the world has reason to be well contented.

When Friendship, therefore, is contracted between men who possess a degree of virtue not inferior to that which adorned those approved personages I have just named, it is productive of unspeakable advantages. "Life would be utterly lifeless," as old Ennius expresses it, without a friend on whose kindness and fidelity one might confidently repose. Can there be a more real complacency, indeed, than to lay open to another the most secret thoughts of one's heart with the same confidence and security as if they were still concealed in his own? Would not the fruits of prosperity lose much of their relish were there none who equally rejoiced with the possessor in the satisfaction he received from them? And how difficult must it prove to bear up under the pressure of misfortunes unsupported by a generous associate who more than equally divides their load? In short, the several occasions to which friendship extends its kindly offices are unbounded, while the advantage of every other object of human desires is confined within certain specific and determinate limits, beyond which it is of no avail. Thus wealth is pursued for the particular uses to which it is solely applicable; power, in order to receive worship; honours, for the sake of fame; sensual indulgences, on account of the gratifications that attend them; and health, as the means of living exempt from pain and possessing the unobstructed exercise of all our corporeal faculties. Whereas Friendship (I repeat again) is adapted by its nature to an infinite number of different ends, accommodates itself to all circumstances and situations of human life, and can at no season prove either unsuitable or inconvenient—in a word, not even fire and water (to use a proverbial illustration) are capable of being converted to a greater variety of beneficial purposes.

I desire it may be understood, however, that I am now speaking, not of that inferior species of amity which occurs in the common intercourse of the world (although this, too, is not without its pleasures and advantages), but of that genuine and perfect friendship, examples of which are so extremely rare as to be rendered memorable by their singularity. It is this sort alone that can truly be said to heighten the joys of prosperity, and mitigate the sorrows of adversity, by a generous participation of both; indeed, one of the chief among the many important offices of this connection is exerted in the day of affliction, by dispelling the gloom that overcasts the mind, encouraging the hope of happier times, and preventing the depressed spirits from sinking into a state of weak and unmanly despondence. Whoever is in possession of a true friend sees the exact counterpart of his own soul. In consequence of this moral resemblance between them, they are so intimately one that no advantage can attend either which does not equally communicate itself to both; they are strong in the strength, rich in the opulence, and powerful in the power of each other. They can scarcely, indeed, be considered in any respect as separate individuals, and wherever the one appears the other is virtually present. I will venture even a bolder assertion, and affirm that in despite of death they must both continue to exist so long as either of them shall remain alive; for the deceased may, in a certain sense, be said still to live whose memory is preserved with the highest veneration and the most tender regret in the bosom of the survivor, a circumstance which renders the former happy in death, and the latter honoured in life.

If that benevolent principle which thus intimately unites two persons in the bands of amity were to be struck out of the human heart, it would be impossible that either private families or public communities should subsist—even the land itself would lie waste, and desolation overspread the earth. Should this assertion stand in need of a proof, it will appear evident by considering the ruinous consequences which ensue from discord and dissension; for what family is so securely established, or what government fixed upon so firm a basis, that it would not be overturned and utterly destroyed were a general spirit of enmity and malevolence to break forth amongst its members?—a sufficient argument, surely, of the inestimable benefits which flow from the kind and friendly affections.

I have been informed that a certain learned bard of Agrigentum published a philosophic poem in Greek, in which he asserted that the several bodies which compose the physical system of the universe preserve the consistence of their respective forms, or are dispersed into their primitive atoms, as a principle of amity, or of discord, becomes predominant in their composition. It is certain, at least, that the powerful effects of these opposite agents in the moral world is universally perceived and acknowledged. Agreeable to this general sentiment, who is there, when he beholds a man generously exposing himself to certain danger, for the sake of rescuing his distressed friend, that can forbear expressing the warmest approbation? Accordingly, what repeated acclamations lately echoed through the theatre at the new play of my host and friend Pacuvius, in that scene where Pylades and Orestes are introduced before the king; who being ignorant which of them was Orestes, whom he had determined to put to death, each insists, in order to save the life of his associate, that he himself is the real person in question. If the mere fictitious representation of such a magnanimous and heroic contention was thus universally applauded by the spectators, what impression must it have made upon their minds had they seen it actually displayed in real life! The general effect produced upon this occasion, clearly shows how deeply nature hath impressed on the human heart a sense of moral beauty; since a whole audience thus unanimously conspired in admiring an instance of sublime generosity in another's conduct, which not one of them, perhaps, was capable of exhibiting in his own.

Thus far I have ventured to lay before you my general notions concerning friendship. If aught remain to be added on the subject (and much there certainly does), permit me to refer you to those philosophers who are more capable of giving you satisfaction.

FANNIUS.—That satisfaction, Laelius, we rather hope to receive from you. For although I have frequently applied to those philosophers to whom you would resign me, and have been no unwilling auditor of their discourses, yet I am persuaded you will deliver your sentiments upon this subject in a much more elegant and enlightening manner.

SCAEVOLA.—You would have been still more confirmed in that opinion, Fannius, had you been present with us at the conference which we held not long since in the gardens of Scipio, upon the subject of government; when Laelius proved himself so powerful an advocate in support of natural justice, by confuting the subtle arguments of the very acute and distinguishing Philus.

FANNIUS.—To triumph in the cause of justice could be no difficult task, certainly, to Laelius, who is, confessedly, one of the most just and upright of men.

SCAEVOLA.—And can it be less easy for him who has deservedly acquired the highest honour by his eminent constancy, affection, and fidelity to his friend, to explain, with equal success, the principles and duties of friendship?

LAELIUS.—This is pressing me beyond all power of resistance; and, indeed, it would be unreasonable, as well as difficult, not to yield to the desires of two such worthy relations, when they request my sentiments upon a point of so interesting and important a nature.

Having frequently, then, turned my thoughts on this subject, the principal question that has always occurred to me is, whether Friendship takes its rise from the wants and weaknesses of man, and is cultivated solely in order to obtain, by a mutual exchange of good offices, those advantages which he could not otherwise acquire? Or whether nature, notwithstanding this beneficial intercourse is inseparable from the connection, previously disposes the heart to engage in it upon a nobler and more generous inducement? In order to determine this question, it must be observed that love is a leading and essential principle in constituting that particular species of benevolence which is termed amity; and although this sentiment may be feigned, indeed, by the followers of those who are courted merely with a view to interest, yet it cannot possibly be produced by a motive of interest alone. There is a truth and simplicity in genuine friendship, an unconstrained and spontaneous emotion, altogether incompatible with every kind and degree of artifice and simulation. I am persuaded, therefore, that it derives its origin not from the indigence of human nature, but from a distinct principle implanted in the breast of man; from a certain instinctive tendency, which draws congenial minds into union, and not from a cool calculation of the advantages with which it is pregnant.

The wonderful force, indeed, of innate propensities of the benevolent kind is observable even among brutes, in that tender attachment which prevails during a certain period between the dam and her young. But their strongest effects are more particularly conspicuous in the human species; as appears, in the first place, from that powerful endearment which subsists between parents and children, and which cannot be eradicated or counteracted without the most detestable impiety; and in the next, from those sentiments of secret approbation which arise on the very first interview with a man whose manners and temper seem to harmonise with our own, and in whom we think we discover symptoms of an honest and virtuous mind. In reality, nothing is so beautiful as virtue; and nothing makes its way more directly to the heart: we feel a certain degree of affection even towards those meritorious persons whom we have never seen, and whose characters are known to us only from history. Where is the man that does not, even at this distance of time, find his heart glow with benevolence towards the memory of Fabricius or Curius, though he certainly never beheld their persons? On the contrary, who is there that feels not emotions of hatred and detestation when he reflects on the conduct of Tarquin, of Cassius, or of Maelius? Rome has twice contended for empire upon Italian ground, when she sent forth her armies to oppose the respective invasions of Pyrrhus and of Hannibal; and yet, with what different dispositions do we review the campaigns of those hostile chiefs! The generous spirit of the former very much softens our resentment towards him; while the cruelty of the latter must render his character the abhorrence of every Roman.

If the charms of virtue, then, are so captivating, as to inspire us with some degree of affection towards those approved persons whom we never saw; or, which is still more extraordinary, if they force us to admire them even in an enemy; what wonder is it that in those with whom we live and converse they should affect us in a still more irresistible manner? It must be acknowledged, however, that this first impression is considerably strengthened and improved, by a nearer intercourse, by subsequent good offices, and by a general indication of zeal for our service—causes which, when they operate with combined force, kindle in the heart the warmest and most generous amity. To suppose that all attachments of this sort spring solely from a sense of human imbecility, and in order to supply that insufficiency we feel in ourselves, by the assistance we hope to receive from others, is to degrade friendship to a most unworthy and ignoble origin. Indeed, if this supposition were true, they who find in themselves the greatest defects would be the most disposed and the best qualified to engage in this kind of connection, which is contrary to fact. For experience shows that the more a man looks for his happiness within himself, and the more firmly he stands supported by the consciousness of his own intrinsic merit, the more desirous he is to cultivate an intercourse of amity, and the better friend he certainly proves. In what respect, let me ask, had Scipio any occasion for my services? We neither of us, most assuredly, stood in need of the other's aid; but the singular virtues I admired in his character, together with the favourable opinion which in some measure, perhaps, he had conceived of mine, were the primary and prevailing motives of that affectionate attachment which was afterwards so considerably increased by the habitudes of intimate and unreserved converse. For although many and great advantages accrued to both from the alliance that was thus formed between us, yet sure I am that the hope of receiving those reciprocal benefits by no means entered into the original cause of our union. In fact, as generosity disdains to make a traffic of her favours; and a liberal mind confers obligations, not from the mean hope of a return, but solely from that satisfaction which nature has annexed to the exertion of benevolent actions, so I think it is evident that we are induced to form friendships, not from a mercenary contemplation of their utility, but from that pure disinterested complacency which results from the mere exercise of the affection itself.

That sect of philosophers who impute all human actions to the same motive which determines those of brutes, and refer both to one common principle of self-gratification, will be very far, I am sensible, from agreeing with me in the origin I have ascribed to friendship. And no wonder, for nothing great and elevated can win the esteem and approbation of a set of men whose whole thoughts and pursuits are professedly directed to so base and ignoble an end.

I shall take no further notice, therefore, of their unworthy tenets, well convinced as I am that there is an implanted sense in man, by which nature allures his heart to the charms of virtue, in whomsoever her lovely form appears. And hence it is, that they who find in themselves a predilection for some particular object of moral approbation are induced to desire a nearer and more intimate communion with that person, in order to enjoy those pure and mental advantages which flow from an habitual and familiar intercourse with the good,—I will add, too, in order to feel the refined satisfaction of inspiring equal and reciprocal sentiments of affection, together with the generous pleasure of conferring acts of kindness without the least view of a return. A friendship placed upon this, its proper and natural basis, is not only productive of the most solid utility, but stands at the same time upon a firmer and more durable foundation than if it were raised upon a sense of human wants and weakness. For if interest were the true and only medium to cement this connection, it could hold no longer than while interest, which is always fluctuating and variable, should continue to be advanced by the same hand; whereas genuine friendship, being produced by the simple efficiency of nature's steady and immutable laws, resembles the source from whence it springs, and is for ever permanent and unchangeable.

This may suffice concerning the rise of friendship, unless you should have anything to object to the principles I have endeavoured to establish.

FANNIUS.—Much otherwise. I will take the privilege, therefore, of seniority to answer for Scaevola as well as for myself, by requesting you in both our names to proceed.

SCAEVOLA.—Fannius has very justly expressed my sentiments, and I join with him in wishing to hear what you have further to observe on the question we have proposed.

LAELIUS.—I will lay before you, then, my excellent young man, the result of frequent conversations which Scipio and I have formerly held together upon the subject. He used to say that nothing is so difficult as to preserve a lasting and unbroken friendship to the end of life. For it may frequently happen not only that the interest of the parties shall considerably interfere, or their opinions concerning political measures widely differ, but age, infirmities, or misfortunes are apt to produce very extraordinary changes in the tempers and dispositions of men. He illustrated this general instability of common friendships by tracing the revolutions they are liable to undergo from the earliest period in which this kind of connection can commence. Accordingly, he observed that those strong attachments which are sometimes formed in childhood were generally renounced with the puerile robe. But should a particular affection contracted in this tender age happen to continue to riper years, it is nothing unusual to see it afterwards interrupted, either by rivalship in a matrimonial pursuit, or some other object of youthful competition, in which both cannot possibly succeed. If these common dangers, however, should be happily escaped, yet others no less fatal may hereafter rise up to its ruin, especially if they should become opposite candidates for the same dignities of the state. For as with the generality of mankind, an immoderate desire of wealth, so among those of a more liberal and exalted spirit, an inordinate thirst of glory is usually the strongest bane of amity; and each of them have proved the occasion of converting the warmest friends into the most implacable enemies.

He added, that great and just dissensions had arisen also in numberless instances on account of improper requests— where a man has solicited his friend to assist him, for example, in his lawless gallantries, or to support him in some other act of equal dishonour and injustice. A denial upon such occasions, though certainly laudable, is generally deemed by the party refused to be a violation of the rights of amity; and he will probably resent it the more, as applications of this nature necessarily imply that the person who breaks through all restraints in urging them is equally disposed to make the same unwarrantable concessions on his own part. Disagreements of this kind have not only caused irreparable breaches between the closest connections, but have even kindled unextinguishable animosities. In short, the common friendships of the world are liable to be broken to pieces by such a variety of accidents, that Scipio thought it required a more than common portion, not only of good sense, but of good fortune, to steer entirely clear of those numerous and fatal rocks.

Our first inquiry therefore, if you please, shall be, " How far the claims of friendship may reasonably extend? " For instance, ought the bosom friends of Coriolanus (if any intimacies of that kind he had) to have joined him in turning his arms against his country; or those of Viscellinus, or Spurius Maelius, to have assisted them in their designs of usurping the sovereign power?

In those public commotions which were raised by Tiberius Gracchus, it appeared that neither Quintus Tubero, nor any other of those persons with whom he lived upon terms of the greatest intimacy, engaged in his faction, one only excepted, who was related to your family, Scaevola, by the ties of hospitality: I mean Blosius, of Cumae. This man (as I was appointed an assessor with the two consuls Laenas and Rupilius) applied to me to obtain his pardon, alleging, in his justification, that he entertained so high an esteem and affection for Gracchus, as to hold himself obliged to concur with him in any measure he might propose. What! if he had even desired you to set fire to the Capitol? " Such a request, I am confident," replied Blosius, " he never would have made." But admitting that he had, how would you have determined? " In that case," returned Blosius, " I should most certainly have complied." Infamous as this confession was, he acted agreeably to it; or rather, indeed, his conduct exceeded even the impiety of his professions, for, not contented with encouraging the seditious schemes of Tiberius Gracchus, he actually took the lead in them, and was an instigator as well as an associate in all the madness of his measures. In consequence of these extravagant proceedings, and alarmed to find that extraordinary judges were appointed for his trial, he made his escape into Asia, where, entering into the service of our enemies, he met with the fate he so justly merited for the injuries he had done to the commonwealth.

I lay it down, then, as a rule without exception, " that no degree of friendship can either justify or excuse the commission of a criminal action." For true amity being founded on an opinion of virtue in the object of our affection, it is scarcely possible that those sentiments should remain, after an avowed and open violation of the principles which originally produced them.

To maintain that the duties of this relation require a compliance with every request a friend shall offer, and give a right to expect the same unlimited concessions in return, would be a doctrine, I confess, from which no ill consequences could ensue, if the parties concerned were absolutely perfect, and incapable of the least deviation from the dictates of virtue and good sense. But in settling the principles by which our conduct in this respect ought to be regulated, we are not to form our estimate by fictitious representations, but to consider what history and experience teaches us that mankind truly are, and to select for our imitation such real characters as seem to have approached the nearest to perfection.

Tradition informs us that Papas Aemilius and Caius Luscinus, who were twice colleagues in the consular and censorial offices, were united also in the strictest intimacy; and that Manius Curius and Titus Coruncanius lived with them, and with each other, upon terms of the strictest and most inviolable friendship. It may well, therefore, be presumed (since there is not even the slightest reason to suspect the contrary) that none of these illustrious worthies ever made a proposal to his friend inconsistent with the laws of honour, or that fidelity he had pledged to his country. To urge that " if any overtures of that nature had ever been made, they would certainly have been rejected, and consequently must have been concealed from public notice," is an objection by no means sufficient to weaken the presumption, when the sanctity of manners which distinguished these venerable persons shall be duly considered; for to be capable of making such proposals would be no less a proof of depravity than actually consenting to them.

Accordingly, we find that both Carbo and Caius Cato, the friends of Tiberius Gracchus, did not refuse to take a part in his turbulent measures, as his brother Caius, although he was not indeed a very considerable actor in the scene at first, is now most zealously engaged in the same unworthy cause.

Let it be established, therefore, as one of the most sacred and indispensable laws of this connection, " never either to make, or to grant, a request which honour and virtue will not justify." To allege, in any instance of deviation from moral rectitude, that one was actuated by a warmth of zeal for his friend, is in every species of criminal conduct a plea altogether scandalous and inadmissible, but particularly in transctions that strike at the peace and welfare of the state. I would the more earnestly inculcate this important maxim, as, from the present complexion of the times, it seems peculiarly necessary to guard against introducing principles which may hereafter be productive of fatal disturbances in the republic; and, indeed, we have already somewhat deviated from that political line by which our wiser ancestors were wont to regulate their public conduct.

Thus Tiberius Gracchus, who aimed at sovereign power—or rather, indeed, who actually possessed it during the space of a few months—opened a scene so totally new to the Roman people that not even tradition had delivered down to them any circumstance in former times which resembled it. Some of the friends and relations of this man, who had concurred with him in his lifetime, continued to support the same factious measures after his death; and I cannot reflect on the cruel part they acted towards Scipio Nasica without melting into tears. I will confess, at the same time, that, in consideration of the punishment which Tiberius Gracchus has lately suffered, I have protected his friend Carbo as far as it was in my power. As to the consequences we have reason to expect from the tribunate of Caius Gracchus, I am unwilling to indulge conjecture; but this I do not scruple to say, that when once a distemper of this kind has broken out in a commonwealth, the infection is apt to spread, and it generally gathers strength the wider it extends. In conformity to this observation, the change which was made by the Gabinian law in the manner of voting was, two years afterwards, you know, carried still farther by the law which Cassius proposed and obtained. And I cannot but prophesy that a rupture between the people and the senate will be the result of both, as the most important affairs of the commonwealth will hereafter be conducted by the caprice of the multitude. It is much easier, indeed, to discover the source from which these disorders will arise, than to point out a remedy for the mischief they will occasion.

I have thrown out these reflections, as well knowing that no public innovations of this pernicious kind are ever attempted, without the assistance of some select and confidential associates. It is, necessary, therefore, to admonish those who mean well to the constitution of their country, that if they should inadvertently have formed an intimacy with men of a contrary principle, they are not to imagine themselves so bound by the laws of amity as to lie under an indispensable obligation to support them in attempts injurious to the community. Whosoever disturbs the peace of the commonwealth, is a just object of public indignation; nor is that man less deserving of punishment who acts as a second in such an impious cause than the principal. No person ever possessed a greater share of power, or was more eminently distinguished among the Grecian states, than Themistocles. This illustrious general, who was commander-in-chief of the Grecian forces in the Persian War, and who by his services upon that occasion delivered his country from the tyranny with which it was threatened, having been driven into exile by the jealousy his great talents had raised, did not acquiesce under the ingratitude of his fellow-citizens with the submission he ought; on the contrary, he acted the same traitorous part under this unmerited persecution as Coriolanus did amongst us about twenty years before. But neither the one nor the other found a coadjutor among their respective friends, in consequence of which just dereliction, they each of them perished by their own desperate hands.

It appears, then, from the principles I have laid down, that these kinds of wicked combinations under the pretended obligations of friendship, are so far from being sanctified by that relation, that on the contrary they ought to be publicly discouraged by the severest punishments; lest it should be thought an allowed maxim, that a friend is to be supported in every outrage he may commit, even though he should take up arms against his country. I am the more earnest to expose the error of this dangerous persuasion, as there are certain symptoms in the present times which give me reason to fear that at some future period the impious principle I am combating may actually be extended to the case I last mentioned; and I am no less desirous that the peace of the republic should be preserved after my death than zealous to maintain it during my life.

The first and great axiom therefore in the laws of amity should invariably be—" never to require from a friend what he cannot grant without a breach of his honour; and always to be ready to assist him upon every occasion consistent with that principle." So long as we shall act under the secure guard of this sacred barrier, it will not be sufficient merely to yield a ready compliance with all his desires; we ought to anticipate and prevent them. Another rule likewise of indispensable obligation upon all who would approve themselves true friends, is, " to be ever ready to offer their advice, with an unreserved and honest frankness of heart." The counsels of a faithful and friendly monitor carry with them an authority which ought to have great influence, and they should be urged not only with freedom, but even with severity, if the occasion should appear to require it.

I am informed that certain Greek writers (philosophers, it seems, in the opinion of their countrymen), have advanced some very extraordinary positions relating to the subject of our present inquiry; as, indeed, what subject is there which these subtle geniuses have not tortured with their sophistry? The authors to whom I allude dissuade their disciples from entering into any strong attachments, as unavoidably creating supernumerary disquietudes to those who engage in them, and as every man has more than sufficient to call forth his solicitude in the course of his own affairs, it is a weakness, they contend, anxiously to involve himself in the concerns of others. They recommend it also in all connections of this kind to hold the bands of union extremely loose, so as always to have it in one's power to straiten or relax them as circumstances and situations shall render most expedient. They add, as a capital article of their doctrine, that " to live exempt from cares is an essential ingredient to constitute human happiness, but an ingredient, however, which he who voluntarily distresses himself with cares in which he has no necessary and personal interest, must never hope to possess."

I have been told, likewise, that there is another set of
pretended philosophers of the same country, whose tenets
concerning this subject are of a still more illiberal and ungenerous cast, and I have already, in the course of this
conversation, slightly animadverted upon their principles.
The proposition they attempt to establish is that " friendship
is an affair of self-interest entirely, and that the proper
motive for engaging in it is, not in order to gratify the kind
and benevolent affections, but for the benefit of that assistance and support which is to be derived from the connection."
Accordingly they assert that those persons are most disposed
to have recourse to auxiliary alliances of this kind who are
least qualified by nature or fortune to depend upon their
own strength and powers; the weaker sex, for instance, being
generally more inclined to engage in friendships than the
male part of our species; and those who are depressed by
indigence, or labouring under misfortunes, than the wealthy
and the prosperous.

Excellent and obliging sages these, undoubtedly. To
strike out the friendly affections from the moral world
would be like extinguishing the sun in the natural, each of
them being the source of the best and most grateful satisfactions that the gods have conferred on the sons of men. But
I should be glad to know what the real value of this boasted
exemption from care, which they promise their disciples,
justly amounts to? an exemption flattering to self-love, I
confess, but which, upon many occurrences in human life,
should be rejected with the utmost disdain. For nothing,
surely, can be more inconsistent with a well-poised and manly
spirit, than to decline engaging in any laudable action, or
to be discouraged from persevering in it, by an apprehension
of the trouble and solicitude with which it may probably
be attended. Virtue herself, indeed, ought to be totally
renounced, if it be right to avoid every possible means that
may be productive of uneasiness; for who that is actuated
by her principles can observe the conduct of an opposite
character, without being affected with some degree of secret
dissatisfaction? Are not the just, the brave, and the good
necessarily exposed to the disagreeable emotions of dislike
and aversion when they respectively meet with instances
of fraud, of cowardice, or of villainy? It is an essential
property of every well-constituted mind to be affected with

pain, or pleasure, according to the nature of those moral appearances that present themselves to observation.

If sensibility, therefore, be not incompatible with true wisdom (and it surely is not, unless we suppose that philosophy deadens every finer feeling of our nature) what just reason can be assigned why the sympathetic sufferings, which may result from friendship, should be a sufficient inducement for banishing that generous affection from the human breast? Extinguish all emotions of the heart and what difference will remain, I do not say between man and brute, but between man and a mere inanimate clod? Away then with those austere philosophers who represent virtue as hardening the soul against all the softer impressions of humanity. The fact, certainly, is much otherwise; a truly good man is upon many occasions extremely susceptible of tender sentiments, and his heart expands with joy or shrinks with sorrow, as good or ill fortune accompanies his friend. Upon the whole, then, it may fairly be concluded, that as in the case of virtue, so in that of friendship, those painful sensations which may sometimes be produced by the one, as well as by the other, are equally insufficient for excluding either of them from taking possession of our bosoms.

There is a charm in virtue, as I have already had occasion to remark, that by a secret and irresistible bias draws the general affection of those persons towards each other in whom it appears to reside, and this instantaneous goodwill is mutually attended with a desire of entering into a nearer and more intimate correspondence; sentiments which, at length, by a natural and necessary consequence, give rise to particular friendships. Strange, indeed, would it be that exalted honours, magnificent mansions, or sumptuous apparel, not to mention other splendid objects of general admiration, should have power to captivate the greater part of our species, and that the beauty of a virtuous mind, capable of meeting our affection with an equal return, should not have sufficient allurements to inspire the most ardent passion. I said " capable of meeting our affection with an equal return; " for nothing, surely, can be more delightful than to live in a constant interchange and vicissitude of reciprocal good offices. If we add to this, as with truth we may, that a similitude of manners is the most powerful of all attractions, it must be granted that the virtuous are strongly impelled towards each other by that moral tendency and natural relationship which subsists between them.

No proposition therefore can be more evident, I think, than that the virtuous must necessarily, and by an implanted sense in the human heart, receive impressions of goodwill towards each other, and these are the natural source from whence genuine friendship can only flow. Not that a good man's benevolence is by any means confined to a single object; he extends it to every individual. For true virtue, incapable of partial and contracted exceptions to the exercise of her benign spirit, enlarges the soul with sentiments of universal philanthropy. How, indeed, could it be consistent with her character to take whole nations under her protection, if even the lowest ranks of mankind, as well as the highest, were not the proper objects of beneficence?

But to return to the more immediate object of our present consideration. They who insist that "utility is the first and prevailing motive which induces mankind to enter into particular friendships," appear to me to divest the associations of its most amiable and engaging principle. For to a mind rightly composed it is not so much the benefits received as the affectionate zeal from which they flow, that gives them their best and most valuable recommendation. It is so far, indeed, from being verified by fact, that a sense of our wants is the original cause of forming these amicable alliances; that, on the contrary, it is observable that none have been more distinguished in their friendships than those whose power and opulence, but above all, whose superior virtue (a much firmer support) have raised them above every necessity of having recourse to the assistance of others. Perhaps, however, it may admit of a question, whether it were desirable that one's friend should be so absolutely sufficient for himself, as to have no wants of any kind to which his own powers were not abundantly adequate. I am sure, at least, I should have been deprived of a most exquisite satisfaction if no opportunity had ever offered to approve the affectionate zeal of my heart towards Scipio, and he had never had occasion, either in his civil or military transactions, to make use of my counsel or my aid.

The true distinction, then, in this question is, that "although friendship is certainly productive of utility, yet utility is not the primary motive of friendship." Those selfish sensualists, therefore, who lulled in the lap of luxury presume to maintain the reverse, have surely no claim to attention, as they are neither qualified by reflection nor experience to be competent judges of the subject.

Good gods! is there a man upon the face of the earth who would deliberately accept of all the wealth and all the affluence this world can bestow if offered to him upon the severe terms of his being unconnected with a single mortal whom he could love or by whom he should be beloved? This would be to lead the wretched life of a detested tyrant, who, amidst perpetual suspicions and alarms, passes his miserable days a stranger to every tender sentiment, and utterly precluded from the heartfelt satisfactions of friendship. For who can love the man he fears? or how can affection dwell with a consciousness of being feared? He may be flattered, indeed, by his followers with the specious semblance of personal attachment, but whenever he falls (and many instances there are of such a reverse of fortune) it will appear how totally destitute he stood of every genuine friend. Accordingly it is reported that Tarquin used to say in his exile, that "his misfortunes had taught him to discern his real from his pretended friends, as it was now no longer in his power to make either of them any returns." I should much wonder, however, if, with a temper so insolent and ferocious, he ever had a sincere friend.

But as the haughtiness of Tarquin's imperious deportment rendered it impossible for him to know the satisfaction of enjoying a faithful attachment, so it frequently happens that the being advanced into exalted stations equally proves the occasion of excluding the great and the powerful from possessing that inestimable felicity. Fortune, indeed, is not only blind herself but is apt to affect her favourites with the same infirmity. Weak minds, elated with being distinguished by her smiles, are generally disposed to assume an arrogant and supercilious demeanour; and there is not in the whole compass of nature a more insufferable creature than a prosperous fool. Prosperity, in truth, has been observed to produce wonderful transformations even in persons who before had always the good sense to deport themselves in a modest and unassuming manner; and their heads have been so turned by the eminence to which they

were raised, as to look down with neglect and contempt on
their old friends, while their new connections entirely engaged
all their attention and favour. But there cannot surely be
a more flagrant instance of weakness and folly than to
employ the great advantages of extensive influence and
opulent possession in the purchase of brilliant equipages,
gaudy raiment, elegant vases, together with every other
fashionable decoration which wealth and power can procure;
and yet neglect to use the means they afford of acquiring that
noblest and most valuable ornaments of human life, a worthy
and faithful friend! The absurdity of this conduct is the
more amazing, as after all the base sacrifices that may have
been made to obtain these vain and ostentatious embellishments, the holding of them must ever be precarious. For
whoever shall invade them with a stronger arm, to him they
will infallibly belong; whereas a true friend is a treasure
which no power, how formidable soever, can be sufficient to
wrest from the happy possessor. But admitting that the
favours of fortune were in their nature permanent and
irrevocable, yet how joyless and insipid must they prove if
not heightened and endeared by the society and participation of a bosom friend.

But not to pursue reflections of this sort any farther, let
me rather observe that it is necessary to settle some fixed
standard or measure, by which to regulate and adjust the
kind affections in the commerce under consideration. To
this intent, three different criterions I find have been proposed. The first is, " that in all important occurrences we
should act towards our friend precisely in the same manner
as if the case were our own: " the second, " that our good
offices should be exactly dealt out, both in degree and value,
by the measure and merit of those we receive from him; "
and the last, " that our conduct in relation to all his concerns
should be governed by the same kind of sentiments with
which he appears to be actuated in respect to them himself."

Now there is not one of these several rules to which I can
entirely give my approbation. The first is by no means I
think just; because there are many things I would undertake
on my friend's account, which I should never prevail with
myself to act on my own. For instance, I would not scruple
on his behalf to solicit, nor even to supplicate a man of a
mean and worthless character, nor to repel with peculiar

acrimony and indignation, any affront or injury that might be offered to him. And this conduct, which I could not hold without blame in matters that merely concerned myself, I very laudably might in those which relate to my friend. Add to this that there are many advantages which a generous mind would willingly forego, or suffer himself to be deprived of, that his friend might enjoy the benefit of them.

With regard to the second criterion, which determines the measure of our affection and good offices, by exactly proportioning them to the value and quality we receive of each, it degrades the connection into a mere mercantile account between debtor and creditor. True friendship is animated by much too liberal and enlarged a spirit to distribute her beneficence with a careful and penurious circumspection, lest she should bestow more abundantly than she receives: she scorns to poise the balance so exactly equal that nothing shall be placed in the one scale without its equivalent in the other.

The third maxim is still less admissible than either of the two former. There are some characters who are apt to entertain too low an opinion of their personal merit, and whose spirits are frequently much too languid and depressed to exert themselves with proper vigour and activity for the promotion of their own interest or honours. Under circumstances of this kind shall the zeal of a friend rise no higher than one's own, but cautiously be restrained within the same humble level? On the contrary, he ought to endeavour by every means in his power to dispel the gloom that overcasts the mind of his desponding associate, and animate his hopes with livelier and more sanguine expectations.

And now, having pointed out the insufficiency of the several criteria I have mentioned, it is necessary I should produce some other more adequate and satisfactory. But before I deliver my opinion in respect to this article, suffer me previously to observe that Scipio used frequently to say there never was a caution advanced more injurious to the principles of true amity than the famous precept which advises, " so to regulate your affection towards your friend as to remember that the time may possibly come when you shall have reason to hate him." He could never, he said, be persuaded that Bias, a man so distinguished for wisdom as to be ranked among the seven celebrated sages of Greece, was really the author, as he is generally supposed, of so unworthy a precaution. It was rather the maxim, he imagined, of some sordid wretch, or perhaps of some ambitious statesman, who, a stranger to every nobler sentiment of the human heart, had no other object in forming his connections but as they might prove conducive to the increase or establishment of his power. It is impossible certainly to entertain a friendship for any man of whom you cherish so unfavourable an opinion as to suppose he may hereafter give you cause to become his enemy. In reality, if this axiom were justly founded, and it be right to sit thus loose in our affections, we ought to wish that our friend might give us frequent occasions to complain of his conduct, to lament whenever he acted in a laudable manner, and to envy every advantage that might attend him, lest unhappily he should lay too strong a hold on our heart. This unworthy rule, therefore, whoever was the author of it, is evidently calculated for the utter extirpation of true amity. The more rational advice would have been, as Scipio remarked, to be always so cautious in forming friendships as never to place our esteem and affections where there was a probability of their being converted into the opposite sentiments. But, at all events, if we should be so unfortunate as to make an improper choice, it were wiser, he thought, not to look forward to possible contingencies than to be always acting upon the defensive, and painfully guarding against future dissensions.

I think, then, the only measures that can be properly recommended respecting our general conduct in the article of friendship is, in the first place, to be careful that we form the connection with men of strict and irreproachable manners; and, in the next, frankly to lay open to each other all our thoughts, inclinations, and purposes without the least caution, reserve, or disguise. I will venture even to add that in cases in which the life or good fame of a friend is concerned it may be allowable to deviate a little from the path of strict right in order to comply with his desires; provided, however, that by this compliance our own character be not materially affected. And this is the largest concession that should be made to friendship; for the good opinion of the public ought never to be lightly esteemed, nor the general affection of our fellow-citizens considered as a matter of little importance in carrying on the great affairs of the world.

Popularity, indeed, if purchased at the expense of base condescensions to the vices or the follies of the people, is a disgrace to the possessor, but when it is the just and natural result of a laudable and patriotic conduct, it is an acquisition which no wise man will ever contemn.

But to return to Scipio. Friendship was his favourite topic, and I have frequently heard him remark that there is no article in which mankind usually act with so much negligence as in what relates to this connection. Everyone, he observed, informs himself with great exactness of what numbers his flocks and his herds consist, but who is it that endeavours to ascertain his real friends with the same requisite precision! Thus, likewise, in choosing the former much caution is commonly used in order to discover those significant marks which denote their proper qualities. Whereas, in selecting the latter, it is seldom that any great attention is exerted to discern those moral signatures which indicate the qualifications necessary to constitute a friend.

One of the principal ingredients to form that character is a "steadiness and constancy of temper." This virtue, it must be confessed, is not very generally to be found among mankind, nor is there any other means to discover in whose bosom it resides than experience. But as this experience cannot fully be acquired till the connection is already formed, affection is apt to take the lead of judgement, and render a previous trial impossible. It is the part of prudence, therefore, to restrain a predilection from carrying us precipitately into the arms of a new friend before we have, in some degree at least, put his moral qualifications to the test. A very inconsiderable article of money may be sufficient to prove the levity of some men's professions of friendship; whilst a much larger sum in contest will be necessary to shake the constancy of others. But should there be a few, perhaps, who are actuated by too generous a spirit to suffer any pecuniary interest to stand in competition with the claims of amity, yet where shall we find the man who will not readily surrender his friendship to his ambition when they happen to interfere? Human nature is, in general, much too weak to resist the charms which surround these glittering temptations; and men are apt to flatter themselves that although they should acquire wealth or power by violating the duties of friendship, the world will be too much dazzled by the splendour of the objects to take notice of the unworthy sacrifice they make to obtain them. And hence it is that real, unfeigned amity is so seldom to be met with among those who are engaged in the pursuit or possession of the honours and the offices of the commonwealth.

To mention another species of trial which few likewise have the firmness to sustain. How severe is it thought by the generality of mankind to take a voluntary share in the calamities of others! And yet it is in the hour of adversity, as Ennius well observes, that Friendship must principally prove her truth and strength. In short, the deserting of a friend in his distress, and the neglecting of him in one's own prosperity, are the two tests which discover the weakness and instability of most connections of this nature. To preserve, therefore, in those seasons of probation, an immovable and unshaken fidelity is a virtue so exceedingly rare that I had almost called it more than human.

The great support and security of that invariable constancy and steadiness which I require in a friend is a strong and delicate sense of honour; for there can be no reliance upon any man who is totally uninfluenced by that principle, or in whom it operates but faintly. It is essential also, in order to form a permanent connection, that the object of our choice should not only have the same general turn of mind with our own, but possess an open, artless, and ingenuous temper; for where any one of those qualities are wanting, vain would it be to expect a lasting and faithful attachment. True friendship, indeed, is absolutely inconsistent with every species of artifice and duplicity; and it is equally impossible it should be maintained between persons whose dispositions and general modes of thinking do not perfectly accord. I must add, as another requisite for that stability I am speaking of, that the party should neither be capable of taking an ill-natured satisfaction in reprehending the frailties of his friend, nor easily induced to credit those imputations with which the malice of others may asperse him.

These reflections sufficiently confirm that position I set out with in this conversation, when I asserted that " true friendship can only be found among the virtuous;" for, in the first place, sincerity is so essential a quality in forming a good—or, if you please, a wise—man (for they are convertible terms), that a person of that character would deem it more generous to be a declared enemy than to conceal a rancorous heart under a smooth brow; and in the next the same generous simplicity of heart would not only induce him to vindicate his friend against the accusation of others, but render him incapable of cherishing in his own breast that little suspicious temper which is ever apt to take offence and perpetually discovering some imaginary violation of amity.

Add to this that his conversation and address ought to be sweetened with a certain ease and politeness of language and manners, that wonderfully contribute to heighten and improve the relish of this intercourse. A solemn, severe demeanour may be very proper, I confess, in certain characters, to give them their proper impression; but friendship should wear a more pleasing aspect, and at all times appear with a complacent, affable, and unconstrained countenance.

And here I cannot forbear taking notice of an extraordinary question which some, it seems, have considered as not altogether without difficulty. It has been asked, " Is the pleasure of acquiring a new friend, supposing him endued with virtues which render him deserving our choice, preferable to the satisfaction of possessing an old one? " On the same account I presume, as we prefer a young horse to one that is grown old in our service, for never, surely, was there a doubt proposed more unworthy of a rational mind! It is not with friendships as with acquisitions of most other kinds, which, after frequent enjoyment, are generally attended with satiety; on the contrary, the longer we preserve them, like those sorts of wine that will bear age, the more relishing and valuable they become. Accordingly the proverb justly says that " one must eat many a peck of salt with a man before he can have sufficient opportunities to approve himself a thorough friend "—not that new connections are to be declined, provided appearances indicate that in due time they may ripen into the happy fruits of a well contracted amity. Old friendships, however, certainly have a claim to the superior degree of our esteem, were it for no other reason than from that powerful impression which ancient habitudes of every kind naturally make upon the human heart. To have recourse once more to the ludicrous instance I just now suggested—who is there that would not prefer a horse whose paces he had been long accustomed to before one that was new and untrained to his hand? Even things inanimate lay a strong hold on the mind by the mere force of custom, as is observable in that rotted affection we bear towards those places, though never so wild and uncultivated, in which a considerable part of our earlier days have been passed.

It frequently happens that there is a great disparity between intimate friends both in point of rank and talents. Now, under these circumstances, " he who has the advantage should never appear sensible of his superiority." Thus Scipio, who stood distinguished in the little group, if I may so call it, of our select associates, never discovered in his behaviour the least consciousness of his pre-eminence over Philus, Rupilius, Memmius, or any other of his particular connections, who were of subordinate abilities or station. And with regard to his brother, Q. Maximus, who, although a man of great merit, and his senior, was by no means comparable with Scipio, he always treated him with as much deference and regard as if he had advanced as far beyond him in every other article as in point of years; in short, it was his constant endeavour to raise all his friends into an equal degree of consequence with himself, and his example well deserves to be imitated. Whatever excellences, therefore, a man may possess in respect to his virtues, his intellectual endowments, or the accidental favours of fortune, he ought generously to communicate the benefits of them with his friends and family. Agreeably to these principles, should he happen to be descended from an obscure ancestry, and see any of his relations in distressed circumstances, or that require the assistance of his superior power or abilities, it is incumbent upon him to employ his credit, his riches, and his talents, to supply their respective deficiencies, and reflect back upon them every honour and advantage they are capable of receiving. Dramatic writers, when the fabulous hero of their play, after having been educated under some poor shepherd ignorant of his true parent, is discovered to be of royal lineage, or the offspring, perhaps, of some celestial divinity, always think it necessary to exhibit the noble youth as still retaining a grateful affection for the honest rustic to whom he had so long supposed himself indebted for his birth; but how much more are these sentiments due to him who has a legitimate claim to his filial tenderness and respect!—In a word, the most sensible satisfaction that can result from advantageous distinctions of every sort is in the pleasure a well-constituted mind must feel by exerting them for the benefit of every individual to whom he stands related, either by the ties of kindred or amity.

But if he who, on account of any of those superiorities which I have mentioned, appears the most conspicuous figure in the circle of his friends, ought by no means to discover in his behaviour towards them the least apparent sense of the eminence on which he stands, so neither should they, on the other hand, betray sentiments of envy or dissatisfaction in seeing him thus exalted above them. It must be acknowledged, however, that in situations of this kind the latter are too apt to be unreasonable in their expectations; to complain that their friend is not sufficiently attentive to their interest, and sometimes even to break out into open remonstrances, especially if they think they are entitled to plead the merit of any considerable services to strengthen their respective claims. But to be capable of reproaching a man with the obligations you have conferred upon him is a disposition exceedingly contemptible and odious; it is his part, indeed, not to forget the good offices he has received; but ill, certainly, would it become his friend to be the monitor for that purpose.

It is not sufficient, therefore, merely to behave with an easy condescension towards those friends who are of less considerable note than oneself; it is incumbent upon him to bring them forward, and, as much as possible, to raise their consequence. The apprehension of not being treated with sufficient regard sometimes creates much uneasiness in this connection; and those tempers are most liable to be disquieted by this suspicion that are inclined to entertain too low an opinion of their own merit. It is the part therefore of a generous and benevolent mind to endeavour to relieve his friend from the mortification of these humiliating sentiments, not only by professions, but by essential services.

The proper measure by which these services ought to be regulated must be taken partly from the extent of our own power, and partly from what the person who is the object of our particular affection has abilities to sustain. For how unlimited soever a man's authority and influence might be, it would be impossible to raise indiscriminately all his friends by turns into the same honourable stations. Thus Scipio, although he had sufficient interest to procure the consular dignity for Publius Rutilius, could not perform the same good office for Lucius, the brother of that consul. But even admitting that you had the arbitrary disposal of every dignity of the state, still it would be necessary well to examine whether your friend's talents were equal to his ambition, and sufficiently qualified him to discharge the duties of the post in question, with credit to himself and advantage to the public.

It is proper to observe that in stating the duties and obligations of friendship, those intimacies alone can justly be taken into consideration which are formed at a time of life when men's characters are decided, and their judgements arrived at maturity. As to the associates of our early years, the companions and partners of our puerile pleasures and amusements, they can by no means, simply on that account, be deemed in the number of friends. Indeed, if the first objects of our affection had the best claim to be received into that rank, our nurses and our pedagogues would certainly have a right to the most considerable share of our regard. Some degree of it is unquestionably due to them, but of a kind, however, far different from that which is the subject of our present inquiry. The truth is, were our early attachments the just foundation of amity, it would be impossible that the union should ever be permanent. For our inclinations and pursuits take a different turn as we advance into riper years; and where these are no longer similar, the true cement of friendship is dissolved. It is the total disparity between the disposition and manners of the virtuous and the vicious that alone renders their coalition incompatible.

There is a certain intemperate degree of affection towards one's friends which it is necessary to restrain, as the indulging of it has frequently, and in very important situations, proved extremely prejudicial to their interest. To exemplify my meaning by an instance from ancient story: Neoptolemus would never have had the glory of taking Troy had his friend Lycomedes, in whose court he had been educated, succeeded in his too warm and earnest solicitations not to hazard his person in that famous expedition. There are numberless occasions which may render an absence between friends highly expedient; and to endeavour, from an impatience of separation, to prevent it, betrays a degree of weakness inconsistent with that firm and manly spirit, without which it is impossible to act up to the character of a true friend. And this is a farther confirmation of the maxim I before insisted upon, that " in a commerce of friendship, mutual requests or concessions should neither be made nor granted, without due and mature deliberation."

But to turn our reflections from those nobler alliances of this kind which are formed between men of eminent and superior virtue, to that lower species which occurs in the ordinary intercourse of the world. In connections of this nature, it sometimes unfortunately happens, that circumstances arise which render it expedient for a man of honour to break with his friend. Some latent vice, perhaps, or concealed ill-humour, unexpectedly discovers itself in his behaviour either towards his friends themselves, or towards others, which cannot be overlooked without participating his disgrace. The most advisable and prudent conduct in situations of this kind is to suffer the intimacy to wear out by silent and insensible degrees; or, to use a strong expression, which I remember to have fallen from Cato upon a similar occasion, " the bands of friendship should be gradually untied, rather than suddenly cut asunder; " always supposing, however, that the offence is not of so atrocious a nature as to render an absolute and immediate alienation indispensably requisite for one's own honour.

As it is not unusual (for I am still speaking of common friendships) that dissensions arise from some extraordinary change of manners or sentiments, or from some contrariety of opinions with respect to public affairs, the parties at variance should be much upon their guard, lest their behaviour towards each other should give the world occasion to remark that they have not only ceased to be cordial friends, but are become inveterate enemies, for nothing is more indecent than to appear in open war with a man with whom one has formerly lived upon terms of familiarity and good fellowship.

Scipio estranged himself from Quintus Pompeius, you well know, solely upon my account; as the dissensions which arose in the republic alienated him also from my colleague Metellus. But in both instances he preserved the dignity of his character, and never suffered himself to be betrayed into the least improper warmth of resentment.

Upon the whole, then, the first great caution in this commerce should be studiously to avoid all occasions of discord; but if any should necessarily arise, the next is to manage the quarrel with so much temper and moderation that the flame of friendship shall appear to have gently subsided, rather than to have been violently extinguished. But above all, whenever a dissension happens between the parties, they should be particularly on their guard against indulging a virulent animosity; as a spirit of this exasperated kind, when unrestrained, is apt to break forth into expressions of the most malevolent contumely and reproach. In a case of this nature, if the language should not be too insulting to be borne, it will be prudent in consideration of their former friendship to receive it without a return, for by this forbearance the reviler, and not the reviled, will appear the person that most deserves to be condemned.

The sure, and indeed the only sure, means to escape the several errors and inconveniences I have pointed out is, in the first place, "never hastily to engage in friendships;" and, in the next, "not to enter into them with those who are unworthy of the connection." Now, he alone is worthy whose personal merit, independent of all other considerations, renders him the just object of affection and esteem. Characters of this sort, it must be confessed, are extremely rare, as indeed every other species of excellence generally is, nothing being more uncommon than to meet with what is perfect in its kind in any subject whatsoever. But the misfortune is that the generality of the world have no conception of any other merit than what may be turned to interest. They love their friends upon the same principle, and in the same proportion, as they love their flocks and their herds; giving just so much of their regard to each as is equal to the profits they respectively produce.

Hence it is they are for ever strangers to the sweet complacencies of that generous amity which springs from those natural instincts originally impressed upon the human soul, and is simply desirable for its own abstracted and intrinsic value. To convince them, however, of the possible existence at least and powerful efficacy of an affection utterly void of all mercenary motives, they need only be referred to what passes in their own bosoms. For the love which every man bears to himself does not certainly flow from any expected recompense or reward, but solely from that pure and innate regard which each individual feels for his own person. Now, if the same kind of affection be not transferred into friendship, it will be in vain to hope for a true friend; as a true friend is no other in effect than a second self.

To these reflections we may add that if two distinct principles universally prevail throughout the whole animal creation, in the first place, that love of self which is common to every sensitive being, and, in the next, a certain degree of social affection, by which every individual of the same species is led to herd with its kind, how much more strongly has nature infused into the heart of man, together with a principle of self-love, this herding disposition! By the latter he is powerfully impelled not only to unite with his species in general, but to look out for some particular associate with whom he may be so intimately blended in sentiments and inclinations as to form, I had almost said, one soul in two bodies.

The generality of mankind are so unreasonable, not to say arrogant, as to require that their friends should be formed by a more perfect model than themselves are able or willing to imitate. Whereas the first endeavour should be to acquire yourself those moral excellences which constitute a virtuous character, and then to find an associate whose good qualities reflect back the true image of your own. Thus would the fair fabric of friendship be erected upon that immovable basis which I have so repeatedly recommended in the course of this inquiry. For what should endanger its stability when a mutual affection between the parties is blended with principles that raise them above those mean passions by which the greater part of the world are usually governed? Being equally actuated by a strong sense of justice and equity, they will at all times equally be zealous to exert their utmost powers in the service of each other, well assured that nothing will ever be required, on either side, inconsistent with the dictates of truth and honour. In consequence of these principles they will not only love, but revere each other. I say revere, for where reverence does not dwell with affection, amity is bereaved of her noblest and most graceful ornament.

It is an error, therefore, that leads to the most pernicious consequences to imagine that the laws of friendship supersede those of moral obligation, and justify a participation with licentiousness and debauchery. Nature has sown the seed of that social affection in the heart of man for purposes far different; not to produce confederates in vice, but auxiliaries in virtue. Solitary and sequestered virtue is indeed incapable of rising to the same height as when she acts in conjunction with an affectionate and animating companion of her generous efforts. They who are thus leagued in reciprocal support and encouragement of each other's moral ambition may be considered as setting out together in the best company and surest road towards those desirable objects in which nature has placed the supreme felicity of man. Yes, my friends, I will repeat it again. An amity ennobled by these exalted principles, and directed to these laudable purposes, leads to honour and to glory, and is productive, at the same time, of that sweet satisfaction and complacency of mind which, in conjunction with the two former, essentially constitute real happiness. He, therefore, who means to acquire these great and ultimate beatitudes of human life must receive them from the hands of Virtue; as neither friendship or aught else deservedly valuable can possibly be obtained without her influence and intervention. For they who persuade themselves that they may possess a true friend, at least, where moral merit has no share in producing the connection, will find themselves miserably deceived whenever some severe misfortune shall give them occasion to make the decisive experiment.

It is a maxim, then, which cannot too frequently nor too strongly be inculcated, that in forming the attachment we are speaking of " we should never suffer affection to take root in our hearts before judgement has time to interpose;" for in no circumstance of our lives can a hasty and inconsiderate choice be attended with more fatal consequences. But the folly is that we generally forbear to deliberate till consideration can nothing avail; and hence it is that after the association has been habitually formed, and many good offices perhaps have been mutually interchanged, some latent flaw becomes visible, and the union which was precipitately cemented is no less suddenly dissolved. Now this inattention is the more blameworthy and astonishing, as friendship is the only article among the different objects of human pursuit the value and importance of which is unanimously, and without any exception, acknowledged. I say the only article, for even Virtue herself is not universally held in esteem; and there are many who represent all her high pretensions as mere affectation and ostentatious parade. There are, too, whose moderate desires are satisfied with humble meals and lowly roofs, and who look upon riches with sovereign contempt. How many are there who think that those honours which inflame the ambition of others are of all human vanities the most frivolous! In like manner throughout all the rest of those several objects which divide the passions of mankind, what some admire others most heartily despise. Whereas, with respect to friendship, there are not two different opinions; the active and the ambitious, the retired and the contemplative, even the sensualist himself (if he would indulge his appetites with any degree of refinement) unanimously acknowledge that without friendship life can have no true enjoyment. She insinuates herself, indeed, by I know not what irresistible charm into the hearts of every rank and class of men, and mixes in all the various modes and arrangements of human life. Were there a man in the world of so morose and acrimonious a disposition as to shun (agreeably to what we are told of a certain Timon of Athens) all communication with his species, even such an odious misanthropist could not endure to be excluded from one associate, at least, before whom he might discharge the whole rancour and virulence of his heart. The truth is, if we could suppose ourselves transported by some divinity into a solitude replete with all the delicacies which the heart of man could desire, but secluded at the same time from every possible intercourse with our kind, there is not a person in the world of so unsocial and savage a temper as to be capable under these forlorn circumstances of relishing any enjoyment. Accordingly, nothing is more true than what Archytas of Tarentum, if I mistake not, is reported to have said, "That were a man to be carried up into heaven, and the beauties of universal nature displayed to his view, he would receive but little pleasure from the wonderful scene if there were none to whom he might relate the glories he had beheld." Human nature, indeed, is so constituted as to be incapable of lonely satisfactions; man, like those plants which are formed to embrace others, is led by an instinctive impulse to recline on his species, and he finds his happiest and most secure support in the arms of a faithful friend. But although in this instance, as in every other, Nature points out her tendencies by a variety of unambiguous notices, and proclaims her meaning in the most emphatical language, yet, I know not how it is, we seem strangely blind to her clearest signals, and deaf to her loudest voice!

The offices of friendship are so numerous, and of such different kinds, that many little disgusts may arise in the exercise of them, which a man of true good sense will either avoid, extenuate, or be contented to bear, as the nature and circumstances of the case may render most expedient. But there is one particular duty which may frequently occur, and which he will at all hazards of offence discharge, as it is never to be superseded consistently with the truth and fidelity he owes to the connection; I mean the duty of admonishing, and even reproving, his friend, an office which, whenever it is affectionately exercised, should be kindly received. It must be confessed, however, that the remark of my dramatic friend is too frequently verified, who observes in his *Andria* that "obsequiousness conciliates friends, but truth creates enemies." When truth proves the bane of friendship we may have reason, indeed, to be sorry for the unnatural consequence; but we should have cause to be more sorry if we suffered a friend by a culpable indulgence to expose his character to just reproach. Upon these delicate occasions, however, we should be particularly careful to deliver our advice or reproof without the least appearance of acrimony or insult. Let our obsequiousness (to repeat the significant expression of Terence) extend as far as gentleness of manners and the rules of good breeding require; but far let it be from seducing us to flatter either vice or misconduct, a meanness unworthy, not only of every man who claims to himself the title of friend, but of every liberal and ingenuous mind. Shall we live with a friend upon the same cautious terms we must submit to live with a tyrant? Desperate indeed must that man's moral disorders be who shuts his ears to the voice of truth when delivered by a sincere and affectionate monitor! It was a saying of Cato (and he had many that well deserve to be remembered) that "some men were more obliged to their inveterate enemies than to their complaisant friends, as they frequently heard the truth from the one, but never from the other;" in short, the great absurdity is that men are apt, in the instances under consideration, to direct both their dislike and their approbation to the wrong object. They hate the admonition, and love the vice; whereas they ought, on the contrary, to hate the vice, and love the admonition.

As nothing, therefore, is more suitable to the genius and spirit of true friendship than to give and receive advice—to give it, I mean, with freedom, but without rudeness, and to receive it not only without reluctance, but with patience—so nothing is more injurious to the connection than flattery, compliment, or adulation. I multiply these equivalent terms, in order to mark with stronger emphasis the detestable and dangerous character of those pretended friends, who, strangers to the dictates of truth, constantly hold the language which they are sure will be most acceptable. But if counterfeit appearances of every species are base and dishonest attempts to impose upon the judgement of the unwary, they are more peculiarly so in a commerce of amity, and absolutely repugnant to the vital principle of that sacred relation; for, without sincerity, friendship is a mere name, that has neither meaning nor efficacy. It is the essential property of this alliance to form so intimate a coalition between the parties that they seem to be actuated, as it were, by one common spirit; but it is impossible that this unity of mind should be produced when there is one of them in which it does not subsist even in his own person, who, with a duplicity of soul which sets him at perpetual variance from himself, assumes opposite sentiments and opinions, as is most convenient to his present purpose. Nothing in nature, indeed, is so pliant and versatile as the genius of a flatterer, who always acts and pretends to think in conformity, not only to the will and inclination, but even to the looks and countenances of another. Like Gnatho in the play, he can prevail with himself to say either yes or no, as best suits the occasion; and he lays it down as his general maxim, never to dissent from the company.

Terence exposes this baseness of soul in the person of a contemptible parasite; but how much more contemptible does it appear when exhibited in the conduct of one who dares usurp the name of friend! The mischief is that there are many Gnathos, of a much superior rank and consequence, to be met with in the commerce of the world; and it is from this class of flatterers that the greatest danger is to be apprehended, as the poison they administer receives additional strength and efficacy from the hand that conveys it. Nevertheless, a man of good sense and discernment, if he will exert the requisite attention, will always be able to distinguish the complaisant from the sincere friend, with the same certainty that he may in any other subject perceive the difference between the counterfeit and the genuine. It is observable in the general assemblies of the people, composed as they are of the most ignorant part of the community, that even the populace know how to discriminate the soothing insidious orator, whose only aim is to acquire popularity, from the firm, inflexible, and undesigning patriot. A remarkable instance of this kind lately appeared, when Caius Papirius proposed a law to enable the Tribunes, at the expiration of their office, to be re-elected for the ensuing year, upon which he employed every insinuating art of address to seduce and captivate the ears of the multitude. Not to mention the part I took myself upon that occasion, it was opposed by Scipio with such a commanding flow of eloquence, and invincible strength of reason, that this popular law was rejected by the very populace themselves. But you were present at the debate, and his speech is in everybody's hands. I cannot forbear giving you another instance likewise, although it is one particularly relating to myself. You may remember that in the consulate of Lucius Mancinus and Quintus Maximus, the brother of Scipio, a very popular law was moved by Caius Licinius, who proposed that the privilege of electing to the sacerdotal offices should be transferred from the respective colleges to the general assemblies of the people; and let me remark, by the way, it was upon this occasion that Licinius, in complaisance to the people, first introduced the practice of addressing them with his back turned upon the Senate-house. Nevertheless, the pious reverence which is due to every circumstance that concerns the worship of the immortal gods, together with the arguments by which I exposed the impropriety of his motion, prevailed over all the specious colourings of his plausible oratory. This affair was agitated during my Prætorship, and I was not chosen Consul till five years afterwards, so that it is evident I owed my success more to the force of truth than to the influence of station.

Now, if in popular assemblies, a scene, of all others, in which fiction and fallacious representations have the greatest scope, and are usually employed with the most success, Truth, when fairly stated and properly enforced, could thus prevail, with how much more reason may she expect to be favourably heard in an intercourse of friendship, the very essence whereof depends upon sincerity! In a commerce of this nature, indeed, if you are not permitted to see into the most hidden recesses of your friend's bosom, and do not with equal unreserve lay open to him the full exposure of your own, there can be no just ground for confidence on either side, nor even sufficient evidence that any affection subsists between you. With respect, however, to that particular deviation from truth which is the object of our present consideration, it must be acknowledged that, noxious as flattery is, no man was ever infected by it who did not love and encourage the offering. Accordingly, there is no turn of mind so liable to be tainted by this sort of poison as a disposition to entertain too high conceit of one's own merit. I must confess, at the same time, that conscious virtue cannot be void of self-esteem, as well knowing her own worth, and how amiable her form appears. But the pretenders to virtue are much more numerous than the really virtuous, and it is of the former only that I am now speaking. Men of that character are particularly delighted with adulation, as confirming their title, they imagine, to the merit they so vainly claim.

It appears then that genuine friendship cannot possibly exist where one of the parties is unwilling to hear truth and the other is equally indisposed to speak it. Friends of this kind are by no means uncommon in the world, and, indeed, there would be neither propriety nor humour in the character of a parasite as exhibited by our comic writers, were a vain-glorious soldier, for example, never to be met with in real life. When the braggart captain in the play asks Gnatho, " Did Thais return me many thanks, say you? " An artless man would have thought it sufficient to answer " many," but the cunning sycophant replies, " immense, innumerable;" for a skilful flatterer perfectly well knows that a pleasing circumstance can never be too much exaggerated in the opinion of the person upon whom he means to practise.

But although flattery chiefly operates on those whose vanity encourages and invites the exercise of it, yet these are not the only sort of men upon whom it may impose. There is a delicate and refined species of adulation, against which even better understandings may not improperly be cautioned. Gross and open obsequiousness can deceive none but fools, but there is a latent and more ensnaring manner of insinuation, against which a man of sense ought to be particularly on his guard. A flatterer of this insidious and concealed kind will frequently gain his point even by opposition; he will affect to maintain opinions which he does not hold, and dispute in order to give you the credit of a victory. But nothing is more humiliating than to be thus egregiously duped. It is necessary, therefore, to exert the utmost attention against falling into these covert snares, lest we should have reason to say, with one of the characters in the *Heiress*, "Never was old dotard on the stage so finely played upon as I have been by you to-day." This, indeed, would be to exhibit the mortifying personage of one of those ridiculous old men in our comedies, who listen with easy faith to every specious tale contrived to impose on their credulity. But I have insensibly wandered from the principal object I had in view, and instead of proceeding to consider Friendship as it appears in perfect characters (perfect, I mean, as far as is consistent with the frailty of human nature), I am talking of it as it is seen in the vain and frivolous connections of the world. I return therefore to the original subject of our conversation, and which it is now time to draw towards a conclusion.

It is virtue, yes, let me repeat it again, it is virtue alone that can give birth, strength, and permanency to friendship. For virtue is a uniform and steady principle ever acting consistently with itself. They whose souls are warmed by its generous flame not only improve their common ardour by communication, but naturally kindle into that pure affection of the heart towards each other which is distinguished by the name of amity, and is wholly unmixed with every kind and degree of selfish considerations. But although genuine friendship is solely the offspring of pure goodwill, and no

motive of advantage or utility has the least share in its pro-
duction, yet many very beneficial consequences result from
it, how little soever those consequences are the objects
primarily in view. Of this disinterested nature was that
affection which, in the earlier season of my life, united me
with those venerable old men, Paulus, Cato, and Gallus, as
also with Nasica and Gracchus, the father-in-law of my late
honoured and lamented friend. That the principle I have
assigned is really the leading motive of true friendship
becomes still more evident when the connection is formed
between men of equal years, as in that which subsisted
between Scipio, Furius, Rupilius, Mummius, and myself.
Not that old men may not also find a generous satisfaction
in living upon terms of disinterested intimacy with the young,
as I have the happiness to experience in the friendship I
enjoy, not only with both of you and Q. Tubero, but even
with Publius Rutilius and Aulus Virginius, who are much
your juniors. One would wish, indeed, to preserve those
friends through all the successive periods of our days with
whom we first set out together in this our journey through
the world. But since man holds all his possessions by a very
precarious and uncertain tenure we should endeavour, as our
old friends drop off, to repair their loss by new acquisitions,
lest one should be so unhappy as to stand in his old age a
solitary, unconnected individual, bereaved of every person
whom he loves and by whom he is beloved. For without a
proper and particular object upon which to exercise the kind
and benevolent affections, life is destitute of every enjoyment
that can render it justly desirable.

As to the loss I have myself sustained by the death of
Scipio, who was so suddenly and so unexpectedly snatched
from me, he is still present in my mind's eye, and present he
will ever remain; for it was his virtues that endeared him to
my heart, and his virtues can never die. But not by me
only, who had the happiness to enjoy a daily intercourse
with them, will they be held in perpetual remembrance; his
name will be mentioned with honour to the latest posterity,
and no man will hereafter either meditate or execute any
great and laudable achievement without proposing to himself
the conduct of Scipio as his brightest and most animating
exemplar. For myself, among all the blessings for which I
am indebted either to nature or to fortune, there is not one

upon which I set so high a value as the friendship in which I lived with Scipio. In him I found a constant associate in public affairs, a faithful counsellor in private life, and upon all occasions the confidential friend from whom my soul received her truest and most solid satisfactions. I am not conscious of ever having given him even the slightest cause of offence; and sure I am that I never heard a word proceed from his lips which I had reason to be sorry he had uttered. We not only lived under the same roof, and ate at the same frugal table, but advanced together through the several military services; and even in our travels, as well as during our recess into the country, we were constant and inseparable companions—not to mention that we were equally animated with the same ardent love of science, and jointly passed every hour of our privacy and leisure in one common pursuit of useful knowledge. If the power of recollecting these pleasing circumstances had become extinct in me at the same time that he expired, it would have been impossible that I could have supported the loss of a man whom I so tenderly loved, and with whom I was so intimately united; but they are indelibly stamped upon my mind, and the oftener they recur to my thoughts the more lively is the impression they leave behind them. But, were I totally deprived of these soothing reflections, my age, however, would afford me great consolation, as I cannot, by the common course of nature, long be separated from him, and short pains, how severe soever they may prove, may well be endured.

I have thus laid before you all that occurs to me on the subject concerning which you desired my sentiments. Let me only again exhort you to be well persuaded that there can be no real friendship which is not founded upon virtuous principles, nor any acquisition, virtue alone excepted, preferable to a true friend.

CATO

OR, AN ESSAY ON OLD AGE

To TITUS POMPONIUS ATTICUS.

> Ah, could my numbers charm thy anxious breast
> And lull the sorrows of thy soul to rest;
> Would'st thou not deem the poet's lenient lay
> More worth than sums of countless gold could pay?

FOR well may I address you, my friend, in those lines of the honest bard,

> Far less for wealth than probity renowned,

with which he opens his poem inscribed to Flamininus. I am sensible at the same time that when the poet adds,

> Each rising sun beholds thy ceaseless grief,
> And night returning brings thee no relief.

he holds a language by no means applicable to you. I perfectly well know the moderation and equanimity you possess; and that you have derived from Athens, not only an honourable addition to your name, but that calm and philosophic spirit which so peculiarly distinguishes your character. Nevertheless, I have reason to believe that the present unpleasing posture of public affairs sometimes interrupts your tranquillity of mind; as it frequently, I confess, discomposes my own. But it is not my present purpose to offer you any consolation upon that subject: the case requires a very powerful application; and I will reserve what I have to say upon it to some future opportunity. My design at this time is only to communicate to you a few reflections concerning Old Age: the infirmities whereof we are now beginning to feel, or at least are advancing fast towards them: and I am desirous of rendering the burthen as easy as possible to you and to myself. I am well convinced indeed that as you have hitherto borne its weight, so you will continue to support its increasing pressure, with the same good sense and composure of mind which you have so happily discovered upon every other important occasion. However, having resolved to publish some reflections upon the subject, I determined to address them to you, who have a peculiar claim to this pledge of my affection: and it is a present to which we may both of us have recourse with equal advantage. For myself, at least, the considerations I now lay before you have had so happy an effect on my own mind, as not only to reconcile me to all the inconveniences of old age, but to render it even an agreeable state to me.

Can we sufficiently then express our sense of the obligations we owe to philosophy, who thus instructs her disciples how to pass through every successive period of human life with equal satisfaction and complacency? The advantages to be derived from her precepts, in other important situations, is a topic upon which I have frequently had occasion to expatiate, and shall often perhaps resume: but in the papers I now send you, my purpose is to consider those advantages with respect only to our declining years. To have put these reflections into the mouth of an imaginary character, like the Tithonus of Aristo, would have made but little impression upon the reader: in order therefore to give them the greater force, I have represented them as delivered by the venerable Cato. To this end I have introduced Scipio and Laelius, as expressing to him their admiration of the wonderful ease with which he supported his old age: and this gives him occasion to enter into a full explanation of his ideas upon the subject. If you should think that he discovers, in this conversation, a richer vein of literature than appears in his own compositions, you must impute it to the acquaintance he afterwards made with the Greek authors, whose language and philosophy, it is well known, he passionately studied in the latter end of his long life. I have only to add, that in delivering the sentiments of Cato, I desire to be understood as fully declaring my own.

Scipio.—I have frequently, Cato, joined with our friend Laelius, in admiring that consummate wisdom and virtue, which upon all occasions so eminently distinguishes your character; but particularly, in that singular ease and cheerfulness with which you seem to bear up under those years which are pressing upon you. I could never observe that they are attended with the least inconvenience to you: whereas the generality of men, at your time of life, usually complain of old age as the heaviest and most insupportable of burthens.

CATO.—There is nothing, my friends, in the circumstance you have remarked, that can justly, I think, deserve your admiration. Those indeed who have no internal resource of happiness, will find themselves uneasy in every stage of human life: but to him who is accustomed to derive all his felicity from within himself, no state will appear as a real evil into which he is conducted by the common and regular course of nature. Now this is peculiarly the case with respect to old age: yet such is the inconsistency of human folly, that the very period which at a distance is every man's warmest wish to attain, no sooner arrives than it is equally the object of his lamentations. It is usual with men at this season of life to complain that old age has stolen upon them by surprise, and much sooner than they expected. But if they were deceived by their own false calculations, must not the blame rest wholly on themselves? For, in the first place, old age surely does not gain by swifter and more imperceptible steps on manhood, than manhood advances on youth; and in the next, in what respect would age have sitten less heavily upon them, had its progress been much slower, and, instead of making his visit at fourscore years, it had not reached them till four hundred? For the years that are elapsed, how numerous soever they may have been, can by no means console a weak and frivolous mind under the usual consequences of long life. If I have any claim therefore to that wisdom which you tell me, my friends, you have often admired in my character (and which I can only wish indeed were worthy of the opinion you entertain of it, and the appellation the world has conferred upon me), it consists wholly in this, that I follow nature as the surest guide, and resign myself with an implicit obedience to all her sacred ordinances. Now it cannot be supposed that nature, after having wisely distributed to all the preceding periods of life their peculiar and proper enjoyments, should have neglected, like an indolent poet, the last act of the human drama, and left it destitute of suitable advantages. Nevertheless, it was impossible but that in the life of man, as in the fruits of the earth, there should be a certain point of maturity, beyond which the marks of decay must necessarily appear: and to this unavoidable condition of his present being, every wise and good man will submit with a contented and cheerful acquiescence. For to entertain desires repugnant to the universal law of our existence; what is it, my friends, but to wage war, like the impious giants, with the gods themselves?

LAELIUS.—You will confer, then, a very acceptable service on both of us, Cato (for I will venture to answer for my friend Scipio as well as for myself), if you will mark out to us by what means we may most effectually be enabled to support the load of incumbent years. For although we are at present far distant from old age, we have reason, however, to expect—at least to hope—that it is a period we shall live to attain.

CATO.—Most willingly, Laelius, I yield to your request, especially as you assure me that my compliance will be equally agreeable to both of you.

SCIPIO.—Yes, my venerable friend; like travellers who mean to take the same long journey you have gone before us, we should be glad (if it be not imposing too much trouble upon you) that you would give us some account of the advanced stage at which you are now arrived.

CATO.—I am ready, Scipio, to the best of my power, to give you the information you desire. And, indeed, I am the more qualified for the task you assign me, as I have always (agreeably to the old proverb) associated much with men of my own years. This has given me frequent opportunities of being acquainted with their grievances; and I particularly remember to have often heard Caius Salinator and Spurius Albinus (men of consular rank and nearly of the same age as myself) bewail their condition. The principal subject of their complaint was, in the first place, that they were no longer capable of enjoying the sensual gratifications without which, in their estimation, life was of no value; and in the next, that they found themselves neglected by those who had formerly paid their court to them with the greatest attention. But they imputed their grievances, I think, to a wrong cause. For had they arisen merely from the circumstance of their age, they would have been common to myself, and to every other man of the same advanced years. But the fact is much otherwise; and I have known many, at that period of life, who passed their time without the least repining—who neither regretted that they were released from the dominion of their passions, nor had reason to think themselves treated with disrespect by any of their connections. In fact, the true grievance, in all complaints of this kind, lies in the man and not in the age. They whose desires are properly regulated, and who have nothing morose or petulant in their temper and manners, will find old age, to say the least of it, is a state very easily to be endured, whereas unsubdued passions and a froward disposition will equally embitter every season of human life.

LAELIUS.—Your observations, Cato, are undoubtedly just. Yet some, perhaps, may be apt to say, that your ample possessions, together with the power and influence of your rank and character, have very much contributed to soften the inconveniences of old age, and render it more than usually easy to you, but that these are advantages which cannot possibly fall to the lot of many.

CATO.—I must acknowledge that the circumstances you mention have some beneficial influence, but I can by no means admit that the whole depends upon them. When a certain native of the paltry island of Seriphos told Themistocles, in an altercation which arose between them, that he was indebted for the lustre of his fame not to the intrinsic splendour of his actions, but to the country in which he had the good fortune to be born. "It may be so," replied the Athenian general, "for if I had received my birth at Seriphos, I could have had no opportunity of producing my talents; but give me leave to tell you, that yours would never have made a figure though you had been born in Athens." The same sentiment is justly applicable to the case in question; for although it must be confessed that old age, under the pressure of extreme indigence, cannot possibly prove an easy state, not even to a wise and virtuous mind, yet without those essential qualities it must necessarily prove the reverse, although it should be accompanied with every external advantage. Believe me, my young friends, the best and surest guard against the inconveniences of old age, is to cultivate in each preceding period the principles of moral science, and uniformly to exercise those virtues it prescribes. The good seeds which you shall thus have sown in the former

seasons of life will, in the winter of your days, be wonderfully
productive of the noblest and most valuable fruit—valuable
not only as a possession which will remain with you even to
your latest moments (though, indeed, that circumstance
alone is a very considerable recommendation), but also as a
conscious retrospect on a long life marked with an uninterrupted series of laudable and beneficent actions affords a
perpetual source of the sweetest and most exquisite satisfaction.

When I was very young I conceived as strong an affection
for Quintus Maximus (the celebrated General who recovered
Tarentum) as if we had been of equal years. There was a
dignity in the deportment of this excellent old man, which
was tempered with singular politeness and affability of
manners, and time had wrought no sort of alteration in his
amiable qualities. He was not, it is true, at a time of life
which could properly be called infirm age when I first began
to cultivate his friendship; but he was certainly, however,
advanced in years, for I was not born till the year before his
first consulate. In his fourth, I served a very young man in
the army he commanded at Capua; and five years afterwards I was his Quæstor at Tarentum. From that post
I succeeded to the Edileship; and four years after, in the
consulate of Tuditanus and Cethegus, I was chosen Prætor.
It was at this period that, by the advice and eloquence of my
venerable friend, who was now become extremely old, the
Cincian law concerning donatives was enacted. This great
man led our troops to battle in his old age with as much spirit
as if he had been in the prime and vigour of life; and when
Hannibal, with all the gaiety of a youthful conqueror, was
exulting in the success of his arms, he gave a check to his
victories by a cool and patient perseverance in avoiding
a general engagement. It is to this part of his judicious
conduct that those famous lines of my friend Ennius
allude:—

> 'Twas his to save the State by wise delay,
> Regardless what the censuring world might say.
> Time proves the merit of the glorious deed,
> His fame still rising as the years succeed.

How wonderful was the judgement he displayed, and the
vigilance he exerted, in retaking the city of Tarentum! I
remember when Salinator (who, after having been driven by

the besiegers from the city, retired to the citadel) was boasting to Maximus, in my presence, that it was by his means he regained possession of the town. "Very true," replied Maximus, with a smile; "for if *you* had not lost it, I certainly could never have recovered it." Nor were his spirit and abilities more conspicuous as a soldier than a statesman. In his second consulship, when C. Flaminius, in direct opposition to the authority of the Senate, was dividing among the soldiers the conquered lands in the provinces of Gaul and Picentia, he had the courage singly, and unsupported by his colleague Carvilius, to withstand, as far as it was possible, the popular measures of that factious tribune. And even when he was Augur, he had the honest boldness, upon a particular occasion, openly to declare that "every omen ought to be considered as favourable or inauspicious, as the interest of the State determined."

But there is no trait among the many shining qualities which adorned this great man's character that I observed with warmer admiration than the fortitude with which he supported the death of his illustrious son. The funeral oration he pronounced upon that affecting occasion is in everybody's hands; and which of the philosophers, I will venture to ask, does not sink in our esteem after the perusing of this admirable performance? The truth is, it was not solely in the conspicuous paths of the world, and when he was acting in the public view, that this excellent man was truly great; he appeared still greater in the private and domestic scenes of life. How pleasing and instructive was his conversation! how profound his knowledge of antiquity! how deep his skill in the laws and institutions concerning augury! To which I may add, that he was better acquainted with the Grecian literature than is usual for a Roman. His memory, too, was so remarkably faithful, that there was not a single event of any note that had happened in the wars, either with our neighbours in Italy or with the more distant nations, with which he was not perfectly well acquainted. In short, from my first connection with him, I as eagerly embraced every opportunity of enjoying his society as if I had then presaged, what the event has verified, that after his death I should never again meet with so wise and informing a companion.

I have entered thus minutely into the character and conduct of Maximus, in order to convince you that it would be an affront to virtue to suppose that old age, to a man endowed with such principles and dispositions, could possibly have been a state of infelicity. It must be acknowledged, at the same time, that it is not in every one's power to be a Maximus or a Scipio; to enliven the gloom of declining years by the animating recollection of the towns he has taken, the battles he has won, and the triumphs that have honoured his successful arms. But it is not the great and splendid actions of the hero or the statesman alone that lead to an easy and agreeable old age; that season of life may prove equally placid and serene to him who hath passed all his days in the silent and retired paths of elegant and learned leisure. Of this kind, we are told, was the old age of Plato, who continued to employ himself with great satisfaction in his philosophical studies, till death put an end to them in his eighty-first year. Such, too, was that of Isocrates, who is said to have composed his famous discourse, intituled "Panathenaicus," in the ninety-fourth year of his age, and his death did not happen till five years afterwards. His preceptor, Leontinus Gorgias, lived to complete his one hundred and seventh year, continuing his studies with undiminished spirit and application to his last moments. This celebrated veteran being asked, Why he did not put an end to such a tedious length of life? "Because," said he, "I find no reason to complain of old age"—an answer truly noble, and altogether worthy of a philosopher! They whose conduct has not been governed by the principles of wisdom and virtue are apt to impute to old age those infirmities for which their former irregularities are alone accountable. Far different were the sentiments of Ennius, whom I just now had occasion to quote; he compares his declining years to those of a generous steed:

> Who victor oft in famed Olympia's fields,
> To sweet repose his age-worn members yields.

You are not too young, my friend, to remember the person of this veteran poet, for his death happened so late as the consulate of Caepio and Philippus, which is not more than nineteen years ago. And let me observe, by the way, notwithstanding I was at that time full sixty-five years of age, I spoke in defence of the Voconian law with great exertion of voice and vehemence of action. But I was going to remark that this venerable bard, who lived to seventy, bore up under age and indigence with such wonderful cheerfulness and good humour, that one would almost have imagined he derived even a satisfaction from those circumstances which the generality of mankind look upon, of all others, as the most dispiriting and oppressive.

When I consider the several causes which are usually supposed to constitute the infelicity of old age, they may be reduced, I think, under four general articles. It is alleged that " it incapacitates a man for acting in the affairs of the world," that " it produces great infirmities of body," that " it disqualifies him for the enjoyment of the sensual gratifications," and that " it brings him within the immediate verge of death." Let us therefore, if you please, examine the force and validity of each of these particular charges.

" Old age," it seems, " disqualifies us from taking an active part in the great scenes of business." But in what scenes? let me ask. If in those which require the strength and vivacity of youth, I readily admit the charge. But are there no other; none which are peculiarly appropriated to the evening of life, and which, being executed by the powers of the mind, are perfectly consistent with a less vigorous state of body? Did Quintus Maximus, then, pass the latter end of his long life in total inactivity? Tell me, Scipio, was your father, and my son's father-in-law, the excellent Lucius Paulus, were the Fabricii, the Curii, and the Coruncanii, utterly bereaved of all useful energy when they supported the interests of the Republic by the wisdom of their counsels and the influence of their respectable authority? Appius Claudius was not only old, but blind, when he remonstrated in the Senate with so much force and spirit against concluding a peace with Pyrrhus, to which the majority of the members appeared strongly inclined. And upon this occasion it was that he broke forth into those animated expostulations which Ennius has introduced into his poem:—

> Shall folly now that honoured Council sway,
> Where sacred wisdom wont to point the way?

together with the rest of those spirited lines with which you are no doubt well acquainted. This celebrated harangue, which is still extant, Appius delivered seventeen years after his second consulate, between which and his first there was an interval of ten years, and prior to both he had exercised the office of Censor. It is evident, therefore, that he must have been a very old man at the time of the Pyrrhic war. And, indeed, the tradition received from our forefathers has always represented him as such.

It appears, therefore, that nothing can be more void of foundation than to assert that old age necessarily disqualifies a man for the great affairs of the world. As well might it be affirmed that the pilot is totally useless and unengaged in the business of the ship, because while the rest of the crew are more actively employed in their respective departments, he sits quietly at the helm and directs its motions. If in the great scenes of business an old man cannot perform a part which requires the force and energy of vigorous years, he can act, however, in a nobler and more important character. It is not by exertions of corporal strength and activity that the momentous affairs of state are conducted; it is by cool deliberation, by prudent counsel, and by that authoritative influence which ever attends on public esteem, qualifications which are so far from being impaired, that they are usually strengthened and improved by increase of years. And in this opinion, my noble friends, I am persuaded I shall have your concurrence, unless, peradventure, you look upon me as an useless and idle member of the commonwealth, because after having regularly passed through the several gradations of military service, from the private soldier to the commander-in-chief, and been concerned in each of those capacities in a variety of engagements, both by sea and land, I now no longer lead forth our armies to battle. But if I forbear to enter personally into the fatigues of war, I represent to the Senate its most proper object, and point out in what manner the operations may best be carried on. In short, I am perpetually urging the expediency of declaring war against the Carthaginians, in order to anticipate them in those hostilities which they have long been meditating against us. As in truth I shall never cease to be apprehensive of that commonwealth till it shall no longer have any existence. And may the glory of extirpating that insidious State be reserved, Scipio, for your arms, that you may have the honour of accomplishing the great work which your illustrious ancestor so happily began! Thirty-three years have now elapsed since the death of that great man, but his virtues are still fresh on the minds of his fellow-citizens, and will be had in honourable remembrance throughout all generations. His death happened the year before I was elected Censor, and nine years after his second consulate, in which office he was chosen my colleague. But had the life of this excellent man been extended even through a whole century, can it be imagined that he would have considered the closing period of such honourable days as a state to be regretted? For it was not agility in the robust and manly exercises, or skill and prowess in the management of arms, it was his judgement, his counsel, and his authority alone which he would then have had occasion to display. If abilities of this latter kind were not the peculiar attributes of old age, our wise ancestors would not surely have distinguished the supreme Council of the State by the appellation of Senate. The Lacedaemonians, for the same reason, give to the first magistrates in their commonwealth the title of Elders. And, in fact, they are always chosen out of that class of men.

If you look into the history of foreign nations you will find frequent instances of flourishing communities, which, after having been well-nigh ruined by the impetuous measures of young and unexperienced statesmen, have been restored to their former glory by the prudent administration of more discreet years. "Tell me," says one of the personages in that dramatic piece of Naevius, called the *School*, addressing himself to a citizen of a certain Republic, "tell me whence it happened that so considerable a State as yours has thus suddenly fallen to decay?" The person questioned assigns several reasons, but the principal is "that a swarm of rash, unpractised young orators had unhappily broken forth and taken the lead among them." Temerity, indeed, is the usual characteristic of youth, as prudence is of old age.

But it is farther urged "that old age impairs the memory." This effect, I confess, it may probably have on those memories which were originally infirm, or whose native vigour has not been preserved by a proper exercise. But is there any reason to suppose that Themistocles, who had so strong a memory that he knew the name of every citizen in the commonwealth, lost his retentive power as his years increased, and addressed Aristides, for instance, by the appellation of Lysimachus? For my own part, I still perfectly well recollect the names, not only of all our principal citizens now living, but of their ancestors also. And I am so little apprehensive of injuring this faculty (as is vulgarly believed) by the perusing of sepulchral inscriptions, that, on the contrary, I find them of singular service in recalling to my mind those persons whom death hath long since removed from the world. In fact, I never yet heard of any veteran whose memory was so weakened by time as to forget where he had concealed his treasure. The aged, indeed, seem to be at no loss in remembering whatever is the principal object of their attention, and few there are at that period of life who cannot readily call to mind what recognisances they have entered into, or with whom they have had any pecuniary transactions. Innumerable instances of a strong memory in advanced years might be produced from among our celebrated lawyers, pontiffs, augurs, and philosophers; for the faculties of the mind will preserve their powers in old age, unless they are suffered to lose their energy and become languid for want of due cultivation. And the truth of this observation may be confirmed not only by those examples I have mentioned from the more active and splendid stations of the world, but from instances equally frequent to be met with in the paths of studious and retired life. Sophocles continued in extreme old age to write tragedies. As he seemed to neglect his family affairs whilst he was wholly intent on his dramatic compositions, his sons instituted a suit against him in a court of judicature, suggesting that his understanding was impaired, and praying that he might be removed from the management of his estate; agreeably to a custom which prevails likewise in our own country, where if a father of a family by imprudent conduct is ruining his fortunes, the magistrate commonly interposes and takes the administration out of his hands. It is said that when the old bard appeared in court upon this occasion he desired that he might be permitted to read a play which he had lately finished, and which he then held in his hand; it was his *Oedipus in Colonos*. His request being granted, after he had finished the recital he appealed to the judges whether they could discover in his performance any symptoms of an insane mind? And the result was that the court unanimously dismissed the complainants' petition.

Did length of days weaken the powers of Homer, Hesiod, or Simonides, of Stesichorus, Isocrates, or Gorgias? Did old age interrupt the studies of those first and most distinguished of the Greek philosophers, Pythagoras or Democritus, Plato or Xenocrates? or, to descend into later times, did grey hairs prove an obstacle to the philosophic pursuits of Zeno, Cleanthes, or that famous stoic whom you may remember to have seen in Rome, the venerable Diogenes? On the contrary, did not all of these eminent persons persevere in their respective studies with unbroken spirit to the last moment of their extended lives?

But not to enter farther into the consideration of old age in respect to the nobler and more exalted application of the human faculties, I could name among my friends and neighbours in the country several men far advanced in life who employ themselves with so much industry and activity in the business of agriculture that they never suffer any of the more important articles of their husbandry to be carried on when they are not themselves present to supervise and direct the work. I will acknowledge, at the same time, that these spirited labours of the persons I allude to are not perhaps a matter of much wonder with regard to those objects of tillage which are sown and reaped within the year, as no man is so far advanced in age as not to flatter himself that he may at least survive to enjoy the benefit of the next harvest. But those rural veterans I am speaking of are occupied also in branches of husbandry, from which they are sure that they themselves cannot possibly live to derive the least advantage:—

> The future shade for times unborn they raise,

as my friend Caecilius expresses it in his play called *The Youthful Companions*. Agreeably to this generous principle, the oldest husbandman when he is asked, " to what purpose he lays out his labours in the business of planting? " may well reply, " In obedience to the immortal gods, by whose bountiful providence as I received these fields from my ancestors, so it is their will that I should deliver them down with improvement to posterity."

The poet's sentiment in the verse I just now repeated is far more just than in those lines he afterwards adds:—

> Severe the doom that length of days impose!
> To stand sad witness of unnumbered woes,
> Ah, had old age no other ills in store,
> Too well might man its dire approach deplore;

for if long life may occasion our being the painful spectators

of many calamities which an earlier death would have
concealed from our view, it may equally afford us the satisfaction of seeing many happy events which could not otherwise have come within our notice. Not to mention that
disagreeable scenes will unavoidably occur to the young no
less than to the old. But the observation of my dramatic
friend is still more unwarrantable when he farther declares
that:—

> Of all the ills which drooping eld await,
> 'Tis sure the worst to stand the scorn, or hate,
> Of happier years.

Why should he suppose that old age necessarily lays us
open to a mortification of this kind? As men of good sense
in the evening of life are generally fond of associating with
the younger part of the world, and when they discover in
them the marks of an amiable disposition, find a sort of
alleviation of their infirmities in gaining their affection and
esteem; so, on the other hand, well-inclined young men
think themselves equally happy to be conducted into the
paths of knowledge and virtue by the guidance and instruction of experienced age. For my own part, at least,
I have reason to believe that my company is not less acceptable to you, my youthful friends, than yours most assuredly
is to me.

But to resume the particular point under consideration.
It appears that old age is so far from being necessarily a
state of languor and inactivity that it generally continues
to exert itself in that sort of occupation which was the
favourite object of its pursuit in more vigorous years. I
will add that instances might be produced of men who in
this period of life have successfully applied themselves even
to the acquisition of some art or science to which they were
before entirely strangers. Thus Solon, in one of his poems
written when he was advanced in years, glories that " he
learnt something every day he lived." And old as I myself
am, it is but lately that I acquired a knowledge of the Greek
language, to which I applied with the more zeal and diligence,
as I had long entertained an earnest desire of becoming
acquainted with the writings and characters of those excellent men to whose examples I have occasionally appealed
in the course of our present conversation. Thus Socrates,
too, in his old age learnt to play upon the lyre, an art which

the ancients did not deem unworthy of their application. If I have not followed the philosopher's example in this instance (which, indeed, I very much regret), I have spared, however, no pains to make myself master of the Greek language and learning.

The next imputation thrown upon old age is, that " it impairs our strength," and it must be acknowledged the charge is not altogether without foundation. But, for my part, I no more regret the want of that vigour which I possessed in my youth, than I lamented in my youth that I was not endowed with the force of a bull or an elephant. It is sufficient if we exert with spirit, upon every proper occasion, that degree of strength which still remains with us. Nothing can be more truly contemptible than a circumstance which is related concerning the famous Milo of Crotona. This man, when he was become old, observing a set of athletic combatants that were exercising themselves in the public circus: " Alas! " said he, bursting into a flood of tears and stretching forth his arm, " alas! these muscles are now totally relaxed and impotent." Frivolous old man; it was not so much the debility of thy body as the weakness of thy mind thou hadst reason to lament, as it was by the force of mere animal prowess, and not by those superior excellences which truly ennoble man, that thou hadst rendered thy name famous. Never, I am well persuaded, did a lamentation of this unworthy kind escape the mouth of Coruncanius, or Aelius, or the late Publius Crassus; men whose consummate abilities in the science of jurisprudence were generously laid out for the common benefit of their fellow-citizens, and whose superior strength of understanding continued in all its force and vigour to the conclusion of their numerous years.

It must be confessed, however, that the powers of an orator (as his function cannot be successfully executed by the force of genius alone, but requires great exertion, likewise, both of voice and gesture) must necessarily become languid and enfeebled by age. Nevertheless, there is a certain sweetness of utterance which, I know not how, is not subject to be impaired by years, and this melody of voice (old as you see I am) I may venture to say I have not yet lost. There is, indeed, a species of calm and composed elocution extremely graceful and perfectly well adapted to advanced years, and I have frequently observed an eloquent old man captivate the attention of his audience by the charms of this soft and milder tone of delivery. But if age should render the orator unequal even to this less laborious application of his talents, they may still be usefully exerted. They may be employed in forming young men of genius (yourself, for instance, Scipio, or our friend Laelius) to a nervous and manly eloquence. And can there be a more pleasing satisfaction to an old man, than to see himself surrounded by a circle of ingenuous youths, and to conciliate by these laudable means their well-merited esteem and affection? It will not, I suppose, be denied that old age has at least a sufficient degree of strength remaining to train the rising generation and instruct them in every duty to which they may hereafter be called, and there cannot, certainly, be a more important or a more honourable occupation. Accordingly, I have always thought it a very considerable happiness to your relations, Cneus and Publius Scipio, together with your two grandfathers, Lucius Aemilius and Publius Africanus, that they were usually accompanied by a train of young nobles, who attended them for the advantage of their instructions. Indeed there is a satisfaction in communicating useful knowledge of every kind, which must render any man happy, how much soever time may have impaired the powers of his body, who employs the talents of his mind to so noble and beneficial a purpose.

But after all, this imbecility of body is more frequently occasioned by the irregularities of youth, than by the natural and unavoidable consequences of long life. A debauched and intemperate young man will undoubtedly, if he live, transmit weakness and infirmities to his latter days. The virtuous Cyrus, in the discourse which Xenophon relates he held when he lay on his death-bed, and which happened at a very late period of life, declares he had never perceived that his old age had been attended with any sensible decay. I perfectly well remember Lucius Metellus when I was a boy. Four years after his second consulate he was chosen chief pontiff, and he presided two and twenty years in the sacred college. This venerable personage preserved such a florid old age to his last moments as to have no reason to lament the depredations of time. If I were to mention myself as an instance of the same kind, it would be only taking an old man's allowed privilege. Homer, you know, represents Nestor, although his years had extended even to the third generation, as frequently boasting of his extraordinary prowess. And, indeed, he might well be indulged in the vanity of being the hero of his own true tale; for, as the poet sings—

Words sweet as honey from his lips distilled.

And let me remark by the way, that in order to pour forth this mellifluous and persuasive eloquence great strength of body was by no means necessary; so much otherwise, that the celebrated general of the Grecian forces never wishes for ten Ajaxes, but for ten such officers as Nestor, to be secure of soon laying the walls of Troy level with the ground.

But I was going to observe that I am now in my eighty-fourth year, and I wish I had reason to boast with Cyrus that I feel no sensible decay of strength. But although I do not possess it in the same degree as when I made my first campaign in the Carthaginian war, in the course of which I was advanced to the rank of questor; or when, during my consulship, I commanded the army in Spain; or when four years afterwards I was military tribune at the battle of Thermopylae; yet I can with truth, you see, affirm that old age has not totally relaxed my nerves and subdued my native vigour. My strength has not yet been found to fail me, either in the Senate or the assemblies of the people, when my country or my friends, my clients or my hosts, have had occasion to require my service. The truth is I have never governed myself by the cautious maxim of that ancient proverb so frequently quoted, which says, " You must be old soon if you would be old long;" on the contrary, I would rather abate some years from that season of my life than prematurely anticipate its arrival. In consequence of this principle I have hitherto been always open to access whenever any person desired to be introduced to me for my advice or assistance in his affairs.

But you will tell me, perhaps, that my strength is much inferior to yours. Undoubtedly it is, and so is yours to that of Pontius the athletic centurion, but is he therefore a more valuable man? A moderate degree of force is sufficient for all the rational purposes of life, and whoever will not attempt to exert his particular portion farther than he is well able, will assuredly have no great cause to regret that he is not endued with a more considerable share. Milo is said to have walked the full length of the course at the Olympic games bearing the whole enormous weight of an ox upon his shoulders. Now tell me which would you choose to possess —this man's extraordinary powers of body or the sublime genius of Pythagoras? In a word, my friends, make a good use of your youthful vigour so long as it remains, but never let it cost you a sigh when age shall have withdrawn it from you; as reasonably, indeed, might youth regret the loss of infancy or manhood the extinction of youth. Nature conducts us, by a regular and insensible progression, through the different seasons of human life, to each of which she has annexed its proper and distinguishing characteristic. As imbecility is the attribute of infancy, ardour of youth, and gravity of manhood, so declining age has its essential properties, which gradually disclose themselves as years increase.

I am persuaded, Scipio, I need not tell you what extraordinary things that ancient host of your ancestors, Massinissa, is still capable of performing. You have heard, no doubt, that although he is at this time ninety years of age, he takes long journeys, sometimes on foot and sometimes on horseback, without once relieving himself throughout the whole way by alternately changing from the one mode of travelling to the other; that he is so exceedingly hardy, that no severity of weather, when he is abroad, can induce him to cover his head; and that having preserved by these means a thin and active habit of body, he still retains sufficient strength and spirits for discharging in person the several functions of his royal station. I particularise these circumstances as a proof, that by temperance and exercise a man may secure to his old age no inconsiderable degree of his former spirit and activity.

If it must be acknowledged that time will inevitably undermine the strength of man, it must equally be acknowledged that old age is a season of life in which great vigour is by no means required. Accordingly, by the laws and institutions of our country, we who are advanced to a certain age are excused from those offices which demand robust powers to discharge. Far from being compelled to undertake what is beyond our force, we are not called upon to exert our strength even to its full extent. If it be alleged that there are numberless old men so totally worn out and decayed, as to be incapable of every kind of civil or social duty, it must be confessed there are; but may not this debility have arisen from an original weakness of constitution? a misfortune by no means peculiar to old age, but common to every period of human life. How great a valetudinarian was that son of Scipio Africanus, who adopted you for his heir; so great indeed, that he scarcely ever enjoyed a day of uninterrupted health. Had he been formed with a less delicate constitution he would have shone forth a second luminary of the Commonwealth, for with all the spirit and magnanimity of his illustrious father he possessed a more improved and cultivated understanding. What wonder then if age is sometimes oppressed with those infirmities from which youth, we see, is by no means secure!

As to those effects which are the necessary and natural evils attendant on long life, it imports us to counteract their progress by a constant and resolute opposition, and to combat the infirmities of old age as we would resist the approaches of a disease. To this end we should be regularly attentive to the article of health, use moderate exercise, and neither eat nor drink more than is necessary for repairing our strength, without oppressing the organs of digestion. Nor is this all: the intellectual faculties must likewise be assisted by proper care, as well as those of the body. For the powers of the body, like the flame in the lamp, will become languid and extinct by time, if not duly and regularly recruited. Indeed the mind and body equally thrive by a suitable exertion of their powers; with this difference, however, that bodily exercise ends in fatigue, whereas the mind is never wearied by its activity. When Caecilius therefore represents certain veterans as " fit subjects for the comic muse," he alludes only to those weak and credulous old doting mortals, whose infirmities of mind are not so much the natural effect of their years as the consequence of suffering their faculties to lie dormant and unexerted in a slothful and spiritless inactivity. The fact in short is plainly this: as irregular indulgences of the amorous passions, although a vice to which youth is in general more prone than age, is a vice, however, with which those young men alone are infected who are unrestrained by principles of virtue; so that species of delirium which is called dotage, is not a common weakness incident to every old man in general, but to those only who have trifled away their frivolous days in idleness and folly. In support of this observation I will instance the venerable Appius. His family consisted of four sons, who were arrived at the state of manhood, and five daughters, together with a numerous train of clients and dependants; yet, far advanced as he was in years, and totally deprived of his sight, he would not commit the management of this very considerable household to any other hands than his own. And he was abundantly equal to the important charge, having kept the spring and energy of his mind in constant action, nor suffered himself tamely to sink down under the weight of incumbent years. In consequence of this spirited conduct he maintained a more than parental authority over his family; his commands were obeyed as so many imperial mandates. In fine, feared by his servants, reverenced by his children, and endeared to all, he exhibited in his house a striking specimen of that simplicity and good order, which so eminently distinguished the domestic economy of our forefathers. Age is truly respectable in the man who thus guards himself from becoming the property of others, vindicates his just rights, and maintains his proper authority to the last moments of his life.

As I love to see the fire of youth somewhat tempered with the gravity of age, so I am equally pleased when I observe the phlegm of age somewhat enlivened with the vivacity of youth; and whoever unites these two qualities in his character, may bear, indeed, the marks of years in his body, but will never discover the same traces in his mind. In pursuance of this maxim, I am now employed in adding a seventh book to my antiquities; in collecting all the ancient records I can meet with that relate to my subject; in finishing a revisal of the speeches I made in the several important causes in which I have been engaged; as also in drawing up some observations concerning the augural, pontifical, and civil law. And in order to exercise my memory, I practise the advice of the Pythagorean philosophers, by recalling to my mind every night all that I have said, or done, or heard, the preceding day. These are the employments by which I keep the faculties of my understanding in play, and preserve them in due vigour: employments in which I have little reason surely to lament the want of mere animal strength. Nor are my occupations wholly confined to those of a sedentary nature:

on the contrary, I not only assist my friends in the courts of judicature, but frequently too, uncalled upon, attend the senate, where I propose such measures for the consideration of that assembly as I have previously weighed and duly matured in my own thoughts. And these I support, not indeed by strength of voice and power of lungs, but by the better force of reason and argument. But were I so worn down by age as to be incapable of exerting myself in the manner I have mentioned, yet one satisfaction nevertheless would still remain with me; the satisfaction of meditating on these subjects as I lay on my couch, and of performing in imagination what I could no longer execute in reality. Thanks, however, to that regular and temperate course of life I have ever led, I am still capable of taking an active part in these public scenes of business. In fine, he who fills up every hour of his life in such kind of labours and pursuits as those I have mentioned, will insensibly slide into old age without perceiving its arrival; and his powers, instead of being suddenly and prematurely extinguished, will gradually decline by the gentle and natural effect of accumulated years.

Let us now proceed to examine the third article of complaint against old age, as " bereaving us," it seems, " of the sensual gratifications." Happy effect indeed, if it deliver us from those snares which allure youth into some of the worst vices to which that age is addicted. Suffer me upon this occasion, my excellent young friends, to acquaint you with the substance of a discourse which was held many years since by that illustrious philosopher Archytas, of Tarentum, as it was related to me when I was a young man in the army of Quintus Maximus, at the siege of that city. "Nature," said this illustrious sage, " has not conferred on mankind a more dangerous present than those pleasures which attend the sensual indulgences; as the passions they excite are too apt to run away with reason, in a lawless and unbridled pursuit of their respective enjoyments. It is in order to gratify inclinations of this ensnaring kind that men are tempted to hold clandestine correspondence with the enemies of the state, to subvert governments, and turn traitors to their country. In short, there is no sort of crimes that affect the public welfare to which an inordinate love of the sensual pleasures may not directly lead. And as to vices of a more private

tendency—rapes, adulteries and every other flagitious violation of the moral duties—are they not perpetrated solely
from this single motive? Reason, on the other hand," continued Archytas, " is the noblest gift which God, or nature,
has bestowed on the sons of men. Now nothing is so great
an enemy to that divine endowment, as the pleasures of sense.
For neither temperance, nor any other of the more exalted
virtues, can find a place in that breast which is under the
dominion of the voluptuous passions. Imagine to yourself
a man in the actual enjoyment of the highest gratification
that his animal nature is capable of receiving; there can be
no doubt that during his continuance in that state, it would
be utterly impossible for him to exert any one power of his
rational faculties." From hence our philosopher inferred
" that the voluptuous enjoyments are attended with a quality
of the most noxious and destructive kind; since, in proportion to their strength and duration, they darken or extinguish every brighter faculty of the human soul."

Archytas expressed these sentiments in a conversation
with Caius Pontius, father of that famous Samnite commander who obtained a victory over the consuls Spurius
Postumius and Titus Veturius, at the battle of Caudium:
and it was related to me by our faithful ally, and my very
worthy host, Nearchus, of Tarentum. My friend assured
me he received this account by tradition from his ancestors:
and he added, that Plato was a party in this conversation.
This circumstance is indeed by no means improbable; as I
find that philosopher visited Tarentum in the consulate of
Lucius Camillus and Appius Claudius.

The inference I mean to draw from the authority I have
cited is, that if the principles of reason and virtue have not
been sufficient to inspire us with a proper contempt for the
sensual pleasures, we have cause to hold ourselves much
obliged to old age at least, for weaning us from those appetites
which it would ill become us to gratify. For the voluptuous
passions are utter enemies to all the nobler faculties of the
soul; cast a mist, if I may so express it, before the eye of
reason, and hold no sort of commerce or communion with the
manly virtues.

To illustrate the truth of this assertion by a particular
instance, I will mention a fact concerning Lucius Flamininus,
who was brother to that brave commander Titus Flamininus.

It was with much regret that seven years after he had been raised to the dignity of consul, I found myself under the necessity of expelling him from the senate; but I thought his scandalous debaucheries ought not to pass without marks of public disgrace. This unworthy man when he commanded, during his consulship, our army in Gaul, was prevailed upon by his pathic at an entertainment, to put to death one of the prisoners who were in confinement for a capital offence; and this infamous act escaped with impunity during the time that his brother Titus was censor. But when I succeeded him in that office, neither myself nor my colleague Flaccus, could by any means be induced to think that so wanton and flagitious an instance of abandoned cruelty and lewdness ought to pass without severe and distinguished animadversion; especially as it reflected dishonour, not only on the base perpetrator himself, but in some measure too on the high office with which he was invested.

I have frequently heard from some of my friends who were much my seniors, a traditionary anecdote concerning Fabricius. They assured me, that in the early part of their lives they were told by certain very old men of their acquaintance, that when Fabricius was ambassador at the court of Pyrrhus, he expressed great astonishment at the account given him by Cineas, of a philosopher at Athens (for a philosopher, it seems, he styled himself), who maintained that the love of pleasure was universally the leading motive of all human actions. My informers added that when Fabricius related this fact to Marcus Curius and Titus Coruncanius, they both joined in wishing that Pyrrhus and the whole Samnite nation might become converts to this extraordinary doctrine, as the people who were infected with such unmanly principles could not fail, they thought, of proving an easy conquest to their enemies. Marcus Curius had been intimately connected with Publius Decius, who in his fourth consulate (which was five years before the former entered upon that office) gloriously sacrificed his life to the preservation of his country. This generous patriot was personally known likewise both to Fabricius and Coruncanius, and they were convinced by what they experienced in their own breasts, as well as from the illustrious example of Decius, that there is in certain actions a natural grace and beauty that captivate by their intrinsic charms; and which, with a noble contempt of what the world calls *pleasure*, every great and generous mind will ardently and invariably pursue.

I have dwelt the longer upon this article, in order to convince you, that the little relish which old age leaves us for enjoyments of the sensual kind, in so far from being a just imputation on this period of life, that on the contrary it very considerably raises its value. If age render us incapable of taking an equal share in the flowing cups, and luxuriant dishes of splendid tables, it secures us too from their unhappy consequences—from painful indigestions, restless nights, and disordered reason. Accordingly, the divine Plato justly represents pleasure as the bait by which vice ensnares and captivates her deluded votaries. But if this enticement cannot always be resisted, if the palate must sometimes be indulged, I do not scruple to say that an old man, although his years will guard him from excess, is by no means excluded from enjoying, in a moderate degree, the convivial gratifications. I remember frequently to have seen, when I was a boy, that illustrious commander who obtained our first naval victory over the Carthaginians, the venerable Duilius, returning from evening entertainments of this festive kind, preceded by a considerable number of flambeaux and instruments of music. He seemed particularly fond of being distinguished by such a pompous and splendid train; and indeed he is the first instance of a man not invested with a public character, that ventured to appear with this sort of ostentatious parade, a privilege, however, which in consideration of his heroic achievements, he might well be allowed to assume.

But to pass from the practice of others to my own, I will acknowledge that I always took a singular satisfaction in frequenting the meetings of those little societies which are known by the name of confraternities, and which were first instituted when I was quaestor, on occasion of the statue of Cybele being received into our public worship. At the return of these anniversary assemblies I used to partake with my brethren of the society in their festive meals—never to excess, indeed; but, however, with a certain freedom natural to the gay spirits which usually animate that period of life, and which gradually subside as more serious years advance. But the principal satisfaction I received from these entertainments arose much less from the pleasures of the palate than from the opportunity they afforded me of enjoying the company and conversation of a very large circle of my friends. Agreeably to this way of thinking our ancestors distinguished these kinds of amicable feasts by the name of convivial banquets, as being chiefly calculated for the more rational purposes of social and friendly intercourse; whereas the Greeks denominate them by a term expressive merely of eating and drinking, as if those two articles, which ought to be considered as the least and lowest objects of the meeting, were first and principal in their estimation. For my own part, I receive so much pleasure from those hours which are thus devoted to cheerful discourse, that I love to prolong my meals, not only when the company is composed of men of my own years (few of which, indeed, are now remaining), but when it chiefly consists of such young persons as yourselves; and I acknowledge my obligations to old age for having increased my passion for the pleasures of conversation at the same time that it has abated it for those which depend solely on the palate. I would not, however, be thought so professed an enemy to the latter as to deny that, within certain limits, they may very reasonably, perhaps, be indulged; and I declare, for the satisfaction of those who are unwilling to part with this kind of gratifications, that I do not find old age is a disqualification for the enjoyment of them. On the contrary, I take delight in joining those social parties where, agreeably to a good old custom instituted by our ancestors, a president of the club is appointed, and am much diverted to hear him deliver out his important edicts. I rejoice, too, in those moderate and refreshing cups which Socrates recommends in Xenophon's Banquet, and am well pleased with those artificial methods of cooling, or warming the wine, as the different seasons of the year invite. Even when I am in the country among my Sabine neighbours I allow myself the same kind of indulgences, as I every day add one to the number of their evening societies, which we generally lengthen out by a variety of amusing conversation till the night is far advanced.

If it be farther objected " that the pleasures of the senses are not so exquisite in old age as in youth," my answer is that neither is the inclination towards them equally strong; and certainly there can be no loss where there is no desire. Sophocles, when he was become old, being asked if he engaged in amorous commerce with the fair sex? " Heaven forbid! "

replied the venerable bard; "and glad I am to have made my escape from the tyranny of so imperious a passion." The truth is, to be deprived of enjoyments of this kind may be an uneasy state perhaps to those who are stimulated by warm desires; but where the passion is sufficiently subdued and extinguished, the privation is more eligible than the fruition—if, indeed, one can properly be said to be deprived of a pleasure who is utterly void of all inclination towards it. I maintain, therefore, that there is more satisfaction in being delivered from the dominion of this passion than in its highest gratification.

If it must be admitted that in the fine season of life the soul receives a stronger and more exquisite impression from the pleasures of the senses, it will also be admitted, in the first place, that these pleasures are in themselves but of little value; and in the next, that notwithstanding old age cannot enjoy them in their utmost extent and perfection, yet it is not absolutely, however, excluded from them. If a spectator who sits in the first row of the theatre enters more thoroughly into the beauties of Turpio's acting than he who is placed in the remotest ranks, the latter, nevertheless, is not totally debarred from all share in the entertainment. In the same manner, if youth holds a less obstructed communication with the sensual gratifications than the circumstances of age will admit, an old man, though not equally, perhaps, affected with delight, feels at least as quick a relish of them as is necessary to content his more subdued desires.

But whatever may be the condition of old age with respect to the instances I have been examining, inestimable surely are its advantages if we contemplate it in another point of view; if we consider it as delivering us from the tyranny of lust and ambition, from the angry and contentious passions, from every inordinate and irrational desire—in a word, as teaching us to retire within ourselves, and look for happiness in our own bosoms; if to these moral benefits naturally resulting from length of days be added that sweet food of the mind which is gathered in the fields of science, I know not any season of life that is passed more agreeably than the learned leisure of a virtuous old age.

It was thus, Scipio, that your father's intimate friend, Caius Gallus, employed himself to the very last moments of his long life; and I saw him expire, I had almost said, in measuring the distances of the heavenly orbs, and determining the dimensions of this our earth. How often has the sun risen upon his astronomical meditations? how frequently has the night overtaken him in the same elevated studies! And with what delight did he amuse himself in predicting to us, long before they happened, the several lunar and solar eclipses! Other ingenious applications of the mind there likewise are—though of a lighter nature, indeed—which may greatly contribute to enliven and amuse the concluding scene of human life. Thus Naevius in composing his poem on the Carthaginian war, and Plautus in writing his two last comedies, filled up the leisure of their latter days with wonderful complacency and satisfaction. I can affirm the same of our dramatic poet, Livius, whom I remember to have seen in his old age, for although the first play he brought upon the stage was in the consulate of Cento and Tuditanus, six years before I was born, yet his death did not happen till I was nearly arrived at manhood. To those venerable personages whom I have already named, I might add Licinius Crassus, celebrated for his consummate skill in the pontifical and civil laws of his country, as also Publius Scipio, who very lately, you know, was elected chief pontiff. These, together with every one of the rest whom I have mentioned, I saw in the last period of life pursuing their respective studies with the utmost ardour and alacrity. But let me not forget to add to this memorable list the example of Marcus Cethegus, whom Ennius justly styled the "soul of eloquence," and whom I likewise saw in his old age exercising even his oratorical talents with uncommon force and vivacity.

Tell me now, can the gay amusements of the theatre, the splendid luxuries of the table, or the soft blandishments of a mistress, supply their votaries with enjoyments that may fairly stand in competition with these calm delights of the intellectual pleasures? pleasures which, in a mind rightly formed and properly cultivated, never fail to improve and gather strength with years. What Solon, therefore, declares in the verse I just now cited, that he "learnt something in his old age every day he lived," is much to his honour; as, indeed, to be continually advancing in the paths of knowledge is one of the most pleasing satisfactions of the human mind.

From the pleasures which attend a studious old age, let

us turn our view to those which at that season of life may be received from country occupations, of which I profess myself a warm admirer. These are pleasures perfectly consistent with every degree of advanced years, as they approach the nearest of all others to those of the purely philosophical kind; they are derived from observing the nature and properties of this our earth, which yields a ready obedience to the cultivator's industry, and returns with interest whatever he deposits in her charge; if not always, indeed, with equal increase, yet always with some.

But the profit arising from this principle of fertility is by no means, in my estimation, the most desirable circumstance of the farmer's labours. I am principally delighted with observing the power, and tracing the process, of Nature in these her vegetable productions. Thus when the ground is sufficiently broken and prepared, the seedsman disseminates the grain, which is afterwards harrowed into the bosom of the earth, by the vital warmth and moisture of which it is gradually expanded and pushed forth into the green blade; this blade shoots up into a knotted stem, which is nourished and supported by the various fibres of the root. The stem terminates in the ear, wherein the grain is lodged in regular order, and defended from the depredations of the smaller birds by a number of little bearded spikes. And let me add (for I take great pleasure in bringing you acquainted with every article that contributes to soothe and alleviate my bending years) that I am particularly entertained with marking the growth of the vine, and following it in its progress from the seed-plot to its perfect maturity. Not to enlarge on that wonderful power with which Nature has endowed every species of the vegetable kingdom—of continuing their several kinds by their respective seeds, and which from the smallest grain, as the fig, or from little stones, as the vine, most amazingly swell into large trunks and branches—not to dwell, I say, on this method of generation common to all the various tribes of plants on the face of the earth, is it possible to observe the different modes of propagating the vine by suckers, by layers, by the root, or by slips, without being affected with the most pleasing admiration? This shrub, which by its form is a trailing plant, must necessarily creep upon the ground, unless it be supported, for this reason: Nature has furnished it with little tendrils, which serve as a sort of claws to lay hold of whatever stands within its reach, in order to raise itself into a more erect posture. And here the art of the husbandman is required to check its luxuriant growth, to train the irregular and depending shoots, and to prevent them, by a judicious pruning, from running into wood. After the vines have undergone this autumnal dressing they push forth in spring from the joints of the remaining branches little buds, which are distinguished by the name of gems. From this gem the future grapes take their rise, which gradually increase in size by the nourishment they draw from the earth, in conjunction with the genial warmth of the sun. At their first appearance they are extremely bitter, but in process of time, and when duly matured, they acquire a most sweet and delicious flavour. In the meanwhile, being covered and guarded by the leaves, they receive a moderate degree of heat without being too much exposed to the solar rays.

There cannot, surely, be a landscape more pleasing to the eye, as well as more profitable to the owner, than a plantation of this kind. It is not, however, as I have already declared, the utility resulting from this species of agriculture with which I am principally charmed; the mere cultivation itself of this generous plant, and the observing of its nature and properties, abstracted from all considerations of emolument, afford me a most amusing occupation; in short, every circumstance that relates to the management of this useful shrub, the regular arrangement of the vine props, the forming of them into arcades, the pruning some of the branches, and fixing layers of others, are employments in which I take much delight. To this I may add the cutting of proper channels for supplying the plantation with water, the stirring of the earth round their roots, and the trenching of the ground— works which are in themselves extremely entertaining, and which greatly contribute at the same time to ameliorate and fertilise the soil. As to the advantage of manure (an article which Hesiod has not taken the least notice of in his poem on husbandry), I have sufficiently explained my sentiments in the treatise I formerly published on the same subject. Homer, however (who flourished, I am inclined to think, many ages before Hesiod), in that part of the *Odyssey* where he represents Laertes as diverting his melancholy for the absence of Ulysses by cultivating his little farm, particularly mentions the circumstance of his manuring it with compost.

But the amusement of farming is not confined to one species of agriculture alone, to the cultivation of vineyards or woodlands, of arable or meadow grounds; the orchard, the kitchen-garden, and the parterre contribute also to diversify its pleasures—not to mention the feeding of cattle and the rearing of bees. And besides the entertainment which arises from planting, I may add the method of propagating trees by the means of engrafting, an art which is one of the most ingenious improvements, I think, that ever was made in the business of horticulture.

I might proceed to point out many other pleasing articles of rural occupations, if I were not sensible that I have already been too prolix. But if the love I bear to this agreeable art, together with that talkative disposition which is incident to my time of life (for I would not appear so partial to old age as to vindicate it from all the infirmities with which it is charged)—if I have dwelt longer, I say, upon this subject than was necessary, I rely, my friends, on your indulgence for a pardon. Suffer me, however, to add that Manius Curius, after having conquered the Samnites, the Sabines, and even Pyrrhus himself, passed the honourable remainder of his declining years in cultivating his farm. The villa in which he lived is situated at no great distance from my own, and I can never behold it without reflecting, with the highest degree of admiration, both on the singular moderation of his mind and the general simplicity of the age in which he flourished. Here it was, while sitting by his fireside, that he nobly rejected a considerable quantity of gold which was offered to him on the part of the Samnites, and rejected it with this memorable saying, " that he placed his glory not in the abundance of his own wealth, but in commanding those among whom it abounded." Can it be doubted that a mind raised and ennobled by such just and generous sentiments must render old age a state full of complacency and satisfaction?

But not to wander from that scene of life in which I am myself more particularly concerned, let us return to our farmers. In those good days I am speaking of, the members of the senate, who were always men advanced in years, were called forth from their fields as often as the affairs of the state demanded their assistance. Thus Cincinnatus was following his plough, when notice was brought to him that he was created Dictator. It was during his exercise of this high office that his master of the horse, Servilius Ahala, in consequence of the spirited orders he received from the Dictator, seized upon Spurius Maelius, and instantly put him to death before he had time to execute his traitorous purpose of usurping the reins of government. Curius, too, and all the rest of the venerable senators of that age, constantly resided at their villas. For which reason a particular officer was appointed (called a courier, from the nature of his employment) whose business it was to give them notice when there was a meeting of the senate.

Now tell me, my friends, could the old age of these respectable patriots, who thus amused their latter years in cultivating their lands, be justly deemed a state of infelicity? In my opinion, indeed, no kind of occupation is more pregnant with happiness; not only as the business of husbandry is of singular utility to mankind in general, but as being attended also (to repeat what I have already observed) with peculiar and very considerable pleasures. I will add, too, as a farther recommendation of rural employment (and I mention it in order to be restored to the good graces of the voluptuous) that it supplies both the table and the altar with the greatest variety and abundance. Accordingly, the magazines of the skilful and industrious farmer are plentifully stored with wine and oil, with milk, cheese, and honey, as his yards abound with poultry, and his fields with flocks and herds of kids, lambs, and porkets. The garden also furnishes him with an additional source of delicacies; in allusion to which the farmers pleasantly call a certain piece of ground allotted to that particular use their dessert. I must not omit, likewise, that in the intervals of their more important business, and in order to heighten the relish of the rest, the sports of the field claim a share in the variety of their amusements.

I might expatiate on the beauties of their verdant groves and meadows, on the charming landscape that their vineyards and their olive-yards present to view; but to say all in one word, there cannot be a more pleasing nor a more profitable scene than that of a well-cultivated farm. Now old age is so far from being an obstacle to enjoyments of this kind that, on the contrary, it rather invites and allures us to the fruition of them. For where, let me ask, can a man in that last stage of life more easily find the comforts in winter of a warm sun or a good fire? or the benefit in summer of cooling shades and refreshing streams?

In respect to the peculiar articles of rural diversions, let those of a more firm and vigorous age enjoy the robust sports which are suitable to that season of life; let them exert their manly strength and address in darting the javelin, or contending in the race; in wielding the bat, or throwing the ball; in riding, or in swimming; but let them, out of the abundance of their many other recreations, resign to us old fellows the sedentary games of chance. Yet if they think proper even in these to reserve to themselves an exclusive right, I shall not controvert their claim; they are amusements by no means essential to a philosophic old age.

The writings of Xenophon abound with a variety of the most useful observations; and I am persuaded it is altogether unnecessary to recommend them to your careful perusal. In his treatise entitled "Oeconomics," with what a flow of eloquence does he break forth in praise of agriculture! an art above all others, you will observe, which he deemed worthy of a monarch's attention. In view to this, he introduces Socrates informing his friend Critobulus, that when Lysander of Lacedaemon, a man of great and eminent virtues, was deputed by the confederate states to the Court of Sardis with their respective presents to the younger Cyrus, that great prince, no less distinguished by his genius than by the glory of his reign, received him in the most gracious manner; and, among other instances of affability, conducted him to an enclosure laid out with consummate skill and judgement. Lysander, stricken with the height and regularity of the trees, the neatness of the walks and borders, together with the beauty and fragrance of the several shrubs and flowers, expressed great admiration not only at the industry, but the genius that was discovered in the scene he was surveying; upon which the prince assured him that the whole was laid out by himself, and that many of the trees were even planted by his own hand. Lysander, astonished at this declaration from the mouth of a monarch whom he beheld arrayed in all the splendour of Persian magnificence, replied with emotion, "O, Cyrus, I am now convinced that you are really as happy as report has represented you; since your good fortune is no less eminent than your exalted virtues."

The good fortune to which Lysander alluded is an article of felicity to which old age is by no means an obstacle; as the pleasure resulting from every rational application of the intellectual faculties, but particularly from the study of husbandry, is consistent even with its latest period. Accordingly tradition informs us that Valerius Corvus, who lived to the age of a hundred, spent the latter part of his long life in the cultivation and improvement of his farm. It is remarkable of this celebrated person that no less than forty-six years intervened between his first and his last consulship, so that his career of honours was equal to that period which our ancestors marked out for the commencement of old age. But his felicity did not terminate with his retiring from public affairs; on the contrary, he was in one respect at least even happier in the latter part of his life than when he filled the first offices of the state; as his great age, at the same time that it exempted him from the fatigue of bearing an active part in the administration of the commonwealth, added weight and influence to his general credit and authority.

The crown and glory of grey hairs is, indeed, that kind of authority which thus arises from a respectable old age. How considerable did this appear in those venerable personages—Caecilius Metellus and Attilius Calatinus! You remember, no doubt, the singular and celebrated eulogy inscribed on the monument of the latter: that " All nations agreed in esteeming him as the first of Romans." The influence he maintained over his fellow-citizens was certainly founded upon the most unquestionable claim, since his merit was thus universally acknowledged and admired. To the instances already mentioned, I might add our late chief pontiff Publius Crassus, together with Marcus Lepidus, who succeeded him in that dignity. And, if it were necessary, I might enlarge this illustrious list with the revered names of Paulus Aemilius, Scipio Africanus, and Fabius Maximus, the latter of whom I have already taken occasion to mention with peculiar esteem. These were all of them men of such approved and respected characters, that even their very nod alone carried with it irresistible authority. In a word, that general deference which is ever paid to a wise and good old man, especially if his virtues have been dignified by the public honours of his country, affords a truer and more solid satisfaction than all the pleasures which attend on the gay season of life.

But let it be remembered, my noble friends, that when I speak thus advantageously of that portion of life we are now considering, I would be understood to mean only that respectable old age which stands supported on the firm foundation of a well-spent youth. Agreeably to this principle, I once declared upon a public occasion that " miserable indeed must that old man be whose former life stood in need of an apology "—a sentiment which, I had the satisfaction to observe, was received by the whole audience with uncommon applause. It is not merely wrinkles and grey hairs which can command that authoritative veneration of which I have been speaking. He alone shall taste this sweet fruit of revered age, whose former years have been distinguished by an uniform series of laudable and meritorious actions.

But besides those more important advantages I have already pointed out as attending an honourable old age, it may be further observed that there are certain customary deferences and attentions which, although they may be considered perhaps as common and insignificant ceremonials, are undoubtedly, however, very honourable marks of general respect. Observances of this kind are strictly practised in our own country, as indeed they likewise are in every other, in proportion to its advancement in civilised and polished manners. It is said that Lysander, whom I just now took occasion to mention, used frequently to remark that Lacedaemon, of all the cities he knew, was the most eligible for an old man's residence; and it must be acknowledged there is no place in the world where age is treated with so much civility and regard. Accordingly it is reported that a certain Athenian, far advanced in years, coming into the theatre at Athens when it was extremely crowded, not one of his countrymen had the good manners to make room for him; but when he approached that part of the theatre which was appropriated to the Lacedaemonian ambassadors, they every one of them rose up and offered him a place among them. Repeated claps of applause immediately ensued from the whole assembly; upon which one of the spectators remarked, " that the Athenians understood politeness much better than they practised it."

There are many excellent rules established in the Sacred College of which I am a member; one of these, as it relates to the particular circumstance immediately under consideration, I cannot forbear mentioning. Every augur delivers his opinion upon any question in debate according to his seniority in point of years; and he takes precedence of all the younger members, even although they should be in the highest degree his superiors in point of rank.

And now I will venture once more to ask if there is a pleasure in any of the mere sensual gratifications which can equal the satisfaction arising from these valuable privileges thus conferred on old age? To which I will only add that he who knows how to enjoy these honourable distinctions with suitable dignity to the conclusion of his days, may be considered as having supported his part on the great theatre of the world with uniform spirit and propriety, and not, like an unpractised player, to have disgracefully failed in the last finishing act of the drama.

I shall be told, perhaps, that if we look into the world, we shall find " petulance, moroseness, and even avarice itself are infirmities which generally break out and discover themselves in old age." But the fact is, these moral diseases of the mind are rather the constitutional imperfections of the man in whom they reside, than necessary defects inseparable from the wane of life. Indeed, this peevishness of temper may—I will not say be justified—but certainly at least in some measure excused from that suspicion which old men are too apt to entertain of their being generally marked by the younger part of the world as objects of their scorn and derision. Add to this, that where the constitution is broken and worn out, the mind becomes the more sensible of every little offence, and is disposed to magnify unintentional slights into real and designed insults. But this captious and irritable disposition incident to this season of life may be much softened and subdued in a mind actuated by the principles of good manners and improved by liberal accomplishments. Examples of this kind must have occurred to every man's experience of the world, as they are frequently exhibited also on the stage. What a striking contrast, for instance, between the two old men in Terence's play called *The Brothers !* Mitio is all mildness and good humour; whereas Demea, on the contrary, is represented as an absolute churl. The fact, in short, is plainly this: as it is not every kind of wine, so neither is it every sort of temper, that turns sour by age. But I must observe at the same time there is a certain gravity of deportment extremely becoming in advanced years, and which, as in other virtues, when it preserves its proper bounds, and does not degenerate into an acerbity of manners, I very much approve. As to avarice, it is inconceivable for what purpose that passion should find admittance into an old man's breast. For surely nothing can be more irrational and absurd than to increase our provision for the road, the nearer we approach to our journey's end.

It remains only to consider the fourth and last imputation on that period of life at which I am arrived. "Old age, it seems, must necessarily be a state of much anxiety and disquietude, from the near approach of death." That the hour of dissolution cannot possibly be far distant from an old man is most undoubtedly certain; but unhappy indeed must he be, if in so long a course of years he has yet to learn that there is nothing in that circumstance which can reasonably alarm his fears. On the contrary, it is an event either utterly to be disregarded, if it extinguish the soul's existence, or much to be wished, if it convey her to some region where she shall continue to exist for ever. One of those two consequences must necessarily ensue the disunion of the soul and body, there is no other possible alternative. What then have I to fear, if after death I shall either not be miserable, or shall certainly be happy? But after all, is there any man, how young soever he may be, who can be so weak as to promise himself, with confidence, that he shall live even till night? In fact, young people are more exposed to mortal accidents than even the aged. They are also not only more liable to natural diseases, but, as they are generally attacked by them in a more violent manner, are obliged to obtain their cure, if they happen to recover, by a more painful course of medical operations. Hence it is that there are but few among mankind who arrive at old age; and this (to remark it by the way) will suggest a reason why the affairs of the world are no better conducted. For age brings along with it experience, discretion, and judgement; without which, no well-formed government could have been established, or can be maintained. But not to wander from the point under our present consideration, why should death be deemed an evil peculiarly impending on old age, when daily experience proves that it is common to every other period of human life? Of this truth, both you and I, Scipio, have a very severe conviction in our respective families: in yours, by the premature decease of your two brothers, who had given their friends a most promising earnest that their merit would one day raise them to the highest honours of the state; and in mine, by the loss of my truly excellent son.

It will be replied, perhaps, that "youth may at least entertain the hope of enjoying many additional years; whereas an old man cannot rationally encourage so pleasing an expectation." But is it not a mark of extreme weakness to rely upon precarious contingencies, and to consider an event as absolutely to take place, which is altogether doubtful and uncertain? But admitting that the young may indulge this expectation with the highest reason, still the advantage evidently lies on the side of the old; as the latter is already in possession of that length of life which the former can only hope to attain. "Length of life," did I say? Good gods! what is there in the utmost extent of human duration that can properly be called long, even if our days should prove as numerous as those of Arganthonius, the king of the Tartessi, who reigned, as history tells us, eighty years, and lived to the age of a hundred and twenty? In my own opinion, indeed, no portion of time can justly be deemed long that will necessarily have an end, since the longest, when once it is elapsed, leaves not a trace behind, and nothing valuable remains with us but the conscious satisfaction of having employed it well. Thus, hours and days, months and years glide imperceptibly away—the past never to return, the future involved in impenetrable obscurity. But whatever the extent of our present duration may prove, a wise and good man ought to be contented with the allotted measure, remembering that it is in life as on the stage, where it is not necessary in order to be approved, that the actor's part should continue to the conclusion of the drama; it is sufficient, in whatever scene he shall make his final exit, that he supports the character assigned him with deserved applause. The truth is, a small portion of time is abundantly adequate to the purposes of honour and virtue. But should our years continue to be multiplied, a wise man will no more lament his entrance into old age than the husbandman regrets, when the bloom and fragrancy of the spring is passed away, that summer or autumn is arrived. Youth is the vernal season of life, and the blossoms it then puts forth are indications of those future fruits which are to be gathered in the succeeding periods. Now the proper fruit to be gathered in the winter of our days is, as I have repeatedly observed, to be able to look back with self-approving satisfaction on the happy and abundant produce of more active years.

But to resume the principal point we were discussing. Every event agreeable to the course of nature ought to be looked upon as a real good, and surely none can be more natural than for an old man to die. It is true, youth likewise stands exposed to the same dissolution, but it is a dissolution contrary to Nature's evident intentions, and in direct opposition to her strongest efforts. In the latter instance, the privation of life may be resembled to a fire forcibly extinguished by a deluge of water; in the former, to a fire spontaneously and gradually going out from a total consumption of its fuel. Or to have recourse to another illustration, as fruit before it is ripe cannot, without some degree of force, be separated from the stalk, but drops of itself when perfectly mature, so the disunion of the soul and body is effected in the young by dint of violence, but is wrought in the old by a mere fulness and completion of years. This ripeness for death I perceive in myself, with much satisfaction; and I look forward to my dissolution as to a secure haven, where I shall at length find a happy repose from the fatigues of a long voyage.

Every stage of human life, except the last, is marked out by certain and defined limits; old age alone has no precise and determinate boundary. It may well therefore be sustained to any period, how far soever it may be extended, provided a man is capable of performing those offices which are suited to this season of life, and preserves at the same time a perfect indifference with respect to its continuance. Old age under these circumstances, and with these sentiments, may be animated with more courage and fortitude than is usually found even in the prime of life. Accordingly Solon, it is said, being questioned by the tyrant Pisistratus, what it was that inspired him with the boldness to oppose his measures, bravely replied, "My old age." Nevertheless,

the most desirable manner of yielding up our lives is when
Nature herself, while our understanding and our other
senses still remain unimpaired, thinks proper to destroy the
work of her own hand, as the artist who constructed the
machine is best qualified to take it to pieces. In short, an
old man should neither be anxious to preserve the small
portion of life which remains to him, nor forward to resign
it without a just cause. It was one of the prohibitions of
Pythagoras " not to quit our post of life without being
authorised by the Commander who placed us in it," that
is, not without the permission of the Supreme Being."

The epitaph which the wise Solon ordered to be inscribed
on his monument, expresses his wish that his death might
not pass undistinguished by the sorrowful exclamations of
his surviving friends. It was natural, I confess, to desire
to be remembered with regret by those with whom he had
been intimately and tenderly connected; yet I am inclined
to give the preference to the sentiment of Ennius, in those
famous lines—

> Nor loud lament nor silent tear deplore
> The fate of Ennius when he breathes no more.

In this poet's estimation, death, which opens the way to
immortality, is by no means a subject of reasonable
lamentation. The act of dying may indeed be attended
with a sense of pain; but a pain, however, which cannot be
of long continuance, especially to a man greatly advanced
in years. And as to the consequence of death, it must either
be a state of total insensibility, or of sensations much to be
desired. This is a truth upon which we ought continually to
meditate from our earliest youth, if we would be impressed
with a just and firm contempt of death; as without this
impression it is impossible to enjoy tranquillity. For as
death is a change which, sooner or later, perhaps even this
very moment, we must inevitably undergo, is it possible
that he who lives in the perpetual dread of an event with
which he is every instant threatened, should know the satisfaction of possessing an undisturbed repose and serenity of
mind?

When I reflect on the conduct of Junius Brutus, who lost
his life in the support of the liberties of his country; on the
two Decii, who rushed to certain death from the same
patriotic principle; on Marcus Attilius, who delivered

himself up to the torture of a most cruel execution, that he might not forfeit his word of honour which he had pledged to the enemy; on the two Scipios, who, if it had been possible, would willingly have formed a rampart with their own bodies against the invasion of the Carthaginians; on Lucius Paulus, your illustrious grandfather, who by his heroic death expiated the ignominy we sustained by the temerity of his colleague at the battle of Cannae; on Marcus Marcellus, whose magnanimity was so universally respected that even the most cruel of our enemies would not suffer his dead body to be deprived of funeral honours—when I reflect, I say, not only on the generous contempt of life which these heroic personages exhibited, but that whole legions of our troops (particular instances of which I have produced in my treatise on Roman Antiquities) have frequently marched, with undaunted courage and even alacrity, to attacks from which they were well persuaded not one of them could live to return, it should seem there is little occasion to enlarge upon the contempt of death. For if the very common soldiers of our armies, who are frequently raw, illiterate young peasants, are thus capable of despising its imaginary terrors, shall old age, with all the superior advantages of reason and philosophy, tremble at the thoughts of its near approach?

The distaste with which, in passing through the several stages of our present being, we leave behind us the respective enjoyments peculiar to each, must necessarily, I should think, in the close of its latest period, render life itself no longer desirable. Infancy and youth, manhood and old age, have each of them their peculiar and appropriated pursuits. But does youth regret the toys of infancy, or manhood lament that it has no longer a taste for the amusements of youth? The season of manhood has also its suitable objects, that are exchanged for others in old age; and these, too, like all the preceding, become languid and insipid in their turn. Now when this state of absolute satiety is at length arrived, when we have enjoyed the satisfactions peculiar to old age, till we have no longer any relish remaining for them, it is then that death may justly be considered as a mature and seasonable event.

And now, among the different sentiments of the philosophers concerning the consequence of our final dissolution, may I not venture to declare my own? and the rather, as the nearer death advances towards me, the more clearly I seem to discern its real nature.

I am well convinced, then, that my dear departed friends, your two illustrious fathers, are so far from having ceased to live, that the state they now enjoy can alone with propriety be called life. The soul, during her confinement within this prison of the body, is doomed by fate to undergo a severe penance. For her native seat is in heaven; and it is with reluctance that she is forced down from those celestial mansions into these lower regions, where all is foreign and repugnant to her divine nature. But the gods, I am persuaded, have thus widely disseminated immortal spirits, and clothed them with human bodies, that there might be a race of intelligent creatures, not only to have dominion over this our earth, but to contemplate the host of heaven, and imitate in their moral conduct the same beautiful order and uniformity so conspicuous in those splendid orbs. This opinion I am induced to embrace, not only as agreeable to the best deductions of reason, but in just deference also to the authority of the noblest and most distinguished philosophers. Accordingly, Pythagoras and his followers (who were formerly distinguished by the name of the Italic Sect) firmly maintained that the human soul is a detached part, or emanation, from the great universal soul of the world. I am further confirmed in my belief of the soul's immortality, by the discourse which Socrates, whom the oracle of Apollo pronounced to be the wisest of men, held upon this subject just before his death. In a word, when I consider the faculties with which the human mind is endowed; its amazing celerity; its wonderful power in recollecting past events, and sagacity in discerning future; together with its numberless discoveries in the several arts and sciences—I feel a conscious conviction that this active comprehensive principle cannot possibly be of a mortal nature. And as this unceasing activity of the soul derives its energy from its own intrinsic and essential powers, without receiving it from any foreign or external impulse, it necessarily follows (as it is absurd to suppose the soul would desert itself) that its activity must continue for ever. But farther: as the soul is evidently a simple uncompounded substance, without any dissimilar parts or heterogeneous mixture, it cannot therefore be divided, consequently it cannot perish. I might add that the facility and expedition with which youth are taught to acquire numberless very difficult arts, is a strong presumption that the soul possessed a considerable portion of knowledge before it entered into the human form; and that what seems to be received from instruction is, in fact, no other than a reminiscence, or recollection, of its former ideas. This, at least, is the opinion of Plato.

Xenophon, likewise, represents the elder Cyrus, in his last moments, as expressing his belief in the soul's immortality in the following terms: " Oh, my sons, do not imagine when death shall have separated me from you that I shall cease to exist. You beheld not my soul whilst I continued amongst you, yet you concluded that I had one, from the actions you saw me perform; infer the same when you shall see me no more. If the souls of departed worthies did not watch over and guard their surviving fame, the renown of their illustrious actions would soon be worn out of the memory of men. For my own part, I never could be persuaded that the soul could properly be said to live whilst it remained in this mortal body, or that it ceased to live when death had dissolved the vital union. I never could believe either that it became void of sense when it escaped from its connection with senseless matter, or that its intellectual powers were not enlarged and improved when it was discharged and refined from all corporeal admixture. When death has disunited the human frame, we clearly see what becomes of its material parts, as they apparently return to the several elements out of which they were originally composed; but the soul continues to remain invisible, both when she is present in the body, and when she departs out of it. Nothing so nearly resembles death as sleep, and nothing so strongly intimates the divinity of the soul as what passes in the mind upon that occasion. For the intellectual principle in man, during this state of relaxation and freedom from external impressions, frequently looks forward into futurity, and discerns events ere time has yet brought them forth—a plain indication this what the powers of the soul will hereafter be, when she shall be delivered from the restraints of her present bondage. If I should not therefore be mistaken in this my firm persuasion, you will have reason, my sons, when death shall have removed me from your view, to revere me as a sacred and celestial spirit. But although the soul should perish with the body, I recommend it to you, nevertheless, to honour my memory with a pious and inviolable regard, in obedience to the immortal gods, by whose power and providence this beautiful fabric of the universe is sustained and governed." Such were the sentiments of the dying Cyrus; permit me now to express my own.

Never, Scipio, can I believe that your illustrious ancestors, together with many other excellent personages, whom I need not particularly name, would have so ardently endeavoured to merit the honourable remembrance of posterity, had they not been persuaded that they had a real interest in the opinion which future generations might entertain concerning them. And do you imagine, my noble friends (if I may be indulged in an old man's privilege to boast of himself), do you imagine I would have undergone those labours I have sustained, both in my civil and military employments, if I had supposed that the conscious satisfaction I received from the glory of my actions was to terminate with my present existence? If such had been my persuasion, would it not have been far better and more rational to have passed my days in an undisturbed and indolent repose, without labour and without contention? But my mind, by I know not what secret impulse, was ever raising its views into future ages, strongly persuaded that I should then only begin to live when I ceased to exist in the present world. Indeed, if the soul were not naturally immortal, never, surely, would the desire of immortal glory be a passion which always exerts itself with the greatest force in the noblest and most exalted bosoms.

Tell me, my friends, whence it is that those men who have made the greatest advances in true wisdom and genuine philosophy are observed to meet death with the most perfect equanimity; while the ignorant and unimproved part of our species generally see its approach with the utmost discomposure and reluctance? Is it not because the more enlightened the mind is, and the farther it extends its view, the more clearly it discerns in the hour of its dissolution (what narrow and vulgar souls are too short-sighted to discover) that it is taking its flight into some happier region?

For my own part, I feel myself transported with the most ardent impatience to join the society of my two departed friends, your illustrious fathers, whose characters I greatly respected, and whose persons I sincerely loved. Nor is this, my earnest desire, confined to those excellent persons alone with whom I was formerly connected; I ardently wish to visit also those celebrated worthies, of whose honourable conduct I have heard and read much, or whose virtues I have myself commemorated in some of my writings. To this glorious assembly I am speedily advancing; and I would not be turned back in my journey, even upon the assured condition that my youth, like that of Pelias, should again be restored. The sincere truth is, if some divinity would confer upon me a new grant of my life, and replace me once more in the cradle, I would utterly, and without the least hesitation, reject the offer; having well-nigh finished my race, I have no inclination to return to the goal. For what has life to recommend it? Or rather, indeed, to what evils does it not expose us? But admit that its satisfactions are many, yet surely there is a time when we have had a sufficient measure of its enjoyments, and may well depart contented with our share of the feast; for I mean not, in imitation of some very considerable philosophers, to represent the condition of human nature as a subject of just lamentation. On the contrary, I am far from regretting that life was bestowed upon me, as I have the satisfaction to think that I have employed it in such a manner as not to have lived in vain. In short, I consider this world as a place which nature never designed for my permanent abode, and I look upon my departure out of it, not as being driven from my habitation, but as leaving my inn.

O, glorious day, when I shall retire from this low and sordid scene, to associate with the divine assembly of departed spirits, and not with those only whom I just now mentioned, but with my dear Cato, that best of sons and most valuable of men. It was my sad fate to lay his body on the funeral pile, when by the course of nature I had reason to hope he would have performed the same last office to mine. His soul, however, did not desert me, but still looked back upon me in its flight to those happy mansions, to which he was assured I should one day follow him. If I seemed to bear his death with fortitude, it was by no means that I did not most sensibly feel the loss I had sustained; it was because I supported myself with the consoling reflection that we could not long be separated.

Thus to think and thus to act has enabled me, Scipio, to bear up under a load of years with that ease and complacency which both you and Laelius have so frequently, it seems, remarked with admiration ; as indeed it has rendered my old age not only no inconvenient state to me, but even an agreeable one. And after all should this my firm persuasion of the soul's immortality prove to be a mere delusion, it is at least a pleasing delusion, and I will cherish it to my latest breath. I have the satisfaction in the meantime to be assured that if death should utterly extinguish my existence, as some minute philosophers assert, the groundless hope I entertained of an after-life in some better state cannot expose me to the derision of these wonderful sages, when they and I shall be no more. In all events, and even admitting that our expectations of immortality are utterly vain, there is a certain period, nevertheless, when death would be a consummation most earnestly to be desired. For Nature has appointed to the days of man, as to all things else, their proper limits, beyond which they are no longer of any value. In fine, old age may be considered as the last scene in the great drama of life, and one would not, surely, wish to lengthen out his part till he sank down sated with repetition and exhausted with fatigue.

These, my noble friends, are the reflections I had to lay before you on the subject of old age, a period to which, I hope, you will both of you in due time arrive, and prove by your own experience the truth of what I have asserted to you on mine.

SELECT LETTERS TO SEVERAL FRIENDS

TO POMPEY THE GREAT

YOUR letter to the senate afforded inexpressible satisfaction, not only to myself, but to the public in general: as the hopes it brought us of a peace, are agreeable to those expectations, which, in full confidence of your superior abilities, I had always encouraged the world to entertain.[1]   I must acquaint you, however, that it entirely sunk the spirits of that party, who, from being formerly your declared enemies, have lately become your pretended friends: as it utterly disappointed their most sanguine hopes.

Notwithstanding the letter which you wrote to me by the same express discovered but very slight marks of your affection; yet I read it with pleasure.   The truth is, I am always abundantly satisfied with the consciousness of having exerted my best offices towards my friends; and if they do not think proper to make me an equal return, I am well contented that the superiority should remain on my side.   But if my utmost zeal for your interests has not been sufficient to unite you to mine, I doubt not that our co-operating together upon the same patriot-principles will be the means of cementing us more strongly hereafter.   In the meantime, it would neither be agreeable to the openness of my temper, nor to the freedom of that mutual friendship we profess, to

[1] Pompey was at this time carrying on the war in Asia against Mithridates, king of Pontus: and the letter to which Cicero alludes, probably brought an account of the progress of the campaign.   Mithridates was a cruel but brave prince, who had given employment to the Roman arms for more than forty years.   Pompey, however, had the good fortune to complete what Sylla and Lucullus, his predecessors in this command, were obliged to leave unfinished: and he not only defeated Mithridates, but annexed to the Roman dominions all that part of Asia which is between the Red, the Caspian, and the Arabian feas.   *Flor.* iii. 5.

conceal what I thought wanting in your letter. I will acknowledge, then, that the public services I performed during my late consulship, gave me reason to expect, from your attachment both to myself and to the commonwealth, that you would have sent me your congratulations: and I am persuaded you would not have omitted them, but from a tenderness to certain persons.[1] Let me assure you, however, that what I have performed for the preservation of my country, has received the concurrent applauses of the whole world. You will find when you return hither, I conducted that important scene with so much spirit and policy, that you, like another Scipio, though far superior, indeed, to that hero in glory, will not refuse to admit me, like a second Laelius,[2] and not much behind him, I trust, in wisdom, as the friend and associate of your private and public transactions. Farewell.

TO TERENTIA, TO MY DEAREST TULLIA, AND TO MY SON [3]

If you do not hear from me so frequently as you might, it is because I can neither write to you, nor read your letters, without falling into a greater passion of tears than I am able to support: for though I am at all times, indeed, completely

---

[1] Cicero was advanced to the consular office the year before the date of this letter; that is, An. Urb. 690. He particularly alludes to the part he acted during his administration, with regard to the suppressing of Cataline's conspiracy. And he had undoubtedly cause to complain of Pompey's unexpected coolness in the present instance: the occasion of which seems to have been this. A very powerful party was now forming against Cicero by Cæsar and Metellus the tribune; and Pompey was considered as a proper person to support their designs of destroying the great authority which Cicero had lately acquired. It is highly probable, therefore, from Pompey's reserve to our author, that he had received some overtures of this sort: and as he was jealous of every power that might obstruct his own, he was by no means disposed, it should seem, to advance Cicero's credit by gratifying him with those applauses which his conduct deserved. *Plut. in vit. Cicero.*

[2] Scipio Africanus the younger, to whom Cicero here alludes, was consul in the year of Rome 605: as Laelius was in the year 612.

[3] The following letters to Terentia were written in our author's exile, and will prove, either that Cicero was a philosopher only in speculation, or that philosophy itself pretends to more than it has power to perform. Perhaps they will prove both; for, as on the one hand they discover the most unmanly dejection of spirit; so it is certain, on the other, that much weaker minds have been able, with the assistance of better

miserable, yet I feel my misfortunes with a particular sensibility upon those tender occasions.

Oh! that I had been more indifferent to life! Our days would then have been, if not wholly unacquainted with sorrow, yet by no means thus wretched. However, if any hopes are still reserved to us of recovering some part at least of what we have lost, I shall not think that I have made altogether so imprudent a choice. But if our present fate is unalterably fixed—Ah! my dearest Terentia, if we are utterly and for ever abandoned by those gods whom you have so religiously adored, and by those men whom I have so faithfully served; let me see you as soon as possible, that I may have the satisfaction of breathing out my last departing sigh in your arms.

I have spent about a fortnight at this place,[1] with my friend Marcus Flaccus. This worthy man did not scruple to exercise the rites of friendship and hospitality towards me, notwithstanding the severe penalties of that iniquitous law against those who should venture to give me reception.[2] May I one day have it in my power to make him a return to those generous services, which I shall ever most gratefully remember.

I am just going to embark, and purpose to pass through Macedonia in my way to Cyzicum.[3] And now, my Terentia,

principles, to support with fortitude far severer trials. Those in which Cicero was at present exercised, were occasioned by Clodius, who procured himself to be elected tribune with the single view of destroying this his avowed adversary. It has already been observed that Cicero in his consulate had put to death some of the conspirators concerned with Cataline, without any formal trial, and upon no other authority than a decree of the senate. And it was upon this charge that Clodius founded his impeachment. Cicero's conduct upon this occasion has also been arraigned by a late very accurate and judicious historian; and it must be acknowledged that, as far as we can be competent judges of it at this distance from the time and scene of action, it seems to have been attended with some circumstances not easily reconcilable to the principles either of justice or good policy. *See Hook's Rom. Hist.* vol. iii. p. 316.

[1] Brundisium: a maritime town in the kingdom of Naples, now called *Brindisi*. Cicero, when he first withdrew from Rome, intended to have retired into Sicily; but being denied entrance by the governor of that island, he changed his direction, and came to Brundisium, in his way to Greece. *Pro Planc.* 40, 41.

[2] As soon as Cicero had withdrawn from Rome, Clodius procured a law, which, among other articles, enacted that "no person should presume to harbour or receive him on pain of death."

[3] A considerable town in an island of the Propontis, which lay so close to the continent of Asia as to be joined with it by a bridge.

thus wretched and ruined as I am, can I entreat you, under all that weight of pain and sorrow with which, I too well know, you are oppressed, can I entreat you to be the partner and companion of my exile? But must I then live without you? I know not how to reconcile myself to that hard condition; unless your presence at Rome may be a mean of forwarding my return; if any hopes of that kind should indeed subsist. But should there, as I sadly suspect, be absolutely none, come to me, I conjure you, if it be possible: for never can I think myself completely ruined, whilst I shall enjoy my Terentia's company. But how will my dearest daughter dispose of herself? A question which you yourselves must consider: for, as to my own part, I am utterly at a lost what to advise. At all events, however, that dear unhappy girl must not take any measures that may injure her conjugal repose,[1] or affect her in the good opinion of the world. As for my son—let me not at least be deprived of the consolation of folding him for ever in my arms. But I must lay down my pen a few moments: my tears flow too fast to suffer me to proceed.

I am under the utmost solicitude, as I know not whether you have been able to preserve any part of your estate, or (what I sadly fear) are cruelly robbed of your whole fortune. I hope Piso [2] will always continue, what you represent him to be, entirely ours. As to the manumission of the slaves; I think you have no occasion to be uneasy. For with regard to your own, you only promised them their liberty as they should deserve it; but, excepting Orpheus, there are none of them that have any great claim to this favour. As to mine, I told them, if my estate should be forfeited, I would give them their freedom, provided I could obtain the confirmation of that grant: but if I preserved my estate, that they should all of them, excepting only a few whom I particularly named, remain in their present condition. But this is a matter of little consequence.

With regard to the advice you give me of keeping up my spirits, in the belief that I shall again be restored to my country; I only wish that I may have reason to encourage so desirable an expectation. In the meantime, I am greatly

---

[1] Tullia was at this time married to Caius Piso Frugi; a young nobleman of one of the best familes in Rome.

[2] Cicero's son-in-law.

miserable, in the uncertainty when I shall hear from you, or what hand you will find to convey your letters. I would have waited for them at this place, but the master of the ship on which I am going to embark, could not be prevailed upon to lose the present opportunity of sailing.

For the rest, let me conjure you in my turn to bear up under the pressure of our afflictions with as much resolution as possible. Remember that my days have all been honourable; and that I now suffer, not for my crimes, but my virtues. No, my Terentia, nothing can justly be imputed to me, but that I survived the loss of my dignities. However, if it was more agreeable to our children that I should thus live, let that reflection teach us to submit to our misfortunes with cheerfulness; insupportable as upon all other considerations they would undoubtedly be. But alas, whilst I am endeavouring to keep up your spirits, I am utterly unable to preserve my own!

I have sent back the faithful Philetærus: as the weakness of his eyes made him incapable of rendering me any service. Nothing can equal the good offices I receive from Sallustius. Pescennius likewise has given me strong marks of his affection: and I hope he will not fail in his respect also to you. Sicca promised to attend me in exile; but he changed his mind, and has left me at this place.

I entreat you to take all possible care of your health: and be assured, your misfortunes more sensibly affect me than my own. Adieu, my Terentia, thou most faithful and best of wives! adieu. And thou my dearest daughter, together with that other consolation of my life, my dear son, I bid you both most tenderly farewell.

BRUNDISIUM, *April the 30th.*

TO TERENTIA, TO MY DEAREST TULLIA, AND TO MY SON

IMAGINE not, my Terentia, that I write longer letters to others than to yourself: be assured at least, if ever I do, it is merely because those I receive from them require a more particular answer. The truth of it is, I am always at a loss what to write: and as there is nothing in the present dejection of my mind, that I perform with greater reluctance in general; so I never attempt it with regard to you and my dearest daughter, that it does not cost me a flood of tears. For how can I think of you without being pierced with grief in the reflection, that I have made those completely miserable whom I ought, and wished, to have rendered perfectly happy? And I should have rendered them so, if I had acted with less timidity.

Piso's behaviour towards us in this season of our afflictions, has greatly endeared him to my heart: and I have, as well as I was able in the present discomposure of my mind, both acknowledged his good offices and exhorted him to continue them.

I perceive you depend much upon the new tribunes: and if Pompey perseveres in his present disposition, I am inclined to think that your hopes will not be disappointed; though I must confess, I have some fears with respect to Crassus. In the meanwhile I have the satisfaction to find, what indeed I had reason to expect, that you act with great spirit and tenderness in all my concerns. But I lament it should be my cruel fate to expose you to so many calamities, whilst you are thus generously endeavouring to ease the weight of mine. Be assured it was with the utmost grief I read the account which Publius sent me, of the opprobrious manner in which you were dragged from the temple of Vesta, to the office of Valerius.[1] Sad reverse indeed! That thou, the dearest object of my fondest desires, that my Terentia, to whom such numbers were wont to look up for relief, should be herself a spectacle of the most affecting distress! and that I, who have saved so many others from ruin, should have ruined both myself and my family by my own indiscretion!

As to what you mention with regard to the Area belonging to my house, I shall never look upon myself as restored to my country, till that spot of ground is again in my possession.[2] But this is a point that does not depend upon ourselves.

---

[1] Terentia had taken sanctuary in the temple of Vesta, but was forcibly dragged out from thence by the directions of Clodius, in order to be examined at a public office, concerning her husband's effects.

[2] After Clodius had produced the law against Cicero already taken notice of, he consecrated the Area where his house in Rome stood, to the perpetual service of religion, and erected a temple upon it to the goddess Liberty.

Let me rather express my concern for what does; and lament that, distressed as your circumstances already are, you should engage yourself in a share of those expenses which are incurred upon my account. Be assured, if ever I should return to Rome, I shall easily recover my estate: but should fortune continue to persecute me, will you, thou dear unhappy woman, will you fondly throw away in gaining friends to a desperate cause, the last scanty remains of your broken fortunes! I conjure you then, my dearest Terentia, not to involve yourself in any charges of that kind: let them be borne by those who are able, if they are willing, to support the weight. In a word, if you have any affection for me, let not your anxiety upon my account injure your health: which, alas! is already but too much impaired. Believe me, you are the perpetual subject of my waking and sleeping thoughts: and as I know the assiduity you exert in my behalf, I have a thousand fears lest your strength should not be equal to so continued a fatigue. I am sensible at the same time that my affairs depend entirely upon your assistance: and therefore that they may be attended with the success you hope and so zealously endeavour to obtain, let me earnestly entreat you to take care of your health.

I know not whom to write to, unless to those who first write to me, or whom you particularly mention in your letters. As you and Tullia are of opinion that I should not retreat farther from Italy, I have laid aside that design. Let me hear from you both as often as possible, particularly if there should be any fairer prospect of my return. Farewell, ye dearest objects of my most tender affection, Farewell!

THESSALONICA, *Oct. the 5th.*

TO FABIUS GALLUS[1]

I HAVE been attacked with a disorder in my bowels, which continued with great violence during ten days: but as it was not attended with a fever, I could not persuade those who had occasion for my services, that I was really indisposed. In order therefore to avoid their importunities, I retired to

---

[1] Gallus is only known by the three or four letters which Cicero has addressed to him.

Tusculanum; having observed so strict an abstinence for two days before, as not to have tasted even a drop of water. Reduced then as I am by my illness and my fasting, I had more reason to hope for a visit from you, than to imagine you expected one from me.

Distempers of every kind I greatly dread, but particularly of that sort for which the Stoics have censured your favourite Epicurus, where he complains of being violently afflicted with the dysentery and the strangury: as the former, they assert, is the consequence of table indulgencies, and the latter of a more shameful intemperance. I had indeed great reason to apprehend a dysentery: but whether it be from change of air, or a relaxation from business, or that the distemper had almost spent itself, I know not; but I am somewhat better since I came hither. You will wonder perhaps what excesses I have been guilty of, to bring upon myself this disorder. I must inform you then, that I owe it to the frugal regulations of the sumptuary law.[1] The products of the earth being excepted out of the restrictions of that act; our elegant eaters, in order to bring vegetables into fashion, have found out a method of dressing them in so high a taste, that nothing can be more palatable. It was immediately after having eaten very freely of a dish of this sort, at the inauguration feast of Lentulus,[2] that I was seized with a diarrhœa, which has never ceased till this day. Thus you see, that I who have withstood all the temptations that the noblest lampreys and oysters could throw in my way, have at last been overpowered by paltry beets and mallows: but it has taught me however to be more cautious for the future. As Anicius found me in one of my sick fits, you must undoubtedly have heard of my illness: I was in hopes therefore you would not have contented yourself with inquiring after my welfare, but would have given me the satisfaction of a visit. I purpose to continue here, till I shall have re-established my health: for I am extremely

---

[1] Manutius conjectures, that the law alluded to is one which is ascribed by Aulus Gellius to Marcus Lucinius Craffus, and which passed in the year of Rome 643. By this law the expenses of the table were regulated both in regard to ordinary and extraordinary occasions, with the express exception mentioned by Cicero in the next sentence, concerning the article of vegetables.

[2] He was son of Publius Cornelius Lentulus, one of the consuls of the present year. He gave this entertainment on occasion of his being chosen a member of the college of augurs.

weakened and emaciated.   But if I can once get the better
of my disorder, I hope I shall find no difficulty in recovering
all the rest.   Farewell.

TO FABIUS GALLUS

I RECEIVED your letter immediately upon my return from
Arpinum, together with one likewise from Avianus, in which
he very generously offers to give me credit as long as I shall
require.   Now let me desire you to imagine yourself in my
situation, and then tell me, whether I can, with a good grace,
ask him to allow me even the least time for the payment of
this money, much less above a year?   Indeed, my dear
friend, I should not have been in this difficulty, if you had not
exceeded the limits of my commission, both in the particulars
and the sum.   However, I am not only willing to ratify the
agreement you have made for the statues you mention, but
am likewise much obliged to you.   I am sensible indeed that
in the zeal of your friendship you have purchased for me what
pleased your own eye, and what you imagined would be
worthy of mine; and I always considered you as a man of the
most judicious and elegant taste in every kind.   Nevertheless, I shall be extremely glad if Damasippus [1] should continue in the resolution of taking these figures off my hands:
for, to own the plain truth, I have no sort of inclination to
them myself.   As you were not apprised of my intentions,
you have actually consented to pay more for these four or
five pieces of sculpture,[2] than I would have given for all the
statues in the universe.   You compare the images of the
priestesses of Bacchus, to those of the Muses which I bought
of Metellus.   But surely, my friend, the two instances are
by no means parallel.   For in the first place the Muses themselves would have condemned me, if I had ever rated them
at so extravagant a price: and in the next, I purchased the

[1] Damasippus was a celebrated virtuoso of these times, who, after
having ruined his fortunes by his extravagant passion for antiques,
turned Stoic.   Horace has ridiculed his character and his conversion
with great humour, in one of his satires.   *Vid. Horat. Sat.* ii. 3.
[2] These statues appear, by what follows, to have been three
Bacchanals, a Mars, and some figure designed for the support of a
table.

figures you mention as bearing an allusion to my studies, and affording a suitable ornament to my library. But where can I, with any propriety, place these Bacchanals? That they are, as you assure me, extremely beautiful, I know full well; for I have frequently seen them: and therefore I should particularly have named them to you, if they had suited my purpose. The purchases which I usually make of this kind are such only as are proper to embellish my Palaestra,[1] in the same manner as the public Gymnasia are generally decorated. But would it not be absurd enough, my good friend, if I, who upon all occasions, you know, have distinguished myself as the friend of peace, should erect a statue of the God of war. It is well there was not a Saturn too; for how could I have expected to have been out of debt, whilst I had lived under the aspect of two such unlucky divinities?[2] Mercury would have been a much more welcome guest: for I should have hoped, by his influence, to have made a more advantageous bargain[3] with Avianus. As to the figure designed for the support of a table, which you intended to reserve for your own use; you shall have it, if you still remain in the same mind; if not, I am ready to take it myself. Upon the whole, however, I had much rather have employed this money in the purchase of a little lodge at Tarracina,[4] that I might not always trouble my friend and host. But this mistake is partly owing to the carelessness of my freedman, in not observing the instructions I gave him; and partly also to Junius: whom I suppose you know, as he is a particular friend of Avianus. As I have

[1] The Palaestra was properly a part of those public buildings which the Grecians (from whom the Romans took them) called Gymnasia: which were originally designed for exercises of various kinds, and in which, in after-times, the philosophers likewise held their schools. What Cicero here calls his *Palaestra*, seems to be the same building which in a letter to Atticus he terms his *Academia*, and which appears to have been some apartments, or perhaps a distinct building, of his Tusculan villa, appropriated principally to the purposes of study, but adapted also to those bodily exercises which the ancients seldom passed a day without practising.

[2] Alluding (as Manutius observes) to the notions of the judicial astrologers: who pretended that Mars and Saturn were unlucky planets.

[3] Mercury was supposed to preside over commerce: from whence it is probable that the *Mercuriales*, mentioned in a letter of Cicero to his brother, were a *company* of merchants.

[4] It is now called *Terracina:* a town in the *campagna di Roma*. It lay in the road from Rome to Cicero's villa at *Formiae*.

lately built some additional apartments to my little portico at Tusculanum,[1] I was desirous of adorning them with a few pictures: for if I take pleasure in anything of this kind, it is in paintings. However, if I must have these statues, let me know where they are, when they will arrive, and by what conveyance you purpose to send them. For if Damasippus should change his intentions of buying them, I shall find, perhaps, some pretender to his taste, who may be glad of the purchase: and I should be willing to part with them even at a loss.

When I received your first letter concerning the house you want to take, belonging to Cassius, I was just setting out from Rome, and therefore I left your commission with my daughter. However, I took an opportunity myself of talking upon this affair with your friend Nicia: who, you know, is very intimate with Cassius. At my return hither, and before I had opened your last letter, I inquired of Tullia what she had done in this matter. She told me, she had applied to Licinia to speak to her brother Cassius: but I believe he is not upon very good terms with his sister. The answer which Licinia gave my daughter was, that her husband being gone into Spain, she durst not remove[2] in his absence and without his knowledge. I am greatly obliged to you for being so desirous of my company as to be impatient to get into a house where you may not only be near me, but actually under the same roof. Be assured, I am no less desirous of having you for my neighbour: and as I am sensible how much it will contribute to our mutual satisfaction, I shall try every expedient for that purpose. If I should have any success, I will let you know: in the meanwhile, I beg you would return me a particular answer to this letter, and tell me at the same time when I may expect to see you. Farewell.

[1] Cicero, if we may credit the invective ascribed to Sallust, expended immense sums on this his favourite villa, which probably was a very fine one when it came into his possession, as it originally belonged to Sylla the dictator. Some considerable remains of it are still shown at Grotta Ferrata.

[2] This lady seems to have been the tenant of the house, which Gallus wanted either to buy or hire.

TO MARCUS MARIUS [1]

IF your general valetudinary disposition prevented you from being a spectator of our late public entertainments; [2] it is more to fortune than to philosophy that I am to impute your absence. But if you declined our party for no other reason than as holding in just contempt what the generality of the world so absurdly admire, I must at once congratulate you both on your health and your jugdement. I say this upon a supposition, however, that you were enjoying the philosophical advantages of that delightful scene, in which, I imagine, you were almost wholly deserted. At the same time that your neighbours, probably, were nodding over the dull humour of our trite farces; my friend, I dare say, was indulging his morning meditations in that elegant apartment, from whence you have opened a prospect to Sejanum, through the Stabian hills. [3] And whilst you are employing the rest of the day in those various polite amusements, which you have the happy privilege to plan out for yourself; we, alas, had the mortification of tamely enduring those dramatical representations, to which Maetius, it seems, our professed critic, had given his infallible sanction! but as you will have the curiosity, perhaps, to require a more particular account; I must tell you, that though our entertainments were extremely magnificent indeed, yet they were by no means such as you would have relished: at least if I may judge of your taste by my own. Some of those actors who had formerly distinguished themselves with great applause, but had long since retired, I imagined, in order to perserve the reputation they had raised, were now again introduced upon

[1] The person to whom this letter is addressed, seems to have been of a temper and constitution, that placed him far below the ambition of being known to posterity. But a private letter from Cicero's hands has been sufficient to dispel the obscurity he appears to have loved, and to render his retirement conspicuous.

[2] They were exhibited by Pompey at the opening of his theatre: one of the most magnificent structures of ancient Rome, and so extensive as to contain no less than 80,000 spectators. It was built after the model of one which he saw at Mitylene, in his return from the Mithridatic war; and adorned with the noblest ornaments of statuary and painting. Some remains of this immense building still subsist.

[3] Sejanum is found in no other ancient author. Stabiae was a maritime town in Campania, situated upon the bay of Naples, from whence the adjoining hills here mentioned took their name.

the stage: as in honour, it seems, of the festival. Among these was my old friend Aesopus: [1] but so different from what we once knew him, that the whole audience agreed he ought to be excused from acting any more. For when he was pronouncing the celebrated oath,

If I deceive, be Jove's dread vengeance hurl'd, etc.

the poor old man's voice failed him: and he had not strength to go through with the speech. As to the other parts of our theatrical entertainments, you know the nature of them so well, that it is scarce necessary to mention them. They had less indeed to plead in their favour than even the most ordinary representations of this kind can usually claim. The enormous parade with which they were attended, and which, I dare say, you would very willingly have spared, destroyed all the grace of the performance. What pleasure could it afford to a judicious spectator, to see a thousand mules prancing about the stage, in the tragedy of Clytaemnestra; or whole regiments accoutred in foreign armour, in that of the *Trojan Horse?* In a word, what man of sense could be entertained with viewing a mock army drawn up on the stage in battle array? These, I confess, are spectacles extremely well adapted to captivate vulgar eyes; but undoubtedly would have had no charm in yours. In plain truth, my friend, you would have received more amusement from the dullest piece that Protogenes could possibly have read to you [2] (my own orations however let me always except) than we met with at these ridiculous shows. I am

---

[1] He excelled in tragedy, and was the most celebrated actor that had ever appeared upon the Roman stage. Cicero experienced the advantage of his friendship and his talents during his exile; for Aesopus being engaged in a part upon the stage, wherein there were several passages that might be applied to our author's misfortunes: this excellent tragedian pronounced them with so peculiar and affecting an emphasis, that the whole audience immediately took the allusion; and it had a better effect, as Cicero acknowledges, than anything his own eloquence could have expressed for the same purpose. But it is not in this instance alone that Cicero was obliged to Aesopus, as it was by the advantage of his precepts and example, that he laid the foundation of his oratorical fame, and improved himself in the art of elocution. The high value which the Romans set upon the talents of this pathetic actor, appears by the immense estate which he acquired in his profession, for he died worth almost £200,000 sterling.

[2] It was usual with persons of distinction amongst the Romans to keep a slave in their family whose sole business it was to read to them. Protogenes seems to have attended Marius in that capacity.

well persuaded at least, you could not regret the loss of our
Oscian and Grecian farces.[1] Your own noble senate will
always furnish you with drollery sufficient of the former
kind:[2] and as to the latter, I know you have such an utter
aversion to everything that bears the name of Greek, that
you will not even travel the Grecian road to your villa.[3]
As I remember you once despised our formidable gladiators,[4]
I cannot suppose you would have looked with less contempt
on our athletic performers:[5] and indeed Pompey himself

[1] The Oscian farces were so called from the Osci, an ancient people of
Campania, from whom the Romans received them.   They seem to have
consisted of low humour.   As to the nature of the Greek farces, the
critics are not agreed.   Manutius supposes they differed only from
the former, as being written in the Greek language.   But it does not
appear that Greek plays were ever represented upon the Roman stage:
and the most probable account of them is, that they were a sort of
pantomimes in imitation of those on the Grecian theatre.

[2] The municipal or corporate towns in Italy were governed by
magistrates of their own, who probably made much the same sort of
figure in their rural senate, as our Burgesses in their town-hall.   This
at least seems to have been the case in that corporation to which Marius
belonged, and to have given occasion to our author's raillery.

[3] Perhaps the Grecian road might be much out of repair, and little
frequented at the time when this letter was written: and on that
circumstance Cicero, it is possible, may have founded his witticism.
Among the many instances of Roman magnificence, that of their public
roads is particularly observable.   They were formed at an immense
cost, and extended to a great distance from all sides of the city.   Lipsius
computes the Appian way at 350 miles, some part of which still remains
as entire as when it was first made; though it has now subsisted above
1800 years.   It is twelve feet broad, and chiefly composed of blue
stones about a foot and a half square.   Criminals of a less atrocious
sort were generally employed in those useful works.

[4] Graevius supposes (and it is a conjecture extremely probable) that
this alludes to some services which Cicero had received from Marius,
in defending him against the outrages of Clodius's mob.
The first show of gladiators exhibited in Rome was given by the
Bruti in honour of their father's obsequies: about 200 years before the
date of this letter.   Originally the unhappy wretches who were exposed
in this manner were either prisoners taken in war, or public criminals:
but in process of time it grew into a profession, and there were men
who hired themselves out for this purpose.   Atticus, who seems to
have omitted no opportunity of improving his finances, had a band of
gladiators which he let out on public occasions, to those who were not
rich enough to maintain them at their own expense.   The passion for
these combats became at length so immoderate, that it was usual to
exhibit matches of gladiators at their private entertainments: and
not only men of the first quality, but even women entered these lists.

[5] The athletic games were of a less cruel kind, as they principally
consisted of running, wrestling, and boxing-matches.   It sometimes
happened indeed that one of the combatants lost his life: but this was
contrary to the laws of the sport; and if it appeared to have been the
effect of design in his adversary, though he was not punished with
death, he was punished in a way still more dreaded, by being deprived

acknowledges, that they did not answer the pains and expense they had cost him. The remainder of our diversions consisted in combats of wild beasts,[1] which were exhibited every morning and afternoon during five days successively; and it must be owned, they were magnificent. Yet after all, what entertainment can possibly arise to an elegant and humanised mind, from seeing a noble beast struck to the heart by its merciless hunter, or one of our own weak species cruelly mangled by an animal of much superior strength? But were there anything really worth observing in spectacles of this savage kind; they are spectacles extremely familiar to you: and those I am speaking of had not any peculiar novelty to recommend them. The last day's sport was composed entirely of elephants: which, though they made the common people stare indeed, did not seem however to afford them any great satisfaction. On the contrary, the terrible slaughter of these poor animals created a general commiseration: as it is a prevailing notion, that these creatures in some degree participate of our rational faculties.[2]

That you may not imagine I had the happiness of being perfectly at my ease during the whole of this pompous festival; I must acquaint you, that while the people were amusing themselves at the plays, I was almost killed with the fatigue of pleading for your friend Gallus Caninius. Were the world as much inclined to favour my retreat, as they showed themselves in the case of Aesopus, believe me I would for ever renounce my art, and spend the remainder of my days with you and some others of the same philosophical turn. The truth of it is, I began to grow weary of this employment, even at a time when youth and ambition prompted my perseverance: and I will add, too, when I was at full liberty to exercise it in defence of those only whom I was inclined to assist. But in my present circumstances, it is absolute slavery. For, on the one side, I never expect to

of the crown that would otherwise have been due to his victory. Pausanias mentions an athletic combatant who having incurred this penalty, was so affected by the disgrace, that he lost his senses.

[1] Beasts of the wildest and most uncommon kinds were sent for upon these occasions, from every corner of the known world: and Dion Cassius relates, that no less than 500 lions were killed at these hunting-matches with which Pompey entertained the people.

[2] This was not merely a vulgar opinion, but entertained by some of the learned among the ancients, as appears from the last cited historian: who likewise takes notice how much the spectators of Pompey's shows were affected by the mournful cries of these poor animals.

reap any advantage from my labours of this kind; and, on the other, in compliance with solicitations which I cannot refuse, I am sometimes under the disagreeable necessity of appearing as an advocate in behalf of those who ill deserve that favour at my hands.[1] For these reasons I am framing every possible pretence for living hereafter according to my own taste and sentiments: as I highly both approve and applaud that retired scene of life which you have so judiciously chosen. I am sensible, at the same time, that this is the reason you so seldom visit Rome. However I the less regret that you do not see it oftener, as the numberless unpleasing occupations in which I am engaged would prevent me from enjoying the entertainment of your conversation, or giving you that of mine: if mine, indeed, can afford you any. But if ever I should be so fortunate as to disentangle myself, in some degree at least (for I am contented not to be wholly released), from these perplexing embarrassments; I will undertake to show even my elegant friends, wherein the truest refinements of life consist. In the meanwhile, continue to take care of your health, that you may be able, when that happy time shall arrive, to accompany me in my litter to my several villas.

You must impute it to the excess of my friendship, and not to the abundance of my leisure, that I have lengthened this letter beyond my usual extent. It was merely in compliance with a request in one of yours, where you intimate a desire that I would compensate in this manner what you lost by not being present at our public diversions. I shall be extremely glad if I have succeeded; if not, I shall have the satisfaction however to think, that you will for the future be more inclined to give us your company on these occasions, than to rely on my letters for your amusement. Farewell.

TO LENTULUS

It is with singular pleasure I perceive by your letter that you are sensible, I will not say of my affection only, but of my devotion towards you. Even that sacred term indeed can but ill express the sentiments you merit from me: and if

[1] Cicero was now wholly under the influence of Pompey and Caesar.

you esteem yourself (as you would persuade me) obliged by my endeavours to serve you, it is your friendship alone which can make you think so. I am sure at least I could not refuse you my best good offices, without being guilty of the most unpardonable ingratitude. You would have experienced, however, much stronger and more powerful instances of my friendship, if, instead of being thus long separated from each other, we had passed this interval together at Rome. It is not only in the particular article you mention, and in which no man is more qualified to shine, that I impatiently wish to receive you as my coadjutor: it is not, I say, in the senate alone that our amicable concurrence would have been distinguished; it would have appeared conspicuous, my friend, in every act of public concernment. Suffer me then to add, previously to the information you request me to give you of my political sentiments and situation, that if fortune had not thus divided us, I should have enjoyed in you a wise and faithful guide; as you would have found in me, a kind, a friendly, and, perhaps, no unexperienced associate. However, I rejoice (as undoubtedly I ought) at the honourable occasion of your absence, and in which your military conduct and success has procured you the illustrious title of *Imperator*.[1] Nevertheless, I must repeat it again, it is owing to this circumstance, that you have not received far more abundant and efficacious fruits of that friendship, to which you have so undisputed a claim. In particular, I should most strenuously have united with you in taking just vengeance on those whose ill offices you have experienced, partly in resentment of your having supported and protected me in my adversity, and partly as they envy you the glory of so generous an action. One of them, however, has sufficiently anticipated our revenge, and drawn down by his own hands the chastisement he merits from ours. The person I mean is that man who has ever distinguished himself by opposing his benefactors, and who, after having received from you the highest services, singled you out as the object of his impotent malice. This man, in consequence of being detected in his late infamous attempts, has entirely and irretrievably lost at once both his honour and his liberty.[2] As to yourself, though

---

[1] History is altogether silent as to the occasion upon which Lentulus was saluted by his army with this title.

[2] The conjecture seems highly probable, that the person to whom Cicero alludes is Caius Cato. But what the secret practices were which

I had much rather you should gain experience by my misfortunes than your own; yet it affords me some consolation
under your present disappointment,[1] that you have not paid
so severe a fine as I did, for being taught the little dependence there is upon the professions of the world. A reflection
this, which may very properly serve as an introduction to the
account you require of the motives of my late transactions.

You are informed then, it seems, that I am reconciled with
Caesar and Appius:[2] a step, you assure me, which you do not
disapprove. But you are at a loss to guess what reasons
could induce me to appear at the trial of Vatinius, not only
as an advocate, but as a witness in his favour.[3] To set this
matter in the clearest light, it will be necessary to trace back
the motives of my conduct to their original source. Let me
observe then, my Lentulus, that when I was recalled from
exile by your generous offices, I considered myself as restored, not only to my friends and to my family, but to
the commonwealth in general. And as you had a right to
the best returns of my affection and gratitude for the distinguished part you acted in that affair; so I thought there
was something more than ordinary due from me to my
country, which had so singularly co-operated with you upon
this occasion. I often took an opportunity, during your
consulate, of publicly declaring these my sentiments in the

had been discovered so much to his disgrace, is a point in which history
does not afford any light.
    [1] In not obtaining the commission to replace Ptolemy on his throne.
    [2] He was embroiled with Appius, as being the brother of his inveter-
ate enemy, Clodius.
    [3] It was customary at trials for the person arraigned to produce
witnesses to his character, who were called *Laudatores:* and ten was
the number requisite for this purpose. Vatinius was tribune of the
people in the consulate of Caesar, and had been in the number of
Cicero's most inveterate enemies, as he was his constant opposer likewise in politics. He was a man of a most abandoned character, and
whose person (as Paterculus assures us) was not less deformed than his
mind. A very learned and polite author, whose just esteem for
Cicero's writings has betrayed him, perhaps, into some partiality
towards his actions, acknowledges that " the defence of Vatinius gave
" a plausible handle for some censure upon Cicero." The truth of it is,
the censure was more than *plausible:* for nothing certainly could discover more meanness of spirit than thus, in compliance with those in
power, not only to defend Vatinius as an advcaote, but to bear public
testimony likewise to his general good conduct. Some colourable
excuse indeed may be given for the former, by considering it in the
light which Valerius Maximus has placed it; as an instance of Cicero's
generosity towards his enemies: but the latter seems to stand beyond
the reach even of a *plausible* justification.

senate: as I always, you well know, expressed myself to the same purpose in our private conversations. Nevertheless, I had many reasons at that time to be highly disgusted. I could not, in truth, but observe the disguised malice of some and the coolness of others, when you were endeavouring to procure a decree for restoring the inscription of that honourable monument of my public services, which had been erected by the senate.[1] But it was not only in this instance that those who had many obligations to concur in your good offices towards me, acted a part I had little reason to expect. They looked indeed with much ungenerous indifference on the cruel outrage which was offered to my brother and myself under our own roof:[2] and the estimate they made in pursuance of the senate's order of the damages I had sustained by these acts of violence, was far unequal to my real loss.[3] This last article of their injustice, though least indeed in my concern, I could not but very sensibly feel amidst the general wreck of my fortunes. But though these mortifying marks of their disposition towards me were much too notorious to escape my observation; they could not efface the more agreeable impressions of their former friendship. For this reason, notwithstanding those high obligations I had to Pompey, of which you yourself were witness, and have often mentioned; notwithstanding also the affection and esteem which I always entertained for him, yet I still firmly adhered to my political principles: nor suffered these considerations of private amity to influence me in favour of his public

[1] Most probably this alludes to the *Atrium Libertatis*, which had been erected by order of the senate as a memorial of Cicero's services in rescuing the commonwealth from the dangerous conspiracy of Cataline. For Clodius had erased the original inscription, and placed his own name in its stead.

[2] Clodius, after having procured a law which declared it treason to vote or take any step towards recalling Cicero from his banishment, proceeded to pillage and burn all his houses both in town and country. Cicero, however, being restored, the senate decreed that his houses should be rebuilt at the public expense. But while the workmen were employed on his Palatine house, and had carried it up almost to the roof, Clodius made a second attack, and, after driving them off, set fire to the adjoining edifice which belonged to Cicero's brother, and wherein he himself likewise at that time was; so that they were both obliged to make their escape with the utmost precipitation.

[3] His house upon the Palatine hill in Rome, together with his Tusculan and Formian villas were jointly estimated at £22,000, a valuation universally condemned as extremely unequitable. But " those who had clipt his wings were not disposed they should grow again."

measures.   Accordingly, when Vatinius (who at the trial of
P. Sextius [1] was examined as a witness against him) intimated
that Caesar's successes had reconciled me to his party; I told
him, in the presence of Pompey, that I preferred the fate of
Bibulus, unhappy as he might esteem it, to all the splendid
triumphs of the most victorious general.[2]   I asserted likewise
upon another occasion (and asserted too in the hearing of
Pompey) that the same persons who confined Bibulus to his
house, had driven me from mine.   Indeed, the whole series
of those interrogatories [3] which I put to Vatinius at this trial,
was entirely designed as an invective against his tribunate:
and I particularly exposed, with much freedom and indignation, his contempt of the Auspices, his corrupt disposal of
foreign kingdoms, together with the rest of his violent and
illegal proceedings.   But it was not only upon this occasion
that I spoke thus unreservedly: I frequently avowed my
sentiments with the same resolute spirit in the senate.   Thus
when Marcellinus and Philippus were consuls,[4] I carried a
motion that the affair of the Campanian lands [5] should be

[1] P. Sextius was a tribune of the people in the consulship of Lentulus,
and a great instrument in restoring Cicero.   He resisted the faction of
Clodius by force of arms, and was, upon that account, in the following
year, accused of public violence by M. Tullius Albinovanus.   Cicero
defended him in an excellent oration, which is still extant, and he was
acquitted by the suffrages of all the judges.

[2] M. Calpurnius Bibulus was joint consul with J. Caesar.   The senate
secured the election of the former, in order to his being a check to the
ambitious designs of his colleague: and it was thought of so much
importance to the republic that he should be chosen, that even Cato
did not scruple upon this occasion to employ methods of bribery for
that purpose.   But Bibulus, after many vain efforts of patriotism,
and being grossly insulted in the forum by Caesar's mob, at length
withdrew from the functions of his office, and voluntarily confined
himself to his own house; tho' by the expression which Tully here
uses, it rather seems as if Caesar had employed some force in keeping
him there.   After which Caesar governed the republic without control.

[3] Cicero, instead of examining Vatinius upon the facts in his evidence
against Sextius, put to him a series of questions in such an artful
manner, that he exposed all the intrigues and iniquity of his tribunate.
This examination is still extant, under the title of *Interrogatio in
Vatinium.*"

[4] They were consuls A. U. 697.

[5] The lands in Campania, a district in Italy, now called the Terra di
lavoro in the kingdom of Naples, were partly appropriated to the use
of the republic, and partly in private hands.   Caesar had procured a
law for dividing the former among 25,000 poor citizens: and for
purchasing the latter in order to distribute them in the same manner.
Both these designs seem to have been very artfully calculated by
Caesar to promote and facilitate his grand purpose of usurping the
supreme power.   For by parcelling out these lands among the common

referred to the re-consideration of a full house,[1] on the 15th
of May following. Now tell me, my friend, could I possibly
have made a bolder or more formidable attack upon this
party? Could I possibly have given a more convincing
evidence, that I had not departed from my old principles,
notwithstanding all I had formerly suffered for their sake?
The truth of it is, this motion greatly exasperated, not only
those whom it was reasonable to expect it would offend, but
others upon whom I did not imagine it would have had any
such effect. Pompey, soon after this decree had passed, set
forward upon his expedition into Sardinia and Africa,[2] without giving me the least intimation of his being disgusted.
In his way thither he had a conference with Caesar at Lucca,[3]
who made great complaints of this motion. He had before,
it seems, been informed of it by Crassus at Ravenna;[4] who
took that opportunity of incensing him against me. And it
appeared afterwards that Pompey was likewise much dissatisfied upon the same account. This I learnt from several

people which belonged to the republic, he secured the populace to his
interest, and at the same time deprived the government of those very
considerable supplies both of money and corn which it derived from
its demesnes in Campania: as on the other side, by purchasing the
remainder of these estates, he must necessarily have weakened those
public treasures which were already much impoverished, and consequently rendered the commonwealth less capable of opposing his
ambitious measures.

[1] A decree of the senate had not its complete force unless it passed
in a full house; that is, when a competent number of the members were
present. The number requisite to make an act valid was 400.

[2] This expedition of Pompey into Sardinia and Africa, was in pursuance of the commission with which he had been invested for supplying
the public magazines with corn.

[3] Lucca was a frontier town in Caesar's province of Cisalpine Gaul,
adjoining to Italy: it still subsists under the same name, and is a
celebrated republic. It was Caesar's policy, at the end of every campaign, to fix his winter-quarters as near Italy as possible, in order to be
within observation of what passed at Rome. A numerous court was
immediately formed around him in these places of his residence, con-
sisting of the most distinguished persons in Rome and the neighbouring
provinces: and no less than 200 senators have been observed among
his attendants upon these occasions. Candidates for offices; young
men who had run out their estates; and, in a word, all whose affairs
of any kind were embarrassed, flocked to him in these cities: and
by liberal concessions to their respective wants and interests, he
strengthened his faction and forwarded his grand enterprise. It was
thus (as the judicious Plutarch observes) he had the address to employ
the forces of the republic against Gaul, and the spoils of Gaul against
the republic.

[4] A city in Cisalpine Gaul, still subsisting under the same name in the
Pope's dominions.

hands, but particularly from my brother, who met him in Sardinia, a few days after he had left Lucca. Pompey told him he was extremely glad of that accidental interview, as he wanted much to talk with him. He begun with saying, that as my brother stood engaged [1] for my conduct, he should expect him to exert all his endeavours to influence me accordingly. Pompey then proceeded very warmly to remonstrate against my late motion in the senate; reminding my brother of his services to us both, and particularly of what had passed between them concerning Caesar's edicts, and of those assurances, he said, my brother had given him of the measures I would pursue with respect to that article. He added, that my brother himself was a witness that the steps he had formerly taken for procuring my recall, were with the full consent and approbation of Caesar. Upon the whole, therefore, he entreated him, if it were either not in my power or my inclination to support the interest and dignity of the latter, that he would at least prevail with me not to oppose them. The account which my brother gave me of this conversation, together with a message I had before received from Pompey by Vibullius, to request that I would not proceed any farther in the affair of the Campanian lands till his return, threw me into a very serious train of reflections. I could not but think, after having performed and suffered so much for my country, that I might now at least be permitted to consider what was due to gratitude and to the honour of my brother: and as I had ever conducted myself with integrity towards the public, I might be allowed, I hoped, to act the same honest part in my more private connections.

During the time I was engaged in these votes and other proceedings with which Pompey appeared thus dissatisfied, I was informed of what passed in the conversations of a set of men, whom you will now guess without my naming. This party, though they approved of my public measures, as being agreeable to what had ever been their professed sentiments; were yet so ungenerous as to express great satisfaction in believing, that my conduct would by no means

---

[1] This alludes to those engagements which Quintus Cicero entered into in behalf of his brother, in order to induce Pompey to favour his recall from banishment. And it appears by what follows, that he promised on the part of Cicero an unlimited resignation to the measures of that ambitious chief.

oblige Pompey, at the same time that it would highly
exasperate Caesar. Well might I resent, indeed, so injurious
a treatment; but much more when I saw them, even before
my face, maliciously encouraging and caressing my avowed
enemy; [1]—mine do I call him? Rather let me say an enemy
to the laws and tranquillity of his country, and to every
character of worth and virtue amongst us.

Their malevolence, however, had not the effect they
intended, and it could not warm me into those transports of
indignation, of which my heart is now, indeed, no longer
susceptible. On the contrary, it only induced me to examine
my situation in all its various circumstances and relations,
with the greatest coolness and impartiality: the process and
result of which I will lay before you, in as few words as
I am able.

There have been times, as experience no less than history
has taught me, when the power of the commonwealth was in
worthless and wicked hands. In such a conjuncture, no
hope of interest (which I have at all times most heartily
contemned) nor fear of danger (which, upon some occasions,
however, has influenced the greatest minds) should prevail
with me to co-operate in their measures: no not though I
were attached to them by the strongest ties of friendship
and gratitude. But when a man of Pompey's distinguished
character presides over the republic; a man who has acquired
that eminence of power and honour by the most heroic
actions, and the most signal services; I could not imagine it
would be imputed to me as a levity of disposition, if in some
few instances I declined a little from my general maxims, and
complied with his inclinations.[2] But my justification, I
thought, would still rise in strength, when it should be
remembered that I favoured his credit and dignity even from
the earliest part of my life; as I particularly promoted them
in my praetorship and consulate: when it should be remem-

---

[1] Clodius.

[2] It appears by what has already been remarked, that Cicero's
compliance can by no means be considered in the favourable light in
which he here represents it; but was in reality a concession most
injurious to his honour and fatal to the liberties of Rome. It is certain
likewise, that it was not from any advantageous opinion of Pompey's
political character and designs, that he was induced to fall in with his
measures. On the contrary, Cicero most undoubtedly had no esteem
for him; and as to his political views, he saw and acknowledged long
before the date of this letter, that they were turned on the destruction
of the republic.

bered, that he not only assisted me with his vote and his influence in the senate during my adversity, but joined his counsels and his efforts with yours, for the same generous purpose: in a word, when it should be remembered, that he has no other enemy in the whole commonwealth, except the man who is my professed adversary.[1] In consequence of these sentiments, it was absolutely necessary for me, you see, to unite with Caesar, as one who was joined in the same views and the same interest. His friendship likewise, which, you are sensible, my brother and I have long shared, together with his humane and generous disposition which I have abundantly experienced both by his late letters and his good offices towards me, contributed greatly to confirm me in these resolutions. To which I must add, that the commonwealth in general seemed to be most strongly averse from giving any opposition to these extraordinary men: more especially after Caesar had performed such great and glorious exploits for the honour of his country. But what had still a farther and very powerful weight in my deliberations, was Pompey's having engaged his word for me to Caesar, as my brother had given the same assurances to Pompey.

Plato, I remembered, lays it down as a maxim in his divine writings, that "the people generally model their manners and their sentiments by those of the great:" a maxim which at this juncture, I thought, merited my particular attention. I was convinced indeed of its truth, when I reflected on the vigorous resolutions which were taken in the senate, on the memorable Nones of December:[2] and it seemed no wonder so noble a spirit should appear in that assembly, after the animating example I had given them upon my first entering on the consular office. I reflected also, that during the whole time which intervened between the expiration of my consulship, and that of Caesar and Bibulus,[3] when I still retained a very considerable authority in the senate, all the

---

[1] Clodius, after having driven Cicero out of Rome, entered most strenuously into the opposition against Pompey and Caesar.

[2] The fifth. It was on this day, in the consulship of Cicero and Antonius, that the senate came to a resolution of inflicting capital punishment on all those who were concerned in Catiline's conspiracy: and it is certain that Rome was indebted to Cicero on this day for one of the greatest deliverances which it had ever received since its foundation; and which nothing perhaps but his vigilance and sagacity could have so happily effected.

[3] Cicero was chosen consul in the year of Rome 690. Caesar and Bibulus in the year 694.

better part of the republic were united in their sentiments. On the other hand, about the time you took possession of your government in Spain, the commonwealth could not so properly be said to be under the administration of consuls, as of infamous barterers of provinces,[1] and the mean vassals and ministers of sedition.   It was then that discord and faction spread through all ranks amongst us: and I was marked out as the victim of party rage.   In this critical season, however, not only every man of worth, but the greater part of the senators, and indeed all Italy in general, rose up with remarkable unanimity in my cause.[2]   What the event proved, I forebear to mention: as in truth it is to be imputed to a complication of errors and artifices.   But this I will say, it was not forces, so much as leaders to conduct them, that were wanting to me at this crisis.   I must add, that whatever censure may justly fall on those who refused me their assistance; most certainly they who first promised it and then deserted me, are not less to be blamed.[3]   In a word, if

[1] The consuls to whom Cicero alludes are Lucius Calpurnius Piso, whose daughter Caesar had married, and Aulus Gabinius, a dependent and favourite of Pompey.   They succeeded Caesar and Bibulus in this office in 695, the year when Cicero went into exile.   Clodius secured them to his measures by a private contract to procure for them, by a grant from the people, two of the best governments of the empire: Piso was to have Macedonia, with Greece and Thessaly; Gabinius, Cilicia.   For this price they agreed to serve him in all his designs, particularly in the oppression of Cicero.

[2] Clodius procured a law, importing, *that whoever had taken the life of a citizen uncondemned and without a trial, should be prohibited from fire and water*.   Though Cicero was not named, yet he was marked out by this law.   His crime was, the putting Catiline's accomplices to death; which, though not done by his single authority, but by a general vote of the senate, and after a solemn hearing and debate, was alleged to be illegal, and contrary to the liberties of the people.   Cicero, finding himself thus reduced to the condition of a criminal, changed his habit upon it, as was usual in the case of a public impeachment; and appeared about the streets in a mourning gown to excite the compassion of his fellow-citizens: whilst Clodius, at the head of his mob, contrived to meet and insult him at every turn.   But Cicero soon gathered friends enough to secure him from such insults; and the whole body of the knights, together with the young nobility to the number of 20,000, headed by Crassus the son, all changed their habit, and perpetually attended him about the city to implore the protection and assistance of the people.

[3] In this number was Pompey himself, who though he had given Cicero the most solemn assurances that he would, at the hazard of his life, protect him against Clodius; yet when afterwards our author solicited the execution of this promise, he treated him with much rudeness as well as great treachery, and absolutely refused to concern himself in the affair.   It seems altogether unaccountable that Cicero should be so injudicious as to touch upon a circumstance that destroys the whole

some of my friends may well be reproached for the timid, though sincere, counsels they gave me; how much more severe must their condemnation prove, who artfully alarmed me with their pretended fears? Let it be noted at the same time to my honour, that zealous as my fellow-citizens showed themselves to rise up in the defence of a man who had formerly stood forth in theirs; yet I would not suffer them to be exposed (unsupported as they were by those who ought to have been their protectors) to the barbarous insults of a lawless banditti. On the contrary, I rather chose the world should judge by the power of my friends in recalling me from my exile, what their honest unanimity could have effected, had I permitted them to have drawn their swords to prevent it.

You were sensible of this general zeal in my favour, when you undertook my cause: and you not only encouraged, but confirmed it, by your influence and authority. I shall always most willingly acknowledge, that you were assisted upon this occasion by some of the most considerable persons in Rome; [1] who, it must be owned, exerted themselves with much greater vigour in procuring my return, than in preventing my banishment. And had they persisted in the same resolute disposition, they might have recovered their own authority at the same time that they obtained my restoration. The spirits, in truth, of the aristocratical part of the republic were at this juncture greatly raised and animated, by the inflexible patriotism of your conduct during your consulship, together with Pompey's concurrence in the same measures. Caesar likewise, when he saw the senate distinguishing his glorious actions by the most singular and unprecedented honours, joined in adding weight to the authority of that assembly. Had these happy circumstances therefore been rightly improved, it would have been impossible for any ill-designing citizen, to have violated the laws and liberties of

force of his apology; so far as he intended to justify his conduct by his friendship to Pompey. For it exceeds all power of credulity to imagine. that he could really be influenced by a motive of that kind with respect to a man, whose insincerity he had so lately and so severely experienced.

[1] Clodius was so elated with his success against Cicero, that he had no sooner driven him out of Rome, than he conceived hopes of rendering himself no less formidable to Caesar and Pompey. Accordingly he entered into an open opposition against them both; which he carried on with so much warmth and petulance, that at length they found it expedient for their purposes to mortify him by recalling Cicero.

the commonwealth. But let me entreat you to reflect a moment on the subsequent conduct of my political associates. In the first place, they screened from punishment that infamous intruder on the matron-mysteries, who showed no more reverence for the awful ceremonies of the goddess in whose honour these sacred solemnities are celebrated, than for the chastity of his three sisters.[1] And thus by preventing a worthy tribune of the people from obtaining that justice upon Clodius which he endeavoured to procure, they deprived future times of a most salutary example of chastised sedition.[2] Did not they suffer likewise that monument, that glorious monument, which was erected, not indeed with the spoils I had gained in foreign wars, but by the generosity of the senate for my civil services; did they not most shamefully suffer it to be inscribed with the name of the cruel and

---

[1] Clodius (as Plutarch relates the story) had an intrigue with Pompeia, Caesar's wife: but as he could not easily gain access to her, he took the opportunity while she was celebrating the mysteries of the *bona Dea* at her own house, to enter disguised in a woman's habit. While he was waiting in one of the apartments for Pompeia, he was discovered by a maidservant of Caesar's mother: who immediately giving the alarm, he was driven out of this female assembly with great indignation.——— The *bona Dea*, as the same author informs us, was supposed to have been a Dryad with whom the God Faunus had an amour. These rites were held in the highest veneration, and conducted with the most profound secrecy. They were celebrated annually by women at the house of the consul or praetor, and it was not lawful for any male to be present. Seneca tells us, they carried this precaution so far, that if there happened to be a picture of any male animal in the room where these mystic ceremonies were performing, it was thought necessary it should be veiled.

[2] Lentulus immediately upon entering on his consular office, A. U. 696, moved the senate that Cicero might be restored: in which he was seconded by Pompey with much zeal, and the whole house unanimously concurred in the motion. Serranus, however, a tribune of the people, interposing his negative, no decree could pass at that time: nevertheless it was with one consent resolved, that on the 22nd of the same month, a law should be proposed to the people for Cicero's recall. When the appointed day arrived, the friends of Cicero found the Forum in the possession of Clodius, who had planted his mob there over-night in order to prevent the promulgation of this law. A very bloody skirmish ensued, in which several lives were lost and many other outrages committed: in consequence of which, Clodius was impeached by Milo as a disturber of the public peace. But Metellus, the colleague of Lentulus, together with Appius the praetor, and Serranus the tribune, determined to screen Clodius: and accordingly, by a most dangerous exercise of their authority, they published their several edicts commanding all farther proceedings in this prosecution to be discontinued. It was a very impolitic power which was lodged in the tribunes, of thus preventing the execution of the laws as well as the passing of them, and which caused infinite mischiefs to the republic.

avowed enemy of his country? [1] Obliged, most certainly, I am to them for having restored me to the commonwealth: but I could wish they had conducted themselves, not only like physicians whose views terminate merely in the health of their patients, but like the Aliptae [2] also who endeavour to establish the spirits and vigour of those under their care. Whereas they have acted with regard to me, as Apelles did in relation to his celebrated picture of Venus: [3] they have finished one part of their work with great skill and accuracy, but left all the rest a mere rude and imperfect sketch.

In one article, however, I had the satisfaction to disappoint my enemies. They imagined my banishment would have wrought the same effect on me, which they falsely supposed a calamity of a like kind produced formerly in Quintus Metellus. This excellent person (whom I look upon to have been a man of the greatest fortitude and magnanimity of any in his times) they represented as broken and dispirited after his return from exile. [4] But if broken he

---

[1] After the suppression of Catiline's conspiracy, the senate decreed that a temple should be erected to liberty, as a public monument of their late happy deliverance. This temple was raised at the foot of Mount Palatine, near Cicero's house. And as the inscription fixed thereon, undoubtedly mentioned Cicero with honour, Clodius erased those words, and placed his own name in their stead.

[2] The *Aliptae* were persons who prepared the bodies of the athletic combatants, by unctions and other proper methods, for rendering them vigorous and active in their gymnastic exercises.

[3] Apelles, one of the greatest masters of painting in ancient Greece, was a native of Cos, and flourished in the 112th Olymp. or about 332 years before Christ. His principal excellency consisted in the inimitable grace which distinguished all his performances. He could even convey ideas which seemed impossible to be raised by colours, and animate his sublime pieces with all the terrors of thunder and lightning. His capital performance was a figure of Venus, which appears to have been at Rome in the times of Augustus. The lower parts of this picture being damaged, no painter would venture to re-touch it. Something of the same kind is mentioned to the honour of Raphael, whose paintings in the little Farnese at Rome being somewhat spoiled, it was with the greatest difficulty that even Carlo Maratti was prevailed upon to restore them. Apelles began a second figure of Venus which he intended should excel his first: but he died before he had proceeded any farther in that design than the head and shoulders.

[4] Q. Caecilius Metellus was in the number of those who opposed the faction of Caius Marius: in consequence of which he was at length driven into exile. The immediate occasion, however, of his sentence was this: Saturninus, a tribune of the people, and creature of Marius, proposed a law in the year 653, which, among other things, enacted, that "the senators should swear to ratify whatever the people ordained." This oath Metellus, with the true spirit of ancient Rome, resolutely refused to take: and when his friends represented to him

really were, it could not be the effect of his adversity: as it is certain he submitted to his sentence without the least reluctance, and lived under it, not only with indifference, but with cheerfulness. The truth is, no man ever equalled him in the strength and heroism of his mind; no, not even the celebrated Marcus Scaurus.[1]   Nevertheless, such as they had heard, or at least chose to imagine Metellus to have been, they figured me to themselves: or, if possible indeed, even yet more abject.   The reverse, however, proved to be the case: and that general concern which the whole republic expressed at my absence, inspired me with more vigorous spirits than I had ever before enjoyed.   The fact is, that the sentence of banishment against Metellus was repealed by a law proposed only by a single tribune of the people: whereas I was recalled from mine upon the motion of the consul himself,[2] and by a law in which every magistrate of Rome concurred.   Let me add likewise, that each order and degree in the commonwealth, headed by the senate, and supported by all Italy, zealously united in one common effort for recovering me to my country.   Yet high as these unexampled honours were, they have never elated my heart with pride, or tempted me to assume an air which could give just offence even to the most malevolent of my enemies.   The whole of my ambition is, not to be wanting either in advice or assistance to my friends; or even to those whom I have

the dangerous consequences which would probably attend his persevering in that honest resolution, he nobly replied, *it is the characteristic of a man of virtue and honour to act rightly, whatever consequences may ensue.*   Accordingly a decree passed in an assembly of the people for his banishment: and when his friends offered him their assistance to withstand this piece of public injustice, he generously refused their aid: *for*, said he, *either public measures will be changed, and the people will repent of the injury they have done me ; and then I shall be recalled with honour : or they will continue in the same sentiments ; and in that case banishment will be a happiness.*   He greatly chose therefore to withdraw himself from the destructive politics of his country; and retiring to Rhodes, he calmly spent his time in philosophical studies. His virtues, however, prevailed at last over the iniquity of his persecutors, and he was restored to the republic notwithstanding all the opposition of Marius.

[1] M. Aemilius Scaurus was advanced a second time to the honour of the consular office in the year of Rome 646, having enjoyed that dignity eight years before.   He is mentioned by Cicero among the orators of that age: but there was more of force and authority in what he delivered, than of grace in his manner, or elegance in his expression.   He was unsuccessfully accused in his latter days of having carried on a traitorous correspondence with Mithridates.

[2] Lentulus, the person to whom this letter is addressed.

no great reason to rank in that number. It is this, perhaps, which has given the real ground of complaint to those who view only the lustre of my actions, but cannot be sensible of the pains and solicitude they cost me. But whatever the true cause may be, the pretended one is, my having promoted the honours of Caesar: a circumstance which they interpret, it seems, as a renunciation of my old maxims. The genuine motives however of my conduct in this instance are, not only what I just before mentioned, but particularly what I hinted in the beginning of my letter, and will now more fully explain.

You will not find then, my friend, the aristocratical part of the republic disposed to pursue the same system as when you left them. That system, I mean, which I endeavoured to establish when I was consul, and which, though afterwards occasionally interrupted, and at length entirely overthrown, was again fully restored during your administration. It is now however totally abandoned by those who ought most strenuously to have supported it. I do not assert this upon the credit only of appearances, in which it is exceedingly easy to dissemble: I speak it upon the unquestionable evidence of facts, and the public proceedings of those who were styled patriots in my consulate. The general scheme of politics therefore being thus changed, it is time, most certainly, for every man of prudence (in which number I have the ambition to be justly accounted) to vary likewise his particular plan. Accordingly, that chief and favourite guide of my principles whom I have already quoted, the divine Plato himself advises, not to press any political point farther than is consonant with the general sense of the community: for methods of violence, he maintains, are no more to be used towards one's country, than one's parent. Upon this maxim, he tells us, he declined engaging in public affairs: and as he found the people of Athens confirmed by long habit in their mistaken notions of government, he did not think it lawful to attempt by force, what he despaired of effecting by persuasion. My situation, however, is in this respect different from Plato's: for on the one hand, as I have already embarked in public affairs, it is too late to deliberate whether I should now enter upon them or not: so on the other, the Roman people are by no means so incapable of judging of their true interest as he represents the

Athenians. It is my happiness, indeed, to be able by the same measures to consult at once both my own and my country's welfare. To these considerations I must add those uncommon acts of generosity, which Caesar has exerted both towards my brother and myself: so much indeed beyond all example, that even whatever had been his success, I should have thought it incumbent upon me, at least to have defended him. But now, distinguished as he is by such a wonderful series of prosperity, and crowned with so many glorious victories, I cannot but esteem it a duty which I owe the republic, abstracted from all personal obligations to himself, to promote his honours as far as lies in my power. And believe me, it is at once my confession and my glory, that next to you, together with the other generous authors of my restoration, there is not a man in the world from whom I have received such amicable offices.

And now, having laid before you the principal motives of my conduct in general, I shall be the better able to satisfy you concerning my behaviour with respect to Crassus and Vatinius in particular: for as to Appius and Caesar, I have the pleasure to find that you acquit me of all reproach.

My reconciliation then with Vatinius was effected by the mediation of Pompey, soon after the former was elected Praetor. I must confess, when he petitioned to be admitted a candidate for that office, I very warmly opposed him in the senate: but it was much less from my resentment to the man himself, than in order to support the honour and interest of Cato.[1] Soon after this, he was impeached: and it was in compliance with the earnest solicitation of Caesar, that I undertook his defence. But you must not inquire why I appeared at this trial, or indeed at any other of the same kind, as a witness in favour of the accused: lest I should hereafter have an opportunity of retorting the question upon you. Though to say truth, I may fairly ask it even now: for do you not remember, my friend, in whose behalf

---

[1] Cato, the year before the date of this letter, had solicited the Praetorship, in order to arm himself with the authority of that important office against the dangerous designs of Crassus and Pompey; who were at that time Consuls. But they were too well aware of the honest purposes of this inflexible patriot, not to obstruct his election: and accordingly they carried it against him in favour of the pliant and worthless Vatinius, whose pretensions they supported by every infamous method of artifice, corruption, and violence.

it was that you formerly transmitted certain honourable
testimonials even from the utmost limits of the Roman
Empire? You need not scruple, however, to acknowledge
the fact: for I have acted, and shall continue to act, the
same part towards those very persons. But to return to
Vatinius: besides the reasons I have already assigned, I was
provoked to engage in his defence, by an opposition of the
same sort which the parasite recommends to the amorous
soldier in the play.[1] The obsequious Gnatho, you know,
advises his friend the captain whenever his mistress
endeavours to pique his jealousy by mentioning his rival
Phaedria, to play off Pamphila upon her in return. Thus,
as I told the judges at this trial, since certain honourable
persons who were formerly much in my interest had thought
proper, by many little mortifying instances in the senate,
to caress my avowed enemy before my face, I thought it
but equitable to have a Clodius on my part, in opposition
to the Clodius on theirs. Accordingly I have upon many
occasions acted suitably to this declaration: and all the
world acknowledges I have reason.

Having thus explained my conduct with regard to
Vatinius, I will now lay before you those motives which
determined me in respect to Crassus. I was willing, for the
sake of the common cause, to bury in oblivion the many and
great injuries I had formerly received from him. Agreeably
to this disposition, as we were then upon good terms, I
should have borne his unexpected defence of Gabinius[2]
(whom he had very lately with so much warmth opposed) if
he had avoided all personal reflections on myself. But
when, with the most unprovoked violence, he broke in upon
me whilst I was in the midst of my speech; I must confess
it raised my indignation: and perhaps I took fire so much
the sooner, as possibly there still remained in my heart some
latent sparks of my former resentment. However, my behaviour in the senate upon this occasion, was much and
generally applauded. Among the rest, I was complimented
likewise by the same men whom I have often hinted at in
this letter; and who acknowledged I had rendered a very
essential service to their cause, by that spirit which I had

---

[1] The Eunuch of Terence.
[2] Aulus Gabinius was consul the same year in which Cicero was so
outrageously persecuted by Clodius; with whom Gabinius most
zealously concurred.

thus exerted. In short, they affected to speak of me in public, as being now indeed restored to the commonwealth in the best and most glorious sense. Nevertheless, they had the malice in their private conversations (as I was informed by persons of undoubted honour) to express singular satisfaction in the new variance that had thus happened between Crassus and myself: as they pleased themselves with imagining it would for ever throw me at a distance from those who were joined with him in the same interest.[1] Pompey in the meantime employed incredible pains to close this breach: and Caesar also mentioned it in his letters, as an incident that gave him much concern. Upon these considerations therefore I thought it expedient to act agreeably both to the dictates of my natural temper, and to that experience which I had gained by my former misfortunes. In pursuance of these sentiments, I consented to a reconcilement: and in order to render it more conspicuous to the world, Crassus set out for his government[2] almost from under my roof: for having invited himself to spend the preceding night with me, we supped together in the gardens of my son-in-law Crassipes. It was for these reasons that I thought my honour obliged me to defend his cause in the senate: and I confess I mentioned him with that high applause, of which, it seems, you have been informed.

Thus I have given you a full detail of the several views and motives by which I am governed in the present conjuncture, as well as of the particular disposition in which I stand with respect to the slender part I can pretend to claim in the administration of public affairs. And, believe me, I should have judged and acted entirely in the same manner, had I been totally free from every sort of amicable bias. For, on the one hand, I should have esteemed it the most absurd folly to have attempted to oppose so superior a force; and on the other, supposing it possible, I should yet have deemed it imprudent to weaken the authority of persons so

---

[1] Caesar and Pompey. The former, finding it necessary for his purposes that Crassus and Pompey should act in concert, procured a reconciliation between them: and by this means, says Plutarch, formed that invincible Triumvirate, which ruined the authority both of the Senate and the people; and of which he alone received the advantage.

[2] The province of Syria was allotted to Crassus, for which he set out a month or two before the expiration of his consulate in the year 698, and from whence he never returned.

eminently and so justly distinguished in the commonwealth. Besides, it appears to me to be the dictates of sound policy, to act in accommodation to particular conjunctures, and not inflexibly pursue the same unalterable scheme, when public circumstances, together with the sentiments of the best and wisest members of the community, are evidently changed. In conformity to this notion, the most judicious reasoners on the great art of government have universally condemned an obstinate perseverance in one uniform tenor of measures. The skill of the pilot is shown in weathering the storm at least, though he should not gain his port: but if shifting his sails, and changing his direction will infallibly carry him with security into the intended harbour, would it not be an instance of most unreasonable tenaciousness to continue in the more hazardous course wherein he began his voyage? Thus (and it is a maxim I have often had occasion to inculcate) the point we ought all of us to keep in view in our administration of the commonwealth, is the final enjoyment of an honourable repose: but the method of securing to ourselves this dignity of retreat, is by having been invariable in our intentions for the public welfare, and not by a positive perseverance in certain favourite modes of obtaining it. To repeat therefore what I just now declared; had I been absolutely uninfluenced by every motive of friendship, I should still have pursued the same public measures in which I am now engaged. But when gratitude and resentment both conspire in recommending this scheme of action to me, I cannot hesitate a moment in adopting it, especially since it appears most conducive to the interests of the republic in general, as well as to my own in particular. To speak freely, I act upon this principle so much the more frequently, and with the less reserve, not only as my brother is Lieutenant under Caesar, but as the latter receives the slightest action or even word of mine in his favour, with an air that evidently shows he considers them as obligations of the most sensible kind. And, in fact, I derive the same benefit from that popularity and power which you know he possesses, as if they were so many advantages of my own. The sum of the whole in short is this: I imagined that I had no other method of counteracting those perfidious designs with which a certain party were secretly contriving to undermine me, than by thus uniting the friendship and protection of the men in power, with those internal aids which have never yet been wanting to my support.

I am well persuaded, had you been in Rome, you would have concurred with me in these sentiments. I know, indeed, the candour and moderation of your temper; and I know, too, that your heart not only glows with friendship towards me, but is wholly untainted with malevolence towards others: in a word, I know that as you possess every sublime and generous affection, you are incapable of anything so mean as artifice and disguise. Nevertheless, even this elevated disposition has not secured you from the same unprovoked malice, which I have experienced in my own affairs. I doubt not, therefore, if you had been an actor in this scene, the same motives would have swayed *your* conduct, which have governed *mine*. But however that may be, I shall most certainly submit all my actions to your guidance and advice, whenever I shall again enjoy your company: and I am sure you will not be less attentive to the preservation of my honour, than you formerly were to that of my person. Of this at least you may be persuaded, that you will find me a faithful friend and associate in all your counsels and measures: as it will be the first and daily purpose of my life, to supply you with additional and more powerful reasons for rejoicing in those obligations you have conferred upon me.

As you desire me to send you those compositions which I have written since you left Rome, I shall deliver some orations into the hands of Menocrates for that purpose. However, not to alarm you, their number is but inconsiderable; for I withdraw as much as possible from the contention of the bar, in order to join those more gentle muses which were always my delight, and are particularly so at this juncture. Accordingly I have drawn up three dialogues upon oratory, wherein I have endeavoured to imitate the manner of Aristotle. I trust they will not prove altogether useless to your son, as I have rejected the modern precepts of rhetoric, and adopted the ancient Aristotelian and Isocratic rules. To this catalogue of my writings I must also add an historical poem which I have lately composed in three cantos, upon the subject of my banishment; and as a lasting memorial likewise of your friendship and my gratitude. This I should long since have transmitted to you, had it been my immediate intention to make it public. But I am discouraged from this design at present, not indeed as fearing the resentment of those who may imagine themselves the objects of my satire (for in this respect I have been extremely tender), but as finding it impossible to make particular mention of every one from whom I received obligations at that season. However, when I shall meet with a proper opportunity, I will send it to you; submitting my writings as well as my actions entirely to your judgment. I know indeed these literary meditations have ever been the favourite employment of your thoughts no less than of mine.

Your family concerns which you recommend to me, are so much a part of my own, that I am sorry you should think it necessary even to remind me of them. I could not therefore read your solicitations for that purpose, without some uneasiness.

I find you were prevented by an indisposition from going the last summer into Cilicia; which was the occasion, it seems, of your not settling my brother's affairs in that province. However you give me assurance that you will now take all possible methods of adjusting them. You cannot indeed oblige him more: and he will think himself as much indebted to you for procuring him this additional farm, as if you had settled him in the possession of his patrimony. In the meantime, I entreat you to inform me frequently and freely of all your affairs, and particularly give me an account of the studies and exercises in which your son is engaged. For be well persuaded, never friend was more agreeable or more endeared to another, than you are to me: and of this truth I hope to render not only you, but all the world, and even posterity itself, thoroughly sensible.

Appius [1] has lately declared in the senate (what he had before indeed often intimated in conversation) that if he could get his proconsular commission confirmed in an assembly of the Curiae, [2] he would cast lots with his colleague for the particular province to which they should respectively succeed:

---

[1] Appius Claudius Pulcher, one of the consuls at this time.
[2] Romulus divided the city into a certain number of districts called Curiae, which somewhat resembled our parishes. When the people were summoned together to transact any business agreeably to this division, it was called an assembly of the Curiae: where the most votes in every Curia was considered as the voice of the whole district, and the most Curiae as the general consent of the people.]

if not, that by an amicable agreement between themselves he had resolved upon yours.[1] He added, that in the case of a consul it was not absolutely necessary, though perhaps it might be expedient, to procure a law of this kind: and as a government had been appointed him by a decree of the senate, he was entitled, he said, in consequence of the Cornelian law, to a military command, till the time of his entrance into Rome. I know not what accounts you may have received of this matter from your other friends: but I find the sentiments of the world are much divided. Some are of opinion, that you are not obliged to resign your government, if your successor should not be authorised by an assembly of the Curiae: whilst others maintain, that notwithstanding you should think proper to leave the province, you may nevertheless depute a person to preside in your absence. As to myself, I am not altogether so clear with respect to the law in question: though I must own at the same time, that my doubts are by no means considerable. Of this however I am perfectly sure, that it is agreeable to your honour, and to that generosity of conduct in which I know you place your highest gratification, quietly to yield up your province to your successor; especially as you cannot in this instance oppose his ambitious views without incurring the suspicion of being influenced by the same motives yourself. But be that as it will, I thought it incumbent upon me to inform you of my sentiments: as I shall certainly defend yours, which ever way they may determine you to act.

After I had finished my letter, I received your last concerning the farmers of the revenues.[2] Your decision appears to me, I must own, perfectly equitable; yet at the same time, I cannot but wish you might be so happy as not to disgust a body of men, whose interest you have hitherto always favoured. However, you may be assured I shall support the decrees you have made upon this occasion: though

---

[1] The senate annually nominated the two provinces to which the consuls should succeed at the expiration of their office; but it was left to the consuls themselves to determine, either by casting lots, or by private agreement, which of the particular provinces so assigned they should respectively administer.

[2] The society of farmers of the public revenues among the Romans was a body of men in high repute, as being composed of the principal persons of the equestrian order. Disputes frequently arose between these and the tributary provinces: and it is to some difference of this kind, wherein Lentulus had given judgement against them, that Cicero seems to allude.

you well know the temper and disposition of these people, and what formidable enemies they proved to the excellent Quintus Scaevola.[1] I would recommend it to you therefore, if possible, to recover their good graces, or at least to soften them. The task, I confess, is difficult: but prudence, I think, requires you should use your best endeavours for that purpose. Farewell.

TO TIRO

NOTWITHSTANDING that I feel the want of your services, in every place and upon all occasions; yet, be assured, your illness gives me far less concern on my own account, than on yours. However, since it has terminated, as Curius informs me, in a quartan ague; I hope, if you are not wanting in proper care, that it will prove a means of more firmly establishing your [2] health. Be so just then to the regard you owe me, as not to suffer any other concern to employ your thoughts but what relates to your recovery. I am sensible, at the same time, how much you suffer from this absence: but believe me, all will be well, whenever you are so. I would by no means therefore have you in so much haste to return to me, as to expose yourself to the dangers of a winter-voyage; nor indeed to the dangers of a sea-sickness, before you shall have sufficiently recovered your strength.

I arrived in the suburbs [3] of Rome on the fourth of January: and nothing could be more to my honour, than the manner in which I was met on my approach to the city. But I am unhappily fallen into the very midst of public dissension, or rather indeed, I find myself surrounded with the flames of a civil war. It was my earnest desire to have composed these

---

[1] There were two very eminent persons of this name in Cicero's time. The first, the most celebrated lawyer and politician of his age, is distinguished by the title of Augur. The other, who was high Priest, was slain at the entrance of the temple of Vesta, as he was endeavouring to make his escape from that general massacre of the senators which was perpetrated by the orders of the young Marius.

[2] A quartan ague was supposed by the ancients to be extremely salutary in its consequences.

[3] As Cicero claimed the honour of a triumph, he was obliged, till his pretensions should be determined, to take up his residence without the walls of the city.

dangerous ferments: and I probably might, if the passions of some in both parties, who are equally eager for war, had not rendered my endeavours ineffectual. My friend Caesar has written a very warm and menacing letter to the senate.[1] He has the assurance, notwithstanding their express prohibition, to continue at the head of his army and in the government of his province: to which very extraordinary measures he has been instigated by Curio. The latter, in conjunction with Quintus Cassius and Mark Antony, without the least violence having been offered to them, have withdrawn themselves to Caesar. They took this step immediately after the senate had given it in charge to the consuls,[2] the praetors, and the tribunes of the people, together with those of us who are invested with proconsular power, to take care of the interests of the republic.[3] And never, in truth, were our liberties in more imminent danger: as those who are disaffected to the commonwealth never were headed by a chief more capable, or better prepared to support them. We are raising forces with all possible diligence, under the authority and with the assistance of Pompey: who now begins, somewhat too late I fear, to be apprehensive of Caesar's power. In the midst however of these alarming commotions, the senate demanded, in a very full house, that a triumph should be immediately decreed to me. But the consul Lentulus, in order to appropriate to himself a greater share in conferring this honour, told them, that he would propose it himself in proper form, as soon as he should have dispatched the affairs that were necessary in the present conjuncture. In the meantime, I act with great moderation: and this conduct renders my influence with both parties so much the stronger. The several districts of Italy are assigned to our respective protections: and Capua is the department I have taken for mine.

[1] The purport of Caesar's letter was, that he declared himself willing to resign his command, provided Pompey did the same: but if this were not complied with, that he would immediately march into Italy, and revenge the injuries done both to himself and to the liberties of the republic.

[2] The consuls of this year were Clodius Marcellus, and Cornelius Lentulus Crus.

[3] By this decree the magistrates therein named were invested with a discretionary power of acting as they should judge proper in the present exigency of public affairs: a decree to which the senate never had recourse but in cases of the utmost danger and distress.

I thought it proper to give you this general information of public affairs: to which I will only add my request, that you would take care of your health, and write to me by every opportunity. Again and again I bid you farewell.

Jan. the 12*th.*

TO TERENTIA AND TO TULLIA

In what manner it may be proper to dispose of yourselves during the present conjuncture, is a question which must now be decided by your own judgements as much as by mine. Should Caesar advance to Rome without committing hostilities, you may certainly, for the present at least, remain there unmolested: but if this madman should give up the city to the rapine of his soldiers, I much doubt whether even Dolabella's credit and authority will be sufficient to protect you. I am under some apprehension likewise, lest whilst you are deliberating in what manner to act, you should find yourselves so surrounded with the army as to render it impossible to withdraw, though you should be never so much inclined. The next question is (and it is a question which you yourselves are best able to determine) whether any ladies of your rank venture to continue in the city: if not, will it be consistent with your character to appear singular in that point? But be that as it will, you cannot, I think, as affairs are now situated, be more commodiously placed, than either with me or at some of our farms in this district: supposing, I mean, that I should be able to maintain my present post. I must add likewise, that a short time, 'tis to be feared, will produce a great scarcity in Rome. However, I should be glad you would take the sentiments of Atticus, or Camillus, or any other friend whom you may choose to consult upon this subject. In the meanwhile let me conjure you both to keep up your spirits. The coming over of Labienus [1] to our party, has given affairs a much better aspect. And Piso having withdrawn himself from the city,

---

[1] Labienus was one of Caesar's principal and most favourite lieutenants in Gaul; where he greatly distinguished himself by his military conduct. The Pompeian party therefore were very assiduous in their applications to gain him over to their cause.

is likewise another very favourable circumstance: as it is a plain indication, that he disapproves the impious measures of his son-in-law.

I entreat you, my dearest creatures, to write to me as frequently as possible, and let me know how it is with you, as well as what is going forward in Rome. My brother and nephew, together with Rufus, affectionately salute you. Farewell.

MINTURNAE,[1] *Jan. the 25th.*

TO TIRO

You will easily judge of our distress when I tell you, that myself and every friend of the republic have abandoned Rome, and even our country, to all the cruel devastations of fire and sword. Our affairs indeed are in so desperate a situation, that nothing less than the powerful interposition of some favourable divinity, or some happy turn of chance, can secure us from utter ruin. If has been the perpetual purpose of all my speeches, my votes, and my actions, ever since I returned to Rome, to preserve the public tranquillity. But an invincible rage for war had unaccountably seized not only the enemies, but even those who are esteemed the friends of the commonwealth: and it was in vain I remonstrated, that nothing was more to be dreaded than a civil war. Caesar, in the meantime, unmindful of his former character and honours, and driven, if should seem, by a sort of phrenzy, has taken possession of Ariminum, Pisaurum, Ancona, and Arretum. In consequence of this, we have all deserted the city: but how prudently, or how heroically, it now avails not to examine. Thus you see our wretched situation! Caesar, however, has offered us the following conditions: in the first place, that Pompey shall retire to his government in Spain; in the next, that the army we have raised shall be disbanded, and our garrisons evacuated. Upon these terms he promises to deliver up the farther Gaul into the hands of Domitius, and the nearer into those of Confidius Nonianus, the persons to whom these provinces have been respectively allotted. He farther engages to resign his right of suing for

[1] A town in Campania.

the consulship in his absence, and is willing to return to Rome in order to appear as a candidate in the regular form. We have accepted these propositions, provided he withdraws his forces from the several towns above mentioned, that the senate may securely assemble themselves at Rome in order to pass a decree for that purpose. If he should think proper to comply with this proposal, there are hopes of peace; not indeed of a very honourable one, as the terms are imposed upon us: yet anything is preferable to our present circumstances. But if he should refuse to stand to his overtures, we are prepared for an engagement: but an engagement which Caesar, after having incurred the general odium of retracting his own conditions, will scarce be able to sustain. The only difficulty will be, to intercept his march to Rome. And this we have a prospect of effecting, as we have raised a very considerable body of troops: and we imagine that he will scarce venture to advance, lest he should lose the two Gauls; every part of those provinces, excepting only the Transpadani, being utterly averse to him. There are likewise six of our legions from Spain, commanded by Afranius and Petreius, and supported by a very powerful body of auxiliaries, that lie in his rear. In short, if he should be so mad as to approach, there is great probability of his being defeated, if we can but preserve Rome from falling into his hands. It has given a very considerable blow to his cause, that Labienus, who had great credit in his army, refused to be an associate with him in his impious enterprise. This illustrious person has not only deserted Caesar, but joined himself with us: and it is said, that many others of the same party intend to follow his example.

I have still under my protection all the coast that extends itself from Formiae. I did not choose to enter more deeply at present into the opposition against Caesar, that my exhortations, in order to engage him to an accommodation, might be attended with the greater weight. If war, however, must, after all, be our lot, it will be impossible for me, I perceive, to decline the command of some part of our forces.[1] To this uneasy reflection, I must add another: my son-in-law Dolabella has taken party with Caesar.

I was willing to give you this general information of public

[1] This, however, Cicero contrived to avoid: and though, after much hesitation, he followed Pompey into Greece, he would accept of no command in his army, nor was he present at any engagement.

affairs: but suffer it not, I charge you, to make impressions upon your mind, to the disadvantage of your health. I have strongly recommended you to Aulus Varro, whose disposition to serve you, as well as whose particular friendship to myself, I have thoroughly experienced. I have entreated him to be careful both of your health and of your voyage, and, in a word, to receive you entirely under his protection. I have full confidence that he will comply with my request, as he gave me his promise for that purpose in the most obliging manner.

As I could not enjoy the satisfaction of your company at a season when I most wanted your faithful services, I beg you would not now hasten your return, nor undertake your voyage either during the winter, or before you are perfectly recovered. For, be assured, I shall not think I see you too late, if I see you safe and well. I have heard nothing of you since the letter I received by Marcus Volusius: but indeed I do not wonder at it, as I imagine the severity of the winter has likewise prevented my letters from reaching your hands. Take care of yourself, I conjure you, and do not sail till your health and the season shall be favourable. My son is at Formiae: but Terentia and Tullia are still at Rome. Farewell.

CAPUA, *January the 29th.*

TO TERENTIA

IN answer to what you object concerning the divorce I mentioned in my last,[1] I can only say, that I am perfectly ignorant what power Dolabella may at this time possess, or what ferments there may be among the populace.[2] However, if you think there is anything to be apprehended from his resentment, let the matter rest: and perhaps the first proposal may come from himself. Nevertheless I leave you to act as you shall judge proper; not doubting that you will take such measures in this most unfortunate affair, as shall appear to be attended with the fewest unhappy consequences. Farewell.

July the 10th.

---

[1] Between Tullia and Dolabella.
[2] Dolabella was at this time tribune of the people, and employing the power and credit with which he was invested by that office, to the most seditious purposes.

TO MARCUS MARIUS

WHENEVER I reflect, as indeed I frequently do, on those public calamities we have thus long endured, and are still likely to endure, it always brings to my thoughts the last interview we had together. It made so strong an impression upon my mind, that I can name the very day: and I perfectly well remember it was on the 10th of May in the consulate of Lentulus and Marcellus, that upon my arrival at my Pompeian villa,[1] I found you waiting for me with the most friendly solicitude. Your generous concern arose from a tenderness both for my honour and my safety; as the former, you feared, would be endangered if I continued in Italy; and the latter, if I went to Pompey. I was myself likewise, as you undoubtedly perceived, so greatly perplexed, as to be incapable of determining which of these measures was most advisable. However, I resolved to sacrifice all considerations of personal safety, to the dictates of my honour; and, accordingly, I joined Pompey in Greece. But I no sooner arrived in his army, than I had occasion to repent of my resolution: not so much from the danger to which I was myself exposed, as from the many capital faults I discovered among them. In the first place, Pompey's forces were neither very considerable in point of numbers,[2] nor by any means composed of warlike troops: and in the next place (I speak however with exception of Pompey himself, and a few others of the principal leaders) they carried on the war with such a spirit of rapaciousness, and breathed such principles of cruelty in their conversation, that I could not think even upon our success without horror. To this I must add, that some of the most considerable officers were deeply involved in debt: and, in short, there was nothing good among them but their cause. Thus despairing of success, I advised (what indeed I had always recommended) that proposals of accommodation should be

[1] This villa of Cicero was situated near Pompeii, upon the eastern coast of the bay of Naples, and at no great distance from the villa of Marius.

[2] Pompey's army at the battle of Pharsalia, was more than double in number to that of Caesar, whose forces amounted only to about 22,000 men.

offered to Caesar: and when I found Pompey utterly averse
to all measures of that kind, I endeavoured to persuade him
at least to avoid a general engagement. This last advice
he seemed sometimes inclined to follow: and probably
would have followed, if a slight advantage which he soon
afterwards gained,[1] had not given him a confidence in his
troops. From that moment all the skill and conduct of this
great man seems to have utterly forsaken him; and he acted
so little like a general, that, with a raw and unexperienced
army, he imprudently gave battle[2] to the most brave and
martial legions. The consequence was, that he suffered a
most shameful defeat: and abandoning his camp to Caesar,
he was obliged to run away, unaccompanied even with a
single attendant. This event determined me to lay down
my arms; being persuaded, that if we could not prevail with
our united forces, we should scarce have better success when
they were broken and dispersed. I declined, therefore, to
engage any farther in a war, the result of which must necessarily be attended with one or other of the following unhappy
consequences: either to perish in the field of battle, to
be taken prisoner by the conquerors, to be sacrificed by
treachery,[3] to have recourse to Juba,[4] to live in a sort of
voluntary exile, or to fall by one's own hand. Other choice
most certainly there was none, if you would not, or durst
not, trust to the clemency of the victor. Banishment, it
must be owned, to a mind that had nothing to reproach
itself with, would have been the most eligible of all these
evils: especially under the reflection of being driven from
a commonwealth, which presents nothing to our view but
what we must behold with pain. Nevertheless, I chose to
remain with my own; if anything now indeed can with propriety be called our *own :* a misfortune which, together with
every other calamity that this fatal war has produced, I long

[1] Before the walls of Dyrrachium. Notwithstanding Cicero speaks
with some sort of contempt of this advantage which Pompey gained
over the troops of Caesar; yet it appears to have been very considerable.

[2] In the plains of Pharsalia.

[3] This seems to allude to the fate of Pompey.

[4] He was a very considerable prince, whose dominions extended, not
only over that part of Africa, which is now called the coast of Barbary,
but southward beyond mount Atlas; and from the Streights mouth
along the Atlantic ocean to the Canary islands. Upon the first breaking out of the civil war, he distinguished himself in supporting the
Pompeian party in Africa, against the army commanded by Curio:
whom he entirely defeated.

since foretold. I returned therefore to Italy, not as to a situation perfectly desirable, but in order, if the republic should in any degree subsist, to enjoy somewhat that had at least the semblance of our country; and if it were utterly destroyed, to live as if I were, to all essential purposes, in a real state of exile. But though I saw no reason that could justly induce me to be my own executioner, I saw many to be desirous of death. For it is an old and true maxim, that "life is not worth preserving, when a man is no longer what he once was." A blameless conscience, however, is undoubtedly a great consolation; especially as I can add to it the double support that arises to my mind, from a knowledge of the noblest sciences, and from the glory of my former actions: one of which can never be torn from me so long as I live; and of the other, even death itself has not the power to deprive me.

I have troubled you with this minute detail, from a full persuasion of the tender regard you bear both to myself and to our country. I was desirous indeed to apprise you fully of the principles by which I have steered, that you might be sensible it was my first and principal aim, that no single arm should be more potent than the whole united commonwealth: and afterwards, when there was one, who by Pompey's mistaken conduct, had so firmly established his power as to render all resistance vain: that it was my next endeavour to preserve the public tranquillity. I was desirous you should know that after the loss of those troops and that general[1] wherein all our hopes were centred, I attempted to procure a total cessation of arms; and when this advice proved ineffectual, that I determined at least to lay down my own. In a word, I was desirous you should know, that if our liberties still remain, I also am still a citizen of the republic: if not, that I am no less an exile, nor more conveniently situated, than if I had banished myself to Rhodes or Mitylene.[2]

I should have been glad to have said this to you in person: but as I was not likely to meet with an opportunity for that purpose so soon as I wished, I thought proper to take this

[1] Pompey.
[2] Rhodes, the metropolis of an island in the Mediterranean, and Mitylene, the principal city of Lesbos, an island in the Aegean sea, were places to which Marcellus and some others of the Pompeian party retired after the battle of Pharsalia.

earlier method of furnishing you with an answer, if you should fall in the way of those who are disposed to arraign my conduct. For notwithstanding that my death could in no sort have availed the republic, yet I stand condemned, it seems, by some, for not sacrificing my life in its cause. But they are those only, I am well assured, who have the cruelty to think, that there has not been blood enough spilt already. If my advice, however, had been followed, those who have perished in this war, might have preserved their lives with honour, though they had accepted of peace upon ever so unreasonable conditions. For they would still have had the better cause, though their enemies had the stronger swords.

And now, perhaps, I have quite tired your patience: I shall think so at least, if you do not send me a longer letter in return. I will only add, that if I can dispatch some affairs which I am desirous of finishing, I hope to be with you very shortly. Farewell.

TO PAPIRIUS PAETUS

Your letter afforded me a very agreeable instance of your friendship, in the concern it expressed lest I should be uneasy at the report which had been brought hither by Silius.[1] I was before indeed perfectly sensible how much you were disturbed at this circumstance, by your care in sending me duplicates of a former letter upon the same subject: and I then returned such an answer as I thought would be sufficient to abate at least, if not entirely remove, this your generous solicitude. But since I perceive, by your last letter, how much this affair still dwells upon your mind, let me assure you, my dear Paetus, that I have employed every artifice (for we must now, my friend, be armed with cunning as well as prudence) to conciliate the good graces of the persons you mention: and if I mistake not, my endeavours have not proved in vain. I receive indeed so many marks of respect and esteem from those who are most in Caesar's favour, that I cannot but flatter myself they have a true

---

[1] Silius, it should seem, had brought an account from the army, that some witticisms of Cicero had been reported to Caesar, which had given him offence.

regard for me. It must be confessed, at the same time, that
a pretended affection is not easily discernible from a real one,
unless in seasons of distress. For adversity is to friendship,
what fire is to gold, the only infallible test to discover the
genuine from the counterfeit: in all other circumstances
they both bear the same common signatures. I have one
strong reason however to persuade me of their sincerity: as
neither their situation nor mine can by any means tempt them
to dissemble with me. As to that person[1] in whom all power
is now centred, I am not sensible that I have anything to
fear from him: or nothing more at least, than what arises
from that general precarious state in which all things must
stand where the fence of laws is broken down; and from its
being impossible to pronounce with assurance concerning any
event which depends wholly upon the will, not to say the
caprice, of another. But this I can with confidence affirm,
that I have not in any single instance given him just occasion
to take offence: and in the article you point out, I have been
particularly cautious. There was a time, 'tis true, when I
thought it well became me, by whom Rome itself was free,[2]
to speak my sentiments with freedom; but now that our
liberties are no more, I deem it equally agreeable to my
present situation, not to say anything that may disgust
either Caesar or his favourites. But were I to suppress every
rising raillery, that might pique those at whom it is directed,
I must renounce, you know, all my reputation as a wit.
And in good earnest, it is a character upon which I do not
set so high a value, as to be unwilling to resign it, if it were
in my power. However, I am in no danger of suffering in
Caesar's opinion, by being represented as the author of any
sarcasms to which I have no claim: for his judgement is much
too penetrating ever to be deceived by any imposition of
this nature. I remember your brother Servius, whom I
look upon to have been one of the most learned critics that
this age has produced, was so conversant in the writings of
our poets, and had acquired such an excellent and judicious
ear, that he could immediately distinguish the numbers of
Plautus from those of any other author. Thus Caesar, I am
told, when he made his large collection of apophthegms,[3]

----

[1] Caesar.
[2] Alluding to his services in the suppression of Catiline's conspiracy.
[3] This collection was made by Caesar when he was very young: and

constantly rejected any piece of wit that was brought to him as mine, if it happened to be spurious: a distinction which he is much more able to make at present, as his particular friends pass almost every day of their lives in my company. As our conversation generally turns upon a variety of subjects, I frequently strike out thoughts which they look upon as not altogether void, perhaps, of spirit or ingenuity. Now these little sallies of pleasantry, together with the general occurrences of Rome, are constantly transmitted to Caesar, in pursuance of his own express directions: so that if anything of this kind is mentioned by others as coming from me, he always disregards it. You see, then, that the lines you quote with so much propriety from the tragedy of Oenomaus,[1] contain a caution altogether unnecessary. For tell me, my friend, what jealousies can I possibly create? Or who will look with envy upon a man in my humble situation? But granting that I were in ever so enviable a state; yet let me observe, that it is the opinion of those philosophers, who alone seem to have understood the true nature of virtue, that a good man is answerable for nothing farther than his own innocence. Now in this respect I think myself doubly irreproachable: in the first place, by having recommended such public measures as were for the interest of the commonwealth; and in the next, that finding I was not sufficiently supported to render my counsels effectual, I did not deem it advisable to contend for them by arms against a superior strength. Most certainly therefore I cannot justly be accused of having failed in the duty of a good citizen. The only part then that now remains for me, is to be cautious not to expose myself, by any indiscreet word or action, to the resentment of those in power: a part which I hold likewise to be agreeable to the character of true wisdom. As to the rest; what liberties any man may take in imputing words to me which I never spoke; what credit Caesar may give to such reports; and how far those who court my friendship, are really sincere: these are points for which it is by no means in my power to be answerable. My

probably it was a performance by no means to his honour. For Augustus, into whose hands it came after his death, would not suffer it to be published.

[1] Written by Accius, a tragic poet, who flourished about the year of Rome 617. The subject of this piece probably turned upon the death of Oenomaus king of Elis, and the marriage of his daughter Hippodamia.

tranquillity arises therefore from the conscious integrity of my counsels in the times that are past, and from the moderation of my conduct in these that are present. Accordingly, I apply the simile you quote from Accius, not only to Envy, but to Fortune: that weak and inconstant power, whom every wise and resolute mind should resist with as much firmness as a rock repels the waves. Grecian story will abundantly supply examples of the greatest men, both at Athens and Syracuse, who have in some sort preserved their independency, amidst the general servitude of their respective communities. May I not hope then to be able so to comport myself under the same circumstances, as neither to give offence to our rulers, on the one hand, nor to injure the dignity of my character on the other?

But to turn from the serious, to the jocose part of your letter.—The strain of pleasantry you break into, immediately after having quoted the tragedy of Oenomaus, puts me in mind of the modern method of introducing at the end of those graver dramatic pieces, the humour of our mimes, instead of the old Atellan farces.[1] Why else, do you talk of your paltry polypus,[2] and your mouldy cheese? In pure good-nature, 'tis true, I formerly submitted to sit down with you to such homely fare; but more refined company has improved me into a better taste. For Hirtius and Dolabella, let me tell you, are my preceptors in the science of the table: as in return, they are my disciples in that of the bar. But I suppose you have already heard, at least, if all the town-news is transmitted to you, that they frequently declaim at my house, and that I as often sup at theirs. You must not however hope to escape my intended visit, by pleading poverty in bar to the admission of so luxurious a guest. Whilst you were raising a fortune indeed, I bore with your parsimonious humour: but now that you are in circumstances to support the loss of half your wealth, I expect that you receive me in another manner than you would one of your compounding debtors.[3] And

---

[1] These Atellan farces, which in the earlier periods of the Roman stage were acted at the end of the more serious dramatic performances, derived their name from Atella, a town in Italy, from whence they were first introduced at Rome.

[2] A sea-fish so extremely tough that it was necessary to beat it a considerable time before it could be rendered fit for the table.

[3] This alludes to a law which Caesar passed in favour of those who had contracted debts before the commencement of the civil war.

though your finances may somewhat suffer by my visit; remember it is better they should be impaired by treating a friend, than by lending to a stranger. I do not insist however that you spread your table with so unbounded a profusion, as to furnish out a splendid treat with the remains: I am so wonderfully moderate, as to desire nothing more than what is perfectly elegant and exquisite in its kind. I remember to have heard you describe an entertainment, which was given by Phameas. Let yours be the exact copy of his: only I should be glad not to wait for it quite so long. Should you still persist, after all, to invite me, as usual, to a penurious supper, dished out by the sparing hand of maternal œconomy; even this, perhaps, I may be able to support. But I would fain see that hero bold who should dare to set before me the villainous trash you mention; or even one of your boasted polypuses, with an hue as florid as vermilioned Jove.[1] Take my word for it, my friend, your prudence will not suffer you to be thus adventurous. Fame, no doubt, will have proclaimed at your villa my late conversion to luxury, long before my arrival: and you will shiver at the sound of her tremendous report. Nor must you flatter yourself with the hope of abating the edge of my appetite by your cloying sweet-wines before supper: a silly custom which I have now entirely renounced; being much wiser than when I used to damp my stomach with your antepasts of olives and Leucanian sausages.—But not to run on any longer in this jocose strain; my only serious wish is, that I may be able to make you a visit. You may compose your countenance, therefore, and return to your mouldy cheese in full security: for my being your guest will occasion you, as usual, no other expense than that of heating your baths. As for all the rest, you are to look upon it as mere pleasantry.

The trouble you have given yourself about Selicius's villa,[2] is extremely obliging: as your description of it was excessively droll. I believe therefore from the account you give me, I shall renounce all thoughts of making that purchase: for though the country, it seems, abounds in salt, the neighbourhood, I find, is but *insipid*. Farewell.

---

[1] Pliny the naturalist mentions a statue of Jupiter erected in the Capitol, which on certain festival days it was customary to paint with vermillion.
[2] In Naples

TO VOLUMNIUS

You have little reason, believe me, to regret the not being present at my declamations: and if you should really envy Hirtius, as you assure me you should if you did not love him, it must be much more for his own eloquence, than as he is an auditor of mine.   In truth, my dear Volumnius, either I am utterly void of all genius, or incapable of exercising it to my satisfaction, now that I have lost those illustrious fellow-labourers at the bar that fired me with emulation when I used to gain your judicious applause.   If ever, indeed, I displayed the powers of eloquence with advantage to my reputation, let me send a sigh when I reflect, with the fallen Philoctetes [1] in the play, that

> These potent shafts, the heroes wonted dread
> Now spend on meaner war their idle force;
> Aim'd at the wing'd inhabitants of air!

However, if you will give me your company here, my spirits will be more enlivened: though I need not add, that you will find me engaged in a multitude of very important occupations.   But if I can once get to the end of them (as I most earnestly wish) I shall bid a long farewell both to the forum and the senate, and chiefly devote my time to you and some few others of our common friends.   In this number are Cassius and Dolabella, who are united with us in the same favourite studies, and to whose performances I with great pleasure attend.   But we want the assistance of your refined judgement, and of that uncommon erudition which has often struck me with awe when I have been delivering my sentiments before you.   I have determined, then, if I

---

[1] Philoctetes was the friend and companion of Hercules, who when he was dying presented him with his quiver of arrows which had been dipped in the hydra's gall.   When the Grecian princes assembled in order to revenge the cause of Menelaus, they were assured by an oracle that Troy could never be taken without the assistance of these arrows. An embassy therefore was sent to Philoctetes to engage him on their side, who accordingly consented to attend their expedition.   But being disabled from proceeding with these heroes in their voyage, by an accidental wound which he received in the foot from one of his own arrows, they ungenerously left him on a desolate island; and it was here that he was reduced to the mortifying necessity of employing these formidable shafts in the humble purposes of supplying himself with food.

should obtain the consent, or at least the permission of Caesar, to retire from that stage on which I have frequently performed a part that he himself has applauded. It is my resolution, indeed, totally to conceal myself in the secret shades of philosophy, where I hope to enjoy with you, and some others of the same contemplative disposition, the honourable fruits of a studious leisure.

I am sorry you shortened your last letter in the apprehension that I should not have patience to read a longer. But assure yourself, for the future, that the longer yours are, the more acceptable they will always prove to me. Farewell.

TO PAPIRIUS PAETUS

YOUR very agreeable letter found me wholly disengaged at my Tusculan villa. I retired hither during the absence of my pupils,[1] whom I have sent to meet their victorious friend,[2] in order to conciliate his good graces in my favour.

As Dionysius the tyrant, after he was expelled from Syracuse, opened a school, it is said, at Corinth; in the same manner, being driven from my dominions in the forum, I have erected a sort of academy in my own house: and I perceive, by your letter, that you approve the scheme. I have many reasons for approving it too, and principally as it affords me what is highly expedient in the present conjuncture, a mean of establishing an interest with those[3] in whose friendship I may find a protection. How far my intentions in this respect may be answered, I know not: I can only say, that I have hitherto had no reason to prefer the different measures which others of the same party with myself have pursued; unless perhaps it would have been more eligible not to have survived the ruin of our cause. It would so, I confess, had I died either in the camp, or in the field: but the former did not happen to be my fate; and as to the latter, I never was engaged in any action. But the inglorious manner in which Pompey, together with Scipio,[4]

---

[1] Hirtius and Dolabella.
[2] Caesar, in his return from the African war.
[3] Particularly Hirtius and Dolabella.
[4] Scipio, after the unfortunate battle of Thapsus, endeavouring to make his escape into Spain, was driven back upon the coast of Africa.

Afranius[1] and your friend Lentulus,[2] severally lost their lives, will scarcely, I suppose, be thought a more desirable lot. As to Cato's death; it must be acknowledged to have been truly noble: and I can still follow his example, whenever I shall be so disposed. Let me only endeavour, as in fact I do, not to be compelled to it by the same necessity:[3] and this is my first reason for engaging in my present scheme. My next is, that I find it an advantage, not only to my health, which began to be impaired by the intermission of exercises of this kind, but also to my oratorical talents, if any I ever possessed: which would have totally lost their vigour, if I had not had recourse to this method of keeping them in play. The last benefit I shall mention (and the principal one, I dare say, in your estimation) is, that it has introduced me to the demolishing of a greater number of delicious peacocks,[4] than you have had the devouring of paltry pigeons in all your life. The truth of it is, whilst you are humbly sipping the meagre broths of the sneaking Aterius, I am luxuriously regaling myself with the savoury soups of the magnificent Hirtius. If you have any spirit then, fly hither, and learn from our elegant bills of fare, how to refine your own: though to do your talents justice, this is a sort of knowledge in which you are much superior to our instructions. However, since you can get no purchasers for your mortgages, and are not likely to fill those pitchers you

where he fell in with a squadron of Caesar's fleet commanded by Hirtius. Scipio was soon overpowered by the strength and number of the enemy's ships: and himself together with the few vessels that attended him were all sunk.

[1] Afranius had been one of Pompey's lieutenants in Spain, and had a command in Scipio's army in Africa. He was taken prisoner in attempting to make his escape after the defeat of that general, and murdered by the soldiers.

[2] This is Lucius Lentulus who was consul with Marcellus for the year in which the civil war broke out. After the defeat at Pharsalia, he fled to the island of Cyprus; where receiving intelligence that Pompey was gone into Egypt, he immediately set sail in order to join him. He arrived on the next day after that unfortunate general had been cruelly assassinated: and being seized the moment he landed, he underwent the same fate with that of his illustrious friend, in pursuance of an order for that purpose from Ptolemy.

[3] The only necessity which Cato was under of putting an end to his life, arose from that uniform opposition he had given to the dangerous designs of the conqueror: and it must be allowed, that Cicero took sufficient care not to fall under the same.

[4] This bird was esteemed by the Romans amongst the most refined delicacies of the table, and no entertainment was thought completely elegant where a peacock did not make one of the dishes.

mention with denarii,[1] it will be your wisest scheme
return hither: for it is a better thing, let me tell you, to be
sick with good eating at Rome, than for want of victuals at
Naples.[2] In short, I plainly perceive that your finances are
in no flourishing situation, and I expect to hear the same
account of all your neighbours: so that famine, my friend,
most formidable famine must be your fate, if you do not
provide against it in due time. And since you have been
reduced to sell your horse, e'en mount your mule (the only
animal, it seems, belonging to you which you have not yet
sacrificed to your table) and convey yourself immediately to
Rome. To encourage you to do so, you shall be honoured
with a chair and cushion next to mine; and sit the second
great pedagogue in my celebrated school. Farewell.

TO PAPIRIUS PAETUS

ARE you not a pleasant mortal to question me concerning
the fate of those estates [3] you mention, when Balbus had just
before been paying you a visit? It is from him, indeed,
that I derive my whole fund of intelligence: and you may
be assured, that where he is ignorant, I have no chance of
being better informed. I might with much more propriety desire you would tell me what is likely to be the fate
of my own possessions, since you have so lately had a person [4]
under your roof, from whom, either in or out of his cups, you
might certainly have discovered that secret. But this, my
dear Paetus, is an article that makes no part of my inquiry;
for, in the first place, I have reason to be well satisfied;
having now almost these four years been indulged with my
life; if life or indulgence it may be called, to be the sad

---

[1] The denarius was a silver coin, equivalent to about eightpence of
our money. Cicero's raillery alludes to the loss which Paetus had
suffered by the late edict of Caesar concerning debtors.

[2] Paetus had a house in Naples, where he appears to have been when
this letter was written.

[3] Probably the estates of the Pompeians that lay about Naples,
where Paetus seems to have been when this letter was written. It
appears that Paetus had been alarmed with a rumour that Caesar
intended to seize these estates, and therefore had applied to Cicero
to learn the truth of this report.

[4] Balbus.

survivor of our country's ruin. In the next place, I believe it is a question I may easily answer myself. For I know it will be just as it shall seem meet to the men in power: and the men in power, my friend, will ever be those whose swords are the most prevailing. I must rest contented therefore with whatever grace it shall be their pleasure to show me: for he who could not tamely submit to such wretched terms, ought to have taken refuge in the arms of death. Notwithstanding, therefore, that the estates about Veii and Capena [1] are actually dividing out (and these, you know, are not far distant from Tusculum [2]), yet it gives me no sort of disquietude. I enjoy my property whilst I may, and please myself with the hope that I shall never be deprived of that privilege. But should it happen otherwise, still however since it was my noble maxim (hero and philosopher as I was!) that life is the fairest of all possessions, I cannot, undoubtedly, but love the man [3] by whose bounty I have obtained the continuance of that enjoyment. It is certain, at the same time, that how much soever he may be disposed perhaps to restore the republic (as we ought all of us most certainly to wish), yet he has entangled himself in such a variety of different connections, that he is utterly embarrassed in what manner to act. But this is going farther into these points than is necessary, considering the person to whom I am writing. Nevertheless I will add, that our chief himself is as absolutely ignorant what measures will finally be resolved upon, as I am who have no share in his councils. For Caesar is no less under the control of circumstances, than we are under the control of Caesar: and it is as much impossible for him to foresee what these may require, as it is for us to penetrate into what he may intend.

You must not impute it to neglect (a fault, you are sensible, of which I am seldom guilty in the article of writing) that I have not said thus much to you before. The single reason for my not sooner answering your inquiry was, that as I could only speak from conjecture, I was unwilling, without a just foundation, either to increase your fears, or to encourage your hopes. But this I can with truth assure you, that I have not heard the least hint of the danger you apprehend. A man of your philosophy, however, ought to hope for

[1] Veii and Capena were cities in Etruria, which is now called Tuscany.
[2] Where Cicero had a villa.　　　　　　　　[3] Caesar.

the best, to be prepared for the worst, and to bear with equanimity whatever may happen. Farewell.

TO PAPIRIUS PAETUS

YOUR letter gave me a double pleasure: for it not only diverted me extremely, but was a proof likewise that you are so well recovered as to be able to indulge your usual gaiety. I was well contented, at the same time, to find myself the subject of your raillery: and, in truth, the repeated provocations I had given you, were sufficient to call forth all the severity of your satire. My only regret is, that I am prevented from taking my intended journey into your part of the world, where I purposed to have made myself, I do not say your guest, but one of your family. You would have found me wonderfully changed from the man I formerly was, when you used to cram me with your cloying antepasts.[1] For I now more prudently sit down to table with an appetite altogether unimpaired: and most heroically make my way through every dish that comes before me, from the egg[2] that leads the van, to the roast veal that brings up the rear.[3] The temperate and unexpensive guest whom you were wont to applaud, is now no more. I have bidden a total farewell to all the cares of the patriot; and have joined the professed enemies of my former principles: in short, I am become an absolute Epicurean. You are by no means however to consider me as a friend to that injudicious profusion, which is now the prevailing taste of our modern entertainments: on the contrary, it is that more elegant luxury I admire which you formerly used to display when your finances were more flourishing, though your farms were not more numerous than

[1] These antepasts seem to have been a kind of collation preparatory to the principal entertainment. They generally consisted, it is probable, of such dishes as were provocatives to appetite: but prudent oeconomists, as may be collected from Cicero's raillery, sometimes contrived them in such a manner as to damp rather than improve the stomach of their guests.

[2] The first dish at every Roman table was constantly eggs; which maintained their post of honour even at the most magnificent entertainments.

[3] It appears that the Romans usually concluded their feasts with broiled or roasted meat.

at present. Be prepared therefore for my reception accordingly: and remember you are to entertain a man who has not only a most enormous appetite, but, who has some little knowledge, let me tell you, in the science of elegant eating. You know there is a peculiar air of self-sufficiency, that generally distinguishes those who enter late into the study of any art. You will not wonder, therefore, when I take upon me to inform you, that you must banish your cakes and your sweetmeats, as articles that are now utterly discarded from all fashionable bills of fare. I am become indeed such a proficient in this science, that I frequently venture to invite to my table those refined friends of yours, the delicate Verrius and Camillus. Nay I am bolder still: and have presumed to give a supper even to Hirtius himself; though, I must own, I could not advance so far as to honour him with a peacock. To tell you the truth, my honest cook had not skill enough to imitate any other part of his splendid entertainments, except only his smoking soups.

But to give you a general sketch of my manner of life; I spend the first part of the morning in receiving the compliments of several both of our dejected patriots, and our gay victors: the latter of whom treat me with great marks of civility and esteem. As soon as that ceremony is over, I retire to my library: where I employ myself either with my books or my pen. And here I am sometimes surrounded by an audience, who look upon me as a man of most profound erudition, for no other reason, perhaps, than because I am not altogether so ignorant as themselves. The rest of my time I wholly devote to indulgencies of a less intellectual kind. I have sufficiently indeed paid the tribute of sorrow to my unhappy country: the miseries whereof I have longer and more bitterly lamented, than ever tender mother bewailed the loss of her only son.

Let me desire you, as you would secure your magazine of provisions from falling into my hands, to take care of your health: for I have most unmercifully resolved that no pretence of indisposition shall preserve your larder from my depredations. Farewell.

TO DOLABELLA, CONSUL[1]

I DESIRE no greater satisfaction, my dear Dolabella, than what arises to me from the disinterested part I take in the glory you have lately acquired: however, I cannot but acknowledge, I am infinitely pleased to find, that the world gives me a share in the merit of your late applauded conduct. I daily meet in this place great numbers of the first rank in Rome, who are assembled here for the benefit of their health, as well as a multitude of my friends from the principal cities in Italy: and they all agree in joining their particular thanks to me, with those unbounded praises they bestow upon you. They every one of them indeed tell me, that they are persuaded it is owing to your compliance with my counsels and admonitions, that you approve yourself so excellent a patriot and so worthy a consul. I might with strict truth assure them, that you are much superior to the want of being advised by any man; and that your actions are the free and genuine result of your own uninfluenced judgement. But although I do not entirely acquiesce in their compliment, as it would lessen the credit of your conduct, if it should be supposed to flow altogether from my suggestions; yet neither do I wholly reject it: for the love of praise is a passion, which I am apt, you know, somewhat too immoderately to indulge. Yet after all, to take counsel of a Nestor, as it was an honour to the character even of that king of kings, Agamemnon himself, it cannot surely be unbecoming the dignity of yours. It is certainly, at least, much to the credit of mine, that while in this early period of your life, you are thus exercising the supreme magistracy with universal admiration and applause, you are considered as directed by my guidance and formed by my instructions.

I lately paid a visit to Lucius Caesar,[2] at Naples; and though I found him extremely indisposed, and full of pain in every part of his body, yet the moment I entered his chamber he

---

[1] Caesar had appointed Dolabella to succeed him in the consulship as soon as he should set out upon his Parthian expedition; and accordingly Dolabella, upon the death of Caesar, immediately assumed the administration of that office.

[2] He was a distant relation to Julius Caesar, and uncle to Mark Antony.

raised himself with an air of transport, and without allowing himself time to salute me, " O my dear Cicero," said he, " I give you joy of your influence over Dolabella, and had I the same credit with my nephew, our country might now be preserved. But I not only congratulate your friend on his worthy conduct, but desire you would return him my particular acknowledgments: as indeed he is the single consul who has acted with true spirit, since you filled that office." He then proceeded to enlarge upon your late glorious action, representing it as equal to the most illustrious and important service that ever was rendered to the commonwealth. And in this he only echoed the general voice of the whole republic. Suffer me then to take possession of those encomiums to which I am by no means entitled, and in some sort to participate with you in that general applause you have acquired. To be serious, however (for you will not imagine that I make this request in good earnest), I would much rather resign to you the whole of my own glory (if there be any indeed I can justly claim) than arrogate to myself the least portion of that which is so unquestionably your due. For as you cannot but be sensible that I have ever loved you, so your late behaviour has raised that affection into the highest possible ardour: as in truth there cannot be anything more engagingly fair, more irresistibly amiable, than the patriot-virtues. I need not tell you how greatly the exalted talents and polite manners, together with the singular spirit and probity of Marcus Brutus, had ever endeared him to my heart. Nevertheless, his late glorious achievement on the ides of March, has wonderfully heightened that esteem I bore him: and which I had always looked upon as too exalted to admit of any farther advance. In the same manner, who would have imagined that my friendship towards yourself was capable of increase? yet it actually has increased so very considerably, that the former sentiments of my heart seem to have been nothing more than common affection, in comparison of that transcendent passion which I now feel for you.

Can it be necessary that I should either exhort you to preserve the glory you have acquired, or agreeably to the usual style of admonition, set before your view some animating examples of illustrious merit? I could mention none for this purpose more forcibly than your own: and you have only to endeavour to act up to the character you have already attained. It is impossible indeed, after having performed so signal a service to your country, that you should ever deviate from yourself. Instead therefore of sending you any unnecessary exhortations, let me rather congratulate you upon this noble display of your patriotism. It is your privilege (and a privilege perhaps, which no one ever enjoyed before) to have exercised the severest acts of necessary justice, not only without incurring any odium, but with the greatest popularity: with the approbation of the lowest, as well as of the best and highest amongst us. If this were a circumstance in which chance had any share, I should congratulate your good fortune: but it was the effect of a noble and undaunted resolution, under the guidance of the strongest and most enlightened judgement. I say this, from having read the speech you made upon this occasion to the people; and never was any harangue more judiciously composed. You open and explain the fact with so much address, and gradually rise through the several circumstances in so artful a manner, as to convince all the world that the affair was mature for your animadversion. In a word, you have delivered the commonwealth in general, as well as the city of Rome in particular, from the dangers with which they were threatened: and not only performed a singular service to the present generation, but set forth a most useful example for times to come. You will consider yourself then, as the great support of the republic; and remember, she expects that you will not only protect, but distinguish those illustrious persons [1] who have laid the foundation for the recovery of our liberties. But I hope soon to have an opportunity of expressing my sentiments to you more fully upon this subject in person. In the meanwhile, since you are thus our glorious guardian and preserver, I conjure you, my dear Dolabella, to take care of yourself for the sake of the whole commonwealth. Farewell.

TO CAIUS CASSIUS

BELIEVE me, my Cassius, the republic is the perpetual subject of my meditations; or to express the same thing in other words, you and Marcus Brutus are never out of my thoughts.

[1] Brutus and Cassius, together with the rest of the conspirators.

It is upon you two, indeed, together with Decimus Brutus, that all our hopes depend. Mine are somewhat raised by the glorious conduct of Dolabella, in suppressing the late insurrection: which had spread so wide, and gathered every day such additional strength, that it seemed to threaten destruction to the whole city. But this mob is now so totally quelled, that I think we have nothing farther to fear from any future attempt of the same kind. Many other fears, however, and very considerable ones too, still remain with us: and it entirely rests upon you, in conjunction with your illustrious associates, to remove them. Yet where to advise you to begin for that purpose, I must acknowledge myself at a loss. To say truth, it is the tyrant alone, and not the tyranny, from which we seem to be delivered: for although the man indeed is destroyed, we still servilely maintain all his despotic ordinances. We do more: and under the pretence of carrying his designs into execution, we approve of measures which even he himself would never have pursued.[1] And the misfortune is, that I know not where this extravagance will end. When I reflect on the laws that are enacted, on the immunities that are granted, on the immense largesses that are distributed, on the exiles that are recalled, and on the fictitious decrees that are published, the only effect that seems to have been produced by Caesar's death is, that it has extinguished the sense of our servitude, and the abhorrence of that detestable usurper: as all the disorders into which he threw the republic still continue. These are the evils, therefore, which it is incumbent upon you and your patriot coadjutors to redress: for let not my friends imagine, that they have yet completed their work. The obligations, it is true, which the republic has already received from you, are far greater than I could have ventured to hope: still however her demands are not entirely satisfied; and she promises herself yet higher services from such brave and generous benefactors. You have revenged her injuries, by the death of her oppressor: but you have done nothing more. For

[1] A few days after Caesar's death, Antony assembled the senate in the temple of Tellus, in order to take into consideration the state of public affairs. The result of their deliberations was, to decree a general act of oblivion of what was past, and to confirm the several nominations to magistracies, and other grants, which had been made by Caesar. This was principally procured by the authority and eloquence of Cicero. But Antony soon perverted it to his own ambitious purposes, disposing of everything as he thought proper, under the authority of this decree.

tell me, what has she yet recovered of her former di
and lustre? Does she not obey the will of that tyrant
he is dead, whom she could not endure when living? And
do we not, instead of repealing his public laws, authenticate
even his private memorandums? You will tell me, perhaps
(and you may tell me with truth), that I concurred in passing
a decree for that purpose. It was in compliance, however,
with public circumstances: a regard to which is of much
consequence in political deliberations of every kind. But
there are some, however, who have most immoderately and
ungratefully abused the concessions we found it thus necessary to make.

I hope very speedily to discuss this and many other points
with you in person. In the meantime be persuaded, that
the affection I have ever borne to my country, as well as my
particular friendship to yourself, renders the advancement
of your credit and esteem with the public extremely my
concern. Farewell.

TO CAIUS CASSIUS

THE malignant spirit of your friend [1] breaks out every day
with greater and more open violence. To instance, in the
first place, the statue which he has lately erected near the
rostrum, to Caesar, under which he has inscribed, TO THE
EXCELLENT FATHER OF HIS COUNTRY; intimating, that you
and your heroic associates are to be considered, not only as
assassins, but parricides. In which number I am likewise
included: for this outrageous man represents me as the
principal adviser and promoter of your most glorious enterprise. Would to heaven the charge were true! for had I
been a party in your councils, I should have put it out of
his power thus to perplex and embarrass our affairs. But
this was a point which depended upon yourselves to determine: and since the opportunity is now over, I can only
wish that I were capable of giving you any effectual advice.
But the truth is, I am utterly at a loss in what manner to
act myself: for to what purpose is resistance, where one
cannot oppose force by force?

[1] Antony.

It is evidently the intent of Caesar's party to revenge his death. And accordingly Antony being on the 2nd of October last presented to the people by Canutius,[1] mentioned the generous deliverers of our country in terms that traitors alone deserve. He scrupled not to assert likewise, that you had acted entirely by my advice; and that Canutius also was under the same influence. He had the mortification, however, to leave the rostrum with great disgrace. In a word, you may judge what are the designs of this faction by their having seized the appointments of your lieutenant:[2] for does not their conduct in this instance sufficiently declare, that they considered this money as going to be remitted to a public enemy? Wretched condition indeed! that we who scorned to submit to a master, should more ignobly crouch to one of our fellow slaves! Nevertheless, I am still inclined to flatter myself, that we are not quite deprived of all hopes of being delivered by your heroic efforts. But where then, let me ask, are your troops? And with this question I will conclude my letter: as I had rather leave the rest to be suggested by your own reflections, than by mine. Farewell.

TO CAIUS CASSIUS

Oh, that you had invited me to that glorious feast you exhibited on the ides of March! Be assured I would have suffered none of it to have gone off untouched.[3] Whereas the part you unhappily spared, occasions me, above all others, more trouble than you can well imagine. I must acknowledge at the same time, that we have two most excellent consuls:[4] but as to those of consular rank, there is not one of them who does not merit the highest reproach. The senate in general, however, exert themselves with spirit: as the lower order of magistrates distinguish themselves by their singular resolution and zeal. In a word, it is impossible to show a better or more vigorous disposition than

---

[1] He was one of the tribunes for the present year.

[2] As proconsul of Syria: to which province Cassius was probably on his way when this letter was written.

[3] Alluding to the conspirators having spared Antony when they destroyed Caesar.

[4] Hirtius and Pansa.

appears in the populace, not only of Rome, but throughout all Italy. But Philippus and Piso, on the contrary, whom the senate deputed with peremptory orders to Antony, have executed their commission in a manner that raises our highest indignation. For notwithstanding that Antony refused to comply with every single article of the senate's injunctions, yet these unworthy deputies had the meanness to charge themselves with bringing back the most insolent demands.[1] This behaviour of theirs has occasioned all the world to have recourse to my assistance, and I am become extremely popular, in a way wherein popularity is seldom acquired: I mean by supporting a good cause.

I am altogether ignorant in what part of the world you are at present, as well as of what schemes you are either executing or meditating. A report prevails that you are gone into Syria: but for this we have no certain authority. We can a little more depend upon the accounts we receive of Brutus, as his distance from us is less remote.[2]

It has been remarked here by men of some pleasantry, and much indignation against Dolabella, that he has shown himself in too great haste to be your *successor* : as he is most uncivilly set out to take *possession* of your government when you have enjoyed it scarce a single month.[3] The case is clear therefore, say they, that Cassius should by no means give him admittance. But to be serious: both you and Brutus are mentioned with the highest applause: as it is generally supposed that each of you has drawn together an army far beyond our expectations.—I would add more, if I knew with certainty the situation of yourself and your affairs: but I hazard this letter merely upon the doubtful

[1] The purport of them was, that the senate should assign lands and rewards to all his troops, and confirm all the other grants which he and Dolabella had made in their consulship: that all his decrees from Caesar's books and papers should be confirmed. On these terms he offered to give up Cisalpine Gaul, provided that he might have the greater Gaul in exchange for five years, with an army of six legions, to be completed out of the troops of Decimus Brutus.

[2] Marcus Brutus, when he found it necessary to leave Italy, withdrew into Macedonia, where he was at this time employed in raising forces in support of the republican cause.

[3] The province of Syria had been intended by Caesar for Cassius: but Mark Antony, after the death of Caesar, had artfully procured it to be allotted to Dolabella. Accordingly, the latter left Rome a short time before the expiration of his consulship the last year, in order to be beforehand with Cassius in getting possession of this government.

credit of common fame. It is with great impatience, therefore, that I wait for better intelligence from your own hand. Farewell.

TO TREBONIUS [1]

WOULD to Heaven you had invited me to that noble feast which you made on the ides of March: no remnants, most assuredly, should have been left behind. Whereas the part you unluckily spared gives us so much perplexity, that we find something to regret, even in the godlike service which you and your illustrious associates have lately rendered to the republic. To say the truth, when I reflect that it is owing to the favour of so worthy a man as yourself, that Antony now lives to be our general bane, I am sometimes inclined to be a little angry with you for taking him aside when Caesar fell [2] as by this mean you have occasioned more trouble to myself in particular, than to all the rest of the whole community. From the very first moment indeed that Antony's ignominious departure from Rome, [3] had left the senate uncontrolled in its deliberations, I resumed the spirit which you and that inflexible patriot your father were wont to esteem and applaud. Accordingly, the tribunes of the people having summoned the senate to meet on the 20th of December, upon other matters, I seized that opportunity of taking the whole state of the republic into consideration: [4] and more by the zeal than the eloquence of my speech, I revived the drooping spirits of that oppressed assembly, and

[1] He was at this time in Asia Minor: of which province he was governor.

[2] As it had been resolved in a council of the conspirators, that Antony's life should be spared, they did not choose he should be present when they executed their design upon Caesar; probably lest he should attempt to assist his friend, and by that means occasion them to spill more blood than they intended. For this reason Trebonius held Antony in discourse at the entrance into the senate, till the rest of the conspirators had finished their work.

[3] Upon the news that two of the four legions from Brundisium had actually declared for Octavius, and posted themselves in the neighbourhood of Rome, Antony left the city with great precipitation; and putting himself at the head of his army, marched directly in order to wrest Cisalpine Gaul out of the hands of Decimus Brutus. Cicero, who was at this time in the country, took the opportunity of Antony's absence to return to Rome.

[4] It was upon this occasion that Cicero spoke his third Philippic.

awakened in them all their former vigour. It was owing to the ardour with which I thus contended in the debates of this day, that the people of Rome first conceived a hope of recovering their liberties: and to this great point all my thoughts and all my actions have ever since been perpetually directed. Thus important however as my occupations are, I would enter into a full detail of our proceedings, if I did not imagine that public transactions of every kind are transmitted to you by other hands. From them therefore you will receive a more particular information; whilst I content myself with giving you a short and general sketch of our present circumstances and situation. I must inform you then, we have a senate that acts with spirit; but that as to those of consular dignity, part of them want the courage to exert themselves in the manner they ought, and the rest are ill-affected to the republic. The death of Servius [1] is a great loss to us. Lucius Caesar, though he is altogether in the interest of liberty, yet in tenderness to his nephew [2] does not concur in any very vigorous measure. The consuls [3] in the meantime deserve the highest commendations; I must mention Decimus Brutus likewise with much applause. The conduct of young Caesar also is equally laudable: and I persuade myself that we have reason to hope he will complete the work he has begun. This at least is certain, that if he had not been so extremely expeditious in raising the veteran forces, and if two legions had not deserted to him from Antony's army, there is nothing so cruel or so flagitious which the latter would not have committed.—But as these are articles which I suppose you are already apprised of, I only just mention them in order to confirm them.

You shall hear farther from me, whenever I can find a more leisure moment. Farewell.

TO CORNIFICIUS

My friendship with Lucius Lamia is well known, I am persuaded, not only to yourself, who are acquainted with all the circumstances of my life, but to every Roman in general. It

---

[1] Servius Sulpicius. He was one of the three consulars whom the senate had lately deputed to Antony; but very unfortunately for that embassy, he died just as he arrived in Antony's camp.

[2] Antony.   [3] Hirtius and Pansa.

most conspicuously appeared, indeed, to the whole world, when he was banished by the consul Gabinius for having, with so remarkable a spirit of freedom and fortitude, risen up in my defence.[1] Our friendship however did not commence from that period: it was from an affection of a much earlier date that he was induced thus generously to expose himself to every danger in my cause. To these his meritorious services I must add, that there is no man whose company affords me a more true and exquisite entertainment. After what I have thus said, you will think it needless, surely, that I should use much rhetoric in recommending him to your favour. You see the just reason I have for giving him so large a share of my affection: whatever terms therefore the strongest friendship can require upon an occasion of this nature, let your imagination supply for me in the present. I will only assure you, that your good offices to the agents, the servants, and the family of Lamia, in every article wherein his affairs in your province shall require them, will be a more acceptable instance of your generosity than any you could confer in my own personal concerns. I am persuaded indeed from your great penetration into the characters of men, that without my recommendation you would be perfectly well-disposed to give him your best assistance. I must confess, at the same time, I have heard that you suspect him of having signed some decree of the senate injurious to your honour. But I must assure you, in the first place, that he never signed any during the administration of those consuls; and in the next, that almost all the decrees which were pretended to be passed at that time, were absolutely forged. The truth is, you might just as reasonably suppose I was concerned in that decree to which my name was subscribed, relating to Sempronius; though in fact I was then absent from Rome, and complained, I remember, of the injury that had been done me, in a letter which I wrote to you upon the occasion. But not to enter farther into this subject; I most earnestly entreat you, my dear Cornificius, to consider the interest of Lamia, in all respects, as mine, and to let him see that my recommendation has proved of singular advantage to his affairs; assuring yourself, that you cannot in any instance more effectually oblige me. Farewell.

[1] When Cicero was persecuted by Clodius.

TO CORNIFICIUS

CORNIFICIUS delivered your letter to me on the 17th of March, about three weeks, as he told me, after he had received it from your hands. The senate did not assemble either on that day or the next; however, on the 9th they met, when I defended your cause in a very full house, and with no unpropitious regards from Minerva.[1] I may with peculiar propriety say so, as the statue of that guardian goddess of Rome, which I formerly erected in the Capitol,[2] and which had lately been thrown down by an high wind, was at the same time decreed to be replaced. Your letter which Pansa read to the senate was much approved, and afforded great satisfaction to the whole assembly. It fired them at the same time with general indignation against the impudent attempts of the horrid *Minotaur*, for so I may well call those combined adversaries of yours, Calvisius and Taurus.[3] It was proposed therefore that the censure of the senate should pass upon them; but that motion was over-ruled by the more merciful Pansa. However, a decree was voted upon this occasion extremely to your honour.

As for my own good offices in your favour, be assured, my dear Cornificius, they have not been wanting from the first moment I conceived a hope of recovering our liberties. Accordingly, when I laid a foundation for that purpose on the 20th of December last,[4] while the rest of those who ought to have been equally forward in that work, stood timidly hesitating in what manner to act, I had a particular view to the preserving you in your present post, and to this end I prevailed with the senate to agree to my motion concern-

---

[1] It was a sort of proverbial expression among the Romans when they spoke of any successful undertaking, to say that it was carried on "not without the approbation of Minerva."

[2] Cicero, a little before his retreat into banishment, took a small statue of Minerva which had long been reverenced in his family as a kind of tutelar deity, and carrying it to the Capitol, placed it in the temple of Jupiter, under the title of *Minerva the guardian of the city*.

[3] Cicero, in allusion to the name of Taurus, who had joined with Calvisius in some combination against Cornificius, jocosely gives them the appellation of the Minotaur.

[4] When he spoke his third and fourth Philippic orations, wherein Cicero endeavoured, amongst other articles, to animate the senate and the people to vigorous measures against Antony.

ing the continuance of the proconsuls in their respective provinces. But my zeal in your cause did not terminate here, and I still continued my attacks upon that person, who, in contempt of the senate, as well as most injuriously to you, had even whilst he himself was absent from Rome, procured your government to be allotted to him. My frequent, or to speak more properly, my incessant remonstrances against his proceedings, forced him, much against his inclinations, to enter Rome, where he found himself obliged to relinquish the hopes of an honour which he thought himself no less sure of than if it had been in his actual possession. It gives me great pleasure that these my just and honest invectives against your adversary, in conjunction with your own exalted merit, have secured you in your government, as I rejoice extremely likewise in the distinguished honours you have there received.

I very readily admit of your excuse in regard to Sempronius, well knowing that your conduct upon that occasion may justly be imputed to those errors to which we were all equally liable, whilst we trod the dark and dubious paths of bondage. I myself, indeed, the grave inspirer of your counsels, and the firm defender of your dignities, even I, my friend, was injudiciously hurried away by my indignation at the times, when too hastily despairing of liberty, I attempted to retire into Greece. But the Etesian winds, like so many patriot-citizens, refused to waft me from the commonwealth, whilst Auster, conspiring in their designs, collected his whole force and drove me back again to Regium. From thence I returned to Rome with all the expedition that sails and oars could speed me, and the very next day after my arrival, I showed the world that I was the only man, amidst a race of the most abject slaves, that dared to assert his freedom and independency.[1] I inveighed indeed against the measures of Antony with so much spirit and indignation, that he lost all manner of patience; and pointing the whole rage of his bacchanalian fury at my devoted head, he at first endeavoured to gain a pretence of assassinating me in the senate, but that project not succeeding, his next resource was to lay wait for my life in private. But

---

[1] This seems to allude to his having refused to pay obedience to a summons from Antony, to attend a meeting of the senate which was held on that day.

I extricated myself from his insidious snares, and drove him, all reeking with the fumes of his nauseous intemperance, into the toils of Octavius.[1] That excellent youth drew together a body of troops, in the first place, for his own and my particular defence; and in the next for that of the republic in general: which if he had not happily raised, Antony, in his return from Brundisium, would have spread desolation, like a wasting pestilence, around the land. What followed I need not add; as I imagine you are well apprised of all that has happened subsequent to that period. To return then to what gave occasion to this digression; let me again assure you, that I am perfectly well satisfied with your excuse concerning Sempronius. The truth is, it was impossible to act with any determined steadiness and uniformity in times of such total anarchy and confusion. "But other days (to use an expression of Terence) are now arrived, and other measures are now required." Come then, my friend, let us sail forth together, and even take our place at the helm. All the advocates of liberty are embarked in one common bottom: and it is my utmost endeavour to steer them right. May prosperous gales then attend our voyage! But whatever winds may arise, my best skill, most assuredly, shall not be wanting: and is it in the power of patriotism to be answerable for more? In the meantime, let it be your care to cherish in your breast every generous and exalted sentiment; remembering always that your true glory must ever be inseparably connected with the republic. Farewell.

---

[1] Octavius, as soon as he returned into Italy after the death of Caesar, endeavoured to secure Cicero in his interest, as Cicero appeared no less forward to embrace the friendship of Octavius.

MADE AT THE TEMPLE PRESS LETCHWORTH IN GREAT BRITAIN

EVERYMAN'S LIBRARY

By ERNEST RHYS

VICTOR HUGO said a Library was 'an act of faith,' and another writer spoke of one so beautiful, so perfect, so harmonious in all its parts, that he who made it was smitten with a passion. In that faith Everyman's Library was planned out originally on a large scale; and the idea was to make it conform as far as possible to a perfect scheme. However, perfection is a thing to be aimed at and not to be achieved in this difficult world; and since the first volumes appeared there have been many interruptions, chief among them Wars, during which even the City of Books feels the great commotion. But the series always gets back into its old stride.

One of the practical expedients in the original plan was to divide the volumes into separate sections, as Biography, Fiction, History, Belles-lettres, Poetry, Philosophy, Romance, and so forth; with a shelf for Young People. The largest slice of this huge provision of nearly a thousand volumes is, as a matter of course, given to the tyrranous demands of fiction. But in carrying out the scheme, publishers and editors contrived to keep in mind that books, like men and women, have their elective affinities. The present volume, for instance, will be found to have its companion books, both in the same class and not less significantly in other sections. With that idea too, novels like Walter Scott's *Ivanhoe* and *Fortunes of Nigel*, Lytton's *Harold*, and Dickens's *Tale of Two Cities*, have been used as pioneers of history and treated as a sort of holiday history books. For in our day history is tending to grow more documentary and less literary; and 'the historian who is a stylist,' as one of our contributors, the late Thomas Seccombe, said, 'will soon be regarded as a kind of Phoenix.'

As for history, Everyman's Library has been eclectic enough to choose its historians from every school in turn, including Gibbon, Grote, Finlay, Macaulay, Motley, and Prescott, while among earlier books may be found the Venerable Bede and the Anglo-Saxon Chronicle. On the classic shelf too, there is a Livy in an admirable translation by Canon Roberts, and Caesar, Tacitus, Thucydides, and Herodotus are not forgotten.

'You only, O Books,' said Richard de Bury, 'are liberal and independent; you give to all who ask.' The variety of authors old and new, the wisdom and the wit at the disposal of Everyman in his own Library, may even, at times, seem all but embarrassing. In the Essays, for instance, he may turn to Dick Steele in *The Spectator* and learn how Cleomira dances, when the elegance of her motion is unimaginable and 'her eyes are chastised with the simplicity and innocence of her thoughts.' Or he may take *A Century of Essays*, as a key to a whole roomful of the English Essayists, from Bacon to Addison, Elia to Augustine Birrell. These are the golden gossips of literature, the writers who learnt the delightful art of talking on paper. Or again, the reader who has the right spirit and looks on all literature as a great adventure may dive back into the classics, and in Plato's *Phaedrus* read how every soul is divided into three parts (like Caesar's Gaul). The poets next, and he may turn to the finest critic of Victorian times, Matthew Arnold, as their showman, and find in his essay on Maurice de Guerin a clue to the 'magical power of poetry,' as in Shakespeare, with his

> daffodils
> That come before the swallow dares, and take
> The winds of March with beauty.

Hazlitt's *Table Talk* may help us again to discover the relationship of author to author, which is another form of the Friendship of Books. His incomparable essay, 'On Going a Journey,' is a capital prelude to Coleridge's *Biographia Literaria*; and so throughout the long labyrinth of the Library shelves one can follow the magic clue in prose or verse that leads to the hidden treasury. In that way a reader becomes his own critic and Doctor of Letters, and may turn to the Byron review in Macaulay's *Essays* as a prelude to the three volumes of Byron's own poems, remembering that the poet whom Europe loved more than England did was, as Macaulay said, 'the beginning, the middle and the end of all his own poetry.' This brings us to the provoking reflection that it is the obvious authors and the books most easy to reprint which have been the signal successes out of the many hundreds in the series, for Everyman is distinctly proverbial in his tastes. He likes best of all an old author who has worn well or a comparatively new author who has gained something like newspaper notoriety. In attempting to lead him on from the good books that are known to those that are less known, the publishers may have at times been even too adventurous. But the elect reader is or ought to be a party to this conspiracy of books and book-men. He can make it possible, by his help and his co-operative zest, to add still more authors, old and new. 'Infinite riches in a little room,' as the saying is, will be the reward of every citizen who helps year by year to build the City of Books. With such a belief in its possibilities the old Chief (J. M. Dent) threw himself into the enterprise. With the zeal of a true book-lover, he thought that books might be alive and productive as dragons' teeth, which, being 'sown up and down the land, might chance to spring up armed men.' That is a great idea, and it means a fighting campaign in which every new reader who buys a volume, counts as a recruit.

> To him all books which lay
> Their sure foundation in the heart of man . . .
> From Homer the great Thunderer, to the voice
> That roars along the bed of Jewish song . . .
> Shall speak as Powers for ever to be hallowed!

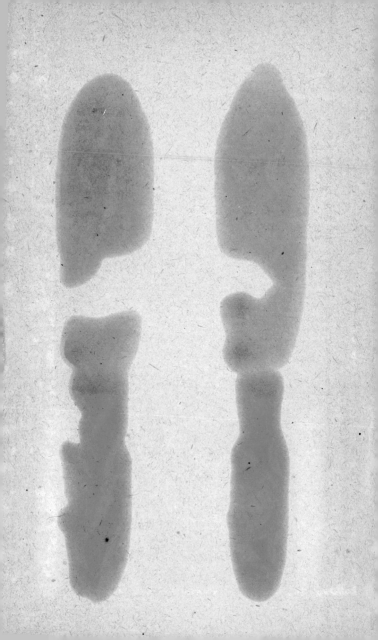